P9-DHT-137

Huon Hooke discovered wine while working as a raw and slightly astringent cadet reporter on *The Murrumbidgee Irrigator* in the NSW Riverina. He followed the flow south to Albury where he matured somewhat (with the help of local tokay) and then across to the Barossa where he further ripened, studying wine marketing in the warm climate of Roseworthy College. He spent a while mellowing in the cellars of Best's and Yellowglen where he worked vintage, finally reaching marketability when he arrived in Sydney in 1982 to work in wine retailing. He has supported himself solely from writing, lecturing, judging and educating for 13 years. Currently, he writes weekly and monthly columns and contributes to various publications including *Decanter* magazine and two overseas wines guides. He judges in about 10 shows a year and runs wine courses in Sydney where he lives. He chairs the judging of Australia's Wine List of the Year Awards (see inside) and occasionally finds time to relax and enjoy a glass of wine while watching the cricket. He published a biography, *Max Schubert Winemaker*, in 1994 and his latest book, *Words On Wine*, hit the shelves in 1997.

After 25 years in the wine industry (15 of them as a full-time wine and spirit writer), even a self-confessed 'wine larrikin' and 'iconoclast' craves respectability. **Mark Shield** has dusted off The Great Australian Novel from the bottom drawer. Publishers stand by for *Betty Boop – The Pistol Packin' Mamma*, a sordid and bizarre tale from the drug-crazed '70s (film rights to the highest bidder). He has also decided to launch a parallel career as a columnist in the field of aviation and the development of aircraft circa World War Two. According to Shield, 'the rejection slips are coming in nicely; it's no different from when I started wine writing'. Since the last edition of this book he has become a regular guest on ABC Radio and has worked on television documentaries. He continues to write several wine columns, do the odd gig as guest chef at the All Nations Hotel and keep life interesting for the other inmates in his notorious abode – the Richmond Rat Shack. He records his greatest pleasure in life as a good glass in good company with good food – and not a computer or editor in sight.

THE PENGUIN
GOOD
AUSTRALIAN
WINE
GUIDE

1997·98
EDITION

HUON HOOKE & MARK SHIELD

PENGUIN BOOKS

Penguin Books Australia Ltd
487 Maroondah Highway, PO Box 257
Ringwood, Victoria 3134, Australia
Penguin Books Ltd
Harmondsworth, Middlesex, England
Viking Penguin, A Division of Penguin Books USA Inc.
375 Hudson Street, New York, New York 10014, USA
Penguin Books Canada Limited
10 Alcorn Avenue, Toronto, Ontario, Canada M4V 3B2
Penguin Books (N.Z.) Ltd
Cnr Rosedale and Airborne Roads, Albany, Auckland, New Zealand

First published by Penguin Books Australia Ltd 1997

10 9 8 7 6 5 4

Typeset in Garamond Adobe by Midland Typesetters, Maryborough, Victoria
Printed in Australia by Australian Print Group, Maryborough, Victoria

ISBN 0 14 026822 7
ISSN 1038-6467

Contents

Acknowledgements

The authors wish to thank all those people in the wine industry who helped make this book possible. Instead of a dedicated list and the risk of omission, thanks to all – including the dedicated folk at Penguin Books who worked on this book.

Introduction

The past year has seen the Australian wine business getting more bullish by the minute. We seem to have entered a new age of wine, an age when people pay outrageous sums for rare and prestigious bottles; when records for exporting are progressively smashed; when vine-planting continues at a breathtaking rate; when wine is a 'sexy' commodity and everybody wants to know about it. There is no field of the wine business that doesn't seem to be booming – except perhaps retailing. Even then, premium wine retailers are doing very well, and it's just the intensity of competition that is preventing the majority from rejoicing in the clover.

At Wine Australia in June 1996 the wine industry, via the Wine Foundation, launched its ambitious Strategy 2025: a target for exports and a plan to become one of the world's most important wine exporters. Just five years ago, many of those in and around the wine business pooh-poohed the industry's objective of exporting $1 billion worth of wine by the year 2000. That target will be reached well before 2000, and the starry-eyed industry planners are now gazing far beyond it. The massive investment in vineyards and winemaking facilities has in fact been forthcoming. There is no slowing of the industry's feverish activity in sight.

Wine styles continue to evolve and subtly change. The latest fad is for ultra-ripe, high-alcohol, blockbuster reds from the warmer regions such as the Barossa, McLaren Vale and Clare. They carry off the major wine show awards with great regularity. But they aren't much in evidence in the 1995 vintage, at least from the southerly regions, because the weather was too cool.

In fact, 1995 was a relatively disappointing year for premium reds; green, underripe characters and lack of fruit generosity are typical problems. The more '95 reds we taste, the more we urge people to grab the generally superb '94s while they last.

The word is that the '96s will be good in all but the cool regions, which again suffered inhospitable weather. The Yarra Valley and Tasmania had a dog of a year, but at least the Yarra pinots got ripe; in fact, they are a superb crop of wines. Speaking of dogs, the Hunter Valley had one in '97, so buy the '96s in preference.

Happily, there are signs of a minor resurgence of interest in riesling, but mainly at the top end of the market. Big companies with large-quantity brands are still having trouble selling riesling, regardless of how good the wines are. This causes us a great deal of wailing and gnashing of teeth. Riesling is so much more enjoyable than unwooded chardonnay, but it seems that the latter is usurping the rightful place of the noble riesling grape in this country. The authors would much rather drink a riesling than 95% of the unwooded chardonnays on offer.

Speaking of chardonnay, it's a sobering thought that in the 12 months to December 1996, chardonnay sales leapt by 8.2%, from 34.2% of the white wine market to 37.0%. That is one hell of a big slice. At the same time, riesling declined from 11.9% of the white wine market to 9.7% – an 18.5% drop. (At least it was heartening to see *Decanter* magazine recognising Aussie riesling as something to write about, with a cover story in its May 1997 edition.)

It's a sign of prosperous times that wine imports are growing, and we suspect that sales of fine imported wine are at an all-time high. In the wake of Chirac's Mururoa, quality Italian imports stole a march on the French, and a glance at bottle shops and restaurant wine lists reveals more smart, new Italians than the now prohibitively expensive Bordeaux and Burgundies.

Takeovers in the past year have been modest, but important. Early on, Southcorp netted Coldstream Hills and the unthinkable happened as James Halliday became an employee of Australia's biggest wine company. After Fosters took over Mildara Blass it also gobbled up Rothbury Wines, with its subsidiaries Saltram, Baileys and St Huberts. Chairman Len Evans immediately pocketed the loot and headed off to rejoin Petaluma as a consultant and to develop his own wine brands (Evans Family, Bulletin Place and Evans Wine Company). On the way he paused to pick up *Decanter* magazine's 1997 Man of the Year Award, his biggest accolade to date. He joins such esteemed company as Robert Mondavi, Hugh Johnson, Michael Broadbent and Piero Antinori.

Before Christmas 1996 we saw Southcorp make Devil's Lair proprietor Phil Sexton an offer no sane person could refuse. Sexton's now off developing breweries in the US and planning his next wine adventure, while Southcorp has big expansion plans for Devil's. Margaret River is very much in the telescopic sights, as BRL Hardy snapped up 50% of Brookland Valley and immediately announced plans to build a winery, to expand plantings and to get into export.

Straight after that, and not pausing to readjust its chequebook, BRL announced a multi-million-dollar venture in the Canberra district: to plant 250 hectares of vines, build a winery and tasting/ sales outlet, and develop Canberra as the next wine tourism destination. Together with local businessman Ron Bell's proposed 60-hectare vineyard, these new plantings will more than double the Canberra district's present total of 150 hectares.

In the King Valley, Victoria's biggest vineyard region outside the Murray River areas, Miranda Wines announced it would build a winery, consolidating its presence in this region where Brown Brothers is the only winery of any size.

A new wine producer appears on the market every week. Not all of them are wineries or have vineyards; some are simply negociant-type brands, but there were more than 50 new ones in 1996.

Demand for premium wine at auctions hit a purple patch in 1996 and continues to boom. At the top end, Penfolds Grange prices have soared and this is reflected in demand for the new vintages. In 1996, for the first time the market set the price of the new Grange ('91 vintage), taking the responsibility for prices out of Penfolds' hands. Then in May 1997 the '92, which might have been expected to retail for about $167 at normal bottle-shop mark-up, opened at an average $250. Retailers pocketed the cream, and the eager market agreed to pay the price. Henschke Hill of Grace is following in Grange's tracks, the latest vintage hitting $100 a bottle.

But the high prices are no longer confined to these prestige leaders. Auctioneers report prices for older vintages of a whole basket of fine, cellarable wines are booming. The fact is that investors have entered the fine wine market in a big way; more's the pity. This is bad news for ordinary Aussie battlers, who will no longer be able to afford the wines they used to.

Australia in the '50s may have ridden on the sheep's back, but these days you can substitute wine for wool. The only things they have in common is that both have four letters, start with 'w' and are agricultural products. While wool was essentially sold as a primary product with little added value for industries in other countries to make profit from, wine is sold as a finished article. It has a retail value of seven times the farm-gate value of the grapes.

Wine exports continue to hum along, and in the 12 months ending April 1997, export volume was up by 24.3%, while value was up by even more: 31.1%. Australia exported 156 million litres of wine, or 3 million bottles each week, to 80 international markets.

Fuelling this growth has been a big task, and grape supply has been under stress. In the lead-up to the 1997 vintage, winemakers were anxious about achieving their grape requirements, especially as a heatwave in February did considerable damage to the grapes on the vines. This caused a loss of yields, but a respectable harvest was still brought in: 800 000 tonnes of grapes, compared with the 1996 record of 880 000. The good news is that the proportion of premium grapes was up: 500 000 tonnes, according to the Winemakers' Federation of Australia.

The pressure was especially hot on premium red grapes because red wine is in big demand both locally and overseas. While total wine sales are up domestically by a healthy 5.9%, red wine is up by an impressive 18.4%. Good news about the health-giving effects of moderate red wine-drinking has had an impact. This applies overseas as well. In a well-reported case in Thailand, the king's doctor suggested a little red wine each day might help the king's heart trouble. When the news leaked out, Thailand trooped down to the local bottle shop en masse. If it's good for the king, it's good for us, they reckoned.

A few years ago there were grave doubts about whether the wine industry would be able to attract the capital investment needed to fund the massive increase in vineyards and the winery capacity necessary to take advantage of frenzied world demand. It's now history that the money has poured in: the Winemakers' Federation of Australia says that over the past four years, some $630 million was spent and 20 000 hectares of vines were planted.

Scary. But, barring some unforeseen disaster, there is no reason why steady export growth shouldn't continue. One risk is that recent price rises could rebound in Australia's face. Accusations of greed have already been heard. However, there is no doubt that when you take the global wine scene into full account, Australian wines still seem good value. Let's hope they always are.

Come June 1998, the second biennial Wine Australia Expo will be held in Melbourne. The first, in Sydney in June 1996, was a big success with 25 000 people attending over the four days, 80% of them general public. What most amazed organisers was the demand for education. As well, the people were young, intelligent, interested, sober and well behaved. It was a far cry from the swilling sessions of the wine expos of the '80s. Educational activities were booked out and many people were turned away. It was a reflection of the level of interest in wine education courses and tutored tastings now seen in the community throughout the year. There's no doubt about the need for such events.

What of the future? The wine industry gets more ambitious every day. Its new goal, enshrined in Strategy 2025 – its long-term plan for expansion – is to achieve annual sales worth $4.5 billion by the year 2025. This would take Australia from the world's 9th largest wine producer to its 5th. Exports today are worth nearly $500 million, so we are talking about nine times the current level! What happens if there's a big exchange-rate shift, a scandal or a major swing in public tastes?

Still, 2025 is a long way off and everybody needs a target to aim for. The war cry is that the goal will be achieved 'by being the world's most influential and profitable supplier of branded wines, pioneering wine as a universal first-choice lifestyle beverage'. It does have the ring of a public relations person with a noseful of coke, running off at the mouth. But it has been said by offshore observers that one of the reasons Australia has already achieved so much is that it plans ahead ... unlike its competitors.

Defining Australia's Wine Regions

Regionalism is a word that's being bandied about with increasing frequency in the wine business. The perception is that wine drinkers throughout the world are more and more interested in drinking wines that have some sort of regional identity. The expectation is that they possess some unique attribute, which means they taste of the region where the grapes were grown. This preoccupation stems from the so-called Old World (Europe – especially France, Italy, Spain and Germany) where centuries of wine production have resulted in certain areas specialising in certain grapes: pinot noir in Burgundy, cabernet sauvignon in Bordeaux, tempranillo in Rioja. With the rest of the world (especially those pesky Australians) making better and better wine and stealing more and more of the markets traditionally 'owned' by the Old World, the French in particular are placing increasing emphasis on the importance of their supposedly unique regional characters.

They say that while Aussies and Californians may make good cabernet, they can never outdo Bordeaux. The same goes for chardonnay and Burgundy. They argue that nobody can better Burgundy because no other place on earth has the same unique combination of soils, slopes, latitude, altitude and climatic characteristics. This is the ultimate defence against those who organise blind tastings concluding that New World wines can rate just as highly as their Old World equivalents.

The corollary is that if Burgundy is unique because of its 'terroir' (the complete growing environment of the vine that has a direct impact on the wine's character), so must Coonawarra, and so on. There is a feeling that Australia needs to promote its wine regions and the characteristics those regions impart to their wines.

That's all very well, but what if there is no consistently perceptible difference between the shirazes of, say, McLaren Vale and the Barossa Valley? Is regional character in Australian wine a phantom?

It's important that Australian winemakers don't pretend 'regional character' exists where it patently does not. But, hopefully, with careful site selection, the suiting of grape varieties and clones to sites, and sensitivity in winemaking, more people will produce wines with distinctive character and individuality, because this is what the consumer increasingly wants – and will want in the future.

Bland uniformity is Australia's hidden enemy. There is a perception in some quarters that our wines are very technically correct, but boringly same-ish. Australian wine has been praised throughout the world for quality and value-for-money. But the way of the future is the production of distinctive wines with special character, and Australia desperately needs more of those.

Geographical Indications

Linked to the notion of regionalism is the nationwide move to define wine regions. In progress at present is the protracted and sometimes controversial exercise of drawing regional boundaries. Inevitably, some wine producers will be disappointed that their vineyards will be left outside the regions they have hitherto considered themselves inside. In Coonawarra, the soul-searching has been especially deep, and in others such as Pemberton, the arguments are more to do with the name of the region than with its geographic limits.

The official title of this complex nest of intrigue is Geographical Indications, and it is overseen by the Geographical Indications Committee (GIC), which is part of the Australian Wine & Brandy Corporation, a key wine industry body.

The need to define wine areas springs from a historic recent bilateral agreement between Australia and the European Union. Australia agreed to respect Europe's regional names, and they reciprocated. The key to this agreement is the phasing out of our use of European generic names such as Burgundy, Champagne, Chablis, Moselle, Port and Sherry on wine labels. Australia also received some trade advantages from the deal.

There are four levels to Geographical Indications: **states** or **territories** (listed below in capital letters); **zones** (listed below in standard type); **regions** (listed below in bold), and mooted **sub-regions** (listed at the end). (It will be a long time before many sub-regions are finally registered.) It goes without saying that we start from the broad, and narrow to the specific.

The broadest description of location – states and territories – are New South Wales, South Australia, Victoria, Tasmania, Queensland, Western Australia, Northern Territory and Australian Capital Territory.

Then come zones. South Eastern Australia is the odd one out. It's something of a catch-all, and includes all of the states of Victoria, Tasmania and New South Wales and part of the states of South Australia and Queensland. It's widely used on labels, especially for large-quantity, multi-state blends, which are usually inexpensive wines from big companies, such as Jacobs Creek.

As of June 1997, these were the zones, regions and sub-regions that had been entered into the Register of Protected Names:

South Eastern Australia

VICTORIA

Gippsland
Central Victoria
North East Victoria
North West Victoria
   Swan Hill
Port Phillip
   Geelong
   Yarra Valley
   Mornington Peninsula
Western Victoria

NEW SOUTH WALES

Big Rivers
   Swan Hill

Western Plains
Northern Slopes
Northern Rivers
Hunter Valley
  Hunter
South Coast
Central Ranges
Southern NSW

SOUTH AUSTRALIA

Adelaide
Mount Lofty Ranges
Fleurieu
Limestone Coast
  Mount Benson
The Peninsulas
Lower Murray
Far North
Barossa

WESTERN AUSTRALIA

Central Western Australia
South West Australia
  Margaret River
  Great Southern
Greater Perth
West Australian South East Coastal
Eastern Plains, Inland & North of WA

Quite a few other regions have been determined but are yet to be finally registered. These are Rutherglen, Grampians, Murray Darling, Pemberton–Warren, Barossa Valley, Eden Valley, Orange, Coonawarra and McLaren Vale.

Only two determinations for sub-regions have been received by the GIC so far. They are Mount Barker (WA Great Southern region) and Broke–Fordwich (Hunter region).

(We expect to be able to use these official regional descriptions in future editions of *The Penguin Good Australian Wine Guide*.)

Once names are registered, the wineries in these areas will be able to use the official names on labels and avoid confusion about regional definitions. This is expected to be especially useful in export markets. Most overseas buyers of Australian wine have yet to learn much about our regions, and if the regional boundary lines are set in stone at the outset, confusion will be averted down the track.

It's worth pointing out that all Australian wines exported to the European Union must carry a geographical indication (GI) of some sort, but it's not mandatory for wine sold in Australia. How specific it is depends on the winemaker's choice. Wines made from grapes grown in a single sub-region (for example, Mount Barker) can use that sub-region's GI, but if blended from more than one sub-region, they may use a more general GI such as a region (for example, Great Southern) or zone (for example, South West Australia). But a winemaker isn't bound to use a sub-region name, even if the wine qualifies. To qualify, at least 85% of the grapes must come from the place specified. He or she can choose to use the sub-region, region, zone or state GI.

Complicated? You bet.

The Price of Wine

For the last 20 years we have been told Australia is the lucky wine country and that our cheap wines are the most drinkable in the world. Just over 10 years ago that was partially true, and it seems to be have been supported by figures of the time. Wine casks accounted for two-thirds of wines sales, and consumption figures were hovering around at an all-time high that was near enough to 22 litres per capita.

Cursory examinations of the figures caused gung-ho articles to be written in the popular press about how Australians were 'Turning on to Wine'. The headline would have been more accurate if it read: 'Wine is the Cheapest Form of Alcohol'. The astute analysts probably realised the headlines should have been: 'Australian Wine Falls Behind the CPI' or even more profoundly: 'Australian Alcohol Consumption Slumps!'

The wine sales figures were painting a deceiving picture. While sales of wine were climbing, beer sales took a crash-dive and spirits remained almost constant. The boom in wine sales was at the lowest end of the market at the expense of beer sales. While not wanting to get bogged down by statistics, over a 20-year period the per-capita consumption of pure alcohol has declined by 22%, and that's not taking the market share of reduced-alcohol beer into account.

We drink less alcohol, and that also apples to wine. Since wine consumption peaked, we have lost around 3 litres per capita, and at the same time the wine industry enjoyed an unprecedented export boom, which more than accounted for any local decline.

Export was so successful that even the base of wine casks was stressed, and we witnessed the phenomenon of wine-cask-quality wines flowing overseas. The shortfall this caused meant cheaper wine imports flowed back to fill the gap. Suddenly the domestic market was drinking a cocktail of local and imported wines at the lower end of the price structure. Wine casks were on allocation, and any chance of competitive discounting evaporated with the shortage.

Another headline of the time could have read: 'Jacobs Creek Flows Around the World'. Orlando Jacobs Creek was the biggest-selling single brand in the UK. There was a sense of affirmation and pride, but that was cold comfort in the bottle shop: the price of Jacobs Creek and its ilk was steadily climbing.

To give another example, a staple red like Wynns Coonawarra Hermitage had a recommended retail price of $6.90 and on special it was selling at $48 a case. Compare this with the current prices in this book and you'll realise you are shopping very well if you pay under $100 a case.

Some producers say 'prices are finally getting real'. Indeed, for a long time they had to survive on prices that did not keep pace with the CPI. During that time they had to suffer for their art and toil at selling bottles. Now they can pick and choose customers, and no doubt they think they have finally triumphed.

You have to pay around $12 to $14 on a good bottle of wine. The next bracket of between $14 to $20 is where the interesting wines can be found, and the great bottles will cost over $20. There are very few absolute bargains and at the top end highway robbery is rife.

Time will tell whether winemakers can sustain these prices; they were not alone in suffering the slings and arrows of depressed prices. Take the price of this book, which is now in its eighth year. It has risen with a gentle curve by $3.00 over the eight-year period and we argue it lasts much longer than a bottle of wine. But we don't begrudge the wine industry; its health is integral to the success of this book. So cheers, wine brothers and sisters – here's to your continued success. Just one word of caution: don't get too greedy!

How much is too much?

No discussion about the upper price limit (if there is one) can avoid a case study involving Penfolds Grange. While the best wine is in the taste buds of the beholder, there is no doubt Grange is our benchmark wine for reasons of style and price.

In 1978, the current Grange was on special for $9.90. To put that in perspective, Penfolds Bin 389 sold for $4.98. The reasoning of the marketing executives of the day was that most people had never tasted the stuff, and that this gave the man and woman in the street a chance to drink it. Experts at the time reported the demise of the line, saying it was forever compromised.

At the time of writing, if you can find a bottle of current vintage Grange for under $300 you are dealing with a true philanthropist. Given that $300 is well above the recommended retail price, there is a considerable amount of profiteering – so much for the demise of the line.

As Grange steams full-speed ahead, many wines are caught in its wake. It could be argued that Henschke Hill of Grace, with its production from fruit grown on pre-phylloxera vines, probably deserves more attention than Grange. It has always been in high demand, and in a marketing ploy to slow the line down the price had risen to dizzying heights. In the case of Hill of Grace, the braking effect from the price increase has been nil. It's like a tyre aquaplaning on a wet road: the speed of sales has increased.

There are also a rash of me-too wines that follow the lead because companies don't want to be seen not to have a super premium wine in their portfolio. These wines have no real claim to their price, which has nothing to do with the cost of manufacture. It's all about buying assumed glamour and, sadly, there will be customers who are prepared to pay the price.

The pundits are already mouthing platitudes like 'the industry needs its benchmarks' and these are 'special wines', and they neglect the coda that reads 'for special people who have pockets with a depth that is inversely proportional to their intelligence'. Don't fall for the hype: many of the wines over $50 a bottle are not worth the money, because you can get the same level of quality for half that price.

Our advice is to trust your palate and forget the fashion statements. By all means use this book as a guide; it points out over 1000 possibilities.

We also caution that all care has been taken with the prices quoted but that given the volatility of the market these can only be used as a rough guide at best. In all cases check with your preferred stockist for an up-to-the-minute quote.

The Rating System

The rating system used in this guide is designed to give you an immediate assessment of a wine's attributes, as they will affect your purchasing decision. The symbols provide at-a-glance information, and the written descriptions go into greater depth. Other wine guides are full of numbers, but this one places importance on the written word.

The authors assess quality and value; provide an estimate of cellaring potential and optimum drinking age; and give notes on source, grape variety, organic cultivation where applicable, decanting, and alcohol content. We list previous outstanding vintages where we think they're relevant.

We assess quality using a cut-down show-judging system, marking out of a possible 10. Wine show judges score out of 20 points – three for nose, seven for colour, 10 for palate – but any wine scoring less than 10 is obviously faulty, so our five-glass range (with half-glass increments) indicates only the top 10 points. When equated to the show system, two and a half to three glasses is roughly equivalent to a bronze medal, and five glasses, our highest award, equals a high gold medal or trophy-standard wine.

Value is arrived at primarily by balancing absolute quality against price. But we do take some account of those intangible attributes that make a wine more desirable, such as rarity, great reputation, glamour, outstanding cellarability, and so on. We take such things into account because they are part of the value equation for most consumers.

If a wine scores more for quality than for value, it does not mean the wine is overpriced. As explained below, any wine scoring three stars for value is fairly priced. Hence, a wine scoring five glasses and five stars is extraordinary value for money. Very few wines manage this feat. And, of course, good and bad value for money can be found at $50 just as it can at $5.

If there are more stars than glasses, you are looking at unusually good value. We urge readers not to become star-struck: a three-glass three-star wine is still a good drink.

Where we had any doubt about the soundness of a wine, a second bottle was always sampled.

Quality

♟♟♟♟♟	The acme of style, a fabulous, faultless wine that Australia should be proud of.
♟♟♟♟?	A marvellous wine that is so close to the top it almost doesn't matter.
♟♟♟♟	An exciting wine that has plenty of style and dash. You should be proud to serve this.
♟♟♟?	Solid quality with a modicum of style; very good drinking.
♟♟♟	Decent, drinkable wine that is a cut above everyday quaffing. You can happily serve this to family and friends.
♟♟?	Sound, respectable wines, but the earth won't move.
♟♟	Just okay, but in quality terms, starting to look a little wobbly.

(Lower scores have not been included.)

Value

★★★★★	You should feel guilty for paying so little: this is great value for money.
★★★★⋆	Don't tell too many people because the wine will start selling and the maker will put the price up.

★★★★ If you complain about paying this much for a wine, you've got a death adder in your pocket.

★★★ᵥ Still excellent value, but the maker is also making money.

★★★ Fair is fair, this is a win–win exchange for buyer and maker.

★★ᵥ They are starting to see you coming, but it's not a total rip-off.

★★ This wine will appeal to label drinkers and those who want to impress the bank manager.

★ᵥ You know what they say about fools and their money . . .

★ Makes the used-car industry look saintly.

Grapes

Grape varieties are listed in dominant order; percentages are cited when available.

Cellar

Any wine can of course be drunk immediately, but for maximum pleasure we recommend an optimum drinking time, assuming correct cellaring conditions. We have been deliberately conservative, believing it's better to drink a wine when it's a little too young than to risk waiting until it's too old.

An upright bottle ▮ indicates that the wine is ready for drinking now. It may also be possible to cellar it for the period shown. Where the bottle is lying on its side ➟ the wine is not ready for drinking now and should be cellared for the period shown.

▮ Drink now: there will be no improvement achieved by cellaring.

▮ 3 Drink now or during the next three years.

- 3–7   Cellar for three years at least before drinking; can be cellared for up to seven years.

- 10+   Cellar for 10 years or more; it will be at its best in 10 years from this book's publication date.

Alcohol by Volume

Australian labelling laws require that alcohol content be shown on all wine labels. It's expressed as a percentage of alcohol by volume, e.g. 12.0% A/V means that 12 per cent of the wine is pure alcohol.

Recommended Retail Price

Prices were arrived at either by calculating from the trade wholesale using a standard full bottle shop mark-up, or by using a maker-nominated recommended retail price. In essence, however, there is no such thing as RRP because retailers use different margins and there are different state taxes. The prices in this book are indicative of those in Sydney and Melbourne, but they will still vary from shop to shop and city to city. They should only be used as a guide. Cellar-door prices have been quoted when the wines are not available in the retail trade.

❤ Organic

The wine has passed the tests required to label it as 'organically grown and made'.

▮ Decant

The wine will be improved by decanting.

⑤ Special

The wine is likely to be 'on special', so it will be possible to pay less than the recommended retail price. Shop around.

Best Wines

Put yourself in our place: you are faced with several wines of equal merit, and judging them becomes a juggling act between style and value. It was worse than ever before; there were so many final contenders for the best wine categories it should be described as the year of the 'could-have-been champions'.

Being ever mindful that readers want to find the winners on bottle shop shelves, wine lists and at cellar doors, many wines had to be eliminated. Discreet but oblique phone calls to potential champions went something like this: 'G'day, finished the pruning? How's the wife and kids? Get much rain? Oh, by the way, got much of your riesling left?'

If we were on the receiving end of such a call we'd probably be tempted to say we had plenty, and we'd dropped the price! We'd then sit back and wait for the handsome certificate to be hung on the cellar door alongside the Sold Out sign.

The decisions are the result of tasting and usually of much discussion, which although never heated, can be spirited. However, there were two categories where there was simply no discussion whatsoever. The Penguin Wine of The Year took as long as it takes to pronounce its name to decide, and the Best Sparkling Wine was another where 'discussion' was limited to the bold statement: 'Name something better'.

As for the rest, there was healthy discussion that was quite often cut short by the issue of availabilty. The wines in short supply are included in the bulk of the book and with luck you may have some in your cellar or find some in a bottle shop.

Finally, when it came to bargains we were forced to shift the goalposts. A bargain wine is no longer under $10 a bottle; under $15 seems to be a more realistic benchmark for today's market.

And now for the best part of compiling this book. It's with great pleasure that we announce the winners . . .

Penguin Wine of the Year & Best White Wine (any grape variety or blend)

Petaluma Chardonnay 1996

The top of the ziggurat – vinous right stuff! This wine can hold its own in global company. The makers should be justly proud and we should all bask in the reflected glory of this great wine. (See page 311).

Best Red Wine (any grape variety or blend)

Wynns Cabernet Sauvignon 1994

This old friend has become a benchmark for value and regional character. It's one of the best examples of the style from a very good year, and the best news is it isn't hard to find. (See page 196.)

Best Sparkling Wine

Clover Hill 1994

An overdue welcome to the winner's rostrum to this sparkling wine, which is a convincing example of the promise of Tasmania. It wins on many counts and takes the word finesse to a high point. (See page 361.)

Best Fortified Wine

Brown Brothers Very Old Tokay

The canny Brown Brothers persisted with this wonderful fortified style when the rest of the market seemed to be losing heart. They are in the happy position of having sheds full of this fine wine. (See page 376.)

Picks of the Bunch

BEST CABERNET SAUVIGNON
Penfolds Bin 407 Cabernet Sauvignon 1994
This vintage was a red-letter year for Penfolds' red wines and this is one of many contenders. It strikes a realistic balance between high quality and affordability. (See page 139.)

BEST PINOT NOIR
De Bortoli Yarra Valley Pinot Noir 1996
A very fine and already complex wine that finds the middle ground as far as style is concerned. It has the bonus of an affordable price. (See page 63.)

BEST SHIRAZ
Fox Creek Reserve Shiraz 1996
Combines fine balance and the exuberance of youth with early drinkability, and there is no doubt about the grape variety. A red ode to joy. (See page 74.)

BEST RED BLEND/OTHER VARIETY
Tim Adams The Fergus 1996
This is mostly grenache and it's as firm as the legendary handshake of the maker. It has slabs of flavour and power, yet it retains finesse and exhibits Clare Valley charm. (See page 180.)

BEST CHARDONNAY
Rosemount Show Reserve Chardonnay 1996
This essay in fruit and oak has been polished to concourse condition. It shows the elegance and richness possible in the Upper Hunter Valley region. (See page 322.)

BEST RIESLING
Crawford River Riesling 1996
Lovely wine from a small winery in a remote corner of Victoria. It has exhilarating flavour and crisp acid, which makes it a good bet for cellaring. (See page 235.)

BEST SEMILLON
Tyrrell's Vat 1 1992
They don't come much better than this! It's still available and shows what an aged Hunter semillon is all about. There is no surprise it's a Tyrrell's wine. (See page 342.)

BEST WHITE BLEND/OTHER VARIETY
Chain of Ponds Sauvignon Blanc Semillon 1997
Fresh and frisky, this wine comes from a new marque that seems hell-bent on establishing a reputation second to none. It's a label to watch. (See page 227.)

Bargains

BEST BARGAIN RED
Richmond Grove Coonawarra Cabernet Sauvignon 1994
Coonawarra cabernet at a pauper's price. It's very easy to drink. (See page 152.)

BEST BARGAIN WHITE
Rouge Homme Chardonnay 1996
You can't ask for any more when you consider the benevolent price – bargains are still possible. (See page 323.)

BEST BARGAIN SPARKLING
Killawarra Premier Vintage Brut 1994
A classy glass of bubbles with subtlety and yeast character, and a fine style that's well above its station. (See page 367.)

BEST BARGAIN FORTIFIED
De Bortoli Show Liqueur Muscat
Looks, smells and tastes like the real thing. The only thing unreal about it is the low price. (See page 380.)

Australia's Wine List of the Year Awards, 1997

When overseas visitors venture to Australia they are amazed at the value-for-money and quality of the food in our restaurants. These days a smorgasbord of fine eateries can be found in Melbourne, Sydney and Adelaide. An essential part of a fine meal is a glass of good wine, and an integral part of any great restaurant is a great wine list.

For the past four years, the co-author of this guide, Huon Hooke, has chaired the Australia's Wine List of the Year Awards, a national competition sponsored and organised by wholesaler Tucker Seabrook, Australia's oldest national fine wine and spirit merchants (established 1838). He reports that the quality of wine lists across the country, the range and value-for-money of their selections, and their actual presentation on the list, has been steadily improving.

The aim of the competition is to encourage higher standards, and entry is voluntary. There were around 400 entrants in 1997 and their lists were judged by 11 judges from Victoria, South Australia, Western Australia, Queensland and New South Wales, including Huon as chief judge, as well as the three international judges. The judges allocated awards for the best wine list from each state and the best list in each of five restaurant categories, as well as the single best wine list in Australia. They also awarded about 100 establishments a recommended wine list rating, scoring out of a possible three wine glasses.

The judging parameters included the quality and range of choice of the wines; pricing; balance; depth of older vintages; number of wines offered by the glass; suitability of the wine to the type of restaurant and cuisine; and – importantly – appearance, layout design and general 'user friendliness'. You can be sure of a decent bottle at a fair price if you go to any of these restaurants.

National Winner

France-Soir Restaurant, Vic. ♟♟♟

HALL OF FAME
Walter's Wine Bar, Vic. (1996 winner) ♟♟♟

Dear Friends Garden Restaurant, WA (1995 winner) ♟♟♟

Cicada, NSW (1994 winner) ♟♟♟

State & Territory Winners

ACT	Caffe Della Piazza ♟♟♟
NSW	Forty One Restaurant ♟♟♟
NT	Raymond's Restaurant ♟
Qld	The Grape Food & Wine Bar ♟♟♟
SA	Universal Wine Bar ♟♟♟
Tas.	Fee & Me ♟♟
Vic.	France-Soir Restaurant ♟♟♟
WA	Stephenies ♟♟♟

Category Winners

BEST RESTAURANT   France-Soir Restaurant, Vic. ♟♟♟

BEST SMALL
RESTAURANT   The Grape Food & Wine Bar, Qld ♟♟♟

BEST CLUB
RESTAURANT   University House, Vic. ♟♟♟

BEST PUB RESTAURANT   The Melbourne Wine Room, Vic. ♟♟♟

BEST CAFE /
BRASSERIE / TRATTORIA   Universal Wine Bar, SA ♟♟♟

VERY HIGHLY RECOMMENDED ♟♟♟
Adams of North Riding Restaurant & Guest House, Vic.; Armstrong's, NSW; Belmondo, NSW; Bistro Moncur, NSW; Blake's Restaurant, SA; Brooklyn Hotel, NSW; Buon Ricordo, NSW; Caffe Della Piazza, ACT; Caffe Grossi, Vic.; Caffe La Strada, Vic.; Charcoal Grill on the Hill, Vic.; Chloe's Restaurant, SA; Cicada, NSW; Claudine's French Restaurant, NSW; Cottage Point Inn Restaurant, NSW; Cracklins on Swan, Vic.; Darley's Restaurant, NSW; Darling Mills, NSW; Dear Friends Restaurant, WA; Dog's Bar, Vic.; Est Est Est, Vic.; Forty One Restaurant, NSW; France-Soir, Vic.; Hotel Australia, Shepparton, Vic.; Jacques Raymond Restaurant, Vic.; Jardines Restaurant, NSW; L'Avventura, NSW; La Grillade Restaurant, NSW; Le Restaurant, Vic.; Marchetti's Latin Restaurant, Vic.; Mask of China, Vic.; Merrony's Restaurant, NSW; Morans Restaurant & Cafe, NSW; One Fitzroy Street, Vic.; Ozone Hotel, Vic.; Pavilion on the Park, NSW; Pier, NSW; Red Wine Bar, SA; Ristorante Roberto, Vic.; St Mount's Guesthouse and Restaurant, NSW; Stella, Vic.; Stephenies, WA; Syracuse Restaurant & Wine Bar, Vic.; The Bathers Pavilion, NSW; The Dolphin Hotel, NSW; The Grape Food & Wine Bar, Qld; The Melbourne Wine Room, Vic.; The Rose Restaurant Bar, Vic.; Universal Wine Bar, SA; University House, Vic.; Walter's Wine Bar, Vic.; Watermark Restaurant, NSW.

HIGHLY RECOMMENDED ♥♥

B-Coz Restaurant, Vic.; Barry's Country Guest House & Restaurant, NSW; Beppi's Restaurant, NSW; Bilson's Restaurant, NSW; Bistro Pave, NSW; Caterina's Cucina E Bar, Vic.; Chesser Cellar, SA; Chinois, Vic.; Courtney's Brasserie, NSW; Durham's Restaurant, SA; Europa Cafe, Vic.; Fee and Me Licensed Restaurant, Tas.; Finches of Beechworth Country Guesthouse, Vic.; Fringe Benefits, ACT; Gekko Restaurant, NSW; Grange Restaurant with Cheong Liew, SA; Iguacu Restaurant & Bar, NSW; Jarmer's Restaurant, SA; Kable's, NSW; La Fontaine, Qld; La Mensa, NSW; Logues Eating House, NSW; Madam Fang, Vic.; Marco Polo East West Cuisine, Qld; No. 44 King Street, WA; Pieroni, Vic.; Raphael's Restaurant, NSW; Roberto Wine Bar & Restaurant, WA; Sails Beach Cafe, Qld; San Francisco Grill, NSW; San Lorenzo Restaurant, WA; Tables of Toowong, Qld; The Old George & Dragon Restaurant, NSW; The Stokehouse, Vic.; The Victory Hotel, SA.

RECOMMENDED ♥

Adams at La Trobe University Club, Vic.; Alex's Italian Restaurant, NSW; Alley Blue Kitchen & Bar, Vic.; Alto Restaurant, Vic.; Antics Restaurant, NSW; Archie's on the Park, NSW; Artis Restaurant, Qld; Becco, Vic.; Between The Flags 'food with a view', NSW; Billy Blue Brasserie, NSW; Bistro Deux, NSW; Bistro Inferno, Vic.; Breezes Restaurant, Qld; Cafe Provincial, Vic.; Caffe Bizzarri, Vic.; Canterbury–Hurlstone Park RSL Club Ltd, NSW; Chez Pok, NSW; Chris's Beacon Point Restaurant & Villas, Vic.; Cibo Ristorante Pastilliera, SA; City Rower's Tavern, Qld; Continental Sorrento Hotel, Vic.; Court Wine Bar, WA; Criterion Restaurant, NSW; D'Marni Restaurant & Bar, Vic.; Daniel Shea's Restaurant, WA; Daniel's Restaurant, Vic.; Daniel's Restaurant, NSW; Delgany Country House Hotel, Vic.; Downs Club Inc., Qld; Dunwoody's Tavern, Qld; Edom, NSW; Edward's Waterfront, Vic.; Fiasco's Restaurant, Qld; Fishermen's Pier, Vic.; Flouch's, Vic.; Fortuna Village Restaurant, Vic.; Fraser's Restaurant, WA; Gowings Grace, Vic.; Grand Mercure Hotel Bowral Heritage Park, NSW; Half Moon, Vic.; Haskins Garden Restaurant, WA; I Marcus, Vic.; Isis Restaurant, Vic.; Jameson's, Qld; Jolleys Boathouse Restaurant, SA; Jonah's, NSW; Juniperberry, ACT; Kingsley's Steakhouse, NSW;

Kingston Hotel Restaurant, Vic.; Lakehouse, Vic.; Le Gourmet Restaurant, Vic.; Lindenderry at Red Hill, Vic.; Lindoni's Ristorante, Qld; Lyrebird Restaurant, Qld; Lyrics Restaurant, SA; Madame Joe Joe Restaurant, Vic.; Marine Cafe, Vic.; Mars Restaurant, NSW; Marylands Country House, Vic.; Mediterraneo, NSW; Metropolitan Hotel, Vic.; Mezzaluna, NSW; Mietta's Queenscliff Hotel, Vic.; Miguel's, Vic.; Milsons Restaurant, NSW; Monty's Restaurant, Qld; Morgans Seafood Restaurant, Qld; Mt Lofty House, SA; Neptune Palace, NSW; Palms Restaurant, Vic.; Paramount, NSW; Paris Match Restaurant, Vic.; Peacock Gardens Restaurant, NSW; Plume Chinese Restaurant, Vic.; Poff's Restaurant, Vic.; Potters Cottage Restaurant, Vic.; R.P.R.'s Restaurant, Qld; Raymond's Restaurant, NT; Red Ochre Grill, SA; Red Ochre Grill, Qld; Reds Restaurant, NSW; Restaurant 98, Qld; Restaurant CBD, NSW; Robert's at Pepper Tree, NSW; Rococo Restaurant and Bar, Vic.; Rubira's Bar Restaurant, Vic.; Sails Restaurant Williamstown, Vic.; Schouten House, Tas.; Shores Restaurant of Middle Harbour, NSW; Siggi's at the Heritage, Qld; Sorrento Golf Club, Vic.; Star Grill Restaurant, NSW; The Boat House by the Lake, ACT; The Boathouse on Blackwattle Bay, NSW; The Candy Bar, Vic.; The Courthouse Restaurant, Qld; The Duxton Brasserie, WA; The East Empress Restaurant and Bar, Vic.; The George, Tas.; The Grand National, NSW; The Grand Pacific Blue Room, NSW; The Hanuman Thai and Nonya Restaurant, NT; The Manse Restaurant, SA; The Mixing Pot Restaurant, NSW; The Near East Restaurant, Vic.; The Oyster Beds River Restaurant, WA; The Republic Restaurant, ACT; The Stag Restaurant, Vic.; The Verandah Restaurant & Wine Bar, Qld; Tory's Seafood Restaurant, NSW; University & Schools Club, NSW; Unley on Clyde Hotel, SA; Villa D'Este Restaurant, WA; Vue Grand Hotel, Vic.; Windows on the Bay, Vic.; Witch's Cauldron Restaurant, WA; Xu Bistro and Bar, NSW; Zarrini, NSW.

Red Wines

Abbey Vale Merlot Shiraz

This ranks along with other mixed marriages like cabernet zinfandel or pinot gris and chardonnay. Never mind, it sorta works. Maker Dorham Mann.

CURRENT RELEASE 1995 The colour is a bright ruby and the nose is dominated by plum and spice. The palate is medium-bodied with sweet fruit flavours, mainly cherry and plums. These are matched by soft tannins on a dry finish. It works well with quail.

Quality	ΥΥΥί
Value	★★★ʁ
Grapes	merlot; shiraz
Region	Margaret River, WA
Cellar	▮ 3
Alc./Vol.	13.0%
RRP	$19.00

Alkoomi Frankland River Shiraz

Alkoomi is a rather remote and isolated vineyard in the Great Southern region of Western Australia.

CURRENT RELEASE 1994 This is a wine that probably reflects the nature of the vintage. It's lean and dominated by herbal and briary characters. The fruit on the palate is subdued, and oak sets the scene on the finish. It's a drink-now proposition that goes well with smoked meats.

Quality	ΥΥΥ
Value	★★★
Grapes	shiraz
Region	Frankland River, WA
Cellar	▮ 2
Alc./Vol.	12.5%
RRP	$21.00

All Saints Aleatico

The search for a summer red goes on, and here is another example. 'Why bother?' is a good question; the notion of chilled red wines in the Australian summer hasn't impinged on consumer consciousness.

CURRENT RELEASE 1996 Tutti-frutti, the colour is a deep pink or a light red. The nose is sweet and fruity with a hint of sherbet. There is clean acid on the finish and this balances the sweetness. It should be served well chilled. Try it with a spicy pizza.

Quality	ΥΥΥ
Value	★★★
Grapes	aleatico
Region	North East Victoria
Cellar	▮ 1
Alc./Vol.	12.5%
RRP	$14.50

Angoves Sarnia Farm Cabernet Sauvignon

Quality	♟♟♟♟
Value	★★★★
Grapes	cabernet sauvignon
Region	Padthaway, SA
Cellar	▮ 5
Alc./Vol.	12.5%
RRP	$19.00

Angoves are a large bulk producer, but it would be wrong to bill this wine as their tilt at respectability. This is a flagship that shows the company is in the premium wine arena, as well as in the bulk wine and brandy arenas.

CURRENT RELEASE 1995   An elegant style with finesse and varietal character. The colour is a medium ruby, and the nose is a mix of mint, blackberry, pepper and mint. The palate is dominated by raspberry and blackberry flavours plus some green herb qualities. Oak on the finish adds coconut and vanilla flavours, and substantial grip. It's great with pasta and a meat sauce.

Annie's Lane Cabernet Merlot

Quality	♟♟♟♟♟
Value	★★★★★
Grapes	cabernet sauvignon; merlot
Region	Clare Valley, SA
Cellar	➦ 1–8+
Alc./Vol.	13.5%
RRP	$15.00 Ⓢ ▮

This is a whopper made with plenty of oak, and is very much in the maker's style. That maker is David O'Leary, ex-Hardys Tintara.

CURRENT RELEASE 1995   Lovely deep, rich, purple–red colour here: the fruit concentration shines through in every way. Sweet, fully ripe blackcurrant fruit shows on the nose with good background oak. It's intensely berryish and weighty in the mouth, concluding with a serious tannin grip. Generous, if not especially elegant. It needs time and will keep long-term. Food: rare kangaroo.

Annie's Lane Shiraz

Quality	♟♟♟♟
Value	★★★★
Grapes	shiraz
Region	Clare Valley, SA
Cellar	➦ 1–5+
Alc./Vol.	13.0%
RRP	$15.00 Ⓢ ▮

Annie's Lane is the latest in a string of Mildara Blass wines named after wells, runs, and sundry geographical landmarks. Maker David O'Leary.

CURRENT RELEASE 1994   One for the lumber lovers: it has richness and smooth, chewy texture in the mouth as a result of all that wood. But the aroma and flavour are all toasty American oak at this stage. Give it time, then serve with nicely chargrilled rump steak.

Antipodean

As night follows day a red wine was sure to follow the successful white. Both wines are designed to match our cuisine and 'hedonistic lifestyle'. Speak for yourself.
CURRENT RELEASE 1996 Brilliant and cheeky cherry-red colour, and a sassy nose that is lifted by ripe fruit, spices and hints of oak. The palate is light- to medium-bodied with fresh fruit and a dash of sweetness. The oak on the finish is subtle, but there is a persistent coating of tannins that linger in the mouth. It drinks well now with a slightly spicy pizza.

Quality	ŸŸŸŸ
Value	★★★★
Grapes	shiraz; mourvèdre; grenache; viognier
Region	Barossa Valley, SA
Cellar	♦ 3
Alc./Vol.	13.0%
RRP	$16.00

Arlewood Cabernet Sauvignon

Newish label (established in 1988) from Margaret River that probably won't win an award for label design, but that keeps the faith as far as style is concerned. There are 4.5 hectares under vine. Maker Mike and Jan Davies (contract).
CURRENT RELEASE 1994 This is typical Margaret River stuff with elegance and length. The nose has black-berry and briar aromas. The medium-bodied palate is dominated by blackberry, and there is a hint of smoky oak. The finish is astringent, but balanced in terms of the volume of fruit. The wine goes well with rare eye fillet steak.

Quality	ŸŸŸ𝟁
Value	★★★𝟁
Grapes	cabernet sauvignon
Region	Margaret River, WA
Cellar	♦ 4
Alc./Vol.	13.0%
RRP	$18.00

Arrowfield Cowra Merlot

Cowra has yet to produce a startling red wine, but that's probably because the main thrust has so far been on whites. There's no reason why it shouldn't also produce good red.
CURRENT RELEASE 1996 Ripe aromas and good, sweet fruit flavours are the feature of this serviceable merlot. The aroma is simple but the plum/cherry notes are spot-on. It's light- to medium-bodied and smooth with, happily, no green characters at all. It could improve further with a year or two in the cellar. Serve with veal cutlets.

Quality	ŸŸŸŸ
Value	★★★★
Grapes	merlot
Region	Cowra, NSW
Cellar	♦ 3+
Alc./Vol.	13.1%
RRP	$15.00 Ⓢ

Arrowfield Hunter Valley Shiraz

Quality	🍷🍷🍷🍷🍷
Value	★★★★★
Grapes	shiraz
Region	Hunter Valley, NSW
Cellar	3–15+
Alc./Vol.	13.8%
RRP	$17.00 (S)

This is a Japanese-owned winery that has had its ups and downs. This wine won a top gold at the National Wine Show in Canberra, and the trophy for the best Hunter red at the Hunter Show, which is some achievement. Alas, they only made 1000 cases.

CURRENT RELEASE 1995 This time Arrowfield hit the nail right on the head! It's a cracker: marvellous concentration and length, massively oaky in its youth but tremendously generous and rich in cherry, plum and licorice flavours. A big wine that carries its masses of toasty, coconutty American oak with ease. Cellar, then drink with aged Reggiano cheese.

Ashton Hills Pinot Noir

Quality	🍷🍷🍷½
Value	★★★
Grapes	pinot noir
Region	Adelaide Hills, SA
Cellar	3
Alc./Vol.	12.5%
RRP	$27.00

The Adelaide Hills is gradually building a track record for pinot. This one is made in tiny quantities by Stephen George and is not easy to track down. Get your name on the mailing list.

Previous outstanding vintages: '94, '95

CURRENT RELEASE 1996 Slightly lollyish medicinal aromas, which suggest a degree of carbonic maceration. Lacks a little weight and intensity compared to the '95, but is a pristine, well-made lighter style which teams well with tuna.

Ashwood Grove Cabernet Sauvignon

Quality	🍷🍷🍷½
Value	★★★½
Grapes	cabernet sauvignon
Region	Swan Hill, Vic.
Cellar	2
Alc./Vol.	12.5%
RRP	$12.95

The vineyards were owned by the Hamilton family, who planted a stand of Ashwood gum trees. The vineyard is now producing wine under its own label.

CURRENT RELEASE 1995 This is a well-balanced style. The colour is a mid-cherry-red, and the nose is fruity and perfumed with a hint of mint. The palate is lightly structured with soft, sweet fruit flavours, and there are gentle tannins on the finish. It's a good spare rib and chop style.

Ashwood Grove Grenache

This is a new label marketing wines that are priced to sell. The reference to Lady Hamilton is a 'small tribute to one of Australia's Wine Pioneers'.
CURRENT RELEASE 1995 This is a soft, fruity style typical of the variety. This has a raspberry-dominated nose and the palate has a juicy character with sweet fruit flavours. The finish is soft with gentle tannins and clean acid. It could be given a slight chill, and it serves well with roast lamb.

Quality	♙♙♙
Value	★★★
Grapes	grenache
Region	Swan Hill, Vic.
Cellar	♦
Alc./Vol.	13.0%
RRP	$11.00

Baileys 1920s Block Shiraz

The founder, Varley Bailey, gave himself a 50th-anniversary present, planting a new vineyard in 1920, a half-century after he began the company. This wine is made from those vines.
Previous outstanding vintages: '91, '92
CURRENT RELEASE 1994 Very tannic and somewhat austere, but not as huge as some Baileys reds can be. The nose combines jammy, sweet, ripe fruit and pep-periness that verges on graphite. There may be a hint of sulfide but it doesn't mar the wine. Could be drunk with a hearty casserole, but better if cellared.

Quality	♙♙♙♙
Value	★★★
Grapes	shiraz
Region	Glenrowan, Vic.
Cellar	➥ 3–10+
Alc./Vol.	14.0%
RRP	$23.00 ▮

Balgownie Estate Cabernet Sauvignon

Mildara doesn't promote Balgownie much these days, but it still produces good and occasionally superb Estate reds, thanks to winemaker Lindsay Ross.
Previous outstanding vintages: '76, '80, '86, '90, '92, '93
CURRENT RELEASE 1994 A marvellous cabernet sau-vignon that remains true to the high-tannin, solid 'n' gutsy Balgownie style. A little more polished than pre-Mildara Balgownies, it's a big wine and happily not dominated by the mintiness of many Bendigo reds. Strong red-berry and oak aromas, sumptuous flavour and luxurious length. Try beef wellington.

Quality	♙♙♙♙
Value	★★★★
Grapes	cabernet sauvignon
Region	Bendigo, Vic.
Cellar	➥ 2–15+
Alc./Vol.	13.5%
RRP	$22.00 ▮

Balgownie Estate Shiraz

Quality	▼▼▼⸮
Value	★★★
Grapes	shiraz
Region	Bendigo, Vic.
Cellar	▮ 4
Alc./Vol.	13.0%
RRP	$20.00 Ⓢ ▮

Although part of the Mildara Blass empire, Balgownie Estate reds are still sourced from the same vineyard. Maker Lindsay Ross.

Previous outstanding vintages: '76, '80, '86, '90, '91, '93

CURRENT RELEASE 1994   Not a big change from last year's note. Tastes like a 'difficult' year, with some acid and leafy/mulberry, green-fruit aromas showing, along with crushed peppercorns. Try it with a T-bone steak.

Bannockburn Pinot Noir

Quality	▼▼▼▼▼
Value	★★★★★
Grapes	pinot noir
Region	Geelong, Vic.
Cellar	▮ 4+
Alc./Vol.	13.0%
RRP	$37.80

Gary Farr makes one of the best, and arguably the most Burgundy-like, Australian pinots. He uses traditional French methods, not only in the winemaking but also in the viticulture.

Previous outstanding vintages: '84, '86, '88, '89, '90, '91, '92, '94

CURRENT RELEASE 1995   Terrific stuff! Serve this to the French and they'd be happy to claim it as their own. The colour is deep and showing some development. There are sweet cherry aromas together with earthy, sappy and peppery characters from the whole-bunch fermentation. It's starting to build gamy overtones. Sumptuous depth of flavour: rich, silky, lush, mouth-watering, and great tannins to finish. A blinder. Try it with truffled squab.

Bannockburn Saignée

Quality	▼▼▼▼
Value	★★★⸓
Grapes	pinot noir
Region	Geelong, Vic.
Cellar	▮ 2+
Alc./Vol.	12.5%
RRP	$18.50

Saigner is the French verb 'to bleed', and in this case it means a small proportion of juice was 'bled' off the fermenter of must before the fermentation began. It's done to concentrate the wine being fermented, while the 'bled' juice makes a nice rosé style.

CURRENT RELEASE 1996   Full of pinot charm, this is a delightful rosé style. The colour is medium salmon-pink; the nose is all sappy, smoky, toasty pinot aroma, with hints of earth and stalk. In the mouth it's light and fruity with strawberry notes and a soft but dry finish, which lingers well. Serve with antipasto.

Bannockburn Shiraz

Since winemaker Gary Farr took to fermenting this shiraz with whole bunches and other traditional Burgundy techniques, it's changed style and become a very elegant, graceful wine.

Previous outstanding vintages: '89, '91, '92, '94

CURRENT RELEASE 1995 Delicious stuff! A fruit-led style that sports beguiling aromas of black pepper, cherry and mixed spices. There is lively acid, which doesn't intrude, plus sweet, ripe fruit flavours of medium weight and luxurious smoothness. Simply yummy! Serve with roast veal loin.

Quality	♟♟♟♟♟
Value	★★★★
Grapes	shiraz
Region	Geelong, Vic.
Cellar	🍶 10
Alc./Vol.	13.0%
RRP	$27.40

Banrock Station Shiraz

This wine is designed to appeal to nature lovers and recyclers, judging by the label and its 'Gee, isn't nature wonderful?' blurb. From the BRL Hardy camp.

CURRENT RELEASE 1994 This has a medium-depth colour and a rather ordinary herbal, wintergreen aroma. It's light and somewhat weak-kneed, showing some development as you might expect, but it's perfectly acceptable around a Sunday BBQ with lots of smoke and dogs and noise.

Quality	♟♟♟
Value	★★★
Grapes	shiraz
Region	Murray Valley, SA
Cellar	🍶
Alc./Vol.	13.5%
RRP	$11.20 Ⓢ

Barratt Pinot Noir

The Barratts sell some of the fruit from their Piccadilly Valley vineyard to Jeffrey Grosset, who also makes their wines for them. The vineyard was planted by the late Ian Wilson.

Previous outstanding vintages: '94

CURRENT RELEASE 1996 Excellent medium–deep purple–red colour, and the impression of depth continues throughout the wine. The nose is very stemmy from whole-bunch fermentation, with some sour cherry and cherry-skin flavours beneath. It has some fruit sweetness and length, but the stalky characters dominate. Better in a year or two. Then serve with hare.

Quality	♟♟♟♟
Value	★★★★
Grapes	pinot noir
Region	Adelaide Hills, SA
Cellar	➡ 1–3+
Alc./Vol.	14.0%
RRP	$29.00

Barwang Cabernet Sauvignon

Quality	♥♥♥♥
Value	★★★★
Grapes	cabernet sauvignon
Region	Young, NSW
Cellar	↑ 8+
Alc./Vol.	13.0%
RRP	$15.70 ⑤

The marketers are obviously trying to create a new and independent identity for Barwang. The McWilliams name is limited to fine print on the back label. Makers Jim Brayne and Russell Cody.

Previous outstanding vintages: '93, '94

CURRENT RELEASE 1995 Last year's won both the Penguin Wine of the Year Award and the Best Bargain Red Award. The '95 is good but has less panache. The colour is medium ruby and there are mulberry, toasty oak and nutty aromas, with a gamy aspect. The palate is showing some development and the woody, dry nutty characters are warm and savoury, finishing with a little acid. Goes with braised beef.

Barwang Shiraz

Quality	♥♥♥♥
Value	★★★★
Grapes	shiraz
Region	Young, NSW
Cellar	➡ 2–8+
Alc./Vol.	14.0%
RRP	$15.70 ⑤

The chaps at McWilliams have been turning out some very useful vino from this high-altitude planting at Young, on the western side of the Great Dividing Range. Maker Jim Brayne.

Previous outstanding vintages: '90, '91, '92, '93, '94

CURRENT RELEASE 1995 A nose of crushed mulberries together with leafy overtones and just a vague whiff of spice this year. The palate is where it all happens. It's big, solid, sweet-fruity, bouncy and generous. Tannin chimes in on the finish, putting in a strong bid for cellaring. Serve with cheddar.

Best's Pinot Meunier

Best's Great Western vineyards have some of the oldest vines in Australia. This comes from the original plantings made by Henry Best in 1869.
CURRENT RELEASE 1993 This is a stunning Burgundian style (despite the fact that they don't grow meunier in Burgundy!), which is just hitting its leathery/gamy, slightly feral and tremendously complex straps at four years of age. There's some nicely integrated oak, and the sumptuous, velvet-smooth palate has beautiful flavour and great length. Exciting stuff. Serve with snails bourguignon.

Quality	♟♟♟♟♟
Value	★★★★★
Grapes	pinot meunier
Region	Grampians, Vic.
Cellar	▮ 5
Alc./Vol.	13.5%
RRP	$29.00

Best's Pinot Noir

Best's makes an unusual pinot, which usually needs time to show its colours, and tends to age better than most. Makers Viv Thomson and Simon Clayfield.
CURRENT RELEASE 1996 The colour is medium–light purple–red, and the nose is fruit-led with cherry and strawberry to the fore. In the mouth it seems lean and somewhat acidic, but it's just a pup, and experience shows that it will be all the better for at least a one- or two-year wait. When young, serve with rare barbecued tuna.

Quality	♟♟♟♟
Value	★★★⯪
Grapes	pinot noir
Region	Grampians, Vic.
Cellar	▮ 5
Alc./Vol.	13.5%
RRP	$19.50

Bethany Grenache Pressings

The story goes that this was the pressings that would normally go into tawny port, until someone thought it'd taste pretty good as an unfortified dry red.
CURRENT RELEASE 1995 The colour is nothing to get excited about (a light purple–red), and the nose has plenty of jammy strawberry and raspberry aromas with no apparent oak. There's an ethereal, herbal note and it's very typical of the variety. The alcohol gives an oily texture, and the palate has an impression of sweetness, making it taste like an unfortified port.

Quality	♟♟♟⯪
Value	★★★
Grapes	grenache
Region	Barossa Valley, SA
Cellar	▮ 2
Alc./Vol.	14.0%
RRP	$14.80

Bethany Shiraz

Quality	�♟♟♟
Value	★★★
Grapes	shiraz
Region	Barossa Valley, SA
Cellar	▮ 4+
Alc./Vol.	12.5%
RRP	$21.40 ▮

The Bethany winery is in an abandoned quarry, high on the eastern side of the Barossa Valley with a stunning view over the village of Bethany and its vineyards.
Previous outstanding vintages: '88, '90, '91, '92, '93
CURRENT RELEASE 1995   Stalky, herbal and gumleafy aromas; quite stylish oak that seems less pronounced than usual. Plenty of straightforward plummy flavour in the mouth, which is soft on the finish. Try it with salt-bush mutton.

Bindi Pinot Noir

Quality	♟♟♟♟
Value	★★★★
Grapes	pinot noir
Region	Macedon, Vic.
Cellar	▮ 2
Alc./Vol.	13.2%
RRP	$20.00 (cellar door)

Bindi is the Macedon vineyard of the Dhillon family. Michael Dhillon has spent a lot of time in Burgundy ferreting out the secrets. Burgundiphile Stuart Anderson consults.
Previous outstanding vintages: '94
CURRENT RELEASE 1995   The '94 was a more successful year, but don't dismiss the '95 out of hand. It has a pale ruby colour, and the palate might be accused of lacking weight and length. But it goes well with food, its tightness and acidity chiming in well with barbecued quail.

Bloodwood Rosé of Malbec

Quality	♟♟♟
Value	★★★
Grapes	malbec
Region	Orange, NSW
Cellar	▮ 1
Alc./Vol.	10.0%
RRP	$14.00

Remember the band Frijid Pink? This is their music, reincarnated as wine. Chill it well.
CURRENT RELEASE 1996   Quite a full purple–red hue for a rosé. The nose offers mixed spices, with cloves and cinnamon predominating. It's clean and fresh with some lollyish flavour and a fair whack of sweetness on the finish. Refrigerate, and serve with bouillabaisse.

Blue Pyrenees Estate

Like a French chateau, this doesn't give away any secrets. No mention of grape varieties anywhere on the container. Maker Vincent Gere.

Previous outstanding vintages: '82, '88, '90, '91, '93

CURRENT RELEASE 1994 This is a rich, distinctive style: oaky, earth/forest-floor, slightly incense-like sandalwood characters, spicy and red-berried. The palate is smooth and fleshy, accessible in youth but with plenty of legs for the future. Serve with venison stew.

Quality	🍷🍷🍷🍷½
Value	★★★½
Grapes	cabernet sauvignon; merlot; shiraz
Region	Pyrenees, Vic.
Cellar	8+
Alc./Vol.	13.0%
RRP	$26.60

CURRENT RELEASE 1995 Tough stuff. The bouquet is green-leafy and it's tight, tense and taut in the mouth; quite unready at present. Whether there is adequate fruit to reward cellaring is uncertain, but it certainly needs time to soften before broaching. Cellar, then try it with a rich casserole.

Quality	🍷🍷🍷½
Value	★★★
Grapes	cabernet sauvignon; merlot; cabernet franc; shiraz
Region	Pyrenees, Vic.
Cellar	3–8+
Alc./Vol.	13.5%
RRP	$29.00

Botobolar Shiraz

Botobolar was the first certified organic vineyard in Australia to promote itself as such. It was the vision of Gil and Vincie Wahlquist, but today it's run by the Karstroms.

CURRENT RELEASE 1994 This is a rich, chunky, generous red in which clean spicy/peppery/berry fruit is attractively wedded to toasty, smoky oak. At three years it's starting to drink well and is building complexity. It's also smooth and friendly in the mouth. Try braised steak and mushrooms.

Quality	🍷🍷🍷🍷
Value	★★★★
Grapes	shiraz
Region	Mudgee, NSW
Cellar	8+
Alc./Vol.	14.0%
RRP	$14.90

Bowen Estate Cabernet Sauvignon

Quality	♟♟♟♟¸
Value	★★★★
Grapes	cabernet sauvignon
Region	Coonawarra, SA
Cellar	▮ 8
Alc./Vol.	13.0%
RRP	$25.35 ▮

The Bowens got all expansionist in 1996–97, buying an established 50-acre vineyard next door. It's on prime terra rossa country and has always been dry grown and, until recently, hand-pruned.

Previous outstanding vintages: '84, '85, '86, '87, '88, '89, '90, '91, '92, '93, '94

CURRENT RELEASE 1995   Despite a difficult year, the Bowens pulled through and made some fine reds. This has a smoky, gunpowder nose due to the French oak, coupled with blackcurrant fruit. There are rich blackberry and blackcurrant mouth flavours, and it's sweet, full, rich and elegant in the mouth. It has a degree of style and tight structure. Goes well with pink lamb.

Bowen Estate Cabernet Sauvignon Merlot Cabernet Franc

Quality	♟♟♟♟
Value	★★★★
Grapes	cabernet sauvignon; merlot; cabernet franc; petit verdot
Region	Coonawarra, SA
Cellar	▮ 5+
Alc./Vol.	13.0%
RRP	$23.60 ▮

Winemaker Doug Bowen is a quietly spoken gent, despite the longwinded name of this wine. His daughter Emma has joined the team of late, and is studying winemaking at Charles Sturt University in Wagga.

CURRENT RELEASE 1995   Similar gunsmoke overtones to the cabernet, amidst a complex perfume of raspberry, mulberry and blackcurrant. There's some cedary French oak and the palate is stylish, being fine, elegant and long in the mouth. It drinks well already and teams with cotechino.

Bowen Estate Shiraz

Shiraz is the grape that built Coonawarra's fame, but these days it's being edged out by cabernet sauvignon and merlot, which are more consistent.

Previous outstanding vintages: '84, '87, '90, '91, '93, '94

CURRENT RELEASE 1995 This is a good wine from a difficult year, and the nose displays cool-year late-ripened characters: Ribena, leafiness and a hint of petrol. The palate is leaner than usual but well endowed with spicy flavour, some savoury oaky flavours on the finish and good drinkability. Try it with osso bucco.

Quality	▼▼▼▼
Value	★★★★
Grapes	shiraz
Region	Coonawarra, SA
Cellar	🍾 5
Alc./Vol.	14.0%
RRP	$23.60 🍾

Brands Laira Cabernet Sauvignon

The Brands wines are some of the least expensive in Coonawarra. In the good vintages they're bargains; in the lesser years they're often still fair value.

Previous outstanding vintages: '94

CURRENT RELEASE 1995 The nose has mulberry and blackcurrant fruit with some leafiness. These fruit flavours reappear in the mouth where the balance is quite good with cedar and cassis flavours, easy-drinking softness and gentle tannins. Try it with pork chops.

Quality	▼▼▼▼
Value	★★★⊬
Grapes	cabernet sauvignon
Region	Coonawarra, SA
Cellar	🍾 4
Alc./Vol.	13.0%
RRP	$16.90 Ⓢ

Brands Laira Shiraz

Shiraz is a marginal grape in Coonawarra, failing to ripen in cool years and struggling in most others. Brands is normally a lighter style, too.

Previous outstanding vintages: '86

CURRENT RELEASE 1995 With a medium purple–red hue, this light-bodied wine has a pepper–spice, cool-year nose and a lean, lively palate of straightforward flavour. Drink young, with spaghetti bolognese.

Quality	▼▼▼
Value	★★★
Grapes	shiraz
Region	Coonawarra, SA
Cellar	🍾 3
Alc./Vol.	12.5%
RRP	$15.30 Ⓢ

Brands Original Vineyard Shiraz

Quality	??????
Value	★★★★
Grapes	shiraz
Region	Coonawarra, SA
Cellar	▌ 4+
Alc./Vol.	12.0%
RRP	$22.00 Ⓢ

The vines were 95 years old when this vintage was produced. Maker Jim Brand.

CURRENT RELEASE 1991   A very fine aged wine of totally distinctive style that reminds us more of a top Hunter shiraz than Coonawarra. Mid-brick-red hue; lovely mature leathery/earthy, slightly gamy complexities; elegant weight in keeping with the house style but of good depth and textural fleshiness. Fine tannin on the finish. Beaut with aged cheeses.

Bridgewater Mill Millstone Shiraz

Quality	????
Value	★★★
Grapes	shiraz
Region	McLaren Vale &
	Langhorne Creek,
	SA
Cellar	▌ 4
Alc./Vol.	14.0%
RRP	$22.50 ▌

This has been a label in search of a style, generally weighing in on the high-alcohol, blockbuster side of the ledger. Maturation in French oak is a departure from the norm.

Previous outstanding vintages: '90, '92

CURRENT RELEASE 1994   Lean and somewhat dry on the palate, this has a slightly fumey, woody bouquet with background spice and earthiness. There's a certain lack of persistence. A savoury style with some porty overtones. A good match with wild duck.

Brokenwood Cabernet Sauvignon

Quality	????
Value	★★★
Grapes	cabernet sauvignon
Region	Coonawarra, SA;
	McLaren Vale, SA;
	Margaret River, WA
Cellar	▌ 5+
Alc./Vol.	13.5%
RRP	$22.50

Iain Riggs is one of the most eclectic blenders you're ever likely to witness. The nickname of this wine is the Area Blend, and it's well earned.

Previous outstanding vintages: '86, '90, '91, '93, '94

CURRENT RELEASE 1995   The nose is full of fruitcake scents, blackcurrant, mint, vanilla and a myriad other berry smells. In the mouth it has a lean and tidy structure, showing some acid but without great power or length. Try it with meatballs.

Brokenwood Graveyard Vineyard

Lots of jokes are made about the name, but it's a deadly serious drink that has earned its place among the great shirazes of this country. We reviewed '95 last year, but it's still the latest release: the '96 is sensibly being held back. Maker Iain Riggs.

Previous outstanding vintages: '83, '85, '86, '88, '89, '90, '91, '93, '94

CURRENT RELEASE 1995 This is a very smart wine, even though it's a few paces behind the '94. It has more Hunter character than usual in a young Graveyard, and the bouquet is earthy and gamy with charred wood, caramel and pepper. In the mouth it's big, brawny and long with firmness, which will take a while to mellow. Food: game pie.

Quality	▼▼▼▼▼
Value	★★★★
Grapes	shiraz
Region	Hunter Valley, NSW
Cellar	➥ 4–10+
Alc./Vol.	13.5%
RRP	$35.00 (cellar door)

Brokenwood Rayner Shiraz

This is a foil for the Graveyard, being a totally different style from a very different region. It comes, amazingly, from unirrigated vines on sand at Blewitt Springs.

Previous outstanding vintages: '94

CURRENT RELEASE 1995 An intriguing wine jammed with chocolate and plum-cake flavours, spices and coconut. The palate is rich and smooth with generous McLaren Vale flavour and some acid on the finish, which makes it seem slightly hollow. A year or two in the cellar will improve it. Serve with civet of hare.

Quality	▼▼▼▼
Value	★★★
Grapes	shiraz
Region	McLaren Vale, SA
Cellar	➥ 2–7+
Alc./Vol.	14.5%
RRP	$30.00 (cellar door)

Brokenwood Shiraz

Another promiscuous blend from the palette of Brokenwood's Iain Riggs. He is also on the board of the Winemakers Federation.

CURRENT RELEASE 1995 A lovely red that combines the best of the Hunter and McLaren Vale. The bouquet has vanilla, crushed peppercorns and plum, and the structure is solid with a big mid-palate and excellent concentration. It makes a forceful statement, which lingers for a long time in the mouth. Food: osso bucco.

Quality	▼▼▼▼▼
Value	★★★★
Grapes	shiraz
Region	McLaren Vale, SA; Hunter Valley, NSW; King Valley, Vic.
Cellar	▮ 10+
Alc./Vol.	13.5%
RRP	$19.35

Brookland Valley Cabernet Merlot

Quality	ŸŸŸŸ?
Value	★★★★
Grapes	cabernet sauvignon; merlot; cabernet franc
Region	Margaret River, WA
Cellar	7+
Alc./Vol.	13.2%
RRP	$24.00

Brookland Valley, established by Malcolm and Dee Jones in 1984, is a 56-hectare property, 20 hectares of which are under vine. It has never had a winery, the wines being made elsewhere, but new partner BRL Hardy will change that.

CURRENT RELEASE 1994   A chunky, high-extract wine with a big finish and marvellous length, this shows Margaret River at its best. There are redcurrant and cherry aromas allied to some meaty characters. The taste is savoury and has long-maceration tannin structure. A generous red to serve with braised venison.

Brown Brothers Cabernet Sauvignon

Quality	ŸŸŸ?
Value	★★★
Grapes	cabernet sauvignon
Region	North East Victoria
Cellar	4
Alc./Vol.	13.0%
RRP	$18.60 $

It seems 1995 was a pretty lean year for the full-bodied red varieties throughout the southern parts of Victoria and South Australia. The better balanced of them will at least provide reasonable early drinking.

CURRENT RELEASE 1995   The colour is an attractive medium–deep purple–red, and there are cherry-like, sweet ripe fruit aromas. A straightforward wine without a lot of depth, which offers respectable drinking now and will possibly improve over the next couple of years. Serve with lamb chops.

Brown Brothers Cellar Door Release Graciano

Quality	ŸŸŸ?
Value	★★★↑
Grapes	graciano
Region	Milawa, Vic.
Cellar	1–5+
Alc./Vol.	12.5%
RRP	$15.00 (cellar door)

Graciano is a Spanish variety, a minor grape in red Rioja. Plantings are in decline these days, but there is evidence that if well handled it can make excellent wine. Only available at the Milawa winery.

CURRENT RELEASE 1994   Very deep purple–red colour. Quite youthful and even a little raw, this has fresh, immature spicy aromas that have most in common with shiraz. There is some overt oak flavour and the palate is lean, with a peppery and slightly acidic finish. Cellar, then serve with barbecued lamb chops.

Brown Brothers Everton

Everton was an old Brown Brothers vineyard, which has long since been abandoned because yields were so low. The fruit for this wine comes from a range of sources. **CURRENT RELEASE 1995** This is a pretty basic, drink-now red, and nothing like the marvellous Everton reds we've drunk from the '60s. The colour is medium–light, and the nose has plain leafy/berry aromas with some malbec stalkiness. It's lean and fairly light on the palate and okay value at the price. Food: pork sausages.

Quality	♀♀♀
Value	★★★
Grapes	cabernet sauvignon 40%; merlot 21%; shiraz 20%; malbec 19%
Region	North East Victoria
Cellar	▮ 2
Alc./Vol.	13.0%
RRP	$13.10

Brown Brothers Politini's Cabernet Sauvignon

Brown Brothers have a whole range of limited production wines that are only available from the Milawa cellar door. They are worth the detour. This is one. **CURRENT RELEASE 1994** Smoky oak and 'cigar butt' vegetal character, coupled with pronounced acidity and leanness, mark this as a cool-climate wine. The overall impression is of austerity. Try it with shish kebabs.

Quality	♀♀♀♀
Value	★★★⊦
Grapes	cabernet sauvignon
Region	King Valley, Vic.
Cellar	⬤ 1–5+
Alc./Vol.	12.5%
RRP	$15.00

Brown Brothers Tarrango

A perennial good-time drop, which never fails to please. Tarrango is a cross between touriga and sultana. Browns can't believe their luck: there's no competition in the tarrango market. **CURRENT RELEASE 1996** The colour is darker this year – a medium–full purple–ruby – and the alcohol higher. The nose is all lollies and cherries with a lacing of spice. There's plenty of fruit and a slight grip, which raises this vintage further out of the rosé class, putting a foot in the Beaujolais door. Good length on the palate. Try it with antipasto.

Quality	♀♀♀⍭
Value	★★★★
Grapes	tarrango
Region	Murray Valley, Vic.
Cellar	▮ 1
Alc./Vol.	12.5%
RRP	$10.40

Cambewarra Estate Cabernet Sauvignon

Quality	♟♟♟♟♟
Value	★★★
Grapes	cabernet sauvignon
Region	south coast New South Wales
Cellar	🍷 3+
Alc./Vol.	13.3%
RRP	$29.00

This new vineyard is near the Shoalhaven River on the New South Wales south coast. The wines are made at Tamburlaine in the Hunter. This is a very impressive first-crop wine, but only 80 cases were produced.

CURRENT RELEASE 1996   A stunner from three-year-old vines, which bodes well for the vineyard. Superbly deep colour; powerful blackcurrant/blackberry cabernet and stylish French oak perfumes; good concentration of beautifully ripened cabernet flavour. There is a hint of stalkiness on the finish, but it's just a babe, and will probably reward a year or so's bottle-ageing. Try it with gourmet sausages.

Cambewarra Estate Chambourcin

Quality	♟♟♟
Value	★★★
Grapes	chambourcin
Region	Central NSW
Cellar	🍷 1
Alc./Vol.	13.1 %
RRP	$18.00

This vineyard was established in 1991. It has 4 hectares under vine and is the labour of love of Geoffrey and Louise Cole. Maker Greg Silkman (contract).

CURRENT RELEASE 1996   A pretty, lolly style that could be served chilled. The colour is a lively purple and the nose is slightly earthy with sweet berry smells. The palate has a lolly character with sweet berry flavour, and the finish is soft. It drinks well with Mexican food.

Campbells Bobbie Burns Shiraz

Quality	♟♟♟♟♟
Value	★★★★★
Grapes	shiraz
Region	North East Victoria
Cellar	➬ 2–6
Alc./Vol.	13.0%
RRP	$18.00

Bobbie Burns was once the core business for this winery, but these days it's just one of many fine red wines that come from the stable. Maker Colin Campbell.

CURRENT RELEASE 1994   More civilised and refined these days, but it still remains a quintessential north-eastern red. Deep ruby colour and strong plum and berry smells. The palate is medium- to full-bodied, with sweet plum flavours laced with spice. The tannin on the finish is quite urbane and well integrated. It goes well with slightly spicy lamb shanks.

Campbells The Barkly

This wine was given some slinky packaging to commemorate 125 years of winemaking by Campbells. Interesting they should choose the variety durif, which is essentially a port component. Maker Colin Campbell.
CURRENT RELEASE 1993   The wine threatens to come on like an enraged gorilla but suddenly shows an urbane, civilised streak. The colour is deep red–purple, and the nose is a mixture of briar patch and berry aromas. The full-bodied palate has sweet berry flavours plus a distinct hint of marzipan. Could the latter be due to the oak treatment? There is firm grip and fine-grained tannin on the finish. It's great with a rich oxtail stew.

Quality	▼▼▼▼▼
Value	★★★★
Grapes	durif
Region	North East Victoria
Cellar	▬ 3–8
Alc./Vol.	13.0%
RRP	$23.00

Canobolas-Smith Alchemy

The vineyard and winery were established in 1986 near Orange. There are 6 hectares under vine.
CURRENT RELEASE 1994   This is a healthy Bordeaux-style blend that has a brilliant ruby colour, a spicy nose and underlying fruit aromas. The palate is light- to medium-weight with dark cherry flavours, hints of tart acid and some toasty oak. The finish has well-tuned grip and fine-grained tannin. It goes well with pan-fried quail.

Quality	▼▼▼▼
Value	★★★⊁
Grapes	cabernet sauvignon; cabernet franc; merlot; shiraz
Region	Orange, NSW
Cellar	▮ 4
Alc./Vol.	13.5%
RRP	$18.00

Canobolas-Smith Alchemy Pinot Noir

Wasn't alchemy the pseudo-science of turning base metal into gold? In this case the lead remains.
CURRENT RELEASE 1994   The colour is a pale cherry-red and the nose has a yeasty brewer's wort aroma. The palate has soft strawberry fruit and there is acid on the finish. The wine is unfiltered and the cork had a large deposit of tartaric acid on the bottom, which made for gritty pouring. Drink now with lamb shanks.

Quality	▼▼▼
Value	★★
Grapes	pinot noir
Region	Orange, NSW
Cellar	▮ 2
Alc./Vol.	13.2%
RRP	$18.00

Cape Mentelle Trinders Cabernet Merlot

Quality	🍷🍷🍷🍷½
Value	★★★★½
Grapes	cabernet sauvignon; merlot
Region	Margaret River, WA
Cellar	6
Alc./Vol.	14.0%
RRP	$21.60

The grapes were grown in the Trinders Vineyard at Margaret River. The objective is to produce a drinkable Bordeaux-style blend.

CURRENT RELEASE 1995 This is the most impressive Trinders to date. It has style and structure, and although you can drink now, cellaring will reward. The nose has juicy, ripe fruit aromas and some distinguished oak. The palate is full-bodied with sweet blackberry and cherry flavours. The finish is a model of French oak and positive grip. It has length and structure. Try it now with lamb shanks in a rich sauce.

Cape Mentelle Shiraz

Quality	🍷🍷🍷🍷½
Value	★★★★½
Grapes	shiraz; grenache
Region	Margaret River, WA
Cellar	3–8
Alc./Vol.	14.00%
RRP	$21.60

This wine label begat one of the most distinguished examples of shiraz in Australia. It has breeding and poise. Maker David Hohnen.

Previous outstanding vintages: '83, '86, '87, '88, '89, '90, '91, '92, '93, '94

CURRENT RELEASE 1995 A very impressive wine that makes much of spice and natural tannin. The colour is a deep crimson with purple tinges, and the nose is spicy with hints of black pepper and vinous grape qualities. The full-bodied palate has ripe plums plus cherries, and there is a handsome load of spices. The finish has soft, fine-grained tannins that linger long. The wine is a youngster that can handle a robust dish like venison sausages.

Cape Mentelle Zinfandel

This marque is one of the few Australian devotees to this remarkable variety. It's a wonderful jolt in the tastebuds that makes no pretence to elegance. Viva la Zin! Maker David Hohnen.

Previous outstanding vintages: '81, '82, '84, '88, '90, '91, '92, '93, '94

CURRENT RELEASE 1995   It's all natural, folks! The exuberance and verve comes straight from the berries. The colour is inky blue–purple. The nose is zesty with loads of spice. The body is big and bold with juicy mouthfilling berry flavours, which are backed up by some mouth-puckering natural tannins. Wood plays only a small part, and there is plenty of grip. It needs more time, but amaze your friends and pull the cork. Try it with devilled kidneys.

Quality	🍷🍷🍷🍷🍷
Value	★★★★★
Grapes	zinfandel
Region	Margaret River, WA
Cellar	🍾 10
Alc./Vol.	15.0%
RRP	$21.60

Capercaillie Cabernet Merlot Franc

A capercaillie is a Scottish grouse. It's also Alasdair Sutherland's new venture in the Hunter Valley at the former Dawson Estate. He used to make wine at Saxonvale for many years.

CURRENT RELEASE 1996   This is just a babe, all arms and legs and quite oaky; should be better for two years' cellaring. Vanilla and coconut aromas indicate liberal use of American oak. The palate has good depth and richness, with a little acidity showing. It's already surprisingly palatable. Try it with spicy sausages.

Quality	🍷🍷🍷¼
Value	★★★
Grapes	cabernet sauvignon; merlot; cabernet franc
Region	Coonawarra, SA; Orange, NSW
Cellar	🍷 2–6+
Alc./Vol.	13.2%
RRP	$19.00 (cellar door)

Carlyle Estate Shiraz

A newish label from Wahgunyah, Victoria. Hopefully the money not spent on label design went into the winemaking.

CURRENT RELEASE 1994   A typically regional style that is fairly big, but not without elegance. The nose is slightly porty with ripe plum aromas. The full-bodied palate is full of plums and pepper. The tannin on the finish imparts a medium grip. It's just perfect with kranski sausages.

Quality	🍷🍷🍷¼
Value	★★★⅟
Grapes	shiraz
Region	North East Victoria
Cellar	🍾 4
Alc./Vol.	13.0%
RRP	$14.95

Cassegrain Reserve Cabernet Merlot

Quality	ΨΨΨΨ
Value	★★★★
Grapes	cabernet sauvignon; merlot
Region	Hastings Valley, NSW
Cellar	➙ 2–6
Alc./Vol.	12.8%
RRP	$23.00

Call in the reserves, because it seems that with Cassegrain, 'Reserve' equates with a tough and uncompromising style. This is a wine with lots of focus, thanks to a dry year.

CURRENT RELEASE 1994 The colour is an intense blood red and the nose has blackberry aromas with a hint of briar. The palate is concentrated with blackberry and redcurrant flavours. The focus is on fine-grained tannins and loads of grip. It needs time, and will become all the more complex with cellaring. Try it with roast squab.

Cassegrain Reserve Chambourcin

Quality	ΨΨΨΨ
Value	★★★★
Grapes	chambourcin
Region	Hastings Valley, NSW
Cellar	➙ 3–6
Alc./Vol.	13.5%
RRP	$23.00

Unusual variety from an unusual location. Cassegrain is an ambitious vineyard that covers 180 hectares in the Hastings Valley. Maker John Cassegrain.

CURRENT RELEASE 1994 You expect a soft, cuddly style from this variety, but this is a tough mutha. It has an intense colour, and the nose has smoke and blackberry aromas. The palate is lean and keen with cherry and blackberry flavours, which are followed by some black-tea-like tannins on a gripping finish. Will it throw a crust and soften? Wait and see, but in the meantime try it with guineafowl, Peking-style.

Quality	ΨΨΨΨ?
Value	★★★★
Grapes	chambourcin
Region	Hastings, NSW
Cellar	➙ 2–6
Alc./Vol.	13.8%
RRP	$23.00

CURRENT RELEASE 1995 There is a bit of breeding here. The normal pink party animal has been vanquished and replaced by a wine with structure. The vinous nose is a mixture of ripe berries and pencil-shaving oak. The palate is medium- to full-bodied with dark cherry and plum fruit flavours. There are lashings of wood and fine-grained tannin on the finish. It's a substantial wine that can handle substantial food like buffalo sausages.

Cathcart Ridge Cabernet Sauvignon

This one was released early because it seemed ready for the outing. It's a very fresh style.
CURRENT RELEASE 1996 The colour is a bright ruby and the nose is dominated by oak. There are vanilla and coconut aromas with a mulberry background. The light body has some sweet, clean berry fruit and this is adorned by coffee-flavoured wood. It drinks well with pink lamb.

Quality	♀♀♀♀
Value	★★★
Grapes	cabernet sauvignon
Region	Grampians, Vic.
Cellar	▌ 3
Alc./Vol.	11.75%
RRP	$16.00

Cathcart Ridge Shiraz

According to CEO David Farnhill they make wine 'the public want to drink'. Indeed they do, as the wines are somewhat softer than most made in the district.
CURRENT RELEASE 1994 A drinkable wine with a fresh, plummy nose. It's quite complex with a minty, chocolate nose and a background of plums. The palate is medium-bodied and chewy in texture, with soft plum-flavoured fruit and coconut oak with a coffee flavour. There are strong tannins, and because of the dry finish it goes well with smoked kangaroo.

Quality	♀♀♀♀
Value	★★★★
Grapes	shiraz
Region	Grampians, Vic.
Cellar	▌ 4
Alc./Vol.	13.0%
RRP	$17.00

Cathcart Ridge Shiraz Cabernet Sauvignon

This 8.5-hectare property was established in 1978 by the local doctor. Since then it has changed hands, with David Farnhill now the CEO/winemaker.
CURRENT RELEASE 1994 The wine is starting to show some bottle development, although the colour remains youthful and the nose has a strong mint component. The palate is showing maturity with plum-flavoured fruit and a medium body. The finish has well-integrated oak and attractive length. It drinks well now with dev-illed kidneys.

Quality	♀♀♀♀
Value	★★★
Grapes	shiraz; cabernet sauvignon
Region	Grampians, Vic.
Cellar	▌ 4
Alc./Vol.	12.5%
RRP	$18.00

Chain of Ponds Amadeus

Quality	♟♟♟♟♟
Value	★★★★
Grapes	cabernet sauvignon
Region	Adelaide Hills, SA
Cellar	➛ 1–7+
Alc./Vol.	13.0%
RRP	$30.00 ▯

Funny name for a vineyard, but Chain of Ponds is named after a place in the Adelaide Hills. Proprietors Caj and Ginny Amadio.
CURRENT RELEASE 1994   This is the Requiem rather than *The Magic Flute*; it's a serious wine of real gravity and structure. Needs air, and then reveals blackberry cabernet fruit and cedary overtones. The palate is very intense with deep flavour and firm tannins. A very promising red that will probably repay cellaring. Try it with rare roast beef.

Chain of Ponds Novello Rosso

Quality	♟♟♟♟♟
Value	★★★★
Grapes	grenache; sangiovese
Region	Adelaide Hills, SA
Cellar	▮ 2
Alc./Vol.	12.8%
RRP	$13.70

The Amadios, who own this vineyard, are of Italian background, hence the name of this 'light red' style and the presence of sangiovese.
CURRENT RELEASE 1996   The colour is medium purple–red, and the nose is perfumed with violets, white pepper and a hint of leafiness. It's a very well-made, soft, light red without appreciable tannin, but with good richness and weight. It would be buono with vitello tonato.

Chapel Hill McLaren Vale Shiraz

Quality	♟♟♟♟♟
Value	★★★★ь
Grapes	shiraz
Region	McLaren Vale, SA
Cellar	▮ 10
Alc./Vol.	13.5%
RRP	$18.00

Maker Pam Dunsford is a deft hand at capturing varietal and regional characters. She has a distinguished career in winemaking that is going from strength to strength.
Previous outstanding vintages: '90, '91, '93, '94
CURRENT RELEASE 1995   Big, bold and beautiful, this is a regional style that also maintains varietal integrity. Deep red colour, and a spicy nose with ripe plum aromas plus a waft of vanillan oak. The palate has ripe plum flavours and an iron tonic character typical of the district. Firm tannin supplies grip on the finish. It needs a robust dish like confit of duck.

Chateau Tahbilk Cabernet Sauvignon

This is a must-visit on a winery tour of the Garden State. It's historic and atmospheric, and now boasts the Len Evans Wine Museum.

CURRENT RELEASE 1994 It's a complex, enjoyable style that entertains in spite of the modest alcohol. The colour is a deep brick red, and the nose is a savoury mix of berries and oak. (It smells like the nose on a wine that has been bottle-aged for over a decade.) The palate is youthful and lively, with blackberry, capsicum and aniseed flavours that are matched by gentle tannins and discreet oak. It drinks well with duck tortellini.

Quality	YYYY
Value	★★★★
Grapes	cabernet sauvignon 90%; cabernet franc 10%
Region	Goulburn Valley, SA
Cellar	▬ 4
Alc./Vol.	11.5%
RRP	$15.00 ⑤

Chateau Tahbilk Shiraz

The bold facts are the vineyard and winery were established in 1860 and have endured phylloxera and financial hard and good times for 137 years. In reality it has become a Victorian wine icon. Maker Alister Purbrick. *Previous outstanding vintages: '71, '76, '80, '82, '85, '86, '90, '92, '93*

CURRENT RELEASE 1994 There is a hint of old times, yet the wine has become a smidgin more contemporary. The wine has a strong brick-red colour, and the nose is full of berries and spices. There is also an element of polished timber à la gentlepersons' clubs. The palate is medium-bodied with berry and licorice flavours that are teamed with soft wood and fine-grained tannins. It's a perfect pasta style.

Quality	YYYY
Value	★★★★
Grapes	shiraz
Region	Goulburn Valley, Vic.
Cellar	▬ 4
Alc./Vol.	12.0%
RRP	$14.00 ⑤

Chestnut Grove Cabernet Merlot

Quality	♟♟♟♗
Value	★★★⟉
Grapes	cabernet sauvignon; merlot
Region	Manjimup, WA
Cellar	▮ 3
Alc./Vol.	13.0%
RRP	$14.50

This label is making a determined marketing push in the eastern states. The vineyard is located at Manjimup. Places given Aboriginal names with the suffix 'up' are those in which permanent water is available.

CURRENT RELEASE 1994   A graceful wine with a medium body and clean fruit flavours. The nose has a pleasant berry aroma plus some dusty oak. The palate has some sweet berry characters and these are matched by some discreet oak. It drinks well now with a lamb and barley casserole.

Chestnut Grove Pinot Noir

Quality	♟♟♟♗
Value	★★★⟉
Grapes	pinot noir
Region	Manjimup, WA
Cellar	▮ 3
Alc./Vol.	14.0%
RRP	$20.50

It's like the plot of a Z-grade thriller: which region in Australia will produce a great pinot noir? Watch this book!

CURRENT RELEASE 1995   Although the alcohol is high it doesn't seem to influence the texture of the wine. The colour is a light cherry-red and the nose is sappy with underlying fruit aromas. The palate is medium-bodied with sweet cherry and strawberry fruit flavours. These are matched by some astringent tannins on a medium-length finish. It drinks well with roast quail.

Cleveland Minus Five

Quality	♟♟♟♗
Value	★★★⟉
Grapes	cabernet sauvignon 70%; cabernet franc 20%; merlot 10%
Region	Macedon, Vic.
Cellar	▮ 3
Alc./Vol.	12.5%
RRP	$21.00

Sounds like a jazz tune circa 1956, but the name actually refers to the temperature at the time of harvest.

CURRENT RELEASE 1995   The colour is a vibrant crimson and the nose has succulent berry aromas tinged with spices. The palate has a sweet berry flavour with cherry and strawberry, and there is a leafy component. The finish is high in fresh acid that adds zest. It drinks well now as a fresh style. Try it with spaghetti and meatballs.

Cleveland Pinot Noir

The Macedon region has to be pinot territory – it's ultra-cool. The vineyard is a diminutive 4 hectares, and a labour of love for ex–airline captain Keith Brien and wife Lynette. Maker Keith Brien.
CURRENT RELEASE 1994   Lovely grub with a great depth of flavour. The colour is deep ruby, and the nose has cherry and strawberry aromas plus a hint of earth and truffles. The palate is sweet and succulent. There are strong, dark cherry flavours, which are supported by oak that adds a cedary element. The tannin is soft compared to the bulk of fruit. It drinks well now, but cellaring should reward. Try it with mushroom risotto.

Quality	♟♟♟♟♟
Value	★★★★★
Grapes	pinot noir
Region	Macedon, Vic.
Cellar	▮ 6
Alc./Vol.	13.5%
RRP	$21.00

Clonakilla Cabernet

The winery was established in 1971 by Dr John Kirk. It has been planted up to 2 hectares. Maker John Kirk.
CURRENT RELEASE 1994   A bit of bottle-age is starting to sneak in, yet the colour remains a bright garnet. The nose has leafy smells and a cassis aroma. The medium-bodied palate offers mature fruit flavours and a dry, dusty oak finish completes the picture. It drinks well now with casserole of kid.

Quality	♟♟♟♟
Value	★★★★
Grapes	cabernet sauvignon
Region	Canberra, ACT
Cellar	▮ 3
Alc./Vol.	13.2%
RRP	$16.00 (cellar door)

Clonakilla Shiraz Pinot Noir Viognier

An unusual blend made from grapes grown on vines that look as though they have been literally willed out of the ground. These are marginal growing conditions.
CURRENT RELEASE 1996 The colour is that of a healthy young red, and the nose is loaded with spices and wild berry flavours. The medium-bodied palate has dark cherries and plum flavours, which are matched by pepper and spice. The oak is there but it isn't obtrusive. Try it with devilled kidneys.

Quality	♟♟♟♟
Value	★★★★
Grapes	shiraz; pinot noir; viognier
Region	Canberra, ACT
Cellar	➡ 2–6
Alc./Vol.	13.0%
RRP	$18.00 (cellar door)

Coldstream Hills Pinot Noir

Quality	♟♟♟♟
Value	★★★★
Grapes	pinot noir
Region	Yarra Valley, SA
Cellar	▮ 4
Alc./Vol.	13.5%
RRP	$22.00

If the mantle for the champion of pinot noir is awarded, it would have to go to the honcho of Coldstream Hills, James Halliday.

CURRENT RELEASE 1996   A fresh style that could be criticised for being a little simple. The colour is a pale ruby, and the nose has strawberry and cherry smells. The palate is lightweight with some sweet cherry flavours, and there is a gentle wash of wood to add some interest. The finish shows some fresh acid and reasonable length. It drinks well now with chargrilled quail.

Coolangatta Estate Cabernet Shiraz

Quality	♟♟♟
Value	★★★
Grapes	cabernet sauvignon; shiraz
Region	Shoalhaven, NSW
Cellar	▮ 3
Alc./Vol.	13.1%
RRP	$16.00

The grapes were grown at Shoalhaven in coastal New South Wales. They were vinified at Tyrrell's in the Hunter Valley.

CURRENT RELEASE 1996   This is a light- to medium-bodied style with a fresh, berry nose. The palate has raspberry and plum flavours, and these are followed by a hint of vanilla (thanks to the oak). The finish is astringent with lingering tannins. It would serve well with pork chops.

Cooperage Hill Estate Shiraz

Quality	♟♟♟
Value	★★★
Grapes	shiraz
Region	Bendigo, Vic.
Cellar	▮ 2
Alc./Vol.	12.8%
RRP	$14.00

This is obviously the original label; notice there is a 'Hill' in the name of the vineyard. It's debatable which label is worse.

CURRENT RELEASE 1994   Considering the other wines from the district, this is a lighter style. The colour is a light cherry-red and the nose has pepper–spice and cherry aromas. The light- to medium-bodied palate has dark cherry and plum flavours dusted with pepper. The oak adds a slightly raw component. It's a drink-now style that goes well with pizza.

Coriole Lalla Rookh Grenache Shiraz

In case you didn't know, Lalla Rookh was a heroine in a Thomas Moore prose-poem. It was also the name of a sailing ship that transported settlers to the Southern Vales district.

CURRENT RELEASE 1995 The maker didn't stint the wood. The colour is a vibrant, dark cherry-red, and the nose has strong raspberry aromas plus some savoury oak. The palate continues the raspberry theme. This is quickly overridden by the oak, which adds firmness to the finish. It's a wine that needs time. At the moment it goes well with oxtail stew.

Quality	♟♟♟♟
Value	★★★★
Grapes	grenache 88%; shiraz 12%
Region	McLaren Vale, SA
Cellar	▮ 4
Alc./Vol.	14.0%
RRP	$18.00

Coriole Redstone

This is not named after the rocket made in the USA. There is lots of red ochre and redstone in the district. This ochre was used as a paint pigment to colour London pillar boxes circa 1880s.

CURRENT RELEASE 1995 Sweet fruit and loads of alcohol combine to make a very affable style. It's a multiple blend, which affords the palate considerable complexity. The palate is full of berries and slight hints of stewed plums, and the nose is sweet and fruity with a waft of alcohol/spirit. The finish has some soft tannins, making it a gentle style. It would be great with a steak and kidney pie.

Quality	♟♟♟♟
Value	★★★★
Grapes	shiraz 45%; cabernet sauvignon 30%; grenache 25%
Region	McLaren Vale, SA
Cellar	▮ 4
Alc./Vol.	14.0%
RRP	$14.00

Coriole Sangiovese

Quality ₸₸₸₸
Value ★★★★½
Grapes sangiovese
Region McLaren Vale, SA
Cellar 3
Alc./Vol. 13.5%
RRP $15.50

This vineyard was the pioneer of this Italian variety in Australia. The object is to make a medium-bodied dry red that will relieve the tedium of the traditional varieties.

CURRENT RELEASE 1995 A very drinkable style that makes few demands on the palate. The colour is a mid-ruby, and the nose has cherry, lavender and spicy oak aromas. The medium-bodied palate is quite sweet with raspberry fruit flavour with a touch of maraschino. The wood on the finish makes for a dusty, dry character. It drinks well schnitzel parma'.

Coriole Shiraz

Quality ₸₸₸₸
Value ★★★★½
Grapes shiraz
Region McLaren Vale, SA
Cellar 6
Alc./Vol. 14.0%
RRP $20.00

Coriole was established in 1969 by the Lloyd family. Today, son Mark is the proprietor and there are 20 hectares under vine. Maker Stephen Hall.

Previous outstanding vintages: too numerous to mention

CURRENT RELEASE 1995 Typical of the marque and the district, and living proof that the 1995 vintage wasn't a total disaster. The colour is vibrant, and there is plenty of sweet berry aroma on the nose that combines with some tangy wood. The palate is rich and mouthfilling, with a flood of ripe plums and blackberry flavours. The wood fits beautifully, adding to the structure but not intruding. There is pleasant grip on the finish and the impeccable balance means it can be drunk now. Try it with liver and bacon.

Craigmoor Cabernet Sauvignon

Forget the so-called 'Mudgee Mud' and 'wine for heroes', which were probably invented by a rival wine district. Mudgee can mean finesse.
CURRENT RELEASE 1995 A very fine style that has good balance and lots of grace. The colour is a deep ruby and the nose has raspberry and dusty wood aromas. The palate has sweet fruit and attractive berry flavours. There is firm oak and drying tannins on a lingering finish. It drinks well with liver and bacon.

Quality	♥♥♥♡
Value	★★★⊦
Grapes	cabernet sauvignon
Region	Mudgee, NSW
Cellar	🍶 4
Alc./Vol.	12.5%
RRP	$14.50

Crofters Cabernet Merlot

Crofters is a new series from Houghton, named after the Houghton homestead that was built in 1863 by Dr Ferguson to resemble a Scottish crofter's farmhouse. Maker Paul Lapsley.
CURRENT RELEASE 1994 This triple gold-medal-winner is a fruit-driven style with a youthful purplish colour and a fresh, undeveloped dark berry, blackcurrant and cedar wood nose. The palate has some acid and tannin lending a firm astringency, and it promises to reward those who are patient. Serve with a rich duck dish.

Quality	♥♥♥♥
Value	★★★★
Grapes	cabernet sauvignon; merlot
Region	Margaret River & Frankland River, WA
Cellar	➡ 1–5+
Alc./Vol.	13.5%
RRP	$16.50 Ⓢ

Cullen Cabernet Sauvignon Merlot

Hallelujah, praise the lord and pass the bottle! This wine has become one of the great reds of Australia in the last few years. Winemaker Vanya Cullen has done away with the Reserve and now all the wine goes into the one label. *Previous outstanding vintages: '84, '86, '90, '91, '92, '93, '94*
CURRENT RELEASE 1995 Watch out! The thick purple colour stains the glass – don't get it on your shirt. This is a very powerful, concentrated, undeveloped red, which needs time. Latent blackberry/blackcurrant flavours – closed-up and dense – with immense potential. We can only guess at its future potential. But we know it's going to be fab-oh.

Quality	♥♥♥♥♥
Value	★★★★★
Grapes	cabernet sauvignon 70%; merlot 23%; cabernet franc 7%
Region	Margaret River, WA
Cellar	➡ 5–15+
Alc./Vol.	13.5%
RRP	$40.00 🍷

Dalfarras Cabernets

Quality	♥♥♥♥
Value	★★★★
Grapes	cabernet sauvignon 75%; cabernet franc 25%
Region	Goulburn Valley, Vic.
Cellar	▬ 4+
Alc./Vol.	13.5%
RRP	$17.60 ▯

Dalfarras is a family affair: wine by Mr Purbrick; label painting by Mrs Purbrick.

CURRENT RELEASE 1993   A little bottle-age is a bonus these days, and this one's nicely mellowed out at four years. The colour is a deep brick red. The nose shows burnt and raisin-like aromas with a touch of honeycomb. The profile is lean and tannic on the finish, and while it's losing its youthful vigour, it's picking up character. Break out a mature cheese.

Dalwhinnie Cabernet

Quality	♥♥♥♥⸵
Value	★★★⸲
Grapes	cabernet sauvignon
Region	Pyrenees, Vic.
Cellar	▬ 3–15
Alc./Vol.	13.0%
RRP	$35.00

The whisky counterpart is a highland single malt of great grace and complexity. The wines here seem to be following the product of Scotland. Maker David Jones.

Previous outstanding vintages: '92

CURRENT RELEASE 1995   Moody, mysterious and very entertaining. The colour is a deep red–purple. The nose has blackberry, chocolate and green leaf smells. The palate has a mouthfilling texture with succulent blackberry fruit flavours and a hint of sweetness. There are fine-grained tannins and some rather foreboding oak on the finish. It needs time in the cellar, but you can try it now with an aged ox steak.

Dalwhinnie Shiraz

Quality	♥♥♥♥♥
Value	★★★★⸲
Grapes	shiraz
Region	Pyrenees, Vic.
Cellar	▮ 8
Alc./Vol.	13.5%
RRP	$35.00

This vineyard is tucked in the Pyrenees behind the relatively massive Taltarni. It's a beautiful, private location and the cellar door is very tranquil. A must-visit if you are in the region.

Previous outstanding vintages: '92

CURRENT RELEASE 1995   It's almost a contradiction: this is so young, yet so soft. The colour is a dense red–purple and the nose has plums, berries and spices. The palate is voluptuous, with intense sweet plum and dark cherry flavours. These are matched by fine-grained tannins on a long finish. It has great balance and is approachable now. Try it with a steak and kidney pie.

d'Arenberg d'Arry's Original Shiraz Grenache

This was the joyfully non-PC d'Arenberg Burgundy, which rolls off the tongue rather nicely . . . until recent times. Maker Chester Osborn.

CURRENT RELEASE 1995   This is a strongly individual style: what some will enjoy as distinctive regional 'cowshed' character, others will see as sulfide/mercaptan. D'Arenberg devotees will love the wine: the rustic gutsiness, graphite-and-earth bouquet, and rich fruit sweetness followed by gripping tannins, are there in abundance. Try saddle of hare.

Quality	▼▼▼℩
Value	★★★ᖮ
Grapes	shiraz; grenache
Region	McLaren Vale, SA
Cellar	▮ 10+
Alc./Vol.	14.0%
RRP	$14.50 ▮

d'Arenberg The Old Vine Shiraz

The Old Vine, huh? Are we expected to believe the entire production came from just one vine? We've heard of the world's biggest vine at Hampton Court, but this is ridiculous.

CURRENT RELEASE 1995   This is d'Arenberg in traditional mode (is there any other?). The trademark feral gaminess is here in abundance, coupled with intense shiraz spice. Underneath that mercaptan-like character there's a mass of fruit. An idiosyncratic style for d'Arenberg devotees.

Quality	▼▼▼
Value	★★★
Grapes	shiraz
Region	McLaren Vale, SA
Cellar	▮ 5+
Alc./Vol.	14.0%
RRP	$14.50 ▮

Darling Estate Koombahla Cabernet Sauvignon

Guy Darling was one of the first farmers to diversify into grapes in the upper King Valley region. He sells fruit to Brown Brothers (who used to have a Koombahla label) and lately makes a little wine of his own.

CURRENT RELEASE 1992   An extractive aroma shows garden mint and suggestions of engine oil, while the tannins are quite aggressive and somewhat forced. It lacks a bit of polish but cellaring may bring some softening effect. Try it with pepper steak.

Quality	▼▼▼
Value	★★★
Grapes	cabernet sauvignon
Region	King Valley, Vic.
Cellar	⟷ 2–5
Alc./Vol.	13.5%
RRP	$14.50 (mailing list) ▮

David Wynn Patriarch Shiraz

Quality	♥♥♥♥♥
Value	★★★★ᵏ
Grapes	shiraz
Region	Eden Valley, SA
Cellar	◊ 10+
Alc./Vol.	13.0%
RRP	$30.00 ◊

Well-named wine, this. David Wynn was one of the great men of the wine business, as well as a key figure in the arts world. Made at Mountadam by Adam Wynn. *Previous outstanding vintages: '92, '93, '94*
CURRENT RELEASE 1995 Marvellously aromatic and fruit-dominated. There are scents of raspberry, spices and other red fruits, and in the mouth it reveals a great complexity of flavours. An unusual style, it's sumptuous and at the same time taut as a violin string. Long, peppery finish. Serve with a pepper steak.

David Wynn Unwooded Shiraz

Quality	♥♥♥ᵏ
Value	★★★ᵏ
Grapes	shiraz
Region	Barossa Valley, SA
Cellar	◊ 5
Alc./Vol.	13.0%
RRP	$13.50

The late David Wynn was almost amused by the obsession of Australian winemakers with small, new oak barrels, especially with chardonnay. He was the first to market an unwooded chardonnay and promote it as such. Maker Adam Wynn.
CURRENT RELEASE 1996 Extraordinary stuff! Green peppercorns, gumleaves, mint ... it's the full herb garden. A hugely aromatic wine which many will find a little confronting, but there's no doubting its volume and clarity of fruit. Lean, lively profile, stacks of personality; almost menthol-like. Light tannin and easy on the gums. Serve it with hamburgers.

De Bortoli Gulf Station Cabernet Sauvignon

Quality	♥♥♥ᵏ
Value	★★★
Grapes	cabernet sauvignon
Region	Yarra Valley, Vic.
Cellar	◊ 3
Alc./Vol.	13.0%
RRP	$17.40 Ⓢ

A new label for De Bortoli's Yarra Valley winery. Gulf Station is so named because De Bortoli's Dixons Creek property was once the summer paddock of the original 1400-acre farm, Gulf Station.
CURRENT RELEASE 1994 The colour shows some development and there are curry-powder spices and some greener, stalky cabernet fruit aromas. It's a generous mouthful of red – soft and drinkable – but not a wine of great finesse. Serve with rabbit stew.

De Bortoli Yarra Valley Cabernet Sauvignon

Assistant winemaker David Slingsby-Smith used to be in charge of the Penfolds red stable, so he should know something about serious red-wine-making.
Previous outstanding vintages: '88, '91, '92, '93
CURRENT RELEASE 1994   A statuesque cabernet of real class. The colour is deep and dark, the bouquet shows off some stylish oak and a hint of blackcurrant, while the taste is rich and seamless and shows excellent concentration. Serve with rare roast beef and mustard.

Quality	♟♟♟♟?
Value	★★★★
Grapes	cabernet sauvignon
Region	Yarra Valley, Vic.
Cellar	▮ 10+
Alc./Vol.	13.0%
RRP	$29.00 Ⓢ ▮

De Bortoli Yarra Valley Pinot Noir

Pinot is increasingly proving to be the variety the Yarra can do better than the others, and 1996 was a blessed vintage for it. Maker Steve Webber.
Previous outstanding vintages: '94, '95
CURRENT RELEASE 1996   Drum roll, please! This is an exceptional pinot. It starts off with a nice deep colour, and there are complex oaky, cherry, smoky, slightly gamy aromas without stalkiness. The palate is deliciously sweet in the middle; ripe-flavoured, silky-smooth and long. A wine to drink more than one glass of. Try it with marinated quail.

Quality	♟♟♟♟♟
Value	★★★★
Grapes	pinot noir
Region	Yarra Valley, Vic.
Cellar	▮ 5
Alc./Vol.	13.5%
RRP	$29.00 Ⓢ

PENGUIN BEST PINOT NOIR

De Bortoli Yarra Valley Shiraz

This is consistently one of the best shirazes in the Yarra, a region in which they should grow more shiraz than they do. De Bortoli is now one of the 10 biggest wine companies in Australia.
Previous outstanding vintages: '92, '93
CURRENT RELEASE 1994   This a yummy shiraz, filled with spicy, peppery, old leather and cedar aromas. The taste is smooth and elegant with a lovely, full mid-palate and savoury ripe-fruit flavours. The finish is firmed up by good tannin, and the balance is very pleasing. Goes well with osso bucco.

Quality	♟♟♟♟♟
Value	★★★★⸱
Grapes	shiraz
Region	Yarra Valley, Vic.
Cellar	▮ 10+
Alc./Vol.	13.0%
RRP	$29.00 Ⓢ ▮

Deakin Estate Cabernet Sauvignon

Quality	♟♟♟
Value	★★★⊢
Grapes	cabernet sauvignon
Region	Murray Valley, Vic.
Cellar	▮ 1
Alc./Vol.	13.0%
RRP	$9.35

The white wines from this company are real eye-openers, and it has to be said the area is better suited to whites than to reds.

CURRENT RELEASE 1996   This has a medium purple–red colour and a fruit-driven aroma of cherries with a herbal, skinsy overtone. The flavour is plain, basic and a trifle short, but at this price it will find many admirers. Serve with frankfurts at a party.

Deakin Estate Grand Prix Shiraz Cabernet

Quality	♟♟♟⊢
Value	★★★⊢
Grapes	shiraz; cabernet sauvignon
Region	Murray Valley, Vic.
Cellar	▮ 2
Alc./Vol.	13.0%
RRP	$12.00

This won't be popular with the friends of Albert Park Lake, and how many petrolheads are into wine, apart from Jeff Kennett?

CURRENT RELEASE 1996   Lovely deep, vivid, red–purple colour coupled with deep, pepper–spice and plum fruit characters. Good concentration of flavour, and some tannin astringency, which will ensure it cellars for a couple of years. Good value and teams well with pie floater.

Deakin Estate Shiraz

Quality	♟♟♟
Value	★★★⊢
Grapes	shiraz
Region	Murray Valley, Vic.
Cellar	▮ 2
Alc./Vol.	13.5%
RRP	$9.30 ⑤

Shiraz from the Riverland needs to be drunk while young and still showing its fruity freshness. Maker Mark Zeppel.

CURRENT RELEASE 1996   Vivid, youthful, clean berry/cherry aromas; quite perfumed and fragrant. There's admirable weight and flavour, no special length of palate but it's an all-round good-value red. Try it with bangers and mash.

Delatite R J

The initials R J are those of the founder Robert John Ritchie, and this wine marks the 21st vintage from the Estate. The vampish label looks a treat.

CURRENT RELEASE 1994 Deep purple colour and a very minty nose, which has become something of a signature for Delatite. The palate is tight and intense with concentrated blackberry fruit. The oak adds spices and some assertive tannins. It's a wine that needs time. Try it with pan-fried kangaroo.

Quality	▼▼▼▼
Value	★★★
Grapes	cabernet sauvignon 60%; merlot 30%; malbec 10%
Region	Mansfield, Vic.
Cellar	➝ 3–6
Alc./Vol.	13.0%
RRP	$24.00

Demondrille Vineyards Purgatory

It's not red, it's not white, but it's somewhere in between – hence the name. Demondrille is a new operation managed by Pam Gillespie on the Canberrra side of Young.

CURRENT RELEASE 1996 Medium–light red–purple in shade, this unusual rosé style has a nose of vanilla and berries with some development creeping in already, giving it a little earthy dullness. It lacks a bit of zip but has some attractive pinot-like flavour and easy-drinking lightness.

Quality	▼▼▼
Value	★★★
Grapes	pinot noir
Region	Hilltops, NSW
Cellar	▮ 1
Alc./Vol.	11.1%
RRP	$15.00

Diamond Valley Blue Label Pinot Noir

David Lance buys grapes from other Yarra Valley vineyards to blend this pinot, which is frequently as good as the estate wine, but in a lighter style.

Previous outstanding vintages: '88, '90, '91, '94

CURRENT RELEASE 1996 A very aromatic pinot with sweet, sappy, cherry and spice perfumes, fine pepper–spice flavours and attractive balance. It's lighter with less oak and tannin than the estate wine, but is a wine of real finesse which drinks beautifully in its youth. Serve with beef carpaccio.

Quality	▼▼▼▼▼
Value	★★★★★
Grapes	pinot noir
Region	Yarra Valley, Vic.
Cellar	▮ 4+
Alc./Vol.	12.8%
RRP	$19.60

Diamond Valley Estate Pinot Noir

Quality	♟♟♟♟♟
Value	★★★★
Grapes	pinot noir
Region	Yarra Valley, Vic.
Cellar	➛ 1–5+
Alc./Vol.	13.0%
RRP	$34.25

This is made each year from a mere two acres of vines grown on the Lance property. It's a blessed patch of vines: the wines have won an amazing 24 show trophies since 1984. Maker David Lance.

Previous outstanding vintages: '86, '87, '90, '91, '92, '93, '94

CURRENT RELEASE 1996   The colour is medium–light purple–red. The bouquet shows peppery/stalky herbal aromas that open out into earthy, woody and cherry scents, with fruit to the fore. The forepalate is rich in sweet fruit, and then acid and tannin firm up the finish. It has charm, balance and zestiness: a babe of real potential, which will improve over several years. Try it with duck.

Dromana Estate Pinot Noir

Quality	♟♟♟♟
Value	★★★
Grapes	pinot noir
Region	Mornington Peninsula, Vic.
Cellar	▮ 2+
Alc./Vol.	13.5%
RRP	$22.50

Dromana is better known as a place to spend a beach holiday, but these days wine is increasingly the thing to pursue on rainy days. Maker Arthur O'Connor.

CURRENT RELEASE 1996   A lighter-weighted pinot with excellent clarity of varietal fruit in the strawberry/ cherry spectrum. It's clean and well balanced with background oak and a trace of fruity sweetness. Suits lighter dishes such as beef carpaccio.

Edencrest Merlot Cabernet 936

Quality	♟♟♟♟
Value	★★★★
Grapes	merlot; cabernet sauvignon
Region	Eden Valley & Barossa Valley, SA
Cellar	▮ 3
Alc./Vol.	13.5%
RRP	$18.00

Sounds a bit like a mid-afternoon TV soapie. It's a label minted by the man who begat Siegersdorf for Hardys. Maker Jim Irvine.

CURRENT RELEASE *non-vintage*   The colour is a deep crimson, and the nose has a strong, fruity element and the perfume of rose petals. The palate offers sweet plum and raspberry flavours. These are matched by some French oak on a soft finish. Try it with steak and kidney.

Elderton Cabernet Sauvignon

Sadly, we must report the death of proprietor Neil Ashmead, who died at age 50 in April 1997. We have shared a wine-soaked table and Neil's robust company on many occasions, so his passing came as a shock.
CURRENT RELEASE 1994   The wine has a deep scarlet colour, and the nose has blackberry and capsicum smells. The palate is medium- to full-bodied, with sweet blackberry fruit and cinnamon spice flavours. American oak adds complexity with a vanillan lift. The wine drinks well after decanting. Try it with game pie.

Quality	▼▼▼▼▼
Value	★★★★
Grapes	cabernet sauvignon
Region	Barossa Valley, SA
Cellar	▮ 6
Alc./Vol.	14.0%
RRP	$20.00 ▮

Elderton Cabernet Sauvignon Shiraz Merlot

There is plenty of can-do at the Elderton winery. From the very start the marketing has been adroit and aggressive. These days the wines seem to measure up to the hype. Maker Jim Irvine (contract).
CURRENT RELEASE 1994   A very complex and rewarding style. The multiple blend means plenty of flavour, yet the wine stays in the elegant zone. There are cherry and blackberry aromas, and these are also the flavours found on the palate. The finish is distinguished with a chalky, dry character that has plenty of length and grip. It's beaut with a game pie.

Quality	▼▼▼▼▼
Value	★★★★
Grapes	cabernet sauvignon 60%; shiraz 30%; merlot 10%
Region	Barossa Valley, SA
Cellar	➡ 2–8 years
Alc./Vol.	14.0%
RRP	$19.00

Elderton Command Shiraz

Your wish is their command – as long as you pay for it, of course. This bit of tall timber is the top of the totem for Elderton. It gets extra oak (three years) and that shows in the final wine.
CURRENT RELEASE 1992   As they say in the Barossa, 'no wood, no good'. There is plenty of timber here, but it's starting to integrate since the last review. It has rich plum aromas and a big vanilla component. The palate is rich with spicy plum flavours, and there is a big whack of oak on the finish. Loads of tannin and splinters, but it's starting to soften. Try it with smoked kangaroo. ▶

Quality	▼▼▼▼▼
Value	★★★
Grapes	shiraz
Region	Barossa Valley, SA
Cellar	➡ 1–6
Alc./Vol.	14.5%
RRP	$41.00 ⑤

Quality	🍷🍷🍷🍷
Value	★★★
Grapes	shiraz
Region	Barossa Valley, SA
Cellar	2–6
Alc./Vol.	14.0%
RRP	$41.00

CURRENT RELEASE 1993 A wine that flatters to deceive. The alcohol is generous, but the palate remains lean, almost restrained. The nose has ripe plum, dark chocolate and vanilla aromas. The medium-bodied palate is quite complex with blackberry, plum, mint and dark chocolate flavours. The finish has a fair jolt of tannin and loads of grip. It needs more time. Try it with tea-smoked duck.

Elderton Shiraz

Quality	🍷🍷🍷🍷½
Value	★★★★★
Grapes	shiraz
Region	Barossa Valley, SA
Cellar	4
Alc./Vol.	14.0%
RRP	$18.00

This is at the slightly lower end of the portfolio. It's the drink-now version of this Barossa style.

Previous outstanding vintages: '86, '88, '89, '90, '91, '92, '93

CURRENT RELEASE 1994 A bit of a softie at heart, even though there is alcohol aplenty. Not much has changed since the last review. The colour is a deep crimson and the nose has plum aromas plus some new oak, pencil-shavings smells. The palate is medium-bodied and the fruit flavours have less depth than the nose would suggest. The oak on the finish is relatively cautious and the wine drinks well now. It can be served with duck in a cherry sauce.

Elsewhere Pinot Noir

Quality	🍷🍷🍷🍷
Value	★★★
Grapes	pinot noir
Region	Tasmania
Cellar	6
Alc./Vol.	13.2%
RRP	$30.00

This 9-hectare vineyard was established in 1984 by Eric and Jette Phillips. It's located at Glaziers Bay, Tasmania, and if you were prone to throwing rocks, maybe that's why you'd rather be elsewhere. Maker Andrew Hood (contract).

CURRENT RELEASE 1994 This is a tough little number with a born-to-be-wild streak. The nose has sap and cherry aromas. The palate is tight with slightly tart, wild cherry and strawberry flavours. The finish is very long and dry to the point of being chalky. It has enough structure to cope with mild bratwurst sausages in onion gravy.

Ermes Estate Cabernet Sauvignon

This is a new label/vineyard on the Mornington Peninsula. It's a small planting that sells mostly by mail order. The label designer shouldn't give up his or her day job. Maker Ermes Zucchet.

CURRENT RELEASE 1995 Cool-climate to the core, the nose has strong tobacco and attractive spices. The palate is light- to middleweight, but not devoid of complexity. There are light berry flavours and a velvety texture. The acid on the finish is strong. It will probably make only modest gains in the cellar. Try it with pan-fried quail.

Quality	🍷🍷🍷
Value	★★★
Grapes	cabernet sauvignon; merlot
Region	Mornington Peninsula, Vic.
Cellar	🍷 3
Alc./Vol.	12.5%
RRP	$17.60

Evans & Tate Gnangara Shiraz

For the E&T empire it all started with the Gnangara vineyard in the Swan Valley. While maintaining the original vineyard they have migrated south to Margaret River in a big way. Maker Brian Fletcher.

CURRENT RELEASE 1995 Very traditional Swan Valley, without the warts. The nose has sweet berry aromas that are tinged with spices. The palate is medium-bodied with sweet plum flavour and zesty spices. There are soft tannins on the finish with a gentle grip. It drinks well now. Try it with a pizza.

Quality	🍷🍷🍷
Value	★★★★
Grapes	shiraz
Region	Swan Valley, WA
Cellar	🍷 4
Alc./Vol.	13.0%
RRP	$19.00

Evans & Tate Margaret River Cabernet Sauvignon

This variety seems to be the life's blood of Margaret River. The pioneers have proved its worth, and E&T have picked up the torch by planting a large vineyard and using the talents of maker Brian Fletcher to put the goods in the bottle.

CURRENT RELEASE 1994 The joy of youth! This is a very youthful style, perhaps a little petulant, but with plenty of potential. The nose has a mixture of herbs, wood and bramble aromas. The palate is tight with blackberry and spice. Fine-grained tannins add astringency to the finish. It drinks well after breathing. Try it with a warm salad of duck breast.

Quality	🍷🍷🍷🍷
Value	★★★★
Grapes	cabernet sauvignon
Region	Margaret River, WA
Cellar	➡ 2–6
Alc./Vol.	13.0%
RRP	$21.00

Evans & Tate Margaret River Shiraz

Quality	♟♟♟♟?
Value	★★★★
Grapes	shiraz
Region	Margaret River, Vic.
Cellar	▮ 6
Alc./Vol.	13.0%
RRP	$23.00

E&T have great faith in this variety planted in the Margaret River district. Could this be Australia's equivalent of the Rhone? Such comparisons with French wines are inescapable but odious: E&T are making Australian wines.

CURRENT RELEASE 1994   Yes, there are some Rhone characters but these are countered by the use of American oak. The nose has cherry and bracken aromas. The palate is rich with cherry flavours, spice and pepper, and the wood adds fine-grained tannins on a lifted finish. It should cellar well but drinking now with rare saddle of hare is no sin.

Evans Family 'Hillside' Pinot Noir

Quality	♟♟♟♟?
Value	★★★★
Grapes	pinot noir
Region	Hunter Valley, NSW
Cellar	▮ 5
Alc./Vol.	13.9%
RRP	$21.00

The Hunter is not many people's idea of the perfect place to plant pinot, but it can occasionally deliver a surprise.

CURRENT RELEASE 1996   A well-structured wine, which delivers authentic pinot flavour and charm. There is some early development in colour and bouquet, the latter already tending savoury, with vanillan oaky complexities. Very good depth of palate flavour and a pleasingly dry finish. Goes well with duck confit.

Eyton on Yarra Cabernet Merlot

Quality	♟♟♟♟
Value	★★★★
Grapes	cabernet sauvignon; merlot
Region	Yarra Valley, Vic.
Cellar	➥ 2–5
Alc./Vol.	12.3%
RRP	$18.95

The Yarra Valley is developing a world reputation, and it seems to hinge on cabernet sauvignon and cabernet blends. The jury is still out where other varieties like pinot noir and shiraz are concerned.

CURRENT RELEASE 1994   Vibrant colour with an aura of health. The nose is slightly closed with some talcum-powder oak aromas and red berry smells. There are some sweet fruit flavours on the palate with raspberry and cherry dominant. The finish is well-tailored, with firm oak and mouth-reviving grip. It's a good rare T-bone steak style (mushroom sauce optional).

Eyton on Yarra Pinot Noir

Sounds like you need a punt to get there. The name is pronounced 'Eye-ton' as in Brighton.
CURRENT RELEASE 1995   Bright lively colours with a cherry-red blush. The nose has a hint of shiraz plum plus sundry berry notes. The palate is medium-bodied with sweet, red berry fruit flavours. There are acid and fine-grained tannins on the finish. It drinks well now, and chargrilled tuna is just the ticket.

Quality	♥♥♥♥
Value	★★★⊢
Grapes	pinot noir
Region	Yarra Valley, Vic
Cellar	🍾 4
Alc./Vol.	12.5%
RRP	$18.95

Eyton on Yarra Shiraz

Shiraz is underrated and some would say under-planted in this region. The climatically kind years produce exciting wines.
CURRENT RELEASE 1994   The colour is a youthful, glowing ruby and the nose is full of pepper, plums and spice. The palate is intense, albeit a tad closed. There are dark cherry flavours, which are combined with black-tea-like tannins on a grippy finish. Time should reward; at the moment try it with venison sausages.

Quality	♥♥♥♥
Value	★★★★
Grapes	shiraz
Region	Yarra Valley, SA
Cellar	↦ 2–6
Alc./Vol.	12.8%
RRP	$18.95

Fermoy Estate Cabernet Sauvignon

This winery is in the Willyabrup area, near the hallowed turf of Moss Wood. The cab is without doubt the most stylish, classical red at Fermoy.
Previous outstanding vintages: '92
CURRENT RELEASE 1994   Tightly packed, firm and quite tannic, this is a complete cabernet of considerable power and length. The fruit is rich, but doesn't overflow into the outrageous jammy opulence of some of the other wines. Good potential too. Try it with hard cheeses.

Quality	♥♥♥♥
Value	★★★★
Grapes	cabernet sauvignon
Region	Margaret River, WA
Cellar	🍾 10
Alc./Vol.	13.5%
RRP	$19.65 🍾

Fermoy Estate Pinot Noir

Quality	🍷🍷🍷🍷
Value	★★★½
Grapes	pinot noir
Region	Margaret River, WA
Cellar	🍾 3+
Alc./Vol.	14.5%
RRP	$21.25

This is a blockbuster thanks to miserable yields of between a half and one tonne to the acre.

CURRENT RELEASE 1995 Michael Kelly has come up with a veritable fruit bomb! It has amazing sweetness due to ripeness, alcohol and glycerine, and massive fruit. It could use a little more structure to hold all that sweet grapiness together. For those who like 'in-ya-face' pinots. Roast turkey and cranberry sauce here.

Fern Hill Estate Cabernet Sauvignon

Quality	🍷🍷🍷
Value	★★½
Grapes	cabernet sauvignon
Region	McLaren Vale, SA
Cellar	🍾 3
Alc./Vol.	12.5%
RRP	$19.00

Sydney businessman Terry Hill bought this McLaren Vale brand, along with Marienberg and Basedow, a few years ago.

CURRENT RELEASE 1994 Developing secondary aged characters now and a brick-red tint to its colour, this smells dusty and tobacco-leafy with some raspberry and Ribena aromas. It's fairly lean on the palate and could use a little more middle. Ready drinking. Try it with braised lamb shanks.

Fern Hill Estate Shiraz

Quality	🍷🍷🍷
Value	★★½
Grapes	shiraz
Region	McLaren Vale, SA
Cellar	🍾 4
Alc./Vol.	13.8%
RRP	$19.00

This is the old Wayne Thomas winery, purchased a few years ago by Sydney winery collector, Terry Hill. Maker Grant Burge.

CURRENT RELEASE 1994 Somewhat green, stalky aromas, together with pronounced pepper/graphite characters, although 13.8% alcohol hardly suggests underripe fruit. The palate is also rather meagre and weedy. Try a mild Indian curry.

Fiddlers Creek Cabernet Shiraz

The name of this label dates back to gold-rush days. Fiddlers Creek actually exists in the district where the maker, Blue Pyrenees Estate, is based.

CURRENT RELEASE 1995 Very appealing for what it is: a light, simple, early-drinking style of red, but attractively plummy and spicy with a hint of graphite. Gentle, fruit-sweet flavour and negligible tannin. Pair it with a pizza.

Quality	🍷🍷🍷
Value	★★★★
Grapes	cabernet sauvignon; shiraz
Region	not stated
Cellar	2
Alc./Vol.	12.0%
RRP	$9.90 (S)

Fire Gully Cabernets Merlot

Pierro's Mike Peterkin makes this wine, and the grapes are grown on the vineyard of the same name by Marg and Ellis Butcher. The swish new label features an original painting.

CURRENT RELEASE 1995 The merlot seems to show through here, with mulberry and vanilla aromas, and a smooth, chunky, fleshy palate. There is rich fruit and ample tannin, finishing quite firm, and some cellaring would not harm it. Then drink with venison casserole.

Quality	🍷🍷🍷🍷½
Value	★★★★
Grapes	cabernet sauvignon; cabernet franc; merlot
Region	Margaret River, WA
Cellar	1–8+
Alc./Vol.	13.0%
RRP	$19.50

Four Sisters Shiraz

Trevor Mast of Mt Langi Ghiran has branched out with this brand of blended wines from various regions, named in honour of his daughters.

CURRENT RELEASE 1996 A decent, straightforward, fruit-driven shiraz with echoes of plums and cherry skins. Good depth of flavour for the money and a nice touch of tannin to close. It's styled with early drinking in mind, but does have length and stuffing. Goes with pork sausages.

Quality	🍷🍷🍷½
Value	★★★½
Grapes	shiraz
Region	Goulburn Valley, Vic.; McLaren Vale, SA
Cellar	4
Alc./Vol.	13.0%
RRP	$16.40

Fox Creek Reserve Cabernet Sauvignon

Quality	ŸŸŸŸ?
Value	★★★⯪
Grapes	cabernet sauvignon
Region	McLaren Vale, SA
Cellar	➛ 3–10+
Alc./Vol.	13.6%
RRP	$25.00 ▮

Winemaker Sparky Marquis wants us to know he left the skins steeping in the wine for 38 days during and after fermentation, which is a very long time. We should interpret this as a warning!

CURRENT RELEASE 1995   Vivid, almost neon purple–red colour introduces a raw, aggressively youthful red, which is quite unready for drinking. The nose has violets, dark berries and plums, coupled with abundant oak character. It's quite astringent, and while it should turn out beautifully, we suggest cellaring first. Then drink with barbecued rump steak.

Fox Creek Reserve Shiraz

Quality	ŸŸŸ?
Value	★★★
Grapes	shiraz
Region	McLaren Vale, SA
Cellar	➛ 2–8+
Alc./Vol.	14.2%
RRP	$22.50 ▮

Fox Creek burst into the spotlight (sorry!) with its '94 shiraz, a sumptuously rich but enormously woody modern McLaren Vale style. It was a hard act to follow. Maker Sparky Marquis.

Previous outstanding vintages: '94

CURRENT RELEASE 1995   This is a take-no-prisoners style of shiraz. Dense, almost opaque purple colour – don't get it on your white shirt! The nose shows raw, unintegrated coconutty American oak, which is quite over the top at this stage. However, there is solid, rich fruit on the tongue, plum and licorice flavours, stacks of tannin, and it could come together with time. Cellar, then serve with barbecued roo backstraps.

Quality	ŸŸŸŸŸ
Value	★★★★★
Grapes	shiraz
Region	McLaren Vale, SA
Cellar	▮ 10+
Alc./Vol.	13.5%
RRP	$22.50

CURRENT RELEASE 1996   **The fox is loose in the McLaren Vale henhouse, scattering feathers in all directions. This is a shamelessly opulent shiraz, loaded with intense spice and plum flavours, enhanced but not overburdened by liberal use of oak. It's seductively sweet and ripe and the tannin is not aggressive. Indeed, it can be enjoyed as a youngster, although we'd prefer to cellar it. Great stuff, and the epitome of the region. Serve with oxtail stew and gusto.**

PENGUIN
BEST
SHIRAZ

Frankland Estate Isolation Ridge

Evocative names are all the go at Frankland. It may be isolated from the rest of humanity but not from other vineyards: Houghton's huge spread is right next door. CURRENT RELEASE 1994 A less opulent, more restrained shiraz than some '94s from this region. Spicy and nutty wood-matured aromas, a fine-boned elegance, and understated oak, leading into a very dry finish. A good drink with osso bucco.

Quality	?????
Value	★★★↑
Grapes	shiraz
Region	Lower Great Southern, WA
Cellar	🍷 4+
Alc./Vol.	13.0%
RRP	$17.70

Frankland Estate Olmo's Reward

Professor Harold Olmo, the American viticulturalist, recommended grapegrowing in Western Australia's southwest, and inspired the early winemakers such as graziers Barrie Smith and Judi Cullam of Frankland Estate.
Previous outstanding vintages: '92, '93
CURRENT RELEASE 1994 A more elegant style than the '93, smelling of crushed leaves, and sweet blackcurrants with a floral high note. Lean, attractive, with smooth tannins and well-ripened fruit. Serve with cheddar.

Quality	?????
Value	★★★
Grapes	cabernet sauvignon; cabernet franc; merlot; malbec; petit verdot
Region	Lower Great Southern, WA
Cellar	🍷 5+
Alc./Vol.	13.0%
RRP	$24.00

Freycinet Pinot Noir

Geoff and Susan Bull have a blessed patch of vines in a dry, sunny position on the Tasmanian east coast. Pinot seems perfectly suited, and yields superb wine most years. Maker Claudio Radenti.
Previous outstanding vintages: '90, '91, '92, '93, '94
CURRENT RELEASE 1995 Developing in an unusual direction, this has a strong vanillan aroma and a hot finish from high alcohol. It's a remarkably big, rich, concentrated and fairly oaky pinot, with tremendous length, but tending almost porty. Not a classic Freycinet but a very good wine all the same. Serve with roast duck.

Quality	?????
Value	★★★↑
Grapes	pinot noir
Region	east coast Tasmania
Cellar	🍷 3
Alc./Vol.	14.0%
RRP	$30.00

Garden Gully Shiraz

Quality	🍷🍷🍷🍷
Value	★★★★
Grapes	shiraz
Region	Great Western, Vic.
Cellar	🍾 5
Alc./Vol.	13.0%
RRP	$18.00

The winery was established in 1987 by the team of Warren Randall and Brian Fletcher, when they were working at Seppelt Great Western. There are 7 hectares under vine. Maker Brian Fletcher.

CURRENT RELEASE 1994 There is a regional theme (plus a dry year) running through the make-up of this wine. The nose is slightly sweaty with blackberry and pepper aromas. The palate is luxurious and soft with sweet blackberry flavours. This is balanced by vanillin oak on a well-integrated finish. It will cellar, but try it now with a T-bone steak and eggs.

Garrett Family Cabernet Merlot

Quality	🍷🍷🍷
Value	★★½
Grapes	cabernet sauvignon; merlot
Region	Padthaway & Barossa Valley, SA
Cellar	🍾 3
Alc./Vol.	12.5%
RRP	$18.00 ($)

Garrett Family was the brand that Andrew Garrett started after he lost control of Andrew Garrett Wines. Mildara ended up buying both of them. It's odds-on Andrew's next venture won't have his name on it!

CURRENT RELEASE 1994 There are signs of early development in this wine. The nose is mainly secondary characters with some earthy notes, and the lean palate has redcurrant and berry flavours with some tannin to finish. It's very soft and just a little short on the finish. Serve with lamb chops and mash.

Garry Crittenden Dolcetto

Quality	🍷🍷🍷🍷½
Value	★★★★½
Grapes	dolcetto
Region	Great Western, Vic.
Cellar	🍾 5
Alc./Vol.	13.0%
RRP	$15.00

Garry Crittenden is not related to the wine-merchant dynasty. He made his fame (and perhaps his fortune) in the field of horticulture before planting his vineyard at Dromana. Maker Garry Crittenden and Arthur O'Connor.

CURRENT RELEASE 1995 Very Italian in design and style. There are cherry and anise aromas on the nose. The palate has maraschino and berry flavours plus a refreshing tartness. The finish is dominated by zesty acid. Close your eyes and you'd think you were in Rome. Have it with spaghetti and meatballs.

Garry Crittenden Riserva

Garry Crittenden was quick to tune in to a growing trend for Italian tastes in wine. The range carrying his name (as opposed to his Estate label) pays direct homage to Italian styles.

CURRENT RELEASE 1995   This is a tart and sassy style that cries out for cheese. The colour is dense and there are strong, dried-fruit and raspberry aromas on the nose. The palate is lively with raspberry flavours that are balanced by zesty acid. It's a very firm style that's great with shaved parmesan.

Quality	YYYY?
Value	★★★★r
Grapes	nebbiolo 80%; barbera 20%
Region	King Valley, Vic.
Cellar	▌ 6
Alc./Vol.	13.5%
RRP	$18.00

Geoff Weaver Cabernet Merlot

The Hills are great for whites and early ripening reds; less so for these varieties, especially cabernet. Maker Geoff Weaver.

Previous outstanding vintages: '93

CURRENT RELEASE 1994   Weaver's best cab merlot yet. It has a rich, deep colour, a ripe and concentrated bouquet of blackcurrant and dark berries, with noticeable but well-balanced oak. It's spicy in the mouth and has more weight and extract than previous vintages. There is some nice drying tannin on a big finish. Food: venison sausages.

Quality	YYYY?
Value	★★★r
Grapes	cabernet sauvignon 75%; merlot 25%
Region	Adelaide Hills, SA
Cellar	▌ 6+
Alc./Vol.	12.5%
RRP	$24.00

Gilberts Shiraz

This is a promising vineyard in the Mount Barker district. The variety is slowly finding form in these relatively new environs.

CURRENT RELEASE 1995   Brilliant colour with great depth, and the nose is a mixture of plums and pepper spice. There is a slight hint of mustiness. The palate is tight with some plum and raspberry fruit, but it's a tad shallow. The oak sits well on the finish and there is some fine-grained tannin grip. Try it with pepper steak.

Quality	YYY?
Value	★★★
Grapes	shiraz
Region	Mount Barker, WA
Cellar	▌ 4
Alc./Vol.	13.0%
RRP	$20.00

Goundrey Reserve Shiraz

Quality	♥♥♥♡
Value	★★★
Grapes	shiraz
Region	Mount Barker, WA
Cellar	➥ 2–6
Alc./Vol.	13.0%
RRP	$23.00

Goundrey is a leading winery in the Lower Great Southern. It has many desirable aspects, including being a crushing facility for fruit from the region.

CURRENT RELEASE 1995   The colour is dark, and the nose has dusty oak aromas with a hint of black tea. The palate has a predominant plum flavour, but tannin is never far away. The finish is very firm with a hint of vanilla, and dry with a strong, astringent grip. Time in the bottle will tell. At the moment try it with hard cheese.

Gralaine Vineyard Merlot

Quality	♥♥♥♥
Value	★★★★
Grapes	merlot
Region	Geelong, Vic.
Cellar	▮ 4
Alc./Vol.	13.8%
RRP	$22.00

The label puts the case quite eloquently: 'One small vineyard, one premium grape variety, one simple aim ... excellence.' The aim is to produce a wine that could grace the best labels from Pomerol. The vineyard is located at Mount Duneed, and the proprietors are Graeme and Elaine Carroll. Maker John Ellis (contract).

CURRENT RELEASE 1993   The nose is sheer joy; it's loaded with seductive perfumes. There are roses, crushed berries and lollies. The palate fumbles slightly. It's medium-bodied and a touch restrained. It has a modest redcurrant flavour and there are chalky characters on the finish, which is dominated by fine-grained tannins. It's great with lamb fillets pan-fried in a lively marinade.

Quality	♥♥♥♥
Value	★★★★
Grapes	merlot
Region	Geelong, Vic.
Cellar	▮ 5
Alc./Vol.	13.9%
RRP	$22.00

CURRENT RELEASE 1994   Shows promise. This is a young, astringent style which in olden days would have been called a 'claret'. The colour is pale ruby, and the nose is vinous with ripe fruit and rose petal aromas. The palate is elegant, with raspberry flavours that are matched by fine-grained tannins and strong acid on a lingering finish. It's great with veal hotpot.

Gramp's Cabernet Merlot

Always a dependable style that can often save the day for an otherwise mundane wine list.

CURRENT RELEASE 1995 Great colour and the nose suggests carbonic maceration with lolly aromas. The palate is light- to medium-weight with sweet, berry fruit flavours that are followed by some undemanding tannins on a gentle finish. It has been made to drink now. Try bangers and mash.

Quality	🍷🍷🍷½
Value	★★★½
Grapes	cabernet sauvignon; merlot
Region	Barossa Valley, SA
Cellar	🍾
Alc./Vol.	13.0%
RRP	$11.00

Gramp's Grenache

Yet another to leap on the grenache bandwagon, and why not? The revival of this variety has gathered a dedicated following.

CURRENT RELEASE 1995 This is a bright, medium-bodied style that was made to drink now. The nose has a sweet raspberry fruit aroma and the colour is a cheeky ruby. The palate has a hint of sweetness as well as succulent berries, and the finish is soft. It could be served with a slight chill. Try crumbed Epping sausages and mash.

Quality	🍷🍷🍷
Value	★★★
Grapes	grenache
Region	Barossa Valley, SA
Cellar	🍾 1
Alc./Vol.	13.5%
RRP	$14.00 (S)

Grant Burge Cameron Vale Cabernet Sauvignon

Quality	♀♀♀♀
Value	★★★★
Grapes	cabernet sauvignon
Region	Barossa Valley, SA
Cellar	▮ 4
Alc./Vol.	13.0%
RRP	$19.00

The wines from Grant Burge take on the names of the vineyards from whence the grapes came. All the vineyards are owned by Grant and Helen Burge.

CURRENT RELEASE 1995   The wine has a bright ruby colour and the nose offers plenty of fruit/berry perfumes. The palate is medium-bodied and complex, with cherry and raspberry fruit flavours interlaced with oak. The finish features bold, fine-grained tannin grip. It's a treat with lamb.

Grant Burge Filsell Shiraz

Quality	♀♀♀♀
Value	★★★★
Grapes	shiraz
Region	Barossa Valley, SA
Cellar	▮ 4
Alc./Vol.	14.0%
RRP	$19.00

The Grant Burge cellar door has quite a history – too long to be recounted here. It's worth a visit just to count the money that has been lavished on the place, not to mention to taste the wine.

CURRENT RELEASE 1995   A refined regional style is an apt description. The colour is a dark plum, and the nose has spices plus crushed berry smells. The medium-bodied palate offers succulent, ripe plum flavours and there is harmonious tannin on the finish. It's hard to see much change in terms of cellar development. Try it with a rack of lamb with wine gravy.

Grant Burge Hillcot Merlot

Quality	♀♀♀⏧
Value	★★★⏧
Grapes	merlot 92%; cabernet
	sauvignon 8%
Region	Barossa Valley, SA
Cellar	▮ 3
Alc./Vol.	12.6%
RRP	$15.50

Barossa Boy makes good. Grant Burge used to ride a horse to school in his native Barossa: now he drives a Porsche to his own cellar door.

CURRENT RELEASE 1995   The nose is floral with ripe, raspberry aromas and the body is medium-weight with sweet raspberry fruit. It's very soft and there is a gentle garnish of oak. The grip is docile and the tannin undemanding. Drink it now with quail risotto.

Grant Burge Shadrach

Dust off the Old Testament and hone up on Nebu-
chadnezzar throwing all 'dose chillin' in de fire'. Unlike
Meshach, there was no Shadrach Burge, and you don't
have to be a biblical scholar to know part of the trio
who were cast into the fiery furnace is not on a label
yet. Stand by. Maker Grant Burge.

CURRENT RELEASE 1993 It's a youthful style with a
slight doughnut effect (hole-in-the-middle palate) that
should fill in with time in the cellar. The nose has strong
blackberry aromas plus hints of wood. The palate is concentrated with blackberry fruit flavours, and there is a
pleasant garnish of oak with fine-grained tannins and
attractive grip. It needs more time, but it's a very pleasant drink beside a casserole of goat.

Quality	⟡⟡⟡⟡⟡
Value	★★★⟡
Grapes	cabernet sauvignon
Region	Coonawarra & Barossa Valley, SA
Cellar	➛ 3–8
Alc./Vol.	13.5%
RRP	$40.00

Greenock Creek Cornerstone Grenache

If you visit the Barossa you must have a drink in the
Greenock pub – it's a beauty. The vineyard is not far
away and it shows all the attributes of old mother
Barossa.

CURRENT RELEASE 1995 Godzilla in a bottle: it's
almost port without fortification. There are strong raspberry aromas, and the palate is sweet and slippery with
bramble, berry and raspberry flavours that flood the
mouth. There is also an amount of residual sweetness
that hints at very ripe grapes. The soft tannins help it
roll down the throat. It's difficult to match with food:
perhaps a game stew or bubble-and-squeak after a B&S
ball.

Quality	⟡⟡⟡
Value	★★★⟡
Grapes	grenache
Region	Barossa Valley, SA
Cellar	▮ 2
Alc./Vol.	15.6%
RRP	$18.00

Greenock Creek Seven Acres Shiraz

Quality	♟♟♟♟♟
Value	★★★★★
Grapes	shiraz
Region	Barossa Valley, SA
Cellar	⬥ 2–10
Alc./Vol.	14.4%
RRP	$18.00

Seven Acres is a vineyard in the Barossa Valley that features old unirrigated vines. This combination tends to deliver classic wines.

CURRENT RELEASE 1994   There are Penfolds Grange elements in the make-up of this wine. It's rich and powerful with pronounced ripe fruit aromas on the nose. There is a load of spice. Plums and dark cherries rule the palate, which is complex with layers of spice and oak-derived flavours. The finish has exuberant tannins that are dry and astringent. The wine shows plenty of poise and goes well with venison sausages.

Green Point Pinot Noir

Quality	♟♟♟♟
Value	★★★
Grapes	pinot noir
Region	Yarra Valley, Vic.
Cellar	▯ 3
Alc./Vol.	13.0%
RRP	$20.00

You can't keep a good table-winemaker down. Green Point is the original name of the Domaine Chandon property, and although it's dedicated to sparkling wine production, table wine will also be produced under this label. Maker Wayne Donaldson.

CURRENT RELEASE 1996   The colour is a mid-ruby and the nose has strong strawberry aromas with hints of cherry. The palate is middleweight with sweet strawberry and fresh cherry flavours. There is also a hint of stalkiness. The finish has green tannins and lingering grip. It drinks well with Turkish food.

Grevillea Estate Merlot

Quality	♟♟♟
Value	★★★
Grapes	merlot
Region	Bega, NSW
Cellar	▯ 1
Alc./Vol.	12.5%
RRP	$14.00

Merlot as a solo act is a difficult wine to quantify: there is no firm Australian style yet to evolve. This one comes from cheese country.

CURRENT RELEASE 1995   The nose is slightly sappy with hints of vegetation and mulched leaf. The medium-weight palate has light raspberry flavours and the oak on the finish acts as a garnish. It drinks well now with pasta.

Hanging Rock Victoria Shiraz

This is the pre-eminent winery in the Macedon region, where ultra-boutiques are the order of the day. Winemaker John Ellis crushed 500 tonnes in 1997.

CURRENT RELEASE 1995 It needs a little air to open up its full spice cupboard, but there's pepper and spice aplenty and it speaks to us of shiraz, clear and true. The palate is lean and lively with well-balanced flavour and gentle tannins in a lighter style. Serve with Wiener schnitzel.

Quality	▼▼▼▼
Value	★★★⊢
Grapes	shiraz
Region	Swan Hill & Heathcote, Vic.
Cellar	▲ 5
Alc./Vol.	12.5%
RRP	$19.60 ▮

Hardys Bankside Grenache

Bankside was Thomas Hardy's first wine cellars in Adelaide, beside the Torrens River. It burnt down in 1905. Maker Stephen Pannell.

CURRENT RELEASE 1994 Slightly bolshie in its youth and needs a year or so to settle. Fresh vanillan oak and stalky-raspberry grenache fruit come through on the bouquet. The taste is smooth enough to enjoy but the flavours are a little raw, and we'd like to see it again in a year. Try it with steak and kidney pie.

Quality	▼▼▼▼
Value	★★★⊢
Grapes	grenache; shiraz
Region	McLaren Vale, SA
Cellar	▲ 1–4+
Alc./Vol.	14.0%
RRP	$17.00 Ⓢ

Hardys Bankside Shiraz

The accompanying insights inform us that this wine was basket-pressed at the Tintara winery.

CURRENT RELEASE 1994 The colour is promisingly dark and dense, while the aromas are soft and dusty with some oak vanilla and shiraz plums. There's a little bitter extraction on the finish and the wine will drink well after a few more months in a dark place. Goes well with grilled lamb chops.

Quality	▼▼▼⸮
Value	★★★
Grapes	shiraz
Region	McLaren Vale, SA
Cellar	▲ 5
Alc./Vol.	14.5%
RRP	$17.00 Ⓢ

Hardys Eileen Hardy Shiraz

Quality	♟♟♟♟♟
Value	★★★★★
Grapes	shiraz
Region	Padthaway & McLaren Vale, SA
Cellar	➡ 2–15+
Alc./Vol.	14.0%
RRP	$45.00 ▮

Eileen Hardy was the matriarch of the Hardy clan, awarded an OBE in 1977 for services to the wine biz. Legend has it she used to favour a glass of fizz when the sun passed over the yardarm. Maker Steve Pannell.

Previous outstanding vintages: '70, '71, '75, '76, '79, '81, '82, '86, '87, '88, '90, '91, '93

CURRENT RELEASE 1994　A great shiraz, perhaps less oaky and not as outrageously minty as the '93, but just as massive. Earth, mixed spices and a hint of mint greet the nose, and the palate holds plum-jam, licorice and prune flavours of enormous power and length. Abundant, but not aggressive, tannins. An outstanding Eileen vintage. Try it with rare kangaroo.

Hardys Insignia Cabernet Shiraz

Quality	♟♟♟
Value	★★★★
Grapes	cabernet sauvignon; shiraz
Region	not stated
Cellar	▮ 2
Alc./Vol.	13.0%
RRP	$10.00

This newie from BRL Hardy has a flash new embossed proprietary bottle. They just keep on minting new brands like there's no tomorrow.

CURRENT RELEASE 1995　A very agreeable bottle of red to kick off a new brand. The nose is full of warm, sweet berries with hints of mulberry and cassis. It tastes lean and light-bodied with pleasant fruit flavour and a nicely dry finish, which doesn't extend further than it has to at the price. It's good-value red. Serve with pork sausages.

Hardys Thomas Hardy Cabernet Sauvignon

The label is positively littered with little gold discs, signifying three trophies and five gold medals. Dare we contradict these august judgements? Maker Stephen Pannell.

Previous outstanding vintages: '89, '90, '91, '92

CURRENT RELEASE 1992 Nice of them to age it for those extra years, but the truth is, it still needs time before you can think about drinking it. A serious, solid red built for the long haul. Forests of oak plus bottle-age result in a sump-oily, meaty bouquet, and the tannin on the finish is very assertive. It will probably always be a food wine. This is about as BIG as Coonawarra gets. Food: chargrilled rump steak.

Quality	🍷🍷🍷🍷
Value	★★★
Grapes	cabernet sauvignon
Region	Coonawarra, SA
Cellar	2–7+
Alc./Vol.	13.5%
RRP	$38.65 (S)

Hay Shed Hill Cabernet Sauvignon

It's a bit hard to take a winery named after a hayshed seriously, but the wines merit serious attention. Maker Peter Stanlake.

CURRENT RELEASE 1995 Tasted from tank just before bottling, this was impressive and a jump up from the '94. Ripe, spicy, vanilla and toasty oak aromas, with a background of dark berries. Full-bodied, with smooth tannins and chocolate/vanilla flavours. Chunky but supple texture. Serve with roast lamb.

Quality	🍷🍷🍷🍷
Value	★★★
Grapes	cabernet sauvignon 88%; cabernet franc 12%
Region	Margaret River, WA
Cellar	7+
Alc./Vol.	13.5%
RRP	$22.40

Hay Shed Hill Pinot Noir

These people go to a lot of trouble to get the right oak for their pinot. This went into Francois Frères and Seguin-Moreau 'Chagny' special pinot barrels.

CURRENT RELEASE 1995 Deep colour for a pinot, and intense, fully-ripe dark cherry and spice aromas, with no sappy or green hints (it's 90% destalked). Excellent flavour, good depth, liberal but not excessive use of oak, smooth long tannins to finish. Try it with Peking duck.

Quality	🍷🍷🍷🍷½
Value	★★★★
Grapes	pinot noir
Region	Margaret River, WA
Cellar	3
Alc./Vol.	13.5%
RRP	$20.00 (cellar door)

Headlands Mourvèdre Shiraz

Quality	♟♟♟
Value	★★★★
Grapes	mourvèdre (mataro); shiraz
Region	South Australia
Cellar	🍶 2
Alc./Vol.	12.3%
RRP	$8.85

What's a Headland? Well, it might be a Liberal Party policy, or an area at the end of vine rows left vacant for turning machinery, maybe. This is a home-brand of wine wholesaler Tucker Seabrook.

CURRENT RELEASE 1996   A light, simple, floral fruited shiraz that won't break the bank. Designed to quaff today, it's plum-skin and red-fruit scented, and a trifle light in colour. At the price, who would quibble? Try it with veal.

Heemskerk Pinot Noir

Quality	♟♟♟♟
Value	★★★
Grapes	pinot noir
Region	northern Tasmania
Cellar	🍶 4
Alc./Vol.	12.2%
RRP	$25.75

The builders have been working overtime at Rochecombe, which will henceforth be the winemaking centre for the Tamar Vineyards group that includes Heemskerk. Maker Gary Ford.

Previous outstanding vintages: '90, '91

CURRENT RELEASE 1995   A refined pinot from a finer year, this has toasty and vanillan oak scents and is building considerable pinot complexities, which it should continue doing with further age. The palate has good flesh and shows a hint of acid. Pair it with beef carpaccio.

Quality	♟♟♟♟
Value	★★★
Grapes	pinot noir
Region	northern Tasmania
Cellar	🍶 5
Alc./Vol.	12.5%
RRP	$25.75

CURRENT RELEASE 1996   A cool, damp year gave the '96 Tassie pinots a distinctive peppery, faintly leafy character and delicacy, both of which this has in abundance. It's spicy, dry and firm to finish, and should fill out further with bottle-age. Good with ham off the bone.

Helm's Cabernet Sauvignon

Ken Helm is something of a spokesman for the small-winery end of the industry. He gained the New South Wales Government's Graham Gregory Trophy this year for services to the state's wine industry.
CURRENT RELEASE 1995 Toasty oak dominates the wine, and the acid is quite noticeable on the finish. There are Ribena and berry-jam flavours, and some fine tannin lending firmness and structure. Won a gold medal in Hobart. Try it with seared kangaroo fillets.

Quality	♟♟♟♗
Value	★★★
Grapes	cabernet sauvignon
Region	Canberra district, NSW
Cellar	☛ 1–5+
Alc./Vol.	12.5%
RRP	$18.00 (cellar door)

Henschke Abbotts Prayer Merlot Cabernet Sauvignon

The label says the grapes were picked in early May, which seems like pushing the prayer thing a bit far. Maker Steve Henschke; viticulture Prue Henschke.
Previous outstanding vintages: '90, '91, '92, '93
CURRENT RELEASE 1994 Still very young for its age, this is stacked with fresh blackcurrant/cassis and cedary new French oak, alongside minty and herbal/leafy merlot flavours. It's very aromatic and has noticeable acid on the palate, which adds life but also a certain leanness. Best with food: try pink veal cutlets.

Quality	♟♟♟♟♗
Value	★★★⯪
Grapes	merlot 70%; cabernet sauvignon 28%; cabernet franc 2%
Region	Adelaide Hills, SA
Cellar	▮ 5+
Alc./Vol.	13.7%
RRP	$47.00 ▮

Henschke Cyril Henschke Cabernet Sauvignon

Winemaker Stephen Henschke named this after his dad. Every self-respecting wine buff these days is squirrelling away a few bottles of 'Squirrel' every year.
Previous outstanding vintages: '81, '86, '88, '90, '91, '93
CURRENT RELEASE 1994 Slathers of very ripe, jammy, berry fruit and high-toast oak coincide with thunderclap impact in this impressive red wine. Opulence is the key word. It's also somewhat firm and astringent and could repay waiting at least two years before drinking. Then serve with Heidi gruyère cheese.

Quality	♟♟♟♟♗
Value	★★★★
Grapes	cabernet sauvignon 77%, merlot 12%, cabernet franc 11%
Region	Eden Valley, SA
Cellar	▮ 10
Alc./Vol.	14.0%
RRP	$61.00 ▮

Henschke Keyneton Estate

Quality	♟♟♟♟
Value	★★★★
Grapes	shiraz 75%; cabernet sauvignon 15%; malbec 10%
Region	Eden Valley & Barossa Valley, SA
Cellar	▸ 12+
Alc./Vol.	13.9%
RRP	$25.00 ▪

Keyneton is a spot in the road near the Henschke winery. The grapes now come from the Barossa floor as well as Eden Valley. Maker Stephen Henschke.
Previous outstanding vintages: '82, '84, '86, '90, '92, '93
CURRENT RELEASE 1994   Sheer magic. The colour is a profound purple–red. Opulent, almost-jammy blackberry and cassis flavours flood the palate. Slight dusty, leafy overtones. There's a lot happening here: voluptuous flavour and ripe, silky tannins. Yum-yum. Try it with rare beef.

Henschke Mount Edelstone Shiraz

Quality	♟♟♟♟♟
Value	★★★⊁
Grapes	shiraz
Region	Eden Valley, SA
Cellar	▸ 7+
Alc./Vol.	14.2%
RRP	$40.00 ▪

We record this out of a sense of duty rather than out of some blind optimism that you'll actually be able to buy a bottle. Henschke reds are blue-chip stock and have stumbled into the collectors' net.
Previous outstanding vintages: '78, '80, '84, '86, '88, '90, '91, '92, '93
CURRENT RELEASE 1994   Trademark Henschke style: sweet, jammy decadence with both fruit and oak in large dollops. Very ripe, but not as big and voluptuous as some vintages. High quality and very attractive drinking. Cellar, then have with aged gruyère.

Hermit's Brook Shiraz

Quality	♟♟♟
Value	★★★⊁
Grapes	shiraz
Region	Hunter Valley, NSW
Cellar	▸ 5
Alc./Vol.	12.0%
RRP	$12.00 Ⓢ

A new label from the Hunter Valley, commissioned and distributed by Marie Brizard, the French liqueur people.
CURRENT RELEASE 1996   This has some sweet, ripe notes in its slightly jammy, licoricey nose, with some plum-skin aspects too. The taste is soft and sweet with, again, evidence of ripe fruit, and some spice joins the cherry/plum flavours on a soft finish. Minimal oak input. Goes with savoury mince on toast.

Hollick Cabernet Merlot

This has reverted to varietal labelling after a few years as simply 'Coonawarra', à la Petaluma. Ian and Wendy Hollick's former partner and winemaker, Pat Tocaciu, left the fold during 1997.

Previous outstanding vintages: '84, '88, '90, '91, '94

CURRENT RELEASE 1995 There was no Ravenswood bottled from '95, so that material is in this wine; however, it fails to help it transcend the lean, mean season. Very dusty, leafy nose and the palate is lean and austere with some green herbal/leafy characters. Food: roasted brisket and mint sauce.

Quality 🍷🍷🍷½
Value ★★½
Grapes cabernet sauvignon 85%; merlot 15%
Region Coonawarra, SA
Cellar 3
Alc./Vol. 12.5%
RRP $19.90

Hotham Valley Cabernet Merlot

The neck tag says 'Sandalwood enhanced', which means maker Jim Pennington has used West Australian sandalwood in the maturation. It's quite a radical innovation. He reckons it lifts the aroma and makes the wine more attractive.

CURRENT RELEASE 1995 The colour is a good, full, purple–red; the nose has a dusty, slightly citrus lift that's subtle yet noticeable; and the medium-bodied palate is smooth and well balanced with a slightly odd sappy aspect. A decent drop, and the sandalwood process is a good talking point.

Quality 🍷🍷🍷½
Value ★★★
Grapes cabernet sauvignon; merlot
Region Darling Ranges, WA
Cellar 4
Alc./Vol. 13.0%
RRP $19.30

Houghton Cabernet Sauvignon

This is the famous one with the red stripe across the label. HH believes the Houghton reds are greatly underestimated. Maker Paul Lapsley.

CURRENT RELEASE 1995 Very much in form in 1995: it has a nose of crushed blackcurrants, is smooth and fruit-sweet in the mouth with underplayed oak, and is ready to go. No frills, but good value. Try it with lamb chops.

Quality 🍷🍷🍷½
Value ★★★★
Grapes cabernet sauvignon
Region Swan Valley, Margaret River, Frankland, Pemberton, Manjimup & Mount Barker, WA
Cellar 3
Alc./Vol. 13.0%
RRP $12.85 (S)

Houghton Cygnet

Quality	♥♥♥⦂
Value	★★★⦁
Grapes	cabernet sauvignon
Region	Frankland River & Darling Ranges, WA
Cellar	▮
Alc./Vol.	10.0%
RRP	$12.85 Ⓢ

A rose by any other name would smell as sweet, etc., etc. Its other name was Houghton Cabernet Rosé, of course. This is an attempt to bypass an untrendy name. CURRENT RELEASE 1996 Jam-packed with early-picked cabernet scents of redcurrant, blackcurrant and definite sauvignon-blanc-like crushed leaf overtones. You could try this blindfolded and think it was a white sauvignon blanc. Some CO_2 gas on palate and a trace of sugar balanced by fresh, zesty acid. Needs a big chill, and serve with antipasto.

Houghton Jack Mann

Quality	♥♥♥♥⦂
Value	★★★⦁
Grapes	cabernet sauvignon; shiraz; malbec
Region	Mount Barker & Frankland, WA
Cellar	➡ 3–12+
Alc./Vol.	13.5%
RRP	$40.00 ▮

This new flagship red commemorates the late Jack Mann, winemaker at Houghton for 50 vintages from the '30s to the '80s. Maker Paul Lapsley.
CURRENT RELEASE 1994 Everything about this wine says Monster! The colour is very dark; the nose is slightly inky; it's jammed with cassis and cedar flavours and tongue-throttling tannins; and the structure is tight and unresolved. Built for the long haul and still unready, so cellar! Then serve with aged cheeses.

Howard Park Cabernet Merlot

Quality	♥♥♥♥♥
Value	★★★★
Grapes	cabernet sauvignon; merlot
Region	Lower Great Southern, WA
Cellar	➡ 2–8+
Alc./Vol.	13.5%
RRP	$46.00 ▮

Howard Park moved into its new state-of-the-art winery just outside Denmark in time for the 1997 vintage. This wine is scarce and it pays to be on the mailing list. (Tasted as a barrel sample.) Maker John Wade.
Previous outstanding vintages: '86, '90, '91, '92
CURRENT RELEASE 1994 One of the greatest reds of the great '94 Australian vintage. A very concentrated wine all round: purple–red hue and classic cabernet blackcurrant-and-violet aromas coupled with stylish oak. Rich, dense palate boasting layers of decadent fruit/oak flavour and smooth ripe tannins, resulting in a fleshy texture. Tremendous length and balance. Cellar, then serve with aged hard cheeses. ▸

CURRENT RELEASE 1995 The '94 vintage set new standards for this stylish wine, and the '95 could turn out just as well. The colour is a dense, purplish red; the nose shows a heap of toasty, smoky oak which will settle down in a year or two, as well as rich, perfectly-ripened fruit. It's dense and almost thick in the mouth with tongue-coating tannins. The spicy flavour has tremendous richness and length to match formidable structure. Drink with chargrilled rump steak.

Quality	▼▼▼▼▼
Value	★★★★
Grapes	cabernet sauvignon; merlot
Region	Lower Great Southern, WA
Cellar	⟷ 5–15
Alc./Vol.	13.5%
RRP	$58.00 ▮

Hungerford Hill Young/Cowra Cabernet Sauvignon

A new label for Hungry Hill, which has been reborn as a New South Wales regional brand, specialising in batches of wine from various, sometimes obscure, sites. Maker Ian Walsh.

CURRENT RELEASE 1994 A tight and nervy cool-climate style, the nose edgy with a whiff of redcurrant and the palate lean and angular, with finer, less-rich flavours and a touch of austerity. Serve with grilled pork chops.

Quality	▼▼▼▼
Value	★★★
Grapes	cabernet sauvignon
Region	Young & Cowra, NSW
Cellar	⟷ 1–4+
Alc./Vol.	13.0%
RRP	$19.80 Ⓢ

Idyll Vineyard Cabernet Sauvignon Shiraz

This wine comes from one of the founding families in the Geelong district. Like their wines, Darryl and Nini Sefton are ageing gracefully. Nini paints the picture on the label.

CURRENT RELEASE 1995 The bright, vibrant colour is an indicator of health. This is a lean style with blackberry and bracken aromas on the nose. The elegant palate has tight, berry fruit flavours and there is an element of high acid on the finish. It's well balanced but it needs time. Serve it with smoked lamb.

Quality	▼▼▼▼
Value	★★★▸
Grapes	cabernet sauvignon; shiraz
Region	Geelong, Vic.
Cellar	⟷ 2–6
Alc./Vol.	13.5%
RRP	$16.50

Ingoldby Cabernet Sauvignon

Quality	ŶŶŶŶ
Value	★★★★
Grapes	cabernet sauvignon
Region	McLaren Vale, SA
Cellar	🍷 5+
Alc./Vol.	13.0%
RRP	$14.50 ⑤

A reliable wine that offers generous, hearty McLaren Vale flavour year in, year out. The winery was acquired by Mildara Blass, reportedly for the grapegrower contracts they had at a time when Mildara (indeed all big companies) were desperate for red grapes.

Previous outstanding vintages: '85, '87, '90, '91, '93, '94

CURRENT RELEASE 1995   Often discounted to around $12, this is good value for money. Minty bouquet, lots of bold American oak; good weight and persistence. The warm, friendly blackberry-like McLaren Vale cabernet flavour, matched by sweet vanillan oak, is hard to fault. Food: saddle of hare.

Ingoldby Grenache

Quality	ŶŶŶŶ
Value	★★★★⊦
Grapes	grenache
Region	McLaren Vale, SA
Cellar	🍷 3+
Alc./Vol.	12.5%
RRP	$13.00 ⑤

Founder Jim Ingoldby was one of the characters of the wine biz, and he sold his winery to a pair of great characters, Walter and Kerry Clappis. Now Mildara Blass holds the reins.

CURRENT RELEASE 1995   A most unusual wine, with animal/gamy characters reminiscent of some Italian reds. The palate has a core of brandied cherry hidden among the savoury flavours and considerable tannins. Fleshy, fruity, sweet and long. A wine of great interest and very well priced. Serve it with steak and kidney pie.

J J McWilliam Cabernet Sauvignon

Quality	ŶŶŶ
Value	★★★
Grapes	cabernet sauvignon
Region	Riverina, NSW
Cellar	🍷 2
Alc./Vol.	12.0%
RRP	$9.90

John James McWilliam planted the Hanwood vineyard in 1913. Hanwood was attractive because it has abundant water and plenty of sunshine.

CURRENT RELEASE 1995   This is a light, fresh style with an attractive cherry-red colour and leafy, berry nose. The lightweight palate has sweet, subtle berry fruit and there is gentle oak on the finish. Drink now with BBQ spare ribs.

J J McWilliam Shiraz

'McWilliam' entered the Australian wine lexicon in 1877 when Sam McWilliam planted the first family vineyard. Son John carried on the family tradition.
CURRENT RELEASE 1995   The wine has a brilliant ruby colour and the nose is full of capsicum, pepper and ripe plums. The palate is medium-bodied with ripe plum flavours and the oak on the finish coats the mouth with slightly fuzzy tannins. It drinks well now with a mixed grill – don't forget the egg.

Quality	♥♥♥♥
Value	★★★★
Grapes	shiraz
Region	Riverina, NSW
Cellar	3
Alc./Vol.	13.5%
RRP	$9.90

Jamiesons Run

A consistent performer from Coonawarra which offers good flavour at a fair price and is often discounted. Maker Gavin Hogg.
Previous outstanding vintages: '86, '88, '90, '91, '93
CURRENT RELEASE 1994   Decent ready-drinking red wine based on oak. Funky, meaty, smoky aromas and a lean, oak-driven palate flavour. Respectable flavour and length. Try it with meatballs.

Quality	♥♥♥♥
Value	★★★★
Grapes	cabernet sauvignon; shiraz; merlot; cabernet franc
Region	Coonawarra, SA
Cellar	3
Alc./Vol.	12.5%
RRP	$16.00 Ⓢ

Jasper Hill Georgia's Paddock Shiraz

Jasper Hill wines enjoy cult status with their followers. They're grown on sustaining volcanic loam near Heathcote. Maker Ron Laughton.
Previous outstanding vintages: '86, '90, '91, '92, '93
CURRENT RELEASE 1995   Ron Laughton must have sneaked a look at the Grange manual. This is a whopper, and it's also liberally endowed with volatile acidity, which purists may take exception to. Huge weight and density of vanilla, plum and dark chocolate aromas, finishing with quite hard tannin astringency that demands it be laid down. Cellar, then drink with hard cheeses. The rating is given with a blind eye to the VA.

Quality	♥♥♥♥♥
Value	★★★★
Grapes	shiraz
Region	Heathcote, Vic.
Cellar	2–10+
Alc./Vol.	14.5%
RRP	$36.25

Jenke Barossa Mourvèdre

Quality	🍷🍷🍷🍷
Value	★★★★
Grapes	mourvèdre
Region	Barossa Valley, SA
Cellar	5
Alc./Vol.	13.1%
RRP	$17.30

The Jenke family have long been growers in the Barossa Valley. In recent times they have turned their hands to making their own wines and marketing them under a family label.

CURRENT RELEASE 1996 This is an interesting change of pace where flavour is concerned. In olden days this variety was called mataro and this is a good example of the girth the variety can develop. It's soft and juicy with sweet plum flavours and soft velvety tannins on the finish. It's great with a rich beef casserole.

Jim Barry Cabernet Sauvignon

Quality	🍷🍷🍷🍷
Value	★★★★
Grapes	cabernet sauvignon
Region	Clare Valley, SA
Cellar	3
Alc./Vol.	13.0%
RRP	$12.50

This is the cooking style: in the jazz, not kitchen, sense. It's a satisfying wine at a reasonable price.

CURRENT RELEASE 1995 A youthful style with a vibrant colour and a redcurrant, capsicum aroma on the nose. The medium-bodied palate has sweet, mulberry fruit flavours that are matched by some discreet wood and lingering grip. It goes well with steak and kidney.

Jim Barry McRae Wood Cabernet Malbec

Quality	🍷🍷🍷🍷
Value	★★★★
Grapes	cabernet sauvignon; malbec
Region	Clare Valley, SA
Cellar	2–6
Alc./Vol.	13.5%
RRP	$22.50

The luck of the Irish? No, there is nothing lucky about this wine: it comes through hard work in a fractious vineyard. Maker Mark Barry.

CURRENT RELEASE 1995 Great colour and loads of nose. There is plenty of ripe berry, pepper and spice. The palate is full-bodied with sweet fruit flavours that are condensed in terms of juicy character. There is also a fleshy quality, thanks to the malbec. The finish shows some dusty oak and a lot of tannic grip. It needs time, but serve it now with air-cured beef.

Jim Barry McRae Wood Shiraz

The Jim Barry enterprise was founded by a man of the same name in 1974. Since then it has grown exponentially and is now administered by the Barry boys.

CURRENT RELEASE 1995 Great stuff! This has all the Clare goodies we've come to love. The nose is plummy with rich spice and pepper characters. The palate is full-bodied with a mouth-filling texture and silky feel. Ripe plum is the major component and there is well-integrated oak on a long, gripping finish. It goes well with roast squab.

Quality	4.5 glasses
Value	★★★★½
Grapes	shiraz
Region	Clare Valley, SA
Cellar	5
Alc./Vol.	13.5%
RRP	$22.50

Jingalla Reserve Shiraz

Jingalla is one of several vineyards clinging to the lower slopes of the Porongurup Ranges near Albany. Winemaking has been done at Goundrey.

CURRENT RELEASE 1994 A lighter wine than generally found in the Great Southern from this crackerjack shiraz vintage. Medium purple–red colour and a light cherry/spice nose, embellished with a little vanillan oak. No lofty aspirations; a good forward, ready-drinking style. Serve with pressed tongue.

Quality	3 glasses
Value	★★★
Grapes	shiraz
Region	Lower Great Southern, WA
Cellar	3
Alc./Vol.	12.5%
RRP	$20.00

Joseph Cabernet Sauvignon Merlot

Joe Grilli of Primo Estate uses the Moda Amarone (air-drying the grapes the same way they do for Italian Amarone) to make this wine. He's developed and improved the style over the last 10 vintages.

Previous outstanding vintages: '84, '86, '90, '91, '93

CURRENT RELEASE 1995 Power, concentration and length are the highlights here. The colour is a deep purple–red, and the bouquet shows excellent fruit/oak integration with a meaty, barbecued inflexion. It's lush, rich, dense and full-bodied in the mouth, with a finish that goes on and on. A satisfying mouthful of red. Serve with aged Reggiano cheese.

Quality	5 glasses
Value	★★★★½
Grapes	cabernet sauvignon 90%; merlot 10%
Region	McLaren Vale, SA 90%; Coonawarra, SA 10%
Cellar	5+
Alc./Vol.	14.0%
RRP	$31.40

Karina Vineyard Cabernet Merlot

Quality	♟♟♟♟
Value	★★★★
Grapes	cabernet sauvignon; merlot
Region	Mornington Peninsula, Vic.
Cellar	▮ 4
Alc./Vol.	12.5%
RRP	$17.50

Value for money and the Mornington Peninsula might seem like a contradiction in terms, but this vineyard breaks the rules by offering reasonably priced, quality wines.

CURRENT RELEASE 1995   The wine that came in from the cold. It's obviously cool-climate with a leafy nose and underlying berries. The medium-bodied palate has sweet blackberry flavours with hints of cherry, and there are dry tannins on a lingering finish. It's a well-balanced style that is a perfect foil for roast lamb.

Katnook Cabernet Sauvignon

Quality	♟♟♟♟
Value	★★★
Grapes	cabernet sauvignon
Region	Coonawarra, SA
Cellar	⊸ 3–7
Alc./Vol.	13.5%
RRP	$28.00

Wine scribes have taken to using adjectives like 'nervous' and 'nervy' when describing wines. The authors of this book are not nervous types, nor are they moody; but this wine certainly seems to have the sulks.
Previous outstanding vintages: '91, '92
CURRENT RELEASE 1994   A deep garnet colour and a leafy nose with dense toasted oak aromas are the introduction to this wine. The palate has blackberry flavours without outstanding depth. Oak is ever-present and strong, dominating the wine. Whether it will marry with the fruit remains to be seen. There is also a slightly stalky element and lots of acid. If served now, a dish like kangaroo will suit.

Quality	♟♟♟♟
Value	★★★
Grapes	cabernet sauvignon
Region	Coonawarra, SA
Cellar	▮ 3
Alc./Vol.	13.0%
RRP	$30.00

CURRENT RELEASE 1995   Not as dire as the year would suggest, but it does show some of the characters of a troubled vintage. The nose is leafy and herbal, and the palate is light- to medium-bodied. The finish is astringent and there are some green characters in the tannin department. It serves well with lamb chops.

Katnook Estate Odyssey Cabernet Sauvignon

A new super premium from this long-established winery in Coonawarra. It's following the trend of other wineries that have established a leading brand. Maker Wayne Stehbens.

CURRENT RELEASE 1991 A very fit and young wine for six years of bottle-age. It's a bit like a vault with the treasures locked firmly inside. The nose has mint, chocolate and mocha aromas. The palate is tight with sweet, blackberry fruit flavours and there is evidence of toasty oak on the astringent finish. It's a lively wine, and the alcohol doesn't intrude. If you serve it now, try it with rare rump and mushroom sauce.

Quality	🍷🍷🍷🍷½
Value	★★★
Grapes	cabernet sauvignon
Region	Coonawarra, SA
Cellar	8
Alc./Vol.	14.0%
RRP	$55.00

Katnook Merlot

The hunt for a Petrus look-alike goes on and some examples are more successful than others. To stand alone merlot has to have considerable power and complexity.

CURRENT RELEASE 1994 An elegant style that shows some of the herbal aspects of the variety. There are tobacco, cedar and crushed rose petal aromas on the nose. The medium-bodied palate has a fresh, redcurrant flavour and some tobacco notes. The finish has a pleasant, dry, almost dusty oak astringency. It drinks well with chargrilled lamb straps in a Middle Eastern marinade.

Quality	🍷🍷🍷🍷
Value	★★★½
Grapes	merlot
Region	Coonawarra, SA
Cellar	6
Alc./Vol.	12.5
RRP	$30.00

CURRENT RELEASE 1995 The nose would have you believe this was a slightly unripe style. It's full of leaf, tobacco and herbs as well as some floral notes. The palate is generous with sweet, ripe fruit flavours, redcurrant being the major component. Fine-grained tannins fill in the grip on the finish. It's perfect for a piece of seared eye fillet.

Quality	🍷🍷🍷🍷½
Value	★★★½
Grapes	merlot
Region	Coonawarra, SA
Cellar	2–6
Alc./Vol.	13.5%
RRP	$35.00

Kay Brothers Block 6 Shiraz

Quality	！！！！！
Value	★★★★
Grapes	shiraz
Region	McLaren Vale, SA
Cellar	▊ 5
Alc./Vol.	14.3%
RRP	$26.10

Block 6 is all about nostalgia. Old vines plus old techniques produce a very old-fashioned style that isn't ashamed to show a few warts in the name of complexity. It's one for those who can remember the black and white version of *The Maltese Falcon*. Maker Colin Kay.
Previous outstanding vintages: '90, '91, '92, '93
CURRENT RELEASE 1994   The colour is deep and the nose offers pepper and plum aromas plus a hint of volatility. The palate is rich and chewy and dominated by plum flavours, and there is that regional iron-medicine character underneath. The finish is loaded with black-tea-like tannins and strong grip. Tea-smoked duck is a blast alongside a glass.

Kay's Amery Cabernet Sauvignon

Quality	！！！！
Value	★★★✦
Grapes	cabernet sauvignon
Region	McLaren Vale, SA
Cellar	▊ 3
Alc./Vol.	14.0%
RRP	$19.00

This is a much overlooked label, and perhaps the wines in the distant past were fairly ho-hum. There have since been great strides in terms of quality and style. Maker Colin Kay.
CURRENT RELEASE 1994   A sunny, honest style that doesn't want for fruit flavours. The colour is a deep crimson, and the nose has strong blackberry fruit and an alcoholic lift. The palate is full of sweet berries and these are attended by slightly disjointed oak. It drinks well now with osso bucco.

Kay's Amery Grenache

Quality	！！！
Value	★★★
Grapes	grenache
Region	McLaren Vale, SA
Cellar	▊ 1
Alc./Vol.	13.4%
RRP	$13.50

In response to the revival of this grape variety it seems that every winery must now make an example. In this case it's the rekindling of tradition.
CURRENT RELEASE 1995   You've got to like grenache to enjoy this one. The nose has a strong raspberry aroma and the palate is quite sweet with intense raspberry fruit flavour. It gets close to confectionery realms. The finish is soft. It could be drunk chilled. Try it with tandoori chops.

Kay's Amery Vineyards Shiraz

Kay's is one of the stalwart pioneering companies from the Southern Vales. It has survived both financial famine and feast, and gives the impression it will be ever thus. CURRENT RELEASE 1995   Plenty of regional and varietal characters in this wine. The colour is a deep red and there are ripe, sweet plum aromas. The palate is medium-bodied, with plum flavours dusted with cinnamon and nutmeg. There are some discreet oak characters on the gentle finish. It drinks well now with devilled kidneys.

Quality	ŸŸŸÝ
Value	★★★⼁
Grapes	shiraz
Region	McLaren Vale, SA
Cellar	🍾 4
Alc./Vol.	13.1%
RRP	$16.50

Killerby Cabernet Sauvignon

There has been a defection in the Killerby camp: winemaker Matt Aldridge and wife Anna (nee Killerby) are now in the Yarra Valley at Eyton on Yarra. CURRENT RELEASE 1994   There is a slightly hard edge to this wine that might soften with time. The colour is dark and there is a blackberry aroma with a hint of briar patch. The palate is medium-bodied with blackberry flavours that are followed by black-tea-style tannins on a finish that imparts loads of grip. It's a good wine to joust with devilled kidneys.

Quality	ŸŸŸÝ
Value	★★★
Grapes	cabernet sauvignon
Region	Capel, WA
Cellar	➡ 3–6
Alc./Vol.	13.5%
RRP	$18.00 🍾

Knappstein Enterprise Shiraz

This is part of the Mildara Blass empire and the new label looks like it's a mock-up for the final design to come. But even if the label does look unfinished, the wine gives the impression of solidarity and style. CURRENT RELEASE 1995   Big wine with typical Clare Valley intensity of colour and nose. There are spices and plums on the nose, and the palate is rich. Plum is the major flavour, and this is laced with dark chocolate and vanilla spices. The finish is a mixture of natural and wood tannins with a black-tea-like element, plus pepper and emphatic grip. It needs time. Try it with squab.

Quality	ŸŸŸŸÝ
Value	★★★★
Grapes	shiraz
Region	Clare Valley, SA
Cellar	➡ 2–6
Alc./Vol.	14.5%
RRP	$22.00

Knight Granite Hills Cabernet

Quality	🍷🍷🍷½
Value	★★★
Grapes	cabernet sauvignon 80%; cabernet franc 15%; merlot 5%
Region	Macedon, Vic.
Cellar	🍾 2 years
Alc./Vol.	13.5%
RRP	$21.50

The vineyard is located on the Burke and Wills Track near Baynton in an ultra-cool location. It's one of the pioneering vineyards that helped put Macedon on the map. Maker Lew Knight.

CURRENT RELEASE 1992 The wine is starting to show some evidence of bottle development. The colour is a mid-brick-red and the nose has a leafy character along with berry aromas. There are mature fruit flavours on the palate, which are matched by some mellow oak and soft tannins on the finish. It's a good pasta (with a meat sauce) style.

Knight Granite Hills Pinot Noir

Quality	🍷🍷🍷
Value	★★★
Grapes	pinot noir
Region	Macedon, Vic.
Cellar	🍾 4
Alc./Vol.	12.5%
RRP	$19.00

Revisionists will have the folks at Granite Hills thinking about producing pinot noir for a sparkling wine base.

CURRENT RELEASE 1995 The colour is a light cherry-red and there is a strong minty element on the nose. The elegant palate has cherry flavours plus mint and a hint of oak caramel. There is strong acid on the finish. It would be good with chargrilled tuna.

Knight Granite Hills Shiraz

Quality	🍷🍷🍷½
Value	★★½
Grapes	shiraz
Region	Macedon, Vic.
Cellar	🍾 3
Alc./Vol.	13.5%
RRP	$21.50

Patriarch Gordon Knight is known in the district as 'Silent Knight', because after one telephone call from Gordon you need to have the telephone surgically removed from your ear! He's one of the great characters in the district.

CURRENT RELEASE 1992 Pass the pepper grinder: that's the distinctive character of the district. In terms of structure the wine has a decidedly Italian feel, thanks to a hint of tartness. The nose shows some mellow bottle development aromas, and the palate is raspberries with black pepper characters. The finish is astringent and tart. It drinks well now with a designer pizza.

Koltz Niseda Cabernet

Sounds a bit like the brand on a rifle you'd use in a book repository in Dallas. This new label belongs to growers who have been in business since 1970. The name might be unfriendly to the tongue, but the wine isn't.

CURRENT RELEASE 1995 The nose is very true to region but it plays you false. It comes on strong with a plummy, porty aroma, yet the palate doesn't follow the nose. It's rich but not jammy, and there is a hint of earth and iron tonic. French and American oak rule the finish. It drinks well now. Try it with a meaty Turkish pizza.

Quality	▾▾▾⟨
Value	★★★⟨
Grapes	cabernet sauvignon
Region	McLaren Vale, SA
Cellar	▮ 4
Alc./Vol.	12.5%
RRP	$14.95

Koppamurra Cabernet Merlot

This area in the Naracoorte Ranges is about to become another wine region discovery. There will be substantial plantings in the near future. This label represents the pioneers.

CURRENT RELEASE 1995 This is a light (claret) style with a pillar-box red colour and an earthy nose. The palate is middleweight with some cherry and raspberry fruit flavours, and these are bound to some black-tea-like tannins on an astringent finish. It's a BBQ chop model.

Quality	▾▾▾
Value	★★★
Grapes	cabernet sauvignon; merlot
Region	Naracoorte Ranges, SA
Cellar	▮ 3
Alc./Vol.	12.7%
RRP	$16.00

Krondorf Family Reserve Cabernet Merlot

What family is this? The Krondorf family? Ain't no such family. The winery was named after a small Barossa Valley settlement of people of German descent. The name means emperor's village.

CURRENT RELEASE 1994 Smoky, toasty oak dominates this wine in a rather attractive way. There are redcurrant and cherry flavours beneath the oak, and it's well balanced, smooth and ready to drink. Try it with lamb kebabs.

Quality	▾▾▾⟨
Value	★★★⟨
Grapes	cabernet sauvignon
Region	McLaren Vale & Barossa Valley, SA
Cellar	▮ 5
Alc./Vol.	13.0%
RRP	$15.00 Ⓢ

Kyeema Cabernet Merlot

Quality	🍷🍷🍷🍷🍷
Value	★★★★⯪
Grapes	cabernet sauvignon; merlot
Region	Canberra district & Hilltops, NSW
Cellar	🍷 7+
Alc./Vol.	13.5%
RRP	$15.00 (ex-winery)

Andrew McEwin buys grapes selectively from around the Canberra and Hilltops regions and his reds have been most impressive in recent years.
Previous outstanding vintages: '94
CURRENT RELEASE 1995   An oak-driven style of real class and depth. Fresh fruit/oak aromas, nutty wood-derived and fully-ripe, sweet berryish fruit flavours, concluding with drying tannins on the finish. A smart red with good persistence. Team it with beef teppanyaki.

Kyeema Shiraz

Quality	🍷🍷🍷🍷🍷
Value	★★★★★
Grapes	shiraz
Region	Canberra district & Hilltops, NSW
Cellar	🍷 8+
Alc./Vol.	13.0%
RRP	$15.00 (ex-winery)

Kyeema's reds have had stunning success in competitions with 10 trophies in the last two years, including three at the '97 Canberra Region Wine Show (two with the '95 shiraz). Maker Andrew McEwin.
Previous outstanding vintages: '94
CURRENT RELEASE 1995   Colour is a promising dark purple–red; indeed the wine has good concentration all round. Vanilla and coconut aromas mingle with varietal spices and the oak is well judged. It's an elegant, seamless shiraz with stacks of ripe, cool-grown shiraz character. Serve it with saddle of hare.

Lark Hill Cabernet Merlot

Quality	🍷🍷🍷🍷🍷
Value	★★★★⯪
Grapes	cabernet sauvignon; merlot
Region	Canberra district, NSW
Cellar	🍷 1–8+
Alc./Vol.	13.5%
RRP	$20.00 (cellar door)

Owners David and Sue Carpenter are looking increasingly to warmer sites on the western side of the Canberra region for grapes for this wine.
Previous outstanding vintages: '88, '91, '93, '94
CURRENT RELEASE 1995   A stylish wine of impressive concentration and overt spicy, cedary oak, which in February needed a few more months to integrate. Sweet blackcurrant cabernet and plummy merlot flavours; excellent length and balance. A complete wine that doesn't suffer from cool-climate greenness. Try it with rare roast beef.

Lark Hill Pinot Noir

The Carpenters of Lark Hill have found their site is a little too cold for cabernet and merlot but pinot noir does much better. Yields are only about a tonne an acre. This took out the pinot trophy at the Sydney Wine Show against all comers. Maker Sue Carpenter.
CURRENT RELEASE 1996 An arrestingly deep colour for a pinot, and the concentration theme continues throughout the wine. It's rich and full in the mouth, with great depth of lush, sweet pinot cherry flavours and an acceptable degree of sappiness. The generosity of fruit is quite remarkable. Serve with Peking duck.

Quality	🍷🍷🍷🍷
Value	★★★★
Grapes	pinot noir
Region	Canberra district, NSW
Cellar	4
Alc./Vol.	13.0%
RRP	$18.00 (cellar door)

Laurel Bank Pinot Noir

From a tiny vineyard at Granton in the Coal Valley, Tasmania, and vinified by Andrew Hood. This is only available by mail order or from the cellar door.
CURRENT RELEASE 1996 The high acidity and less-ripe, dusty/capsicum aromas typical of the vintage are evident here. It has surprising richness and gravity in the mouth, with chunky cherry and vanilla flavours. A good wine considering the difficulties of the year. Serve with veal sweetbreads.

Quality	🍷🍷🍷
Value	★★★
Grapes	pinot noir
Region	Coal Valley, Tas.
Cellar	3+
Alc./Vol.	12.8%
RRP	$19.00 (ex-winery)

Leasingham Bin 61 Shiraz

Opulence is the key word for Leasingham reds these days. Show judges love them too: this won a trophy at the '96 Cowra Show. Maker Richard Rowe.
Previous outstanding vintages: '90, '91, '92, '93, '94
CURRENT RELEASE 1995 Straight back in the groove. First thing that hits you is the dense purple colour; then the noseful of ripe plums, spices and vanillan oak; then finally the rich, chunky, concentrated flavour. Heaps of grip and fleshiness; big and tannic – but balanced. Not a wine of subtlety! It goes well with beef wellington.

Quality	🍷🍷🍷🍷
Value	★★★★
Grapes	shiraz
Region	Clare Valley, SA
Cellar	8+
Alc./Vol.	13.0%
RRP	$17.40 Ⓢ

Leasingham Classic Clare Cabernet Sauvignon

Quality	🍷🍷🍷🍷🍷
Value	★★★★★
Grapes	cabernet sauvignon
Region	Clare Valley, SA
Cellar	➡ 3–13
Alc./Vol.	13.5%
RRP	$28.00 🍶

Richard Rowe has breathed fire into all the Leasingham reds since he took over the winemaking reins in the early '90s.
Previous outstanding vintages: '91, '92, '93, '94
CURRENT RELEASE 1995 The colour is a youthful, dense purple–red, the first sign of the quality and fruit concentration that are hallmarks of this label. Toasty, charry oak dominates the nose at this early stage. There is massive flavour and tannin in a muscular, powerful framework, and it needs years before it will hit its peak. Then serve with aged cheddar.

Leasingham Classic Clare Shiraz

Quality	🍷🍷🍷🍷🍷
Value	★★★★★
Grapes	shiraz
Region	Clare Valley, SA
Cellar	➡ 2–10
Alc./Vol.	14.0%
RRP	$28.00 🍶

A Jimmy-Watson-Trophy-winner that lives up to the loftiest expectations. It will probably escalate in price rapidly, putting it in collector territory, but there's no doubt about the quality.
Previous outstanding vintages: '91, '92, '93
CURRENT RELEASE 1994 Dense purple colour, and powerful bouquet packed with pepper, spices and sweet, ripe berries. Forests of oak also, which indicates a year or two to fully integrate. A wine of concentration and opulence: what the Americans might call decadent. Cellar, then serve with aged cheeses.

Quality	🍷🍷🍷🍷🍷
Value	★★★★★
Grapes	shiraz
Region	Clare Valley, SA
Cellar	➡ 3–10+
Alc./Vol.	13.5%
RRP	$28.00 🍶

CURRENT RELEASE 1995 Concentrated wine in every way: dense colour, latent undeveloped aromas of rich plummy fruit and coconut/vanilla oak. It's very tannic in the mouth but promises great things with adequate time in the cellar. Plum and licorice flavours ad infinitum. Cellar, then serve with rare rump steak.

Leconfield Cabernet

This is a past Penguin-Award-winner. Maker Ralph Fowler has quickly built Leconfield a reputation for quality and consistency.
Previous outstanding vintages: '80, '82, '91, '92, '93, '94
CURRENT RELEASE 1995 A pretty wine, not one with a lot of legs for the future, but a pleasant early drinker. The nose is typical Leconfield: aromatic, perfumed oak, and leafy, minty fruit, which has some peppery nuances. It may lack a little richness but the lean, tight structure has good balance. Try it with roast lamb and mint sauce.

Quality	♉♉♉♉
Value	★★★
Grapes	cabernet sauvignon; merlot; cabernet franc; petit verdot
Region	Coonawarra, SA
Cellar	▮ 3
Alc./Vol.	13.5%
RRP	$22.50

Leconfield Merlot

This has been matured in French oak barriques made in Burgundy, according to the blurb. Sorry to be pedantic, but a barrique is a Bordeaux style of barrel.
CURRENT RELEASE 1995 This has a fairly light colour for its age, a medium purple–red, and there are leafy, raspberry and cherry-pip aromas coupled with trademark Leconfield aromatic oak. The raspberry flavour reappears in the mouth, where it's quite lean and somewhat ungiving. Perhaps it's the year showing itself. Serve with lighter meats such as veal.

Quality	♉♉♉♉
Value	★★★
Grapes	merlot
Region	Coonawarra, SA
Cellar	▮ 3
Alc./Vol.	13.0%
RRP	$20.00

Leeuwin Estate Art Series Cabernet Sauvignon

Leeuwin's cabernets are a boots-and-all style, built for drinking rather than tasting. They invariably appear like tannic monsters when tasted without food. Maker Bob Cartwright.
Previous outstanding vintages: '79, '82, '87, '89, '91, '92
CURRENT RELEASE 1993 The nose has a pungent, dusty, herbaceous high-note, plus earthy development and a lot of oak. A big wine with toasty, nutty flavours, and the tannin monsters the tastebuds, leaving an austere astringency on the finish. Cellar, or at least serve with strong food like venison.

Quality	♉♉♉♉
Value	★★⟟
Grapes	cabernet sauvignon
Region	Margaret River, WA
Cellar	➥ 2–7+
Alc./Vol.	14.0%
RRP	$37.00 ▮

Leeuwin Estate Art Series Pinot Noir

Quality 🍷🍷🍷🍷
Value ★★★
Grapes pinot noir
Region Margaret River, WA
Cellar 3
Alc./Vol. 13.5%
RRP $33.00

Each year all the wines in the art series have a different original painting at the top of their label. Go to the restaurant in the winery and you'll see them hung all around the walls.

Previous outstanding vintages: '89, '91, '92

CURRENT RELEASE 1994 A rather oaky pinot, which shows stewy, sappy fruit on the nose and chocolate on the palate. It has considerable grip on the finish, thanks to the oak tannin. It lacks a little in the complexity department, but certainly has weight. Try it with BBQ lamb chops.

Leeuwin Estate Prelude Cabernet Sauvignon

Quality 🍷🍷🍷½
Value ★★★
Grapes cabernet sauvignon
Region Margaret River, WA
Cellar 1–5+
Alc./Vol. 14.5%
RRP $22.00

This is more about Wagner at his gravest than a tinkling Chopin prelude. It tries hard to be more than it is. Maker Bob Cartwright.

CURRENT RELEASE 1993 Maturity shows here with a brick-red colour and a bouquet of old boots. The palate is swingeingly tannic (thanks, Michael Broadbent) and leathery with a searingly dry finish. A bit tough, so we recommend further cellaring. Then serve with a hearty casserole.

Lengs & Cooter Old Bush Vines Grenache

Quality 🍷🍷🍷
Value ★★★
Grapes grenache
Region Clare Valley, SA
Cellar 2
Alc./Vol. 13.6%
RRP $15.20

Bush vines are supposed to give the best grenache grapes by virtue of being close to the ground, and low in vigour and yield. They tend also to be old and unirrigated.

CURRENT RELEASE 1996 A lightish but vivid purple–red colour, and the nose is pungent in strawberry/raspberry grenache fruit aroma. There's a hint of pepper–spice as well. The palate weight is lightish and the flavour is typically floral grenache. A fruit-bomb, which is nice, but it lacks depth and complexity. Goes with devilled kidneys.

Lengs & Cooter Old Vines Shiraz

At least it's a distinctive name: you wouldn't remember Smith and Jones as easily. The wines are pretty scarce, so you'll have to look hard. The oldest vines were planted in 1892.
CURRENT RELEASE 1995 A bawling infant. This is impressively concentrated but needs time to soften a slight toughness. Vivid purple colour, a closed-up, dusty, cough-medicine-like aroma, and quite a tannic, structured palate. Cellar, then try it with braised venison.

Quality	▼▼▼₵
Value	★★★
Grapes	shiraz
Region	Clare Valley, SA
Cellar	➠ 2–7+
Alc./Vol.	13.5%
RRP	$20.00

Lenswood Vineyards Cabernets

Cabernet is a challenge in the cool Adelaide Hills, but a healthy dollop of merlot in the blend helps. Maker Tim Knappstein.
CURRENT RELEASE 1994 This has concentration in spite of its dusty, leafy, herbaceous notes. There are blackberry aromas too, and the palate is youthfully astringent with mouth-puckering tannin. Could repay a couple of years in the cellar. Then try it with rabbit casserole.

Quality	▼▼▼▼
Value	★★★
Grapes	cabernet sauvignon 81%; merlot 19%
Region	Adelaide Hills, SA
Cellar	▮ 5+
Alc./Vol.	12.5%
RRP	$28.00

Lenswood Vineyards Pinot Noir

Tim Knappstein flies a canary-yellow Boeing Stearman biplane. A similar aircraft does a spectacular prang in the film *The English Patient*.
Previous outstanding vintages: '91, '93, '94
CURRENT RELEASE 1995 This has good depth of colour but is a leaner, meaner style than the '94. It's dominated by stalky/vegetable characters, probably derived from whole-bunch (including stalks) fermentation. The palate profile is lean and savoury, almost Italianate. Lacks a bit of charm now, but could be better in a year. Try it with spit-roast pigeon.

Quality	▼▼▼₵
Value	★★₭
Grapes	pinot noir
Region	Adelaide Hills, SA
Cellar	▮ 2+
Alc./Vol.	12.5%
RRP	$32.50

Lenton Brae Cabernet Merlot

Quality	ÝÝÝÝ¿
Value	★★★★
Grapes	cabernet sauvignon; merlot
Region	Margaret River, WA
Cellar	▮ 6+
Alc./Vol.	12.7%
RRP	$19.75

Sounds like a good name for a malt whisky. Perhaps the owners should consider opening a distillery as well? Maker William Shields.

CURRENT RELEASE 1996   This seems to be made as a softer, earlier-drinking red than the straight cabernet. Although very young, it's a real charmer. Sweet black-currant and blackberry nose and flavour. The taste is smooth and seamless, the oak gently handled, and there is just enough tannin to firm the finish. It has the elegance to partner veal.

Lenton Brae Cabernet Sauvignon

Quality	ÝÝÝÝ¿
Value	★★★★
Grapes	cabernet sauvignon
Region	Margaret River, WA
Cellar	▮ 7+
Alc./Vol.	13.0%
RRP	$19.75 ▮

This is the more highbrow of the two Lenton Brae cabernet styles. It's an attempt at a red with real structure and legs.

CURRENT RELEASE 1994   A complex red that has seen a lot of wood. There are toasty, barbecued-meat and also earthy, savoury aromas. The taste is likewise savoury and dry, with oak-influenced richness, extract and generosity. It has a tonne of flavour and grip, thanks in no small part to wood. It has excellent length and should team well with harder cheeses.

Leo Buring Barossa Coonawarra Cabernet Sauvignon

Quality	ÝÝÝ¿
Value	★★★
Grapes	cabernet sauvignon
Region	Barossa Valley & Coonawarra, SA
Cellar	▮ 5
Alc./Vol.	13.0%
RRP	$16.25 Ⓢ ▮

The Southcorp marketers have dropped the bin numbers off the entire Buring range: this used to be bin DR505. Maker Geoff Henriks.

CURRENT RELEASE 1993   Starting to show some attractive bottle development, but still rather oak-dominated. There is a certain Southcorp style about the wine, and the finish is strong on wood tannins. There's plenty of flavour and depth, and it goes well with seared kangaroo fillets.

Leydens Vale Pinot Noir

This is the second label of Blue Pyrenees Estate, and the wines are made from local as well as brought-in grapes. Makers Vincent Gere and Kim Hart.
CURRENT RELEASE 1993   Good colour for its age: full red with a tinge of purple. There's a slight volatile lift but also lots of vanilla and chocolate flavour, much of it due to oak. Lean, slightly angular palate, with a firm grip on the finish. Slightly dry reddish (lacking varietal signature), but a good drink with country-style terrine.

Quality	ΨΨΨ⸮
Value	★★★
Grapes	pinot noir
Region	Pyrenees, Vic.
Cellar	◊ 2
Alc./Vol.	13.3%
RRP	$17.60

Leydens Vale Shiraz

Another label from Blue Pyrenees Estate, signifying good-value blended wines from various regions, produced to a price. Makers Vincent Gere and Kim Hart.
CURRENT RELEASE 1994   This is a remarkable wine at the price. Evoking Rhone Valley wines such as Crozes-Hermitage, it has a dense colour, and pungent intensity of pepper–spice aromas overlying sweet red-berry, cherry fruit. It's ripe and fragrant with elegant weight and fine balance. Serve with seared kangaroo fillets.

Quality	ΨΨΨΨΨ
Value	★★★★★
Grapes	shiraz
Region	not stated
Cellar	◊ 5+
Alc./Vol.	13.9%
RRP	$15.00

Lillydale Vineyards Cabernet Merlot

Since the McWilliams takeover, Lillydale has opened a new restaurant in which to entertain visitors.
CURRENT RELEASE 1995   The bouquet shows toasted oak and shy, red-berry aromas; the palate is lean, narrow and a trifle hollow. Okay flavour and teams well with beef ravioli.

Quality	ΨΨΨ
Value	★★★
Grapes	cabernet sauvignon; merlot
Region	Yarra Valley, Vic.
Cellar	◊ 4
Alc./Vol.	12.0%
RRP	$15.30 Ⓢ

Lillydale Vineyards Pinot Noir

Quality	♛♛♛♛
Value	★★★★
Grapes	pinot noir
Region	Yarra Valley, Vic.
Cellar	▮ 3
Alc./Vol.	13.0%
RRP	$15.30 Ⓢ

At last, an affordable pinot with good flavour and pinot character. It's not in the league of the Yarra's best, but it's an improver.

CURRENT RELEASE 1996   Sweet strawberry and cherry aromas with a hint of maceration bubblegum, which will settle down with short bottle-age. A fruit-driven style with nice, tight structure and a little bitterness on the finish, which should soften out quickly. Very promising. Try it with beef carpaccio.

Lindemans Bin 50 Shiraz

Quality	♛♛♛
Value	★★★
Grapes	shiraz
Region	not stated
Cellar	▮ 2
Alc./Vol.	13.0%
RRP	$9.75 Ⓢ

This is part of the Bin range that includes the tearaway Bin 65 Chardonnay, which is selling up a storm in the US.

CURRENT RELEASE 1995   Medium–light colour and showing some development, this has a nose of earth and forest floors, together with a leanish, light–medium-weight palate. It's soft and ready to drink. Modest character and length, but good value. Try it with steak pie and sauce.

Lindemans Hunter River Shiraz

Quality	♛♛♛♛
Value	★★★
Grapes	shiraz
Region	Hunter Valley, NSW
Cellar	➥ 2–8
Alc./Vol.	13.0%
RRP	$20.00 Ⓢ ▮

The Lindemans Hunter shirazes took on a new persona when they discovered new American oak. The price has also gone up in leaps and bounds.

CURRENT RELEASE 1994   Bin 8803. The nose is dominated by a planky, freshly sawn oak character at present. This adds a certain sweetness to the flavour as well. Medium-bodied and smooth in the mouth, it could reward cellaring. As it is, we'd prefer to let it age and hope the oak settles in and the wine develops some of the complexities we love in typical Hunter shiraz. Serve with a mild Thai curry.

Lindemans Hunter River Steven Vineyard Reserve Shiraz

This increasingly busy label has more titles than the House of Lords, so we left the Bin 8625 out. Maker Patrick Auld.

Previous outstanding vintages: '90, '91

CURRENT RELEASE 1994   Medium red–purple colour, and dusty, subdued nose with a slight whiff of wood. Arid and savoury on the tongue with some coconutty oak flavour, it's lean and has drying tannins on the finish, although there's a core of sweetness hidden inside. Needs time: cellar for three years, then serve with smoked cheddar.

Quality	▼▼▼?
Value	★★ʳ
Grapes	shiraz
Region	Hunter Valley, NSW
Cellar	⬤ 3–8+
Alc./Vol.	12.0%
RRP	$22.00 🍾

Lindemans Limestone Ridge

We suspect most of this wine will be drunk long before the wood has a chance to integrate properly, which is a great pity. Maker Greg Clayfield.

Previous outstanding vintages: '82, '86, '88, '90, '91

CURRENT RELEASE 1993   This has won four gold medals, but it's hard to see how the judges could get past the oak. It's very woody, and the palate seems just a trifle lean and lacking on the finish to balance the timber. We would not be investing $31.50 on it. Strictly one for the gamblers.

Quality	▼▼▼
Value	★★ʳ
Grapes	shiraz; cabernet sauvignon
Region	Coonawarra, SA
Cellar	⬤ 2–5+
Alc./Vol.	13.0%
RRP	$31.50 Ⓢ 🍾

Lindemans Padthaway Cabernet Merlot

Padthaway initially came to notice with white wines. These days, as the vines mature, the reds are increasingly impressive.

Previous outstanding vintages: '93, '94

CURRENT RELEASE 1995   Definitive blackcurrant cabernet flavour here, enriched by toasty oak. There are some floral notes to the berry fruit. It has satisfying power and grip, finishing with fine tannins. Works well with a standing rib roast of beef.

Quality	▼▼▼▼?
Value	★★★★ʳ
Grapes	cabernet sauvignon; merlot
Region	Padthaway, SA
Cellar	🍾 5+
Alc./Vol.	13.0%
RRP	$15.60 Ⓢ

Lindemans Padthaway Pinot Noir

Quality	♟♟♟♟
Value	★★★★
Grapes	pinot noir
Region	Padthaway, SA
Cellar	▮ 4+
Alc./Vol.	13.0%
RRP	$15.60 ⑤

This discounts in price to around $12, making it one of the best-value pinots around. Maker Greg Clayfield.

CURRENT RELEASE 1996   Oak has long been the Lindeman way, and while this is a red wine of good weight, smoothness and drinkability, it would be a better pinot with a little less overt oak character. Vanilla is the dominant theme, with some sweet berry poking through. Serve with duck confit.

Lindemans Pyrus

Quality	♟♟♟♟♟
Value	★★★⟵
Grapes	cabernet sauvignon; merlot; cabernet franc; malbec
Region	Coonawarra, SA
Cellar	⟵ 1–12
Alc./Vol.	13.5%
RRP	$31.50 ⑤ ▮

This style was created in an emergency following the Melbourne Wine Show, when a sample from the '85 vintage – a laboratory blend thrown together just for the show – jagged the Jimmy Watson Trophy.
Previous outstanding vintages: '85, '86, '91, '92
CURRENT RELEASE 1993   An interesting wine of some charm. Floral, slightly jammy nose featuring sweet vanillan oak and crushed berries. Good weight and concentration. Savoury, heavily oak-matured flavours and a nicely arid finish. Try it with squab.

Madfish Bay Premium Dry Red

Quality	♟♟♟
Value	★★★⟵
Grapes	not stated
Region	Great Southern, WA
Cellar	▮ 2
Alc./Vol.	13.5%
RRP	$16.00

This is the second label from the folks behind Howard Park. Maker John Wade consults for so many vineyards it's hard to know when he gets time for his own wines.

CURRENT RELEASE 1995   Bold red in colour and a nose that blossoms with fruit aromas. The palate is succulent with sweet plum and cherry fruit flavours that are matched by some soft tannins on a moderate finish. It's great for a beef casserole.

Maglieri Cabernet Sauvignon

This company built fortune – if not fame – on the production of cheap sparkling styles like Gully Spumante. These days it's seeking fame in the quality end of the market.

CURRENT RELEASE 1995   There is a touch of class with this wine. The nose is dominated by blackberry aromas on a leafy background. The palate has sweet berry flavours and a spicy element. There is some smoky oak on the finish and the wood also contributes a vanilla flavour. It drinks well now with a mince pie.

Quality	♟♟♟♟
Value	★★★★
Grapes	cabernet sauvignon
Region	McLaren Vale, SA
Cellar	▮ 4
Alc./Vol.	13.5%
RRP	$15.00

Maglieri Shiraz

When the going gets tough the shiraz gets going. It's a generalisation to suggest 1995 was not a kind year in Australia, but there are many disappointments. Shiraz seems to be an exception, particularly in McLaren Vale.

CURRENT RELEASE 1995   A very fruity style that is a delight to drink. What it lacks in downright guts is made up for by attractive fruit and complexity. The nose is a mixture of berries, plums and pepper. The medium-weight palate has sweet berry flavours, which are matched by some chocolate characters. The oak adds spice and some discreet tannin. Drink it now with rare kangaroo fillets.

Quality	♟♟♟♟♟
Value	★★★★⯪
Grapes	shiraz
Region	McLaren Vale, SA
Cellar	▮ 5
Alc./Vol.	$13.5%
RRP	$15.00

Majella Coonawarra Cabernet

Quality	YYYY
Value	★★★
Grapes	cabernet sauvignon
Region	Coonawarra, SA
Cellar	4
Alc./Vol.	13.0%
RRP	$22.00

This is proof that eventually most grapegrowers can't resist the urge to become proprietors of their own label. Brian Lynn was a grower for 25 years before he made the transition.

CURRENT RELEASE 1995   The year has influenced the style, and the wine is elegant and slightly lean. The nose has blackberry and grenadine aromas with a dusting of wood. The light- to medium-bodied palate has the classic cabernet hole in the centre. The major flavour is blackberry and there is some dry dusty oak on the finish. There is fine astringent grip. It's a wine that would go well with pink lamb chops.

Majella Shiraz

Quality	YYYY
Value	★★★
Grapes	shiraz
Region	Coonawarra
Cellar	3
Alc./Vol.	13.0%
RRP	$18.00

There are 40 hectares under vine at this estate, and even with the relatively low yields from Coonawarra, it's not a hobby farm by any means.

Previous outstanding vintages: '91, '92, '93

CURRENT RELEASE 1995   Probably lighter than usual (thanks to the nature of the vintage), but there is finesse and flavour. The colour is a light ruby and the nose has a mixture of mint and earth. The medium-bodied palate has dark cherry flavours and there is fine-grained tannin on the astringent finish. It drinks well now with smoked kangaroo.

Mandurang Valley Cabernet Sauvignon

Quality	YYYY
Value	★★★★
Grapes	cabernet sauvignon
Region	Bendigo, Vic.
Cellar	5
Alc./Vol.	12.4%
RRP	$17.90

The exuberance of youth – right down to the stand-out label. Some people will be attracted, others repelled, but there is no doubting Mandurang Valley is now available.

CURRENT RELEASE 1994   Vibrant, young, purple–red colour and a nose that is full of cassis and leaf aromas. The medium- to full-bodied palate has sweet fruit flavours and a hint of tobacco. There is some boss oak on the back palate and plenty of grip. It needs a little more time. At the moment it can handle game dishes like squab.

Marienberg Cabernet Mourvèdre Grenache

This is showing all the hallmarks of becoming a trendy blend thanks to the re-discovery of grapes like mourvèdre, nee mataro, which was the varietal name in old winespeak.

CURRENT RELEASE 1995 This is an interesting luncheon style that is very easy to drink. The nose is fruity, as is the palate. It's book-of-verse stuff with a gentle finish and a quaffing capacity. Try it with a platter of cold meats.

Quality	🍷🍷🍷
Value	★★★
Grapes	cabernet sauvignon; mourvèdre; grenache
Region	not stated
Cellar	🍾
Alc./Vol.	11.5%
RRP	$11.00

Marienberg Reserve Shiraz

The Reserve range from this marque is reserved for fruit from the McLaren Vale district. It's said to 'reflect its essence'.

CURRENT RELEASE 1994 Pretty typical of the district, although slightly less substantial than most. The colour is a medium garnet, and the nose has capsicum and cracked pepper aromas. The palate is medium-bodied with some sweet plum flavours and a light dusting of spice. Oak lurks underneath, but the tannin on the finish is quite civilised. It drinks well now with continental sausages.

Quality	🍷🍷🍷½
Value	★★★½
Grapes	shiraz
Region	McLaren Vale, SA
Cellar	🍾 3
Alc./Vol.	13.5%
RRP	$21.00

Maritime Estate Cabernet Sauvignon

Simple but distinctive label for this Mornington Peninsula vineyard located at Red Hill and made by an almost ubiquitous winemaking team. Maker Kevin McCarthy and Kath Quealy (consultants).

CURRENT RELEASE 1995 A wine with its cool-climate hem showing. The colour is mid-ruby and the nose has sweet berry aromas. The palate is a bit of a let-down, being a trifle thin and wan. Add a leafy element and you've got the cool-climate syndrome. There is plenty of acid on the finish. It could be served now with pink lamb.

Quality	🍷🍷🍷
Value	★★★
Grapes	cabernet sauvignon
Region	Mornington Peninsula, Vic.
Cellar	🍾 3
Alc./Vol.	12.5%
RRP	$19.00

McWilliams Maurice O'Shea Shiraz

Quality	♙♙♙♙
Value	★★★★
Grapes	shiraz
Region	Hunter Valley, NSW
Cellar	▯ 8
Alc./Vol.	13.5%
RRP	$27.00

The late Maurice O'Shea is one of our wine icons, and rightly so. He changed the face of Australian winemaking in the '40s and mid-'50s, particularly concerning red wines. Maker Phillip Ryan.

CURRENT RELEASE 1993 This is serious shiraz with great regional character. The colour is a deep brick red and the nose has strong plum and strong spice aromas. The palate is a little tight, but there is a great depth of varietal flavours. The oak treatment adds starch, giving the wine backbone and grip. There is plenty of cellar promise but it also drinks well with a rare eye fillet steak.

McWilliams Mount Pleasant Merlot

Quality	♙♙♙
Value	★★★
Grapes	merlot
Region	Hunter Valley, NSW
Cellar	▯ 2
Alc./Vol.	12.0%
RRP	$15.50

It seems that everyone is getting into the merlot act, and why not? McWilliams have a long history of pioneering grape varieties in the Hunter Valley.

CURRENT RELEASE 1995 This wine is something of a misfire. It's a pleasant, light red but it misses some varietal character. The colour is a pale cherry-red, and the nose has some sweet berry and soft wood aromas. The palate is lightweight with simple, sweet fruit flavours that are matched by gentle oak on a delicate finish. It drinks well with casserole of quail.

McWilliams Mount Pleasant Phillip

Quality	♙♙♙♙
Value	★★★★
Grapes	shiraz
Region	Hunter Valley, NSW
Cellar	▯ 4
Alc./Vol.	13.0%
RRP	$13.95 ⑤

A real comfort style and a baby boomer refuge. This wine has changed little in terms of style, but the technology has kept pace with the times. Maker Phillip Ryan.

Previous outstanding vintages: too numerous to mention

CURRENT RELEASE 1991 The colour is a deep brick red and the nose has ripe plum aromas plus a dash of earth and leather. The palate has generous mouth feel with sweet plum flavours and gentle spice. It also offers a maturity factor that adds mellowness. The oak is discreet but supportive. It goes well with a hearty casserole or confit of duck.

McWilliams Mount Pleasant Rosehill Shiraz

The burgeoning McWilliams range of wine is nothing if not confusing. There are several labels at several levels and it takes thought to sort out what goes where. For once price can be used as a guide, because McWilliams is realistic and fair.

CURRENT RELEASE 1991   Old-fashioned and ready to go. This is typical aged Hunter Valley red with a perfumed leather and spice-dominated nose. The palate is mellow with concentrated fruit juice flavours; juicy plums laced with spice. The oak on the soft finish has integrated beautifully. The wine is soft, warm and cuddly – perfect for a lamb and barley casserole.

Quality	▼▼▼▼
Value	★★★★
Grapes	shiraz
Region	Hunter Valley, NSW
Cellar	🍾 3
Alc./Vol.	$12.5%
RRP	$27.00

Meadowbank Cabernet Sauvignon

Like most Tasmanian vineyards the weather is critical to the final quality of the wine. Tasmania cries out for warmth and sunshine. Maker Greg O'Keefe.

Previous outstanding vintages: '94

CURRENT RELEASE 1995   Not a kind year in terms of fruit flavours. It's lean and sculptured. The nose is a mixture of crushed leaves and blackberry. The palate is light- to medium-bodied with blackberry flavours and hints of wintergreen. The finish shows some discreet tannins and a moderate grip.

Quality	▼▼▼
Value	★★
Grapes	cabernet sauvignon
Region	Derwent Valley, Tas.
Cellar	🍾 3
Alc./Vol.	12.0%
RRP	$22.00

Merrivale Cabernet Malbec Shiraz

The vineyard was established in the hills of McLaren Vale in 1971 and there are now 8 hectares under vine. Maker Brian Light.

CURRENT RELEASE 1995   A gentle style that was made for easy drinking – lunch stuff. The colour is a bright garnet and the nose has crushed berry aromas. The palate is light- to medium-weight with sweet fruit flavours. There are benign tannins on a caressing finish. It's a good BBQ style; don't burn the chops.

Quality	▼▼▼
Value	★★★
Grapes	cabernet sauvignon; malbec; merlot
Region	McLaren Vale, SA
Cellar	🍾 2
Alc./Vol.	13.0%
RRP	$13.00

Milburn Park Grenache

Quality	♟♟♟⸲
Value	★★★⸲
Grapes	grenache
Region	Mildura, Vic.
Cellar	▮ 2
Alc./Vol.	13.0%
RRP	$11.00

Lazarus with a triple bypass? That's the lot of grenache in the present wine climate. Once it was an outcast, now its revival seems to be at hand. Maker Bob Shields.

CURRENT RELEASE 1995   The colour is a vibrant light ruby and the nose has strong raspberry aromas. The palate is light- to medium-bodied and succulent raspberry fruit is the main feature. The finish has clean acid. It's a refreshing style that can be served chilled. Try it with a rabbit stew.

Mildara Alexanders

Quality	♟♟♟♟⸲
Value	★★★★
Grapes	cabernet sauvignon; merlot; cabernet franc
Region	Coonawarra, SA
Cellar	▮ 5+
Alc./Vol.	13.5%
RRP	$28.70 ⑤

Alexander was the name of one of the small block-holders in John Riddoch's visionary Coonawarra Fruit Colony late last century. This is a distinctive style that is always released with some bottle-age. Maker Gavin Hogg.

Previous outstanding vintages: '85, '86, '88, '90, '91

CURRENT RELEASE 1992   Attractive matured complexities here with aged development and liberal oak combining stylishly. Smoky, toasty, game and beef stock feature in the bouquet. It's smooth in the mouth with good depth and concentration, and more grip than usual for Alexanders. Drink with aged Reggiano parmesan.

Miranda High Country Merlot

Quality	♟♟♟♟
Value	★★★★⸲
Grapes	merlot
Region	King Valley, Vic.; Barossa Valley, SA
Cellar	▮ 3
Alc./Vol.	13.0%
RRP	$12.00

High country from the valleys? Growing pains from a large company trying to grow market share in mid-range segment. The prices are very competitive.

CURRENT RELEASE 1995   This is a light, stylish red that drinks well now. The colour is a mid-cherry-red and the nose has herbaceous aromas plus raspberry smells. The palate has more raspberry and there is some evidence of green herbs. The finish is slightly stalky, with fine-grained, astringent tannins. It's the perfect pasta style.

Miranda Show Reserve Old Vine Shiraz

There is a money-back guarantee on the front label, which must rank along with 24 hours' roadside assistance or unlimited kilometres.
CURRENT RELEASE 1993   The wine doesn't really say Barossa, but it's a very drinkable shiraz that shows the benefits of bottle-age. The colour is a deep ruby with some hints of brown. The nose has sweet berry aromas and concentrated fruit juice characters. The palate is medium-bodied with ripe plum and cherry flavours, and these are matched by some well-integrated oak on a dry finish. It's ready to go. Try it with a curried beef pie.

Quality	🍷🍷🍷
Value	★★★⊦
Grapes	shiraz
Region	Barossa Valley, SA
Cellar	🍷 3
Alc./Vol.	13.0%
RRP	$19.00

Mirrool Creek Cabernets Shiraz

If ever there was a need for fighting brands in the marketplace it's now, and this one is pulling on the gloves. It has been made to a price.
CURRENT RELEASE 1995   This is a soft, red wine that is ready to drink. It has light berry aromas plus leaf on the nose. The palate is sweet with raspberry fruit flavours, and there are soft tannins on the finish. Try it with BBQ chops.

Quality	🍷🍷🍷
Value	★★★
Grapes	cabernet franc; cabernet sauvignon; shiraz
Region	Griffith, NSW
Cellar	🍷 1
Alc./Vol.	12.5%
RRP	$9.90

Mitchell Peppertree Vineyard Shiraz

Proprietor Jane Mitchell is one sassy dude who is very adept at promotion. The label continues to gain strength locally and overseas, and with good reason – there have been some great wines. Maker Andrew Mitchell.
Previous outstanding vintages: '84, '86, '87, '90, '91, '92, '93
CURRENT RELEASE 1995   This wine is like a rotating mirrored ball with many flashes of flavour. The nose does indeed have a pepper quality plus much more. The nose is a conglomeration of plums, cherries, and pepper and spice aromas. The palate continues the complexity with dark cherry, blackberry, plum, pepper and spices. These are adorned by French oak, which provides the grip on the finish. It should be decanted and treated with reverence. Love it with confit of duck.

Quality	🍷🍷🍷🍷🍷
Value	★★★★★
Grapes	shiraz
Region	Clare Valley, SA
Cellar	🍷 10
Alc./Vol.	13.5%
RRP	$18.00

Mitchelton Goulburn Valley Shiraz

Quality	🍷🍷🍷🍷
Value	★★★★
Grapes	shiraz
Region	Goulburn Valley, Vic.
Cellar	2–6
Alc./Vol.	13.3%
RRP	$21.00

One of the unsung winemaking heroes lives in the shadow of this tower on the banks of the Goulburn River. Don Lewis, take a bow.

CURRENT RELEASE 1994 This is a combination of power and elegance. The colour is bright red and the nose has ripe plum and cherry aromas. The medium- to full-bodied palate is rich with sweet plum flavours, and there are astringent tannins on a dry and lingering finish. It should cellar with aplomb, and the steak and kidney pie will taste all the better for its company.

Mitchelton III

Quality	🍷🍷🍷🍷
Value	★★★★★
Grapes	shiraz; grenache; mourvèdre
Region	Goulburn Valley, Vic.
Cellar	4
Alc./Vol.	13.5%
RRP	$19.00

The change of ownership seems to have meant little to the course plotted by the previous owners. Here an ongoing flirtation with a Rhone Valley style. Maker Don Lewis.

CURRENT RELEASE 1994 This is a very complex wine that conjures up many images: marzipan, cinnamon, mint, cherry, vanilla and caramel all apply. The nose is spicy, and the medium-bodied palate is complex indeed. The finish is dry with discreet oak and impressive length. It's great with a rabbit and mushroom stew.

Mitchelton Print Label

Let's face it, a print is a bloody common or garden print. No-one is going to say, 'Come up and see my prints . . . ', so why devote the flagship wine to the commemoration of a print?

CURRENT RELEASE 1993 Not much change since last year; the development in the bottle is slow. It's a well-structured, rich style with strong berry flavours and dark cherries. The oak is beautifully matched with the weight of fruit, and there is a marked astringency on the grainy finish. It needs more time, but have a go with veal shanks in a rich sauce.

Quality	▼▼▼▼▼
Value	★★★★
Grapes	cabernet sauvignon
Region	Goulburn, Vic.
Cellar	➥ 2–8+
Alc./Vol.	13.8%
RRP	$24.00

Montrose Black Shiraz

Does the name of this wine pay homage to Robert O'Callaghan of Rockford fame? In truth this is a mild-mannered Mudgee shiraz.

CURRENT RELEASE 1994 It's no tub thumper and perhaps the 'black' comes from the black pepper characters. The colour is a mid-ruby, and the nose has plum and pepper aromas. The palate is medium-bodied but the flavour is intense. Plums and cracked pepper are the major features and the American oak on the finish adds vanilla. It drinks well now with rare roast beef.

Quality	▼▼▼▼
Value	★★★★
Grapes	shiraz
Region	Mudgee, NSW
Cellar	▮ 3
Alc./Vol.	12.5%
RRP	$13.50

CURRENT RELEASE 1995 What's black about this stuff? It's ruby-red to begin with. The nose is plummy and there is a wet wood and vanilla aroma. The light to medium body has sweet cherry and plum flavours and these are balanced by some astringent oak on a dry finish. It drinks very well now with a goulash.

Quality	▼▼▼?
Value	★★★⊦
Grapes	shiraz
Region	Mudgee, NSW
Cellar	▮ 3
Alc./Vol.	12.5%
RRP	$13.50

Montrose Poet's Corner

Quality 🍷🍷🍷
Value ★★★
Grapes shiraz; cabernet sauvignon; cabernet franc
Region Mudgee, NSW
Cellar 1
Alc./Vol. 13.0%
RRP $10.00

Henry Lawson is the poet in question and Mudgee/Gulgong was his stamping ground. This is an enjoyable commercial style.

CURRENT RELEASE 1995 The colour is a light cherry-red, and the nose has soft berry aromas and sweet fruit smells. The middleweight palate has succulent berry flavours and the oak on the finish fits perfectly, making an amusing couplet. Drink now with a Yorkshire hotpot.

Moorilla Estate Cabernet Sauvignon

Quality 🍷🍷🍷½
Value ★★½
Grapes cabernet sauvignon
Region southern Tasmania
Cellar 5
Alc./Vol. 13.6%
RRP $22.00

The quest in any Tasmanian vineyard is to ensure the grapes are ripe at the time of picking. In some years a sun lamp seems in order.

CURRENT RELEASE 1994 The colour is a dense ruby and the nose has tobacco, leaf and cassis aromas. There are sweet blackberry flavours on the palate with a background of tobacco and vegetation. There are astringent tannins on the long, dry finish and acid adds to its power. It could be cellared. Try it with rare roast beef with horseradish dressing.

Mornington Vineyards Estate Pinot Noir

Quality 🍷🍷🍷
Value ★★★
Grapes pinot noir
Region Mornington Peninsula, Vic.
Cellar 3
Alc./Vol. 13.0%
RRP $19.00

The label will no doubt get some attention; such things are not a matter for argument. Let's call this the enigma of the retail shelves.

CURRENT RELEASE 1995 The colour is a light ruby/cherry pink. The nose has strawberry and sap aromas, and the medium-bodied palate has soft, sweet berry fruit flavours that are backed by acid and soft tannins. Drink it now with pan-fried tuna. ►

CURRENT RELEASE 1996   To pull the cork is cradle-snatching at this stage; in fact, you can still see the nappy rash, because the wine is slightly unsettled and difficult to assess. The colour is a pale cherry-red. The nose has strawberry and some ferment characters. There is sweet fruit on the palate and the flavours include dark cherry and strawberry. The finish is spicy with some gentle oak. It should be given time. Try it with pink lamb.

Quality	♟♟♟
Value	★★☆
Grapes	pinot noir
Region	Mornington Peninsula, Vic.
Cellar	➥ 2–4
Alc./Vol.	13.0%
RRP	$23.00

Morris Cabernet Sauvignon

Although this is part of the Orlando/Wyndham group and despite having seen many previous owners, there is still a nice, old-world feel to the winery. And a Morris is usually still floating around the place.
CURRENT RELEASE 1994   The colour is deep and the nose has plenty to ponder. There are black-tea aromas as well as blackberries, mulberries and undergrowth smells. The palate is a middleweight, with sweet black-berry fruit with a note of cherry-pip flavour. The finish has modest grip. It drinks well now with liver and bacon.

Quality	♟♟♟♟
Value	★★★★
Grapes	cabernet sauvignon
Region	Rutherglen, Vic.
Cellar	▮ 4
Alc./Vol.	13.5%
RRP	$12.50

Morris Durif

This is traditionally a port grape, but it makes an interesting table wine with plenty of character. This is a gentle example.
CURRENT RELEASE 1994   A big wine, but not demanding. The colour is inky-black, and the nose has sweet berry aromas and a waft of spice. The palate is full-bodied and juicy with loads of chewy fruit characters. Plums and blackberry are matched by drying tannins on a moderately grippy finish. It will cellar, but drink it now with kangaroo.

Quality	♟♟♟♟
Value	★★★★
Grapes	durif
Region	Rutherglen, Vic.
Cellar	▮ 4
Alc./Vol.	13.5%
RRP	$12.50

Morris Shiraz

Quality	♟♟♟♟
Value	★★★★
Grapes	shiraz
Region	Rutherglen, Vic.
Cellar	🍶 4
Alc./Vol.	13.0%
RRP	$12.50

Seasoned (some would say well-marinated) drinkers would expect a blood-and-guts red from the north-east of Victoria. They are living in the past: elegance is now not out of the question.

CURRENT RELEASE 1994   Ample proportions but no excessive tannins. The colour is a dark plum, and the nose has fruit and spice aromas. The palate is sweet and juicy with plum and spice flavours. The tannin on the finish is relatively restrained but it makes its presence felt. The wine drinks well now with a traditional beef casserole.

Moss Brothers Moses Rock Red

Quality	♟♟♟♟
Value	★★★★
Grapes	cabernet sauvignon; pinot noir; grenache
Region	Margaret River, WA
Cellar	🍶 1
Alc./Vol.	12.5%
RRP	$12.95

The search goes on for a luncheon red that could even be served chilled. Sometimes unlikely bedfellows (in terms of grape varieties) can make a winning trio. Maker David and Jane Moss.

CURRENT RELEASE 1995   The colour is a mid-ruby and the nose has sweet berry aromas. The palate has sweet berry flavours. Strawberry is the major flavour, and this is framed by soft tannins. It could be served chilled in summer, and it goes well with an antipasto platter.

Moss Wood Cabernet Sauvignon

Quality	♟♟♟♟
Value	★★★⸍
Grapes	cabernet sauvignon; merlot; cabernet franc; petit verdot
Region	Margaret River, WA
Cellar	➘ 3–10+
Alc./Vol.	13.5%
RRP	$34.50 🍶

The Moss Wood cabernets have been heading in a curious direction lately. The '94 was even more feral than this, with gamy/animal characters which age may reveal to be simply another face of the complex terroir of the region. Maker Keith Mugford.

Previous outstanding vintages: '75, '76, '77, '80, '83, '85, '86, '87, '90, '91, '92, '93

CURRENT RELEASE 1995   The colour is a medium-depth red–purple, and the bouquet has a meaty note which may be related to highly toasted oak. It has a leaner palate structure than usual for Moss Wood, with considerable astringency and a hint of greenness or bitterness to close. There is no doubting the fruit concentration, and it may simply need time to settle down. The track record of the vineyard is, of course, impeccable.

Mount Ararat Estate Shiraz

This is the fighting brand or second label for Cathcart Ridge. It's a drink-now, bistro style.

CURRENT RELEASE 1994   The colour is a mid-ruby-red and the nose has sweet, simple berry fruit, which is balanced by some drying tannins on an astringent finish. It drinks well with spaghetti bolognese.

Quality	♥♥♥
Value	★★★
Grapes	shiraz
Region	various, Victoria
Cellar	▲ 3
Alc./Vol.	12.5%
RRP	$12.00

Mount Benson Vineyard

The shape of things to come, this vineyard is located between Robe and Kingston on the south coast of South Australia. It was planted by Margaret and Bill Wehl in 1989. The wine is made at Brands Laira.

CURRENT RELEASE 1994   Swashbuckling style, even though the alcohol is relatively low and the vines are obviously young. The nose is a complex mixture of oak, leaf and blackberry with maybe a hint of VA (volatile acidity) to give it a subtle lift. The palate is intense with a great concentration of blackberry flavour. New oak adds tannin to the finish. It's well balanced and goes down a treat with duck.

Quality	♥♥♥♥
Value	★★★
Grapes	cabernet sauvignon
Region	Mount Benson, SA
Cellar	▲ 4
Alc./Vol.	12.0%
RRP	$22.85

CURRENT RELEASE 1995   Being on the cool and lean style, this wine skirts disaster. The colour is bright crimson and the nose has tobacco and cigar-box aromas. The palate is a little fruit-shy. There are lean blackberry flavours and slightly green tannins on the finish. It probably won't change much with cellaring. Try it now with warm salad of rare beef.

Quality	♥♥♥
Value	★★☆
Grapes	cabernet sauvignon
Region	Mount Benson, SA
Cellar	▲ 2
Alc./Vol.	12.5%
RRP	$22.85

Mount Horrocks Cabernet Merlot

Quality 🍷🍷🍷🍷½
Value ★★★★½
Grapes cabernet sauvignon; merlot
Region Clare Valley, SA
Cellar ➡ 2–5
Alc./Vol. 13.5%
RRP $19.00

This is a small, enduring winery near Watervale in the Clare Valley. It was established in 1981. Maker Jeffrey Grosset (contract).

CURRENT RELEASE 1995 Great colour that shows the wine is full of promise. There is also a typical Clare Valley nose: lots of dark cherry and rich, sweet earth characters. The palate is a slight anticlimax in terms of weight, but the flavours of redcurrant and wild cherry are very attractive. There is plenty of tannin on the finish, supplying loads of grip. It drinks well with kidneys in a red wine sauce.

Mountadam Pinot Noir

Quality 🍷🍷🍷½
Value ★★★
Grapes pinot noir
Region High Eden, SA
Cellar 🍾 3
Alc./Vol. 13.0%
RRP $28.00

Proprietor Adam Wynn has been having some literary fun on his back labels. Try this for size: 'This wine will flower beautifully with more years in the bottle, ensuring intense gastronomic pleasure once the corkscrew performs its pretty pirouette'. Adam – don't give up your day job!

Previous outstanding vintages: '89, '90, '91, '93, '94

CURRENT RELEASE 1995 A leaner style than previous years and that's probably to do with the nature of the vintage. The colour is a pale red, and the nose has wild raspberry and sappy aromas. The light- to middleweight palate has raspberry and cherry flavours. There is plenty of acid on the finish, which has admirable length. It's a style that suits a mushroom risotto.

Mountadam The Red

This is a difficult wine to approach and even more difficult to describe in words. It's an uncompromising style that is clearly in the winemaker's sights year after year. It will be interesting to taste a fully developed example.
Previous outstanding vintages: '89, '90, '91
CURRENT RELEASE 1994   This is a big, tough mutha that gives no beg-pardons. The colour is deep, with brick-red and ruby hues. The nose is dominated by wood, with a strong smell of burnished wood-panelling and a gentleperson's club cigar atmosphere. The palate is tight with raspberry and cherry flavours, and the wood gives a wet undergrowth of characters. The finish is long and firm. Try it with venison steaks.

Quality	♟♟♟
Value	★★★
Grapes	cabernet sauvignon; merlot
Region	High Eden, SA
Cellar	● 2–6
Alc./Vol.	15.0%
RRP	$35.00

Mt William Cabernet Franc

This vineyard was established in 1987 and it covers 4 hectares. Obviously the production is small and the labelling could be mistaken as being French (it's simple, but it works). Maker Murray Cousins and M. Cope-Williams (contract).
CURRENT RELEASE 1995   It might look light but it's a powerful wine. The nose is strong and pervasive. There are flower garden and orchard smells: it's all roses and crushed berries. In terms of body, the palate is light to medium, yet the depth of fruit is profound. Cherry is the major flavour. The finish is dry, yet soft. It's a well-balanced wine that goes well with a cassoulet.

Quality	♟♟♟♟
Value	★★★★
Grapes	cabernet franc
Region	Macedon, Vic.
Cellar	▮ 3
Alc./Vol.	12.5%
RRP	$17.00

Mt William Pinot Noir

Quality	♟♟♟
Value	★★★
Grapes	pinot noir
Region	Macedon, Vic.
Cellar	▮ 3
Alc./Vol.	13.0%
RRP	$23.00

Yet another cradle for this troublesome variety. The climatic conditions in the cool Macedon district indicate this is a suitable place for the variety. In ultra-cool years it can be used as a sparkling wine base. In warm years it makes good table wine.

CURRENT RELEASE 1995   A supple style with a deep brick-red colour and hints of cherry and earth on the nose. The palate is light- to medium-bodied, with cherry and strawberry flavours and hints of sap and earth. The oak is supportive rather than combative. Try it with mushroom risotto.

Murray Robson Wines Cabernet Sauvignon

Quality	♟♟♟
Value	★★★
Grapes	cabernet sauvignon
Region	Hunter Valley, NSW
Cellar	▮ 5
Alc./Vol.	11.9%
RRP	$23.00

Murray Robson was part of the first wave of small vineyards that broke on vinous shores in the late '60s. He was famous for his Squire vineyard.

CURRENT RELEASE 1996   This is a lighter style with sweet berry fruit aromas on the nose. The palate is light with delicate, sweet berry flavours, which are matched by supple tannins on the finish. It will probably have a long cellar life, but the changes and gains will be small.

Murray Robson Wines Shiraz

Quality	♟♟♟
Value	★★★
Grapes	shiraz
Region	Hunter Valley, NSW
Cellar	▮ 3
Alc./Vol.	12.5%
RRP	$23.00

Murray Robson rides again, or should that be is still in the saddle? He is marketing small parcels under his old label.

CURRENT RELEASE 1996   The nose is slightly volcanic with earth and sweaty leather characters. The palate is light- to medium-bodied with some sweet plum flavours. There are also signs of early development, and the finish displays soft tannins and modest grip. Try it with a rabbit stew.

Murrindindi Cabernets

Proprietor Hugh Cuthbertson has come a long way since the days when he used to run the Talavera wine company. These days he is a knob in the Mildara Blass group and you have to make an appointment to see him. Maker Hugh Cuthbertson.

CURRENT RELEASE 1993 A tough number that needs time. It's deep in colour and the nose is a mixture of berries and coffee oak. The palate is lean, with blackberry and raspberry fruit that is mixed with toasted oak flavours. The wine should develop well and is solid enough to cope with venison steaks.

Quality	▼▼▼▼
Value	★★★★
Grapes	cabernet sauvignon; cabernet franc; merlot
Region	Yarra Valley, SA
Cellar	➥ 3–6
Alc./Vol.	12.5%
RRP	$24.00

Normans Bin C106 Cabernet Sauvignon

The 'white label' is Normans' fighting varietal range, and while they don't scale the heights, they do offer decent-value current drinking. Maker Brian Light has recently stepped down.

CURRENT RELEASE 1995 Fairly light colour presages a straight-up-and-down wine, with a leafy/stalky, herbal nose and a lean, plain, uncomplicated flavour. Okay value when discounted. Serve with pork sausages.

Quality	▼▼▼
Value	★★★
Grapes	cabernet sauvignon
Region	not stated
Cellar	▮ 2
Alc./Vol.	13.0%
RRP	$13.70 ⑤

Normans Bin C107 Pinot Noir

When the rest of the wine industry is trying to jettison bin numbers, Normans is just starting to use them. Are they still living in the '50s?

CURRENT RELEASE 1996 Attractive medium purple–red colour, and a fruit-dominant, cherry-pip aroma which is true to the variety. It's a straightforward style, well made and fruity, and perfectly good at the price. Serve with beef carpaccio.

Quality	▼▼▼▼
Value	★★★★
Grapes	pinot noir
Region	not stated
Cellar	▮ 2
Alc./Vol.	12.0%
RRP	$13.70 ⑤

Normans Chais Clarendon Cabernet Sauvignon

Quality	ϤϤϤϤ
Value	★★★
Grapes	cabernet sauvignon
Region	McLaren Vale, SA
Cellar	▮ 9+
Alc./Vol.	12.5%
RRP	$28.00 Ⓢ

Chais is a French word used in the Bordeaux region to denote a winery. Clarendon is where the Normans winery is situated. Maker Brian Light.

CURRENT RELEASE 1995 This is the top of the tree at Normans, an elegant wine with fruit to the fore. The colour is deep and youthful, the nose a matter of fresh, dark berries and blackcurrants, coupled with stylish oak. The structure is smooth and supple, rounded and ripe-flavoured with savoury secondary flavours. Tannin dries a well-balanced finish. It goes with pink lamb fillets.

Normans Chais Clarendon Shiraz

Quality	ϤϤϤϤ
Value	★★★★
Grapes	shiraz
Region	McLaren Vale, SA
Cellar	▮ 7+
Alc./Vol.	13.0%
RRP	$27.70 Ⓢ

The Chais Clarendon range is Normans' flagship and has always offered premium quality, although fame has been elusive. Maker until recently was Brian Light.

CURRENT RELEASE 1995 Nice concentration of cherry and dark berry fruit aromas, with coconutty oak and youthful freshness. It has good weight and chunky mouth-feel, solid flavour (if lacking complexity at this early stage), and a nice, dry tannic finish. It would repay cellaring. Serve with aged gruyère cheese.

Normans Merlot Bin C108

Quality	ϤϤϤϞ
Value	★★★▸
Grapes	merlot
Region	various, SA
Cellar	▮ 3
Alc./Vol.	12.5%
RRP	$13.70 Ⓢ

Oh dear! Not another meaningless *new* bin number? We thought the demystification of Aussie wine had left them far behind. Not so.

CURRENT RELEASE 1995 This has soaked up a lot of oak flavour, and for those who like a fairly wood-influenced red, it's good drinking. There's a hint of mint in the bouquet; the taste is soft and well-rounded with fair balance and good length. And it's hard to argue about the price. Goes well with pork sausages.

Normans Old Vine Shiraz

The age of the vines was between 26 and 42 years. But old vines do not of themselves guarantee great wine. CURRENT RELEASE 1995 Vanillary American oak dominates the nose, which smells like vanilla ice-cream. The palate is dominated by drying tannins and oak flavour, resulting in a dry, savoury finish. There is attractive fleshiness and length to the wine. It could reward short-term cellaring. Food: roast pigeon.

Quality	ŸŸŸ̈
Value	★★★
Grapes	shiraz
Region	McLaren Vale, SA
Cellar	▮ 4
Alc./Vol.	13.5%
RRP	$17.00

Orlando Jacobs Creek

'Today the world, tomorrow the universe!' What more is there to be said? They'll be drinking this on Mars in the next decade.
CURRENT RELEASE 1995 Very bright colour and a sweet berry nose are a friendly introduction to a very gentle wine. There are sweet berries on the palate and these are matched by some subtle oak on a balanced finish. It drinks like a charm. Try it with sausages and mash.

Quality	ŸŸŸ̈
Value	★★★★
Grapes	shiraz, cabernet sauvignon
Region	not stated
Cellar	▮ 2
Alc./Vol.	12.5%
RRP	$8.90 Ⓢ

Orlando Russet Ridge Cabernet Shiraz Merlot

The name is a longstanding leg-pull, in the same league as 'Mount Coonawarra'. If you've ever been to the region you will know the topography is as flat as the proverbial night carter's hat.
CURRENT RELEASE 1994 A neat style that is ready to drink. The colour is a glowing ruby and the nose is a little smelly at first. This breathes off and there are berry and leaf aromas. The light to medium body has sweet raspberry fruit flavours in the shade of coconut oak. There is pleasant grip on the finish and the wine drinks very well now. Try it with liver and bacon. ▸

Quality	ŸŸŸ̈
Value	★★★ｋ
Grapes	cabernet sauvignon; shiraz, merlot
Region	Coonawarra, SA
Cellar	▮ 4
Alc./Vol.	13.5%
RRP	$16.00 Ⓢ

Quality	♟♟♟♙
Value	★★★⸤
Grapes	cabernet sauvignon; shiraz; merlot
Region	Coonawarra, SA
Cellar	🍷 4
Alc./Vol.	12.5%
RRP	$15.50

CURRENT RELEASE 1995   Great young colour of ruby and purple. The nose is a tad subdued with hints of stalks, and leafy soft berry aromas. The light- to medium-weight palate has some attractive fruit flavours centred on blackberry. The wood works in harmony to produce a mildly astringent finish. It's perfect for pink lamb chops.

Orlando St Hugo Cabernet Sauvignon

Quality	♟♟♟♟♙
Value	★★★★
Grapes	cabernet sauvignon
Region	Coonawarra, SA
Cellar	🍷 7
Alc./Vol.	12.5%
RRP	$24.00

Hugo Gramp was killed in an air disaster in the '40s. He and other prominent members of the wine industry were in transit to Canberra to lobby the government when a DC2 crashed in rough weather near Melbourne. *Previous outstanding vintages: '82, '86, '88, '90, '91*
CURRENT RELEASE 1993   Nothing has changed since last year; perhaps there is a little more elegance. It remains a typical regional style with a mulberry nose with a leafy background. The palate is complex and elegant with blackberry and mulberry fruit, which is integrating with the oak on the soft finish. It drinks very well now with pink barbecued lamb straps.

Osborne's Harwood Cabernet Sauvignon

Quality	♟♟♟♙
Value	★★★
Grapes	cabernet sauvignon
Region	Mornington Peninsula, Vic.
Cellar	🍷 4
Alc./Vol.	13.0%
RRP	$21.00

The number of Mornington Peninsula wineries keeps growing at a mind-boggling pace. Will they all find an economic place in the sun? Time will tell.
CURRENT RELEASE 1994   Autumn leaves drift by my window . . . Typical of the Peninsula in a cool year, it's leafy and herbaceous on the nose. The palate has blackberry with hints of tobacco and leafy notes. The finish is astringent, showing plenty of acid. It's a good style for a designer pizza.

Osborne's Harwood Pinot Noir

Interesting label design but somewhat difficult to read in less-than-direct light. It's also curious: could that be a bird of paradise, and if so, what is it doing on the Mornington Peninsula?

CURRENT RELEASE 1995   A gentle style that opens up with decanting. The colour is light cherry-red, and the nose has strawberry and cherry aromas as well as leafy elements. The palate is medium-bodied. Cherry is the major flavour and there are hints of leaf and sap. Acid dominates the finish and it drinks well now with pan-fried quail.

Quality	▼▼▼▼
Value	★★★
Grapes	pinot noir
Region	Mornington Peninsula, Vic.
Cellar	3
Alc./Vol.	13.0%
RRP	$21.00

Pankhurst Cabernet Merlot

The Pankhurst vineyard is at Hall (west of Canberra) in one of the region's warmer locations. The wines are made by Sue Carpenter at Lark Hill, who also takes some of the grapes for her wines.

CURRENT RELEASE 1995   This has attractive, sweet berry aromas and a slight grassy/herbal tinge to the fruit. Good support from fresh oak, and the palate has appealing depth, richness and fruit-sweetness. An elegant red to serve with veal.

Quality	▼▼▼▼
Value	★★★★
Grapes	cabernet sauvignon; merlot
Region	Canberra district, NSW
Cellar	5
Alc./Vol.	12.5%
RRP	$17.00

Paringa Estate Pinot Noir

This is a regular winner on the Victorian Wine Show circuit and is simply one of the best pinots in Australia. Maker Lindsay McCall produced last year's Penguin Best Pinot Noir Award for Port Phillip Estate.

Previous outstanding vintages: '91, '92, '93, '94

CURRENT RELEASE 1995   Rates with '93 as the equal-best Paringa pinot to date, with great intensity of ripe cherry and spicy oak flavours, lovely fleshy richness and an immensely long carry. Concentrated fruit and magical balance. Great with braised duck.

Quality	▼▼▼▼▼
Value	★★★★✦
Grapes	pinot noir
Region	Mornington Peninsula, Vic.
Cellar	5
Alc./Vol.	12.5%
RRP	$28.00 (cellar door)

Parker Estate Terra Rossa First Growth

Quality	♥♥♥
Value	★★
Grapes	cabernet sauvignon; merlot; cabernet franc
Region	Coonawarra, SA
Cellar	▮ 3
Alc./Vol.	13.5%
RRP	$45.00

A cheeky name, and as far as we know it's the first time anyone outside France has had the gall to declare their own wine a first growth.

Previous outstanding vintages: '88, '90, '91, '93

CURRENT RELEASE 1994   This is a hiccup in what has been a stunning run. There is simply too much green fruit, giving herbaceous aromas and a lean, light-bodied leafy/tobacco taste that falls away fast, leaving unbalanced tannin. An okay red, but not a first growth.

Passing Clouds Angel Blend

Quality	♥♥♥♥
Value	★★★⸙
Grapes	cabernet sauvignon; cabernet franc; merlot
Region	Bendigo, Vic.
Cellar	▮ 7+
Alc./Vol.	13.0%
RRP	$17.00 ▮

The name is a whimsical reference to the local clouds, which pass over without shedding rain on the parched vines. Maker Graeme Leith has figured in some of Tourism Victoria's advertising.

CURRENT RELEASE 1994   Cassis and blackberry jam are the dominant scents, and the fruit takes precedence over the oak. Its profile is trim and there's a touch of elegance to what can in some years be a rather butch wine. Won a gold medal at the Melbourne Wine Show in 1996. Try it with steak and kidney pie.

Passing Clouds Pinot Noir

Quality	♥♥♥⸙
Value	★★★⸙
Grapes	pinot noir
Region	Central Victoria
Cellar	▮ 4
Alc./Vol.	13.0%
RRP	$18.00

The place is so named because the clouds do just that. Think dry vineyard with limited production. Maker Graeme Leith.

CURRENT RELEASE 1996   Straight down the middle as far as varietal character is concerned. The colour is a pale ruby and the nose has sweet strawberry flavours. The middleweight palate has plum and cherry flavours, and there is evidence of a high acid level on the astringent finish. It could be served chilled if you wish. Try it with roast chicken.

Pattersons Pinot Noir

This Mount Barker vineyard does increasingly impressive things with chardonnay and pinot. The wines are made at Plantagenet.
CURRENT RELEASE 1995 A superb pinot, mouthfilling and loaded with fruit and authentic pinot charm. Slightly jammy, ripe berry smells coupled with earthy development and dusty, cedary oak. The palate has that elusive pinot silkiness, is smooth and round and fills the mouth. Yum! Serve it with barbecued king prawns with plenty of garlic and olive oil.

Quality	♟♟♟♟♟
Value	★★★★★
Grapes	pinot noir
Region	Mount Barker, WA
Cellar	♦ 3+
Alc./Vol.	13.0%
RRP	$22.00

Pattersons Shiraz

Arthur and Sue Patterson are schoolteachers in the Mt Barker district; the vineyard is their weekend diversion. All things considered, it yields surprisingly good wine.
CURRENT RELEASE 1994 Further proof that '94 was a great shiraz year in the sou' west. The colour is deep and youthful; the bouquet has abundant spices and Rhone-like gamy overtones, with a twist of vegetal regional character. The taste is elegant and beautifully balanced, fruit-driven and smooth with a nicely judged dryness to finish. Serve with pepper steak.

Quality	♟♟♟♟♟
Value	★★★★
Grapes	shiraz
Region	Lower Great Southern, WA
Cellar	♦ 7+
Alc./Vol.	12.5%
RRP	$21.00 ▮

Paul Osicka Cabernet Sauvignon

There was a time when this vineyard was confused with north-east Victoria. Then came the Heathcote plantings. But Osicka didn't really belong – it remains an entity unto itself.
CURRENT RELEASE 1994 An elegant, minty style with a bright scarlet colour and a minty nose with a touch of bracken and leaves. The medium-weight palate has a strong redcurrant flavour, and the oak is well tailored without being obtrusive. The wine can handle a hearty shepherd's pie.

Quality	♟♟♟♟
Value	★★★★
Grapes	cabernet sauvignon
Region	Graytown, Vic.
Cellar	♦ 5
Alc./Vol.	13.5%
RRP	$18.90

Paul Osicka Shiraz

Quality	♥♥♥♥
Value	★★★★
Grapes	shiraz
Region	Central Victoria
Cellar	▮ 6
Alc./Vol.	13.0%
RRP	$18.90

This vineyard is located at Graytown, which some mastermind calculated to be the geographical centre of Victoria. This knowledge is of no particular use and we throw it in free of charge. The vineyard was established in 1955 and has 13 hectares under vine.

CURRENT RELEASE 1995   Big mint on the nose and a great crimson colour greet you from the glass. The palate is medium-bodied with wild, dark cherry laced with spice. The oak plays a subordinate role but adds support and grip. It shows great balance and drinks well now. Try it with roast beef.

Pauletts Andreas

Quality	♥♥♥♥♥
Value	★★★★⋆
Grapes	shiraz
Region	Clare Valley, SA
Cellar	➡ 2–10
Alc./Vol.	13.7%
RRP	$33.00

A new label for a much respected winemaker in Clare. This is the top of the Paulett Christmas tree. It won't happen every year: only when the weather is kind. Maker Neil Paulett.

CURRENT RELEASE 1995   This is already very complex, but many years away from its peak. The nose is minty, with an underlay of fruit and a suggestion of wood. The palate has a silky texture with fresh fruit and sweet berry flavours. There are some toasted qualities on the finish but these add rather than intrude. It has outstanding length and should develop into a national treasure. Try it now with eye fillet in a pepper sauce.

Pauletts The Quarry

Quality	♥♥♥♥⋆
Value	★★★★⋆
Grapes	mourvèdre 95%; shiraz 5%
Region	Clare Valley, SA
Cellar	▮ 4
Alc./Vol.	13.5%
RRP	$17.00

Not as tough as stone or even flinty – the Kelly vineyard is adjacent to the Clare quarry. Maker Neil Paulett.

CURRENT RELEASE 1996   This is a great change of pace and living proof that this variety doesn't have to be dull and boring. The nose is a powerful mixture of spice and fruit. The palate is soft and mouthfilling. There are ripe plums and cherry flavours, and loads of spice. This is followed by some soft tannins on a dry finish. It's generous and drinkable. Try it with chargrilled kangaroo.

Pearson Vineyards Cabernet Franc

This is an unusual solo act: usually franc is a filler and fragrance enhancer in a blend.

CURRENT RELEASE 1994   Great colour – a veritable feast for the eye in red and purple. The nose is slightly mulchy with leaf and bracken aromas. The middleweight palate has soft, berry flavours and the usual varietal shortness. The finish is gentle with some soft tannins. It's a decent pasta style.

Quality	♥♥♥♡
Value	★★★¢
Grapes	cabernet franc
Region	Clare Valley, SA
Cellar	╏ 2
Alc./Vol.	13.5%
RRP	$17.00

Peel Estate Shiraz

This winery is a conundrum: it makes some sensational reds like this one, but others are distinctly ordinary, for example the '93 cabernet, which has a sulfide problem.

CURRENT RELEASE 1993   The colour is youthful for its years with a strong purple tint. The nose shows deep cherry, plum and spice with slightly aggressive American oak. In the mouth it is powerfully flavoured, vibrant and fresh for its age. A full-bodied shiraz with balanced tannins and impressive depth of flavour. Serve it with osso bucco.

Quality	♥♥♥♥♡
Value	★★★¢
Grapes	shiraz
Region	south-west coast, Western Australia
Cellar	╏ 10
Alc./Vol.	14.3%
RRP	$27.00

Pegasus Bay Pinot Noir

Professor Ivan Donaldson is firstly a Christchurch neurologist, and then a winemaker and wine judge. He also writes a newspaper wine column.

Previous outstanding vintages: '94

CURRENT RELEASE 1996   Amazingly deep colour introduces a most impressive pinot noir. The bouquet shows rich, ripe, black-cherry fruit and obvious oak; there's excellent concentration in the mouth and tremendous length. Needs time for the oak to meld and the perfume to build. Try serving it with grilled quail.

Quality	♥♥♥♥♥
Value	★★★★
Grapes	pinot noir
Region	Canterbury, NZ
Cellar	➥ 1–5+
Alc./Vol.	13.0%
RRP	$38.00

Pendarves Pinot Noir

Quality	▼▼▼⸮
Value	★★★⸮
Grapes	pinot noir
Region	Hunter Valley, NSW
Cellar	▮ 2
Alc./Vol.	12.5%
RRP	$16.50

Doctor Phil Norrie, the evangelist preacher of the health-giving effects of moderate wine-drinking, has his own vineyard in the Hunter. This is one of his better efforts. CURRENT RELEASE 1995 Developing medium brick-red colour, with dusty, earthy, dry aged bouquet and a slightly leathery, developed palate flavour that carries attractive sweetness and a degree of complexity. Slight tannin to close. It's not especially pinoid, but we like the flavour. Try it with a doner kebab.

Penfolds Bin 128 Coonawarra

Quality	▼▼▼▼⸮
Value	★★★★
Grapes	shiraz
Region	Coonawarra, SA
Cellar	▮ 10+
Alc./Vol.	13.5%
RRP	$19.45 Ⓢ ▮

Penfolds is noted as a multi-regional (and often multi-variety) blender, so this Coonawarra shiraz is out of the ordinary. Maker John Duval and team.
Previous outstanding vintages: '71, '78, '80, '82, '86, '88, '90, '91, '93
CURRENT RELEASE 1994 One of the better Bin 128s we can recall. Excellent colour, and deep, solid aromas with rich fruit and oak aplenty. The palate is sweet and fleshy, showing good concentration. Heaps of stuffing and a firm, well-balanced finish. Good with cassoulet.

Penfolds Bin 28 Kalimna

Quality	▼▼▼▼▼
Value	★★★★⸮
Grapes	shiraz
Region	Barossa Valley, McLaren Vale & Langhorne Creek, SA
Cellar	▮ 10+
Alc./Vol.	13.5%
RRP	$19.40 Ⓢ ▮

Kalimna is the name of Penfolds' best vineyard in the Barossa Valley. It has a long history, stretching back to the turn of the century.
Previous outstanding vintages: '82, '83, '86, '87, '88, '90, '91, '92, '93
CURRENT RELEASE 1994 Typical Bin 28 style, showing some development in colour, and complex earthy, gamy and beef-stock aromas of mellowing shiraz. The oak is integrating well and there is sweet fruit aplenty on the mid-palate: full-bodied, smooth and generous. Some rustic overtones and great length. Should cellar well, but you can drink now with steak and kidney pie.

Penfolds Bin 389 Cabernet Shiraz

This used to be nicknamed 'The poor man's Grange', but its price probably doesn't appeal to the penurious any longer. Maker John Duval and team.

Previous outstanding vintages: '66, '71, '80, '83, '86, '87, '90, '91, '92

CURRENT RELEASE 1994   A complex, oak-driven red which bears the Penfolds hallmarks: smoky, toasty oak bouquet coupled with dark berries. It has full body, abundant tannin, marvellous intensity of savoury, multi-layered flavour, and a persistent aftertaste. Best if cellared a few years, then drink with standing rib roast of beef.

Quality	▼▼▼▼▼
Value	★★★★
Grapes	cabernet sauvignon; shiraz
Region	Coonawarra, McLaren Vale & Barossa Valley, SA
Cellar	➡ 3–12+
Alc./Vol.	13.5%
RRP	$25.00 ⑤ 🍾

Penfolds Bin 407 Cabernet Sauvignon

This was created in 1990 to fill the shoes of the upwardly mobile (and increasingly rare) Bin 707 Cabernet. Maker John Duval and team.

Previous outstanding vintages: '90, '91, '92, '93

CURRENT RELEASE 1994   This is more than a poor man's 707: it's a truly superb wine, bursting with classic Coonawarra cabernet aromas of blackcurrant, blackberry and cedar, although the wood is not at all dominant. Great depth of flavour, discreet but firm tannin, and exceptional length. Serve with rare roast beef and all the trimmings.

Quality	▼▼▼▼▼
Value	★★★★★
Grapes	cabernet sauvignon
Region	mainly Coonawarra & Barossa Valley, SA
Cellar	🍾 12+
Alc./Vol.	13.5%
RRP	$22.00 ⑤ 🍾

PENGUIN BEST CABERNET SAUVIGNON

Penfolds Bin 707 Cabernet Sauvignon

Quality	ΥΥΥΥΥ
Value	★★★
Grapes	cabernet sauvignon
Region	Coonawarra &
	Barossa Valley, SA;
	Mount Barker, WA
Cellar	➥ 5–20+
Alc./Vol.	13.5%
RRP	$80.00 ▮

Okay, so the price has doubled in three years; but at least the wine is good. A helluva good wine, actually. It's just a shame it's doing a Grange and sliding into investor territory, so we ordinary mortals will never again be able to afford it. Befriend a millionaire today.

Previous outstanding vintages: '64, '76, '80, '83, '84, '86, '87, '90, '91, '92, '93

CURRENT RELEASE 1994 This is what winemakers affectionately term a glass-stainer! Monstrous purple–red colour that will ruin your new shirt; massive, solid, very full-bodied and grippingly tannic, it demands cellaring. In true 707 style it's more about coconut/vanilla American oak than cabernet as a youngster, and possesses formidable power and flavour concentration. When mature, serve with aged cheddar.

Penfolds Grange

Quality	ΥΥΥΥΥ
Value	★★★ǐ
Grapes	shiraz
Region	Barossa Valley,
	Coonawarra &
	McLaren Vale, SA
Cellar	➥ 5–15+
Alc./Vol.	13.5%
RRP	$200–$350 ▮

Australia's most sought-after wine, but not necessarily its greatest any longer. There are many pretenders to the throne but few can match Grange's longevity, investment potential or ability to improve with 20+ years' ageing. Maker John Duval and team.

Previous outstanding vintages: '52, '53, '55, '62, '63, '66, '71, '76, '83, '86, '88, '90, '91

CURRENT RELEASE 1992 Not a front-rank Grange, but still a superb red wine. The trademarks are there: forests of dominant toasty American oak, rich concentrated fruit and tongue-crunching tannin. As ever, it has the spirited aggression of youth and phenomenal length. It appears remarkably immature – its colour parallels most shirazes at three years, let alone five. It has smoky, toasty American oak, vanilla, cherry/plum, earth and licorice flavours. These finish with forbidding astringency that should ward off any who aspire to open it too soon. For full reward, put it down for at least five years. Then serve with aged hard cheeses.

Penfolds Koonunga Hill Shiraz Cabernet

This label has been extraordinary value for money for many years, although the price is creeping up of late. Maker John Duval and team.

CURRENT RELEASE 1995 Smooth, round, easy-drinking red wine that offers more depth and character than usual in its price range. Has a teasing hint of the trademark Penfolds toasty, coconutty oak. Drink with designer hamburger.

Quality	ᵀᵀᵀᵀ
Value	★★★★
Grapes	shiraz; cabernet sauvignon
Region	various, SA
Cellar	🍶 4
Alc./Vol.	13.5%
RRP	$14.00 ⑤

Penfolds Magill Estate Shiraz

This wine was designed by Max Schubert and Don Ditter in the early '80s to justify the retention of the remaining vineyard at Magill. They meant it to be an alter ego for Grange.

Previous outstanding vintages: '83, '86, '87, '88, '89, '90, '91, '92

CURRENT RELEASE 1993 In olden days this might have been termed a burgundy style. The bouquet shows toasty/earthy age development and oak vanillin. It's supple and round in the mouth, with oak again fairly evident but in no sense overdone. Supple and savoury, it would be fine with a meaty casserole.

Quality	ᵀᵀᵀᵀ
Value	★★★
Grapes	shiraz
Region	Adelaide foothills, SA
Cellar	🍶 5+
Alc./Vol.	12.0%
RRP	$40.25 ⑤ 🍶

Penley Estate Phoenix Cabernet Sauvignon

If this newie is Kym Tolley's second label, we can't wait to taste his top cabernet. And who said '95 wasn't a good year in the 'Warra?

CURRENT RELEASE 1995 Don't be put off by the rather middling colour. Cool-year green notes surface on the nose, which is crushed leaf joined by blackcurrant. This is an aromatic style with considerable charm. Surprising fruit-sweetness and suppleness; an all-round winner. Try it with braised lamb shanks.

Quality	ᵀᵀᵀᵀᵀ
Value	★★★★★
Grapes	cabernet sauvignon
Region	Coonawarra, SA
Cellar	🍶 5+
Alc./Vol.	12.5%
RRP	$19.00

Petaluma Coonawarra

Quality	🍷🍷🍷🍷
Value	★★★
Grapes	cabernet sauvignon 60%; merlot 40%
Region	Coonawarra, SA
Cellar	➟ 3–8+
Alc./Vol.	13.5%
RRP	$41.85 🍾

Minimalism is 'in', and besides, who needs to know what's in the bottle? We should all be very grateful that it comes from Coonawarra, via the god-like hand of Mr Brian Croser.

Previous outstanding vintages: '79, '82, '88, '90, '91, '92, '93

CURRENT RELEASE 1994 As always, an immaculate colour for its age: a profound and youthful purple–red. The nose is shy and somewhat reticent: some nutty oak, some shy, dark berries. The mouth is lean and elegant, quite tannic and with an underdeveloped, nascent concentration that shows good ripeness and depth. More a matter of potential than here-and-now. Try it with beef wellington.

Peter Lehmann Clancy's Gold Preference

Quality	🍷🍷🍷
Value	★★★★
Grapes	shiraz; cabernet sauvignon; merlot; cabernet franc
Region	Barossa Valley, SA
Cellar	🍷 3+
Alc./Vol.	13.0%
RRP	$14.50 Ⓢ

The label is a tribute to Banjo Paterson's *Clancy of the Overflow*, but the connection is a loose one. At least the Lehmanns, Pete and Doug, wear Akubras.

CURRENT RELEASE 1995 As usual, fine value for your $14 here, with bigger depth of mid-palate flavour than normally found at the price these days. Nice deep crimson colour and a nose of berries, cherry, plum and cedar. There's a whisper of wood, and the finish carries a mild but positive tannin handshake. Good value with a gourmet hamburger.

Peter Lehmann Shiraz

Quality	🍷🍷🍷🍷
Value	★★★
Grapes	shiraz
Region	Barossa Valley, SA
Cellar	🍷 7
Alc./Vol.	13.0%
RRP	$16.20

Barossa Valley shiraz grapes cost more than cabernet to buy by the tonne these days. Ten years ago, no-one would have believed that would ever happen. Maker Andrew Wigan.

Previous outstanding vintages: '92, '93, '94

CURRENT RELEASE 1995 The oak level seems to have crept up in this wine, but it's still mild compared to some. There are toasty, smoky aromas and a degree of rusticity to the palate, which concludes with drying tannins on a savoury finish. It's just starting to drink well. Try it with T-bone steak and mushrooms.

Pewsey Vale Cabernet Sauvignon

Pewsey used to be one of the premium brands of S. Smith & Son (alias Yalumba) but it has slipped down the hierarchy over the years. Maker Simon Adams.
CURRENT RELEASE 1995   An elegant-weight red with a juxtaposition of leafy, early-picked characters and riper blackcurrant aromas. There is some fleshiness, and it's a fruit-driven style with just a hint of oak on the palate. There's a degree of elegance, and moderate length to the finish. Try it with lamb kebabs.

Quality	ΥΥΥℓ
Value	★★★⅃
Grapes	cabernet sauvignon
Region	Eden Valley, SA
Cellar	♦ 4
Alc./Vol.	12.5%
RRP	$13.00 ⑤

Phillip Island Wines 'The Nobbies' Pinot Noir

Despite the name, this is not made from Phillip Island grapes. It's a new brand struck by the Lances of Diamond Valley, who were the first to grow grapes on the island. The wines are only available from the island winery.
CURRENT RELEASE 1996   Pinot specialist David Lance has done it again. This is a delicious pinot, with full purple–red colour, captivating aromas of game and spice together with cherry, plum and vanilla, and admirable weight and length in the mouth. There are hints of stalks, and the oak and alcohol come back on the finish. Goes with washed-rind cheese, such as Lactos Red Square.

Quality	ΥΥΥΥℓ
Value	★★★★
Grapes	pinot noir
Region	Gippsland & Yarra Valley, Vic.
Cellar	♦ 4
Alc./Vol.	13.0%
RRP	$17.00

Picardy Pinot Noir

Picardy is Bill Pannell's exciting new venture at Pemberton. The Moss Wood founder's son Dan is winemaker, and a new winery has been erected on the vineyard. This is from first-crop fruit off three-year-old vines. (This was tasted as a barrel sample.)
CURRENT RELEASE 1996   Tasted before bottling, this was most impressive for a first effort from a new and pioneering vineyard. It had a full purple–red colour, a shy but sweet, estery, cherry/violet aroma, and a sweet, silky palate with excellent flavour intensity and a long tail of tannin.

Quality	ΥΥΥΥℓ
Value	★★★★
Grapes	pinot noir
Region	Pemberton, WA
Cellar	♦ 3+
Alc./Vol.	13.0%
RRP	$28.30

Pierro Cabernets

Quality	🍷🍷🍷🍷
Value	★★★
Grapes	cabernet sauvignon; cabernet franc; merlot; petit verdot; malbec
Region	Margaret River, WA
Cellar	2–7+
Alc./Vol.	13.5%
RRP	$39.50

This is the first vintage for this label. Winemaker Mike Peterkin used the grapes for other things until the vines reached eight years old.

CURRENT RELEASE 1994 A shy, closed-up wine that needs time. There is subdued fruit/oak interplay in the aroma, and the palate has promising density and firm tannin to finish. Could reward with several years in the cellar. Then drink with roast leg of lamb.

Pipers Brook Pellion Pinot Noir

Quality	🍷🍷🍷🍷
Value	★★★
Grapes	pinot noir
Region	Pipers Brook, Tas.
Cellar	3
Alc./Vol.	12.7%
RRP	$24.00

Doctor Andrew Pirie, maestro of Pipers Brook, has a theory that humidity plays an important role in the suitability of Tasmania for growing fine wine grapes.

Previous outstanding vintages: '91, '92, '94

CURRENT RELEASE 1995 The colour is medium–light brick red, and the nose offers a complex melange of briary, leafy, strawberry and meaty pinot characters. There's good volume of flavour, with some spicy palate flavours and a certain leanness, accentuated by quite high acidity. Will the acid mellow or become more obvious with age? We'd prefer to drink it young, with truffled quail.

Pirramimma Stocks Hill Shiraz

Stocks Hill is a bump in the Southern Vales landscape and the highest point of the Pirramimma empire. Maker Geoff Johnston.

CURRENT RELEASE 1995 This is a friendly regional shiraz with lots of flavour. The nose is plummy with lashings of spice. The full-bodied palate has sweet, ripe fruit flavours, which are matched by vanilla and spice. The finish has soft, comely grip and the whole package drinks well. Try it with lamb and barley casserole.

Quality	♥♥♥♥
Value	★★★★
Grapes	shiraz
Region	Southern Vales, SA
Cellar	▮ 4
Alc./Vol.	14.0%
RRP	$14.50

Plantagenet Cabernet Sauvignon

The coat of arms on the Plantagenet label is the same as that of the UK's royal Plantagenet family. The wines are made by Gavin Berry.

Previous outstanding vintages: '79, '81, '85, '86, '88, '90, '91, '93

CURRENT RELEASE 1994 This won a trophy at the '96 Sheraton Perth awards, and looks to be in the top line of Plantagenet cabernets. While there's a lot of crushed leaf in the bouquet, the palate structure is full and rich with no greenness or lack of weight. The mid-palate is full of nicely concentrated ripe-berry flavour, the oak is notable and in fine balance, and the finish carries a firm tannin grip. It would go well with roast lamb and pesto.

Quality	♥♥♥♥♥
Value	★★★★
Grapes	cabernet sauvignon 91%; merlot 9%
Region	Lower Great Southern, WA
Cellar	▮ 8+
Alc./Vol.	14.0%
RRP	$22.15

Plantagenet Omrah Merlot Cabernet

Quality	▼▼▼▼
Value	★★★★
Grapes	merlot; cabernet sauvignon
Region	Lower Great Southern, WA
Cellar	▐ 4+
Alc./Vol.	13.0%
RRP	$16.90

Omrah is a brand name – although hardly one to excite a marketer. It's no longer the source of the grapes as it's been bought by BRL Hardy. Maker Gavin Berry.

CURRENT RELEASE 1995   Chocolate and vanilla aromas here, which don't really speak of the cool Great Southern area, but it's a fine, soft, rich, cuddly red. A slightly lactic quality does not mar it. Smooth, fleshy palate structure finishing with drying tannins. Try it with a mixed grill.

Plantagenet Shiraz

Quality	▼▼▼▼▼
Value	★★★★★
Grapes	shiraz
Region	Lower Great Southern, WA
Cellar	▐ 10+
Alc./Vol.	13.5%
RRP	$22.50 ▐

This leading West Australian winery recently announced plans to more than double its production over the next five years. This has always been a fruit-driven style, aged in subtler French oak. Maker Gavin Berry.

Previous outstanding vintages: '76, '77, '83, '84, '85, '88, '90, '91, '92, '93, '94

CURRENT RELEASE 1995   A superb wine to follow up the great '94. The colour is dense and there are rich, ripe, meaty and spicy characters in the bouquet. Decadent flavours abound on the palate, which is sumptuously fleshy. The fruit flavours are complex, lush and layered. An exciting wine and worth tracking down. Serve with a complex casserole.

Preece Cabernet Sauvignon

Quality	▼▼▼
Value	★★★
Grapes	cabernet sauvignon
Region	King Valley & Goulburn Valley, Vic.
Cellar	▐ 3
Alc./Vol.	13.5%
RRP	$14.65 Ⓢ

This is the fighting varietal brand from Mitchelton. When we see the miniature Preece labels we get all teary and feel like passing around the hat for poor old Mitchelton. Maker Don Lewis.

CURRENT RELEASE 1995   A fresh, youthful style tailored for ready drinking. Straightforward red cherry and currant nose, with a light hand on the oak. Smooth, gentle, rounded palate, which has a slight doughnut hollowness. A tad short, but the price is right. Serve with a veal chop.

Preece Merlot

Colin Preece probably never crushed a merlot grape in his life, but we're sure he would have approved of this effort. In his later years, Preece was the original winemaking consultant at Mitchelton when it was established in 1974.

CURRENT RELEASE 1995 This is probably the best value merlot on the market. It has a fine deep colour, attractive sweet berry/floral aromas, a fair complement of oak, and a flavoursome palate with good structure and tannin firmness. It fills the mouth and avoids the greenness that still besets most merlots in this country. Goes well with a doner kebab.

Quality	♥♥♥♥
Value	★★★★⯨
Grapes	merlot
Region	King Valley & Goulburn Valley, Vic.
Cellar	▮ 3+
Alc./Vol.	13.9%
RRP	$14.65 Ⓢ

Redbank Fighting Flat Shiraz

The name and concept of this wine hark back to central Victoria's gold-rush days of the 1860s. Maker Neill Robb.

CURRENT RELEASE 1994 Lightish red–purple colour and a pepper–spice, cool-grown shiraz aroma. Stalky beginning, then some attractive and Cotes-du-Rhone-like spice and berry flavours in the middle. Just lacks a little in length and dimension. Serve with rissoles.

Quality	♥♥♥⯨
Value	★★★
Grapes	shiraz
Region	various, Victoria
Cellar	▮ 3
Alc./Vol.	11.5%
RRP	$17.50 (cellar door)

Redbank Long Paddock Shiraz

Long Paddock is a bit of a jape: the label says it's a reference to droving days when the roadsides were known as the long paddock. But it could also refer to the grapes that are sourced from far and wide. Maker Neill Robb.

CURRENT RELEASE 1995 This is a pleasing ready-drinker, with more character than most in its league. The nose has meaty, gamy spice and oak interactions, and the smooth, subtly wooded palate ends with some grainy tannin. Nice fleshy texture. Serve it with shish kebabs.

Quality	♥♥♥⯨
Value	★★★★
Grapes	shiraz
Region	'Australia's southern vineyards'
Cellar	▮ 4
Alc./Vol.	12.5%
RRP	$11.60

Redbank Sally's Paddock

Quality	♟♟♟♟♟
Value	★★★★⸠
Grapes	cabernet sauvignon; shiraz; merlot; cabernet franc; malbec
Region	Pyrenees, Vic.
Cellar	▮ 15
Alc./Vol.	11.5%
RRP	$35.50 ▮

This is named after winemaker Neill Robb's wife. It comes from a single patch of vines at the front of the property beside the drive. They are naturally low-yielding and unwatered, and have produced some sensational wines.

Previous outstanding vintages: '80, '81, '82, '86, '88, '90, '91, '92, '93, '94

CURRENT RELEASE 1995   A typical top-year Sally's, this is fragrantly fruit-driven, subtly oaked, and remarkably low in alcohol considering its intensity and power. Fresh berries and lightly minty, briary aromas. Smooth, sweet, gentle, well-balanced flavour, with length and elegance, and a firm finish. Drinks well now, with roast rack of veal.

Redbank Spud Gully Pinot Noir

Quality	♟♟♟
Value	★★★
Grapes	pinot noir
Region	Pyrenees, Vic.
Cellar	▮ 2
Alc./Vol.	13.0%
RRP	$14.50 (cellar door)

Redbank's Neill and Sally Robb come up with some delightfully rustic brand names to match the individual style of their wines. This is Exhibit A.

CURRENT RELEASE 1995   Straight out of left field, this doesn't toe any conventional pinot noir lines. The colour has some development and is slightly opaque. There are sour cherries and plum stones to sniff, and abundant ripe pinot fruit in the mouth, which turns slightly jammy/pruney on a slightly extractive finish. It could team well with pork spare ribs.

Redman Cabernet Sauvignon Merlot

Quality	♟♟♟⸠
Value	★★⸠
Grapes	cabernet sauvignon; merlot
Region	Coonawarra, SA
Cellar	▮ 4+
Alc./Vol.	13.5%
RRP	$23.00 Ⓢ ▮

The Redman style has changed dramatically, at least with this blend. New oak, a no-no during Owen Redman's tenure, is very much a part of the style.

CURRENT RELEASE 1993   The obvious toasty oak treatment reminds us more of Southcorp than Redman. The question is: will it come into harmony with time? There is some development starting to show and the finish is quite strong on oak tannin. Serve with gourmet hamburgers.

Redman Shiraz

This is one of the more down-market Coonawarras, and while it won't set any hearts aflutter, it must be said that it's cheaper than most Coonawarras.
CURRENT RELEASE 1995 Medium–light red colour reflects a pretty ordinary year for shiraz in the 'Warra. Slightly fumey on the nose, without a lot of freshness, and the palate is all up-front, fairly simple and short on the finish. Try it with a doner kebab.

Quality	♟♟♟
Value	★★★
Grapes	shiraz
Region	Coonawarra, SA
Cellar	↓ 2
Alc./Vol.	12.5%
RRP	$14.50 Ⓢ

Reynolds Hunter Orange Cabernet Merlot

Cabernet is probably not going to be the great grape of Orange, which is a cool, high-altitude region in New South Wales. Maker Jon Reynolds.
CURRENT RELEASE 1995 Minty, tomato-sauce-like nose, with some more grapey flavours coming through on the palate. It's quite aromatic, and the medium-weight palate finishes with some astringency. Try it with meat pie and tomato sauce.

Quality	♟♟♟♟
Value	★★★
Grapes	cabernet sauvignon 60%; merlot 35%; cabernet franc 5%
Region	Orange, NSW 65%; Hunter Valley, NSW 35%
Cellar	↓ 4
Alc./Vol.	13.0%
RRP	$18.35

Reynolds Orange Cabernet Sauvignon

Jon and Jane Reynolds have been buying Orange grapes for several years. These come from the Bloodwood and Bantry Grove vineyards.
CURRENT RELEASE 1994 Tomato sauce and greenish mulberry, minty aromas that betray the cool climate. It's lean and slightly acidic with some hardness on the finish. Not a wine of fullness and flesh; more a salute to cool-climate viticulture. Try it with a designer pizza.

Quality	♟♟♟
Value	★★⋆
Grapes	cabernet sauvignon
Region	Orange, NSW
Cellar	↓ 4+
Alc./Vol.	13.0%
RRP	$22.50

Reynolds Shiraz

Quality	♥♥♥⁍
Value	★★★
Grapes	shiraz
Region	Hunter Valley, NSW
Cellar	▮ 7+
Alc./Vol.	13.0%
RRP	$18.35 ▮

Jon and Jane Reynolds have a winery in the Upper Hunter, but they increasingly use grapes from the Orange district. This one's true-blue Hunter.

CURRENT RELEASE 1995 Plums and oak, earth and forest-floor overtones with some slightly rough extraction. A gutsy, rustic red with grainy tannins and plenty of flavour. Goes well with shepherd's pie.

Richard Hamilton Burton's Vineyard Grenache Shiraz

Quality	♥♥♥♥
Value	★★★★
Grapes	grenache; shiraz
Region	McLaren Vale, SA
Cellar	⬤ 1–4+
Alc./Vol.	13.5%
RRP	$13.50

Burton was Richard's father, and he started planting this block in 1947, which means the 'old vines' statement is no idle boast.

Previous outstanding vintages: '93, '95

CURRENT RELEASE 1996 A rather raw wine that needs a little time. There is a hint of volatility amid simple aromas of sweet jammy fruit and some alcohol. Big and without pretence to elegance, it has solid structure, a degree of richness and slightly hard tannins. Cellar, then serve with pan-fried calf's liver.

Richard Hamilton Hut Block Cabernet

Quality	♥♥♥♥⁍
Value	★★★★⊦
Grapes	cabernet sauvignon
Region	McLaren Vale, SA
Cellar	⬤ 2–7
Alc./Vol.	12.8%
RRP	$16.00

This winery has entered into a joint venture with the Rhone Valley firm Chapoutier. Selected clones of Chapoutier's vinestock are being imported, and Michel Chapoutier is making wine for an export label.

CURRENT RELEASE 1996 It's a pity wines like this are released so young. It's just a baby; very fresh and just a tad raw. But there's no denying the pristine cabernet character: blackcurrants galore to sniff, good fruit concentration on the palate, sweet, some tannin grip but a slightly acidic finish. Food: braised beef.

Richard Hamilton Marion Vineyard Grenache Shiraz

The Marion vineyard is in the Adelaide suburban municipality of the same name. It's one of the few plots of vines left where once there were many. Maker Ralph Fowler.

CURRENT RELEASE 1996 This is similar to the '95 edition: deep youthful colour, dark-berry and fresh new wood aromas, spices and berries, and a rather astringent finish. There is good depth of flavour in the middle, but the finish is all acid and hard tannins. Cellar, then serve with shish kebabs.

Quality	▼▼▼
Value	★★▸
Grapes	grenache; shiraz
Region	Adelaide, SA
Cellar	➾ 2–5+
Alc./Vol.	13.6%
RRP	$25.75 ▮

Richard Hamilton Reserve Merlot

Last year's debut release '95 was a cracker; so is this one. There is a lack of merlots with real guts on the market. Maker Ralph Fowler.

Previous outstanding vintages: '95

CURRENT RELEASE 1996 Rich colour and a sweet, ripe noseful of berries with nicely trimmed oak. The palate is serious, with concentrated flavour that is also soft and sensuous, concluding with assertive tannins. Slightly lactic to sniff, but a delicious drop of wine. Serve with carpetbag steak.

Quality	▼▼▼▼
Value	★★★★
Grapes	merlot
Region	McLaren Vale, SA
Cellar	▮ 5+
Alc./Vol.	14.0%
RRP	$21.00

Richard Hamilton Reserve Old Vine Shiraz

Gee, that's smart marketing! They've got two of the important buzz-words of the moment on the same label. In fact, all the premium Hamilton labels are getting very busy these days. Maker Ralph Fowler.

CURRENT RELEASE 1995 Lovely, big, bouncy shiraz! McLaren Vale at its best, with a big purple–red colour and rich, sweet, plums-and-spices shiraz flavour to burn. The palate is rich and has good density augmented by liberal oak. Smooth and up-front with a touch of acid on the finish. Serve with beef satays.

Quality	▼▼▼▼
Value	★★★
Grapes	shiraz
Region	McLaren Vale, SA
Cellar	➾ 1–7+
Alc./Vol.	13.0%
RRP	$25.00 Ⓢ

Richard Hamilton Shiraz

Quality	♟♟♟
Value	★★★
Grapes	shiraz
Region	McLaren Vale, SA
Cellar	➥ 2–5
Alc./Vol.	14.0%
RRP	$15.30 Ⓢ

No doubt there are pressures on wineries to release reds younger in order to maintain supply in a world that's increasingly thirsty for red wine. But it would be nice to see them released with more than one year's age.

CURRENT RELEASE 1996 Vivid, youthful purple–red colour; lifted and somewhat raw aroma with shavings-like oak plus spices. It's still estery and needs more time. The palate is fiercely astringent and almost tastes unfinished. Cellar, then have it with pepper steak.

Richmond Grove Coonawarra Cabernet Sauvignon

Quality	♟♟♟♟♟
Value	★★★★★
Grapes	cabernet sauvignon
Region	Coonawarra, SA
Cellar	▮ 5
Alc./Vol.	13.0%
RRP	$15.50 Ⓢ ▮

PENGUIN BEST BARGAIN RED

The corporate meandering that saw a Hunter brand come to have a Coonawarra wine is too difficult to track in this space. Suffice it to say that this is now an Orlando Wyndham brand. Maker John Vickery.

CURRENT RELEASE 1994 This is a classic blackcurranty regional style of cabernet, medium- to full-bodied with tight tannin structure and a balanced, dry finish. It's a lovely wine of considerable depth; a gold-medal-winner (as a finished wine) in Canberra in 1996. It'll provide great drinking for the next seven or eight years. Serve with grana padano cheese.

Riddoch Shiraz

Quality	♟♟♟♟
Value	★★★★
Grapes	shiraz
Region	Coonawarra, SA
Cellar	▮ 6
Alc./Vol.	13.5%
RRP	$15.30

John Riddoch, the father of winegrowing at Coonawarra, has had his name on several fine wine labels over the years. Maker Wayne Stehbens.

CURRENT RELEASE 1994 Katnook doesn't produce a shiraz, so you might say this is the best of their shiraz material – not the offcuts. Smoked oyster, vanilla, game and spices on the nose. Sweet entry and abundant smooth, ripe, berry/plum flavours that seduce the senses. Clean soft-tannin finish. Try it with spit-roast lamb. ▶

CURRENT RELEASE 1995   Strong toasted oak dominates this wine at present, and the palate is lean and a trifle simple. Caramel and vanilla flavours prevail in the mouth. It appears to be a light-year wine pumped up with toasty oak. Try it with a well-charred hamburger.

Quality	♀♀♀
Value	★★★
Grapes	shiraz
Region	Coonawarra, SA
Cellar	▮ 4
Alc./Vol.	12.5%
RRP	$15.30

Robertson's Well Cabernet Sauvignon

Windmills, wells, wide-brown-land colours: this is a very Aussie-looking package with a quite stylish wine inside. Maker Gavin Hogg.
Previous outstanding vintages: '93
CURRENT RELEASE 1994   Fairly obvious oak-meets-leafy, blackcurranty cabernet fruit, and an elegant wine is the happy result. A foil for Mildara's white label and Jamieson's Run, it's a handsome red with some oaky firmness on the finish. Serve with vitello tonato.

Quality	♀♀♀♀
Value	★★★ᖰ
Grapes	cabernet sauvignon
Region	Coonawarra, SA
Cellar	▮ 4
Alc./Vol.	13.0%
RRP	$18.85 Ⓢ

Rockford Basket Press Shiraz

This cult wine kicked off the rediscovery of the basket press and shiraz – and to some extent, the Barossa Valley. Maker Robert O'Callaghan.
Previous outstanding vintages: '92
CURRENT RELEASE 1994   Another masterpiece from Rocky: the old vines have once again summoned fruit of sumptuous concentration and opulence. It opens with a sprinkle of coconut/vanilla oak, and unfolds marvellously rich, supple plum flavours that linger long and finish with alcohol warmth and satisfying resonance. Suits venison braised with cherries.

Quality	♀♀♀♀♀
Value	★★★★★
Grapes	shiraz
Region	Barossa Valley, SA
Cellar	▮ 10+
Alc./Vol.	14.5%
RRP	$20 (cellar door) ▮

Romsey Park Pinot Noir

Quality	♥♥♥♡
Value	★★★
Grapes	pinot noir
Region	Macedon, Vic.
Cellar	▲ 3
Alc./Vol.	12.7%
RRP	$22.00

Rochford winery in the Macedon region is the source of this brand. It's effectively a Rochford second label. Maker Bruce Dowding.

CURRENT RELEASE 1995   Pale-coloured and with a shy, slightly herbal aroma, this is a lightweight pinot from a cooler year. The taste is lean, savoury and sinewy with some astringency to finish. Try it with tuna steaks.

Rosabrook Estate Cabernet Merlot

Quality	♥♥♥♥
Value	★★★★
Grapes	cabernet sauvignon; merlot
Region	Margaret River, WA
Cellar	▲ 7
Alc./Vol.	13.0%
RRP	$17.00 ▲

Margaret River is a booming wine district, and between the wineries, the natural bush, the surf and unspoilt coastline, it comes close to paradise on earth.

CURRENT RELEASE 1995   Once you get past the odd herbal, vegetable/tomato bush bouquet, there are spices and pepper, smooth berry-fruit flavours and gentle tannins. It tastes better than it smells, and on balance is a very attractive red. Try it with braised lamb shanks.

Rosabrook Estate Shiraz

Quality	♥♥♥♥♡
Value	★★★★⊦
Grapes	shiraz
Region	Margaret River, WA
Cellar	⊶ 1–8+
Alc./Vol.	13.5%
RRP	$17.00 ▲

A newcomer to Margaret River. The wines were made until recently by Dan Pannell, member of a very accomplished West Australian winemaking family.

CURRENT RELEASE 1995   A teeth-stainer that pushes oak to the max. Dense, thick purple–red colour; dominant oak aroma, but does have the fruit to balance with another year or two in the bottle. Solidly built, firmly structured. Abundant tannin is balanced with rich, ripe fruit galore. Serve with seared kangaroo fillets.

Rosemount Balmoral Syrah

Rosemount's foray into McLaren Vale some years ago and the purchase of the Ryecroft winery has paid off handsomely with a bevy of sumptuous reds. None better than this one.

Previous outstanding vintages: '89, '90, '91, '92, '93

CURRENT RELEASE 1994   High-toast American oak features prominently on the bouquet, but does not overpower the rich fruit in the mouth. It needs time to mellow out, but there is no hurry; the wine has a great future. Dense colour; huge volume of sweet fruit; persistent, smooth, ripe tannins. A voluptuous red that should turn out beautifully with age. Serve with rare steak.

Quality	▼▼▼▼▼
Value	★★★⋆
Grapes	shiraz
Region	McLaren Vale, SA
Cellar	➡ 2–8+
Alc./Vol.	13.5%
RRP	$45.00 ▮

Rosemount Cabernet Sauvignon

Rosemount's diamond label reds offer extraordinary value for money year in, year out. This won a gold medal at the '96 Adelaide Show.

CURRENT RELEASE 1995   A slightly jammy nose of rich, red fruits well interwoven with oak, and a dusty, earthy aspect that is probably McLaren Vale regional character. Good weight and structure with tannin grip and muscle, although a touch straightforward. Good with steak, and has potential for the future.

Quality	▼▼▼▼
Value	★★★★
Grapes	cabernet sauvignon
Region	various
Cellar	▮ 6+
Alc./Vol.	13.5%
RRP	$16.00 ⑤

Rosemount Grenache Shiraz

This is part of the 'split label' range in which Rosemount shows off its labelling machinery as much as its ability to make wine to a budget.

CURRENT RELEASE 1996   A slightly feral nose: gamy, spicy and peppery with a touch of graphite. The taste is soft, quite round and oily in texture, with sweet-berry grenache fruit character and some astringency to close. A decent rustic red at the price. Try it with a hamburger.

Quality	▼▼▼
Value	★★★
Grapes	grenache 65%; shiraz 35%
Region	McLaren Vale, SA; Murray Valley, Vic.
Cellar	▮ 3
Alc./Vol.	13.5%
RRP	$12.60 ⑤

Rosemount GSM

Quality 🍷🍷🍷🍷🍷
Value ★★★★½
Grapes grenache; shiraz; mourvèdre
Region McLaren Vale, SA
Cellar 6+
Alc./Vol. 13.8%
RRP $19.30

The initials stand for the grape varieties, and '94 is the debut vintage for what promises to be a new addition to the ranks of the classics. Maker Philip Shaw and team.
CURRENT RELEASE 1994 Swags of oak, which is integrating and developing with the fruit to reveal more interesting gamy, beef-stocky complexities, together with lush berries and spices. The palate has superb depth of sweet fruit and a smooth, lingering finish. A most impressive debut. Try it with game pie.

Rosemount Mountain Blue Shiraz Cabernet

Quality 🍷🍷🍷🍷🍷
Value ★★★★
Grapes shiraz; cabernet sauvignon
Region Mudgee, NSW
Cellar 2–10+
Alc./Vol. 13.0%
RRP $35.00

Rosemount claimed this wine, with seven golds and a trophy, was the most awarded wine ever to come out of Mudgee, which ain't true. Huntington Estate can top that record. Maker Philip Shaw.
CURRENT RELEASE 1994 A stunning debut that's worth all the hoo-haa. This is a massive wine, packed to the gunnels with flavour and tannin; structured for the long haul. Large helpings of coconut/vanilla oak are balanced by equally large licks of chunky, spicy, berry fruit and assertively gripping tannins. Impressive stuff to help herald the re-emergence of Mudgee as a force. Barbecue some juicy steaks and enjoy.

Rosemount Orange Vineyard Cabernet Sauvignon

Quality 🍷🍷🍷½
Value ★★★
Grapes cabernet sauvignon
Region Orange, NSW
Cellar 3
Alc./Vol. 13.0%
RRP $21.00 (S)

Rosemount's winemaker Philip Shaw started this vineyard – Orange's biggest – in the '80s. It's 900 metres up on New South Wales's central highlands.
CURRENT RELEASE 1993 Some aged development is starting to show, adding to the matured character gained from barrel ageing. There's a burnt-capsicum note as well. The bouquet is dusty, earthy and slightly meaty, and the flavour is deep, rich and very dry. Teams well with Irish stew.

Rosemount Reserve Shiraz

These days Rosemount is moving its red-grape focus increasingly to McLaren Vale, while its Hunter vineyards are still numero uno for whites, especially chardonnay. CURRENT RELEASE 1994 Yet another stunning Rosemount shiraz; they are as predictable as the sun coming up. Deep colour, youthful toasty American oak and plummy fruit nose, generous flavour, and mouth-coating tannin finish. The intense and stylish flavour is not compromised by the drying tannin aftergrip. It could cellar well. Serve with venison pot roast.

Quality	??????
Value	★★★⋆
Grapes	shiraz
Region	McLaren Vale, SA
Cellar	🍾 10
Alc./Vol.	13.0%
RRP	$25.00 🍾

Rosemount Shiraz

This has rightly earned a place among the most consistent bargains of Australian wine. It's had more *Wine Spectator* Best Buy berths than any other Aussie red. *Previous outstanding vintages: '88, '90, '91, '92, '94* CURRENT RELEASE 1995 One of the very best of a strong line. Youthful purple–red; spicy/peppery shiraz nose with a degree of style; stacks of sweet, spicy shiraz flavour in the mouth plus a modicum of elegance. Good balance and a positive, yet not tannic, finish. Serve with saddle of hare.

Quality	?????
Value	★★★★★
Grapes	shiraz
Region	various
Cellar	🍾 5+
Alc./Vol.	13.0%
RRP	$16.00 Ⓢ

Rosemount Shiraz Cabernet

The colour codes of the split-label range are supposed to match the wines inside, hence this one has a purple theme. *Previous outstanding vintages: '95* CURRENT RELEASE 1996 An unusual wine that seems a trifle raw and unfinished. It has a sweetish, grapey, plum-juice taste, but is quite attractive as a fresh youngster for early drinking. The aromas are of flowers and plum-skins. Try it with spaghetti bolognese.

Quality	???
Value	★★★
Grapes	shiraz; cabernet sauvignon
Region	not stated
Cellar	🍾 2
Alc./Vol.	13.0%
RRP	$12.55 Ⓢ

Rosemount Show Reserve Cabernet Sauvignon

Quality	♛♛♛♛♛
Value	★★★★
Grapes	cabernet sauvignon
Region	Coonawarra, SA
Cellar	➥ 1–8+
Alc./Vol.	13.5%
RRP	$25.00 🍾

Another wine that showcases the wide-ranging talents of winemaker Philip Shaw. He's equally at home with McLaren Vale or Orange, with shiraz, grenache, cabernet, semillon or chardonnay.

Previous outstanding vintages: '87, '88, '90, '91, '92, '93

CURRENT RELEASE 1994 This is a serious, firm style with an authoritative grip. The colour is impressively dark and there is a wealth of toasty oak in the bouquet. The flavours are savoury, with shades of earth, oak, plum, berries and coconut. The fruit is hidden somewhat under tannin. Give it time, then drink with aged cheddar.

Rosemount Traditional

Quality	♛♛♛♛♛
Value	★★★★
Grapes	cabernet sauvignon; merlot; petit verdot
Region	McLaren Vale, SA
Cellar	🍷 7+
Alc./Vol.	13.5%
RRP	$19.30

This started life as a Ryecroft brand, and since Ryecroft became part of Rosemount, the banner has shifted. Ryecroft is now just a quaffing brand.

CURRENT RELEASE 1994 This has an earthy, dusty, long-time wood-matured bouquet. It's savoury and also has a leafy/plummy aspect. It turns blackberry jammy in the mouth. Nicely balanced oak and plenty of grip and muscle. A chunky wine of real flavour. Serve with lamb spit roast.

Rothbury Estate Reserve Shiraz

Quality	♛♛♛♛
Value	★★★⋆
Grapes	shiraz
Region	Hunter Valley, NSW
Cellar	➥ 1–5+
Alc./Vol.	12.5%
RRP	$22.00 Ⓢ 🍾

The prices have been tumbling since the Mildara Blass takeover; we've seen this wine discounted heavily. The first three Reserves were most impressive, but the '94 is not up to the same mark.

Previous outstanding vintages: '89, '91, '93

CURRENT RELEASE 1994 Peppery shiraz fruit and earthy Hunter regional overtones meet coconutty American oak on the bouquet, and there is good depth of elegant flavour in the tightly-knit palate. Cherry and spice flavours, restrained and nicely balanced. This will benefit from a few years in the cellar. Food: oxtail stew.

Rouge Homme Cabernet Sauvignon

Winemaker Paul Gordon has steadily improved the Rouge Homme reds over recent years and they are now quite superb. Coming out of the same winery, they give Lindemans' Coonawarra premium reds serious competition in price and quality.

CURRENT RELEASE 1994 An elegant, powerful, beautifully crafted wine, which has structure for keeping plus enough early appeal to drink young. Full purple–red, it has coffee, toasty oak and red-berry fruit on the nose, and smooth, rich, complex palate flavour that finishes forcefully. It drinks well despite the tannin, with matured secondary flavours starting to appear. Food: bistecca fiorentina.

Quality	🍷🍷🍷🍷
Value	★★★★
Grapes	cabernet sauvignon
Region	Coonawarra, SA
Cellar	🍷 10+
Alc./Vol.	13.5%
RRP	$18.65 Ⓢ

Rymill Cabernet Sauvignon

This marque has gone from Rymill to Riddoch Run and back to Rymill again. Although Peter Rymill's second name is Riddoch and he's a direct descendant of John Riddoch, there were just too many Riddoch wines around. Maker John Innes.

CURRENT RELEASE 1994 A full-bodied, slightly angular wine, which is nicely perfumed with smoky, toasty oak and dark berries. Although there's some acid showing on the palate it's a tidy wine and goes well with chargrilled steak.

Quality	🍷🍷🍷🍷
Value	★★★★
Grapes	cabernet sauvignon
Region	Coonawarra, SA
Cellar	🍷 5+
Alc./Vol.	13.7%
RRP	$18.50

Rymill Merlot Cabernets

The new Rymill winery at the northern extremity of the Coonawarra strip is a grand structure and a showpiece for the region.

CURRENT RELEASE 1994 An oak-driven style which opens up slightly sweaty and airs to reveal lots of coconutty American oak. The profile is lean and the palate is on the lighter side, soft enough to drink young. Try it with lamb's fry.

Quality	🍷🍷🍷
Value	★★★
Grapes	merlot; cabernet franc; cabernet sauvignon
Region	Coonawarra, SA
Cellar	🍷 3+
Alc./Vol.	13.4%
RRP	$16.90

Sacred Hill Shiraz Cabernet

Quality	♟♟♟?
Value	★★★★ʳ
Grapes	shiraz; cabernet sauvignon
Region	Riverina, NSW
Cellar	▮ 1
Alc./Vol.	12.0%
RRP	$6.50 ⑤

The De Bortoli family have scored a few wins with this cheapie red over the years, and this vintage has a Brisbane silver medal to its credit.

CURRENT RELEASE 1996   Spicy, plum-skin and earthy aromas are very pleasing, with fruit to the fore, and the taste is equally easy on the gums. Soft, lightweight and somewhat short, it nevertheless has tremendous appeal at the price. Take a few bottles to a BBQ.

Saddler's Creek Bluegrass Cabernet Sauvignon

Quality	♟♟♟♟
Value	★★★
Grapes	cabernet sauvignon
Region	Hunter Valley, NSW
Cellar	▮ 5
Alc./Vol.	13.0%
RRP	$24.00

Kentucky Bluegrass is a brand of bourbon barrel coopered from American oak. Its character tends to dominate anything you put into it. Stylish packaging is a feature of this producer.

CURRENT RELEASE 1995   The overwhelming aroma is the vanilla/coconut smell of toasted American oak, so this is one for lumber lovers. There is, however, a swag of redeeming sweet, ripe fruit on the palate, which combines with the wood to give a silky-rich, sensuous, fleshy texture and mint/vanilla flavour that many will love.

Salitage Cabernet Merlot

Quality	♟♟♟♟?
Value	★★★ʳ
Grapes	cabernet sauvignon; cabernet franc; merlot; petit verdot
Region	Pemberton, WA
Cellar	⊸ 3–8+
Alc./Vol.	13.7%
RRP	$32.00 ▮

There were just 1400 cases bottled of this first release. Whether cabernet is a suitable grape for Pemberton remains to be seen, but there's no doubt it's chardonnay and pinot noir country. Maker Patrick Coutts.

CURRENT RELEASE 1995   The colour is a very dense, concentrated purple–red, and the density theme is repeated on the nose and palate. It's rich and solid with plenty of fruit sweetness and only a whisper of cool-climate mintiness. The gravelly soil and Scott Henry trellis have done well. It just needs time for the astringency to soften.

Salitage Pinot Noir

Owner John Horgan believes the ironstone in the soil at Salitage acts as a heat bank to help get his grapes fully ripe. The property has made impressive wines from day one.

Previous outstanding vintages: '93, '94

CURRENT RELEASE 1995 This has benefited from bottle-age since last year's review. The colour has deepened and the bouquet shows cherry and earthy characters with hints of undergrowth. There are chocolate and vanilla flavours in the mouth and the very firm tannins are starting to smooth out, but they still have a way to go. A muscular wine which needs food. Try pink lamb chops.

Quality	▼▼▼▼
Value	★★★
Grapes	pinot noir
Region	Pemberton, WA
Cellar	▮ 3+
Alc./Vol.	13.9%
RRP	$30.40

Saltram Barossa Reserve Shiraz

Yet another change of ownership (which must make the employees dizzy), but at the moment it seems to be business as usual. Maker Nigel Dolan.

CURRENT RELEASE 1994 A very well-made wine that is generous yet taut in structure. It has cherry and plum aromas on the nose. The palate has black cherry flavours as well as pepper spices. The tannins on the finish have a black-tea character. It needs plenty of time in the bottle to give of its best. Drink it now after decanting with tea-smoked duck.

Quality	▼▼▼▼
Value	★★★★
Grapes	shiraz
Region	Barossa Valley, SA
Cellar	► 2–8
Alc./Vol.	13.6%
RRP	$20.00 ▮

Sandalford Cabernet Sauvignon

Quality	ỶỶỶỶ⍦
Value	★★★★⍦
Grapes	cabernet sauvignon
Region	Mount Barker & Margaret River, WA
Cellar	▲ 4
Alc./Vol.	13.0%
RRP	$18.50

Founded in 1840 on the banks of the Swan River, Sandalford has three vineyards. Margaret River (120 hectares), Swan Valley (20 hectares) and Mount Barker (64 hectares) all contribute to a growing portfolio of wine. Maker Bill Crappsley.

Previous outstanding vintages: '94

CURRENT RELEASE 1995 A very civilised style that makes the most of the regions involved. The nose has sweet, ripe fruit aromas and some savoury wood smells. The berries promise and deliver a medium to full palate. It has ripe blackberry and redcurrant flavours, and these are augmented by vanilla from the wood treatment. It's a stylish wine that is easy to drink. Try it with pink lamb chops.

Sandalford Margaret River Mount Barker Shiraz

Quality	ỶỶỶỶ
Value	★★★★
Grapes	shiraz
Region	Margaret River & Mount Barker, WA
Cellar	▲ 6
Alc./Vol.	13.0%
RRP	$18.95

To put this place in historic perspective: it was founded 20 years before Chateau Tahbilk in Victoria, 13 years before Thomas Hardy, and two years after Chateau Reynella in South Australia.

CURRENT RELEASE 1995 A very agreeable style that makes for easy drinking. The colour is a bright and healthy deep red. The nose has spice and pepper as well as ripe berry aromas. The medium- to full-bodied palate has rich, ripe, plum fruit flavours, which are matched by some velvety tannins. Although it drinks well now, it should also cellar. Try it with a lamb and barley casserole.

Sandhurst Ridge Cabernet Sauvignon

The Marong region of Central Victoria has been appearing sporadically on labels from other districts for the last 20 years. This label and winery are located in the district. CURRENT RELEASE 1995 Pity about the slightly fishy, musty nose. The colour is bright ruby-red, and the palate offers sweet fruit and excellent berry flavours. The oak is well integrated and the tannin is clean and lingering. If it weren't for the nose this wine would have scored much higher. Try it with BBQ chops.

Quality	♀♀♀
Value	★★ｒ
Grapes	cabernet sauvignon
Region	Bendigo, Vic.
Cellar	♦ 3
Alc./Vol.	12.5%
RRP	$16.00

Sandhurst Ridge Shiraz

Brand-new label (the ink is just dry) and there are no details in the Wine Industry Directory as yet. CURRENT RELEASE 1995 A youthful and somewhat restrained style with a beautiful young colour. The nose has strong mint and smoky oak aromas. The palate has a medium body with dark cherry and raspberry flavours, and there are fine-grained tannins on a grippy finish. It has plenty of cellar potential and goes well with emu sausages.

Quality	♀♀♀♀
Value	★★★★
Grapes	shiraz
Region	Bendigo, Vic.
Cellar	➡ 2–6
Alc./Vol.	12.5%
RRP	$16.00

Scarpantoni School Block

The winery was established in 1979 with 32 hectares under vine. It has made steady and impressive progress up the quality ladder. Maker Michael Scarpantoni. CURRENT RELEASE 1995 A drink-now style with a light cherry-red colour. There are hints of carbonic maceration/lolly/berry aromas. The palate has juicy fruit with ripe berry and spice flavours. There are modest tannins on the finish. You could chill it a bit and serve it with tacos.

Quality	♀♀♀♀
Value	★★★★
Grapes	cabernet sauvignon; shiraz; merlot
Region	McLaren Vale, SA
Cellar	♦ 2
Alc./Vol.	13.5%
RRP	$12.50

Scotchmans Hill Cabernet Sauvignon Merlot

Quality	♟♟♟♟
Value	★★★★★
Grapes	cabernet sauvignon; merlot
Region	Geelong, Vic.
Cellar	▮ 5
Alc./Vol.	13.5%
RRP	$21.00

This vineyard seldom puts a foot wrong in terms of releasing top-flight wines. They have demanding standards and these start in the vineyard and end in the bottle. Maker Robin Brockett.

Previous outstanding vintages: '90, '91, '92, '93

CURRENT RELEASE 1994   Lovely red with a perfumed nose that sings a siren's song. It's all about exotic berries and rose gardens. The palate is complex with a medium body and great finesse. Cherry and blackberry are the major flavours and these are laced with spices. The oak is like the faithful butler: discreet but ever-present and supportive. It's too elegant for roo or stew. Try it with a steak tartare.

Scotchmans Hill Pinot Noir

Quality	♟♟♟♟
Value	★★★★
Grapes	pinot noir
Region	Geelong, Vic.
Cellar	▮ 5
Alc./Vol.	13.1%
RRP	$20.00

Established in 1982, this is a picture-postcard vineyard that has been subjected to much revisionism as far as plantings of varieties are concerned. Maker Robin Brockett.

Previous outstanding vintages: '90, '91, '92, '93, '94

CURRENT RELEASE 1996   A delicious wine with some Burgundian characters, but in the end it's Australia uber alles. There are cherry and truffle aromas on the nose. The palate is full-flavoured with sweet, wild cherry flavours laced with dark chocolate. The finish shows soft, toasty elements and caressing wood tannins. Further cellar age will up the complexity. At the moment it serves well with a mushroom risotto.

Seaview Cabernet Sauvignon

The magicians at Seaview have pulled another rabbit out of the hat during a difficult vintage. This wine is always great value for money.

CURRENT RELEASE 1995 Balance and poise for a few pence. The nose has strong blackberry aromas plus a hint of caramelised oak. The palate is medium- to full-bodied with blackberry and cherry flavours and a hint of toast for the oak. The wood on the finish is discreet, yet it adds structure. It's ready to flow, so pull the plug and try it with scotch eggs.

Quality	♟♟♟♟
Value	★★★★⊦
Grapes	cabernet sauvignon
Region	McLaren Vale, SA
Cellar	▮ 3
Alc./Vol.	13.0%
RRP	$12.00

Seaview Edwards & Chaffey Cabernet Sauvignon

This, along with the shiraz, is the top of the Seaview ziggurat. It's meant to be cellared at the bottom of the stack because it'll be a while before it's ready to drink – in the most delightful way. (Apologies to Mary Poppins.)

CURRENT RELEASE 1994 The wine doesn't want for colour: it's incredibly dense with red and purple hues. The nose is a mixture of berries, leaves and oak aromas. The palate is medium- to full-bodied with strong black-berry flavours mixed with vanilla. The oak adds to the tannic cacophony that directs the finish. It needs time at the moment. It can handle duck and pistachio nut sausages.

Quality	♟♟♟♟
Value	★★★★
Grapes	cabernet sauvignon
Region	McLaren Vale, SA
Cellar	➥ 2–6
Alc./Vol.	13.5%
RRP	$24.50

Seaview Edwards & Chaffey Shiraz

Quality	❦❦❦❦❦
Value	★★★★
Grapes	shiraz
Region	McLaren Vale, SA
Cellar	➟ 2–6
Alc./Vol.	13.5%
RRP	$22.00

Why buy this book, when for further information and some corporate window-dressing you can simply try http://www.seaview.com.au? But don't expect a critical assessment. Maker Mike Farmilo.

CURRENT RELEASE 1994   This wine is a convincing regional display of why you should grow shiraz in the McLaren Vale region. It has a dense colour and an attractive nose with strong vanilla and ripe plum aromas. The palate is medium- to full-bodied with strong blackberry fruit and plum flavours. There is evidence of brand-new oak on the dry finish. It needs more time. Try it with prime ox steak.

Seaview Shiraz

Quality	❦❦❦❦❦
Value	★★★★★
Grapes	shiraz
Region	McLaren Vale, SA
Cellar	3
Alc./Vol.	13.5%
RRP	$11.00 $

Wine snobs tune out: this is some of the best value for money on the market. Great stuff when you want to pocket some change.

CURRENT RELEASE 1995   Lovely grub: drinks like a dream. The nose has a waft of spice plus sweet berry aromas. The palate is open and sunny with sweet plum and raspberry fruit flavours, which are adorned by some subtle oak. The finish is soft but satisfying. Bloody good drink with a pizza and your favourite video on a Friday night.

Seppelt Great Western Shiraz

A famous label is etched in time and label purists like us are not sure what to make of the labelling changes. Like a new dog on the block, it's all about new brand managers marking their territory. Yuck! Maker Ian McKenzie.

Previous outstanding vintages: '54, '62, '67, '71, '85, '86, '88, '91

CURRENT RELEASE 1992 If this was a car it would be a Bentley. The wine is already showing the benefits of bottle-age. The colour is deep and the nose smells of ripe plums, dressed leather and seasoned oak. The palate is round and soft with sweet, mature fruit aligned with an integrated oak treatment. While it can be cellared with confidence, it drinks well now. Give it a whirl with a beef casserole.

Quality	▼▼▼▼
Value	★★★⋆
Grapes	shiraz
Region	Great Western, Vic.
Cellar	🍷 5
Alc./Vol.	13.0%
RRP	$22.00

Seppelt Terrain Series Cabernet Sauvignon

New label, more confusion. The label states, 'Great wine begins in the vineyard'. Fair enough. The label also states that the grapes were grown in various South Australian vineyards. Shouldn't it read, 'Great wine is a blend that begins in various vineyards'? Maker Ian McKenzie.

CURRENT RELEASE 1995 An agreeable style with an emphasis on varietal fruit. The colour is a deep plum-red and the palate is dominated by blackberry flavour. Well-integrated oak that doesn't intrude, but which adds soft tannins. It's a good wine for a rare T-bone steak.

Quality	▼▼▼⋆
Value	★★★⋆
Grapes	cabernet sauvignon
Region	not stated
Cellar	🍷 3
Alc./Vol.	13.0%
RRP	$10.00

Serventy Shiraz

Quality	♟♟♟♟
Value	★★★★
Grapes	shiraz
Region	Margaret River, WA
Cellar	🍷 4
Alc./Vol.	13.0%
RRP	$17.00

It's welcome to the ranks for this organic vineyard planted in the West. It was established in 1984 with 5 hectares under vine. Maker Peter Serventy.

CURRENT RELEASE 1995   A gentle basket-pressing has produced a soft, yet satisfying, wine. The colour is a sprightly garnet and the nose has perfumed fruit aromas and a waft of cinnamon. The palate is dominated by cherry and plum flavours, which are matched by fine-grained tannins on the finish. It drinks well now with a chicken and mushroom pie.

Seville Estate Cabernet Sauvignon

Quality	♟♟♟♟♟
Value	★★★★
Grapes	cabernet sauvignon
Region	Yarra Valley, Vic.
Cellar	➽ 4–10
Alc./Vol.	13.5%
RRP	$40.00

The news here is that this long-established label (by Dr McMahon) is now under the Brokenwood umbrella. Maker Peter McMahon and Iain Riggs.

CURRENT RELEASE 1995   Very convincing wine with loads of style. It's reminiscent of a young Bordeaux. The colour is dense, and the nose has blackberry, charred oak and herbal aromas. The palate is intense, with an amalgam of fruit flavours closely interlocked with charred oak. It's well balanced, albeit a tad forbidding, at the moment. Time will tell; it's a shame to drink it now.

Seville Estate Pinot Noir

Quality	♟♟♟♟♟
Value	★★★★
Grapes	pinot noir
Region	Yarra Valley, Vic.
Cellar	🍷 4
Alc./Vol.	13.0%
RRP	$28.00

Winemaker Iain Riggs is a self-confessed pinot nut, so we can expect this style to develop under his tutelage.

CURRENT RELEASE 1995   Very pleasant surprise considering the fractious nature of the vintage. The colour is a rich garnet, and the nose has cherry and strawberry aromas. The palate is substantial and complex. There are dark cherry and strawberry flavours, and these have a solid oak backup on a long, lingering finish. It drinks well with a duck risotto.

Seville Estate Shiraz

This estate was established in 1972 and there are 4 hectares under vine. Right from the outset it aimed to be the jewel in the Yarra Valley's crown.

Previous outstanding vintages: too numerous to mention

CURRENT RELEASE 1995   Lovely wine with great structure and much potential. The colour is deep, and the nose has strong berry, plum and briar aromas. The palate is intense with strong berry fruit and loads of spice. There is impressive oak integration on a lengthy finish. The grip shows the use of classy oak. It needs time, but try it now with pigeon pie.

Quality	🍷🍷🍷🍷🍷
Value	★★★★
Grapes	shiraz
Region	Yarra Valley, Vic.
Cellar	�‑ 4–10
Alc./Vol.	13.0%
RRP	$45.00

Sharefarmers Vineyard

The farmers are hardly bib-and-brace tractor drivers – they are professional people who funded this project under the supervision of Brian Croser. Although Coonawarra appears on the label, there is an ongoing dispute as to whether the vineyard will lie in the yet-to-be-established boundaries.

CURRENT RELEASE 1994   This vintage is more substantial than the last model. The nose is heady and enchanting with crushed berry aromas plus wafts of savoury wood. The palate is medium-bodied and quite complex, with blackberry as the major flavour. The finish is marked by fine-grained tannins on a dry, astringent finish. It's a good bistro style that would cope with osso bucco.

Quality	🍷🍷🍷🍷
Value	★★★★
Grapes	malbec 34%; cabernet sauvignon 31%; merlot 23%; cabernet franc 12%
Region	Coonawarra, SA
Cellar	🍾 4
Alc./Vol.	13.5%
RRP	$14.50

Shottesbrooke McLaren Vale Cabernet Sauvignon, Merlot, Malbec

Named after a parish in England that has a significance for the winemaker's family. The fruit is supplied by contract growers.

CURRENT RELEASE 1995   This is a very soft, drinkable style with the emphasis on fruit. There are some earthy, regional aromas and leafy tones on the nose. The palate has succulent fruit with hints of earthy characters. There are fine-grained tannins on an astringent finish. It's a good roast beef style.

Quality	🍷🍷🍷🍷
Value	★★★★
Grapes	cabernet sauvignon; merlot; malbec
Region	McLaren Vale, SA
Cellar	🍾 4
Alc./Vol.	13.0%
RRP	$19.00

Shottesbrooke McLaren Vale Merlot

Quality	♟♟♟♟
Value	★★★★
Grapes	merlot
Region	McLaren Vale, SA
Cellar	♟ 4
Alc./Vol.	13.0%
RRP	$18.00

This is a winemaker label; that is, it started as a private venture for a winemaker who was engaged by another company and given permission to use the facilities and buy grapes to make a wine that would be marketed separately. In this case the label was started by Nick Holmes when he was working for Ryecroft.

CURRENT RELEASE 1995   There is a strong hint of mint, which is somewhat atypical for the region. The eucalyptus/mint on the nose is followed by a slightly tart palate with tangy cherry flavours. There is clean acid and subtle tannins on the finish. It drinks well now with pumped mutton.

Skillogalee The Cabernets

Quality	♟♟♟
Value	★★★
Grapes	cabernet sauvignon; cabernet franc; malbec
Region	Clare Valley SA
Cellar	♟ 4
Alc./Vol.	12.5%
RRP	$17.50 ♟

'Skilly' or 'Skillogalee' was a type of broth or gruel that was the lot of the Irish settlers in the Clare Valley. The wines from this label are a bit above humble gruel. Maker Dave Palmer.

CURRENT RELEASE 1994   Very tough style at the moment but maybe it will blossom with time. The nose has leaf and berry aromas, and the palate is as tight as a locked door. It's as if the oak has walled away the shy fruit aromas. The finish has plenty of fine-grained tannins. Decant, shake, rattle and rev. It can be served with a sharp cheddar.

St Francis Coonawarra Cabernet Merlot

Quality	♟♟♟♟
Value	★★★⊦
Grapes	cabernet sauvignon
Region	Coonawarra, SA
Cellar	♟ 3
Alc./Vol.	12.5%
RRP	$13.90

This is a fruit import for this Southern Vales winery. It was established in 1852 and has experienced many changes of ownership since then.

CURRENT RELEASE 1995   The colour is a mid-ruby and the nose has berry aromas plus a hint of earth. The palate is medium-bodied and there are succulent fruit flavours (mainly cherry). The finish has some dry oak. It drinks well now, and a steak and kidney pie isn't out of the question.

Stanley Brothers John Hancock Shiraz

The vineyard is located near Tanunda and there are 10 hectares under various varieties of vine. Forgive us for not knowing the significance of John Hancock, but there is no clue on the label.

CURRENT RELEASE 1995 Big, deep colour and a rich, sweet nose that borders on being jammy. The palate is rich and mouthfilling with sweet plum fruit flavours, spices and a hint of alcoholic warmth. The finish has some subtle oak and drying tannins. It drinks well now and needs a rich dish like cassoulet.

Quality	🍷🍷🍷🍷½
Value	★★★
Grapes	shiraz
Region	Barossa Valley, SA
Cellar	6
Alc./Vol.	14.0%
RRP	$24.00

Stanley Brothers Thoroughbred Cabernet Sauvignon

The vineyard was originally established in 1986 as Kroemer Estate. It's now under the direction of Lindsay Stanley formerly from Anglesey Wines who also handles the winemaking chores.

CURRENT RELEASE 1994 This is an attractive middleweight with plenty of style. The colour is a mid-ruby, and the nose has ripe cherry and plum aromas with a hint of vanilla. The palate is medium-bodied with restrained raspberry and plum fruit flavours. The finish is all about American oak, which adds a touch of vanilla and caramel sweetness. It's a well-balanced style perfect for roast lamb.

Quality	🍷🍷🍷🍷
Value	★★★½
Grapes	cabernet sauvignon
Region	Barossa Valley, SA
Cellar	4
Alc./Vol.	13.0%
RRP	$20.00

Stephen John Cabernet Sauvignon

We would expect no less from a winemaker of his experience. Hopefully, with a kind bank manager who can understand the need for oak and equipment, this label will flourish.

CURRENT RELEASE 1995 A convincing style with both fruit and structure. It has a beautiful colour with a cherry- and spice-laden nose. The palate is soft and supple with dry, cherry-pip flavours and sweet fruit. Astringent tannins make for a very long and grippy finish. It needs more time, but try it now with smoked mutton.

Quality	🍷🍷🍷🍷½
Value	★★★★½
Grapes	cabernet sauvignon
Region	Clare Valley, SA
Cellar	2–6
Alc./Vol.	12.0%
RRP	$17.50

Stephen John Shiraz

Quality	♥♥♥♥
Value	★★★★
Grapes	shiraz
Region	Clare Valley, SA
Cellar	▮ 5
Alc./Vol.	13.0%
RRP	$17.50

Young Stephen (well, middle-aged Stephen) and his wife set up shop after he spent his working life with large companies. He finds the freedom of doing one's own thing 'very heady indeed'.

CURRENT RELEASE 1995   A bawling, healthy babe of a wine (not the porker kind). It has a bright crimson colour with a touch of amethyst. The nose is spicy and full of capsicums. The medium-bodied palate has rich fruit flavours – mainly plum and dark cherry – and these are measured by some fine-grained tannins on a lingering finish. It drinks well with a game dish like hare.

Stonier's Cabernet

Quality	♥♥♥♥⅛
Value	★★★★⅛
Grapes	cabernet sauvignon 85%; cabernet franc 15%
Region	Mornington Peninsula, Vic.
Cellar	▮ 6
Alc./Vol.	14.0%
RRP	$19.00

This is a curtain-raiser to the Reserve bottling, and when the dare-we-say 'cooking' version is exciting, there usually is a blockbuster to follow.

CURRENT RELEASE 1994   The nose smells like the harbinger of doom with leaf, tobacco and muted berry aromas. The palate contradicts the nose with abundant berry fruit. Blackcurrants are mingled with some exotic oak. The wood makes a classy contribution to the fine-grained tannins on the finish and there is plenty of persistent grip. It's great with squab in a reduction sauce.

Stonier's Pinot Noir

Quality	♥♥♥⅛
Value	★★★
Grapes	pinot noir
Region	Mornington Peninsula, Vic.
Cellar	▮ 3
Alc./Vol.	13.0%
RRP	$19.00

This is the great red hope for the Mornington Peninsula. The climate is right most of the time, so it boils down to winemaking interpretation of the variety.

CURRENT RELEASE 1996   The colour is a pale ruby and the nose has fresh cherry aromas and hints of strawberries. The palate is light- to medium-bodied, and there are cherry and modest wood flavours. The finish has soft tannins. It drinks well now with tripe – Italian style.

Stonier's Reserve Cabernet Sauvignon

This is the acme of the cabernets produced at this winery. It has been hand selected and given the oak equivalent of royal jelly. Maker Tod Dexter.
Previous outstanding vintages: '88, '90, '91
CURRENT RELEASE 1993   The nose is potent with strong mint, briar and red berry aromas. The palate has weight and substance. There are redcurrant and mulberry flavours which are mingled with wood spices and smoky elements. The finish has plenty of tannin and good grip. It should cellar well and become one of the more memorable reds from the region. Drink now and serve with venison sausages.

Quality	♛♛♛♛♛
Value	★★★★★
Grapes	cabernet sauvignon 85%; cabernet franc; merlot 15%
Region	Mornington Peninsula, Vic.
Cellar	▲ 5
Alc./Vol.	14.0%
RRP	$30.00

Stonier's Reserve Pinot Noir

There will come a day for the great Australian pinot noir shoot-out when the Yarra Valley, Mornington Peninsula and Adelaide Hills stage a contest to determine the best pinot in the land. MS says: 'Include me out and give me a shiraz with a beer chaser'.
CURRENT RELEASE 1995   All the elements are present for a memorable wine and it has been put together well. The colour is a medium, bright cherry-red and the nose offers sweet fruit and earthy truffle aromas. The palate is medium-bodied with wild cherry flavours and strawberry tones. The finish has well-integrated oak and complex tannins. It's a supple but steely wine that drinks well now. Try it with quail casserole.

Quality	♛♛♛♛♛
Value	★★★★
Grapes	pinot noir
Region	Mornington Peninsula, Vic.
Cellar	▲ 5
Alc./Vol.	13.0%
RRP	$28.00

Stonyfell Metala

Quality	♟♟♟♟
Value	★★★★
Grapes	shiraz
Region	Langhorne Creek, SA
Cellar	↓ 8
Alc./Vol.	13.5%
RRP	$18.50

This label is one of Australia's icons, and there is a neat symmetry in that the current winemaker, Nigel Dolan, is the son of the first winemaker Skip Dolan.
Previous outstanding vintages: too numerous to mention
CURRENT RELEASE 1994 Old-fashioned wine that really is a comfort to those who can remember. It has a deep colour and spicy nose. The palate has intense blackberry and cherry flavours, and the finish is marked by a strong tannin grip. It should cellar well. Goes well with an old-fashioned lamb roast with spuds and all the trimmings.

Strathbogie Vineyards Merlot

Quality	♟♟♟
Value	★★★
Grapes	merlot
Region	Strathbogie Ranges, Vic.
Cellar	↓ 2
Alc./Vol.	12.5%
RRP	$16.50

This small vineyard was the eighth to be established in the Strathbogie Ranges at a level above 600 metres.
CURRENT RELEASE 1994 A gentle, slightly hollow style with a nose that is a real tease. It's abundant with perfumed rose petals and ripe berries. The palate is a letdown, being a tad thin with some gentle redcurrant flavours and oak that doesn't overly intrude. It makes the wine a very drinkable pizza style.

Taltarni Cabernet Sauvignon

Quality	♟♟♟♟♟
Value	★★★★
Grapes	cabernet sauvignon 85%; cabernet franc 13%; merlot 2%
Region	Pyrenees, Vic.
Cellar	↓ 10+
Alc./Vol.	13.0%
RRP	$22.00 ↓

This is a past Penguin-Award-winner ('93 vintage). It's a good example of the labelling laws: to be labelled by a single grape variety, a wine must be at least 85% of that variety.
Previous outstanding vintages: '78, '79, '81, '82, '84, '86, '88, '90, '93
CURRENT RELEASE 1994 Typical Taltarni developed, savoury style. The colour shows some brick-red tints and the bouquet has earthy, dusty, oak-matured characters. The wine is all about secondary flavours rather than primary fruit. The taste is mellow with savoury undergrowth notes and dry tannins. A good drink now, with blanquette de veau, but has long cellaring potential.

Taltarni Merlot

Taltarni is one of several wineries selling a merlot as their top-priced red, which to us is a rather strange trend. Could it be something to do with rarity?

CURRENT RELEASE 1993   Seems to be ageing rather quickly. The colour is brick red of modest intensity, and there are savoury tobacco, earth and plum scents in the bouquet that translate into raspberry and leafy-green mint characters on the palate. There are firm tannins to close. Try Wiener schnitzel.

Quality	♀♀♀⁄
Value	★★⊦
Grapes	merlot; cabernet franc
Region	Pyrenees, Vic.
Cellar	▮ 1
Alc./Vol.	13.7%
RRP	$25.75 ▮

CURRENT RELEASE 1994   A quite similar wine to the '93 with a developed, mid-brick-red colour and a subdued, earthy, mature bouquet which has some vegetal notes. There are trademark savoury flavours and dry tannins, although the structure is quite lean and somewhat hollow. Vanilla and tannin dominate the finish. Try it with aged gruyère cheese.

Quality	♀♀♀⁄
Value	★★⊦
Grapes	merlot; cabernet franc
Region	Pyrenees, Vic.
Cellar	▮ 2
Alc./Vol.	13.3%
RRP	$25.75 ▮

Taltarni Merlot Cabernet

Merlot is all the rage, and the rush to get its name on a label is reminiscent of the early days of chardonnay. Makers Greg Gallagher and Dominique Portet.

CURRENT RELEASE 1994   This wine is built around oak, with a rich, earthy, chocolatey wood-linked bouquet and some attractive sweetness among the oak and tannin. The palate is slightly hollow but also lean, lively and smooth – made to be drunk young. Serve with osso bucco.

Quality	♀♀♀⁄
Value	★★★
Grapes	merlot; cabernet sauvignon
Region	Pyrenees, Vic.
Cellar	▮ 5+
Alc./Vol.	13.2%
RRP	$17.70 ▮

Taltarni Reserve des Pyrenees

The Taltarni vineyard is the biggest in the Avoca/Moonambel district, known as the Pyrenees. This is their budget-priced, everyday red.

CURRENT RELEASE 1995   Very typical Taltarni style, smelling woody, earthy, with a lot of maturation effect on the nose, and a dry, savoury taste ending with a pronounced tannin grip. Very good depth and intensity at the price. Serve with osso bucco.

Quality	♀♀♀⁄
Value	★★★★
Grapes	cabernet sauvignon; merlot
Region	Pyrenees, Vic.
Cellar	▮ 4
Alc./Vol.	12.2%
RRP	$12.00

Tapestry McLaren Vale Cabernet Sauvignon

Quality	🍷🍷🍷🍷
Value	★★★★
Grapes	cabernet sauvignon
Region	McLaren Vale, SA
Cellar	🍾 6
Alc./Vol.	13.5%
RRP	$15.00

Expect big things from this label: it's the product of a very experienced winemaker from a very reliable vineyard. Maker Brian Light.

CURRENT RELEASE 1994 Still on the young side and very varietal in make-up. The nose has cassis and blackberry aromas, and herbaceous touches. The palate is full of sweet, succulent berries with blackcurrant being the major flavour, and there are fine-grained tannins on a long finish. It should cellar well. Try it now with oxtail stew.

Tapestry McLaren Vale Shiraz

Quality	🍷🍷🍷🍷
Value	★★★★
Grapes	shiraz
Region	McLaren Vale, SA
Cellar	🍾 5
Alc./Vol.	13.5%
RRP	$15.00

This label and Merrivale are almost one and the same. The former was minted when Brian Light worked for Normans.

CURRENT RELEASE 1995 Great colour: deep and vibrant with an equally obvious nose. There is a forceful aroma of ripe plums and spices. The palate is a regional blueprint with intense plum fruit and loads of complex spice. The oak fits well, making for a very drinkable style. Try it with cheddar.

Tarrawarra Pinot Noir

Quality	🍷🍷🍷🍷
Value	★★★
Grapes	pinot noir
Region	Yarra Valley, Vic.
Cellar	🍾 5
Alc./Vol.	13.5%
RRP	$31.40

The Yarra Valley has quickly established itself as one of the leading pinot noir regions in the country. Fastidious producers such as Tarrawarra are in the vanguard. Maker Mike Kluczko.

Previous outstanding vintages: '88, '90, '91, '92, '94

CURRENT RELEASE 1995 An impressive wine, although not quite up to the lovely '94. Sweet vanilla, coconut and cherry aromas, and a tightly wound, firmly structured palate that packs an unusually large tannin wallop, which unbalances it a trifle. A pinot built to age? Serve with Peking duck.

Tatachilla Cabernet Sauvignon

Tatachilla retains the services of expatriate Aussie Daryl Groom as a consultant. Groom is now one of the most successful winemakers in the United States.
Previous outstanding vintages: '94
CURRENT RELEASE 1995 A stylish wine, although the dominant flavours in its youth are spices and white pepper, as though a small percentage of aromatic shiraz has been thrown in. It's lively and fresh with stacks of berry fruit and a generous complement of oak. Needs time for the pieces to fall into place. Then serve with Thai beef salad.

Quality	🍷🍷🍷🍷½
Value	★★★★
Grapes	cabernet sauvignon
Region	McLaren Vale, SA
Cellar	1–8+
Alc./Vol.	14.0%
RRP	$17.60

Tatachilla Clarendon Vineyard Merlot

It's interesting that some of the best merlots are now coming out of McLaren Vale; we might have expected the cooler regions to have sewn up this area of the market. Maker Michael Fragos.
CURRENT RELEASE 1995 The nose is a riot of sweet blackcurrants overlaid with cloves and other spices. This is an intense, vibrant red wine with stacks of fruit, and one that could easily be mistaken for a cabernet. Smooth, supple palate and drinks very well in its youth. Try it with stirfry.

Quality	🍷🍷🍷🍷½
Value	★★★★
Grapes	merlot
Region	McLaren Vale, SA
Cellar	5+
Alc./Vol.	13.0%
RRP	$17.60

Tatachilla Keystone Grenache Shiraz

Made from dry-grown McLaren Vale vines, this style is Australia's answer to Chateauneuf-du-Pape. Maker Michael Fragos.
CURRENT RELEASE 1996 The colour is deep and full of promise. The floral, raspberry-like aroma of young grenache is here in force, and the shiraz puts in a spicy element. The gutsy palate has a slight bitterness and it would benefit from a year in the cellar. Then serve with game.

Quality	🍷🍷🍷🍷
Value	★★★★
Grapes	grenache; shiraz
Region	McLaren Vale, SA
Cellar	1–5+
Alc./Vol.	14.0%
RRP	$15.30

Taylors Cabernet Sauvignon

Quality	♟♟♟♟
Value	★★★★★
Grapes	cabernet sauvignon
Region	Clare Valley, SA
Cellar	🍾 10
Alc./Vol.	14.0%
RRP	$16.00 ⑤ 🍾

It amazes us how keen some retailers are to give away profit. One high-profile Sydney retailer was discounting this for $9.99. But it doesn't need to be slashed to sell. CURRENT RELEASE 1994   A top vintage in Clare makes this even better value than usual. Taylors cab is among the six best-selling bottled red wines in Australia. Smoky, earthy, toasty, developing flavours; some beef stock and redcurrants. Rich, high-extract palate; solid and fleshy with slightly rough tannins. A big, friendly lump of a wine to serve with steak and kidney pie.

Quality	♟♟♟
Value	★★★
Grapes	cabernet sauvignon
Region	Clare Valley, SA
Cellar	🍾 3
Alc./Vol.	13.0%
RRP	$16.00 ⑤

CURRENT RELEASE 1995   Grab the '94 while you can: this isn't nearly as good. The colour is fairly weak and the bouquet lacks freshness. The somewhat dull flavour falls away towards a dry finish. Take it to a very smoky barbecue.

Taylors Pinot Noir

Quality	♟♟♟
Value	★★★
Grapes	pinot noir
Region	Clare Valley, SA
Cellar	🍾 2
Alc./Vol.	12.5%
RRP	$16.00 ⑤

Clare is not an easy place to produce fine pinot noir. The best that can be hoped for is a decent medium-bodied dry red of indeterminate personality. CURRENT RELEASE 1996   The colour is medium–light purple–red; the nose opens with stalky/herbal green notes and airs to reveal some cherry and strawberry. The palate is quite lightweight and angular, with some herbal flavours that turn slightly bitter on the finish. Oak vanillin lingers. Serve with spicy sausages.

Thomas Mitchell Triple Blend

Named after the explorer Major Mitchell, who crossed the Murray River near Mitchelton. In less PC times, the label used to show him shooting Aborigines.
CURRENT RELEASE 1995 A respectable cheapie without setting the world on fire. It has some meaty aromas and traces of older wood and earthiness among the cherry fruit, and the palate has decent flavour and balance. Very drinkable at the price, and goes with meatballs.

Quality	❡❡❡
Value	★★★
Grapes	cabernet sauvignon; shiraz; cabernet franc
Region	not stated
Cellar	▮ 2
Alc./Vol.	12.8%
RRP	$12.50 Ⓢ

Tim Adams Shiraz

Adams' is one of the newer labels in Clare. He's proved himself a reliable maker of traditional gutsy Clare reds, and he's generous enough to name his grapegrowers on the back labels.
Previous outstanding vintages: '88, '90, '92, '94
CURRENT RELEASE 1995 A worthy follow-up to last year's crackerjack '94. Somewhat sappy on the nose, with herbal and minty wintergreen aromas. The palate starts off nice and sweet, with richer, riper flavour than the nose indicates, and winds up with a definite finish and long follow-through. Try it with game pie.

Quality	❡❡❡❡
Value	★★★★
Grapes	shiraz
Region	Clare Valley, SA
Cellar	▮ 10
Alc./Vol.	13.0%
RRP	$16.00 ▮

Tim Adams The Aberfeldy

The Aberfeldy is a vineyard planted in 1904 with a solid history for producing the goods.
CURRENT RELEASE 1995 Tim has turned down the mint and balanced the fruit on the nose. The colour is a voluptuous dark cherry, and the nose has a wood component as well as the afore-mentioned mint. The palate is full-bodied with ripe raspberry and blackberry flavours, and there is some grippy oak on the long finish. It should be cellared long and hard, but try it now with kangaroo and field mushroom sauce if you wish.

Quality	❡❡❡❡❡
Value	★★★★★
Grapes	shiraz
Region	Clare Valley, SA
Cellar	➟ 3–8
Alc./Vol.	14.0%
RRP	$34.00 ▮

Tim Adams The Fergus

Quality	?????
Value	★★★★✦
Grapes	mainly grenache, with cabernet sauvignon; cabernet franc; shiraz; malbec
Region	Clare Valley, SA
Cellar	▯ 6
Alc./Vol.	14.0%
RRP	$14.50

The grapes were grown by Ferg and Vyv Mahon, begorrah. Tim Adams has always been very fair to acknowledge his grapegrowers on his back-labels.
Previous outstanding vintages: '94, '95
CURRENT RELEASE 1996 A lovely rich, joyous bundle of flavour, perfumed with peppermint and filled with youthfully aggressive, but smooth and rich fruit-dominant, flavour. Ends with a soft tannin finish. A very complete wine, with more depth and style than the average grenache. Try it with herbed saltbush mutton.

Tisdall Mount Helen Cabernet Merlot

Quality	????
Value	★★✦
Grapes	cabernet sauvignon; merlot
Region	Strathbogie Ranges, Vic.
Cellar	▯ 5
Alc./Vol.	13.0%
RRP	$22.00 Ⓢ ▯

Mount Helen was the first major vineyard in the high altitudes of the Strathbogie Ranges, near Victoria's Goulburn Valley. Maker Toni Stockhausen.
CURRENT RELEASE 1994 This needs air to show its best, so decant first. Full purple–red colour and slightly muffled cabernet varietal character. Lean but clean in the mouth with dark berry flavours that grew in the glass. A decent red, but not what we expected at the price. Try it with oxtail stew.

Tisdall Mount Ida Shiraz

This is part of the labyrinth that is the Mildara Blass group. It's something of a sleeper that should not be overlooked. The original owner of the vineyard was the artist Leonard French. Maker Toni Stockhausen.

Previous outstanding vintages: '91, '92

CURRENT RELEASE 1994 Typical of the district, displaying outstanding colour and strength of flavour. The nose has strong berry, cinnamon and plum aromas. The palate is full and rich with concentrated fruit flavours that are matched by swashbuckling tannins on the assertive finish. It has plenty of brio, and cellaring will add to the complexity. It's great with both sides of the national emblem: emu and kangaroo.

Quality	▼▼▼▼?
Value	★★★★+
Grapes	shiraz
Region	Heathcote, Vic.
Cellar	⊸ 2–8
Alc./Vol.	13.5%
RRP	$21.00 Ⓢ

Tollana Show Reserve Shiraz

This is a true show reserve: with a trophy and three gold medals under its belt it can afford to be more expensive than the standard Tollana shiraz.

CURRENT RELEASE 1993 The complex toasty, oaky bouquet is very Southcorp. It has a deep blackish-red colour, abundant sweet, ripe plum and cherry flavours, and a smooth, open structure. Quite delicious flavour, verging on jammy and unashamedly cuddly. Serve with lamb shanks.

Quality	▼▼▼▼?
Value	★★★+
Grapes	shiraz
Region	Eden Valley, SA
Cellar	▮ 4+
Alc./Vol.	13.0%
RRP	$20.40 Ⓢ ▮

Tollana TR 222 Cabernet Sauvignon

Quality	?????
Value	★★★★
Grapes	cabernet sauvignon
Region	Eden Valley, SA
Cellar	▮ 7
Alc./Vol.	13.0%
RRP	$18.00 Ⓢ

Tollana started life as the wine brand of distillers Tolley, Scott & Tolley in the days when brandy was more lucrative than table wine. Maker Neville Falkenberg.

Previous outstanding vintages: '82, '84, '87, '88 '90, '91, '92, '93

CURRENT RELEASE 1994   Here's a red with oodles of character. There's a stack of blackberry, mint, leafy and cassis aromas, and even some jammy overripe notes. In the mouth there is very generous fruit coupled with some aromatic oak, ending with subtle but positive tannin. Great with grilled lamb chops.

Trentham Estate Cabernet Merlot

Quality	????
Value	★★★★
Grapes	cabernet sauvignon; merlot
Region	Murray Valley, NSW
Cellar	▮ 3+
Alc./Vol.	13.5%
RRP	$12.90

Trentham wines are very keenly priced, thanks to the misconception that the Riverlands only grow cask-quality wine.

CURRENT RELEASE 1995   Fragrant, sweet, cabernet blackberry and raspberry-jam flavours are soft and easy on the gums. There's a twist of green-tinged merlot on the afterpalate, and the oak is nicely underplayed. Good drinking now, with lamb satays.

Trentham Estate Merlot

Quality	???
Value	★★★
Grapes	merlot
Region	Murray Valley, NSW
Cellar	▮ 3
Alc./Vol.	13.5%
RRP	$12.90

Trentham is the substantial Murphy family vineyard near Mildura, across the water from Lindemans Karadoc. Winemaker Tony Murphy did his hard yards with Mildara at Merbein.

CURRENT RELEASE 1995   High-toned oak and youthful raspberry fruit aromas, the oak lending vanilla and caramel shades. There is some acid hardness on the palate, but the acid certainly gives it life and intensity. Needs food: try it with rissoles.

Trentham Estate Shiraz

Old, low-vigour 45-year-old vines, sparing irrigation and careful winemaking enable the Murphys to make a consistently fine shiraz in an area that's noted for very ordinary shiraz.

Previous outstanding vintages: '91, '93, '94

CURRENT RELEASE 1995 Promising dark red colour, rich flavours with chocolate and vanilla to the fore, some varietal spice and fleshy, dark-chocolate afterpalate flavours. Fleshy, well-textured wine. Some licorice along with plentiful tannin on the finish. A triumph! Serve with saltbush mutton.

Quality	▼▼▼▼
Value	★★★★
Grapes	shiraz
Region	Murray Valley, NSW
Cellar	▐ 4+
Alc./Vol.	14.0%
RRP	$14.50

Twin Valley Estate Shiraz

There is life in the old cellars yet. This winery is enjoying new management and the development of a new label.

CURRENT RELEASE 1994 Big and brawny but not totally without finesse. The colour is a deep red, and the nose has ripe plum, pepper and spice aromas. The palate has dark cherry and stewed plum flavours. Oak takes a secondary role to the fruit, and there are some chewy tannins and a warmth of alcohol on the finish. It's a decent osso bucco style.

Quality	▼▼▼▼
Value	★★★
Grapes	shiraz
Region	Barossa Valley, SA
Cellar	▐ 3
Alc./Vol.	14.8%
RRP	$19.50

Twin Valley QC Cabernet Merlot

Not, as the QC suggests, from courtroom to you, but rather self-proclaimed 'quality and consistency' at the cellar door.

CURRENT RELEASE 1993 The colour remains youthful and the nose is starting to show the action of bottle-age. There are mellow fruit and wood smells. The middle-weight palate has sweet cherry and raspberry fruit flavours. The oak is passive, adding support but not much tannin. It's a good casserole style.

Quality	▼▼▼
Value	★★★
Grapes	cabernet sauvignon; merlot
Region	Barossa Valley, SA
Cellar	▐ 2
Alc./Vol.	12.0%
RRP	$16.00

Tyrrell's Old Winery Pinot Noir

Quality	♟♟♟
Value	★★★
Grapes	pinot noir
Region	Hunter Valley, NSW; McLaren Vale & Barossa, SA
Cellar	🍷 2
Alc./Vol.	13.0%
RRP	$14.50 ⑤

Bruce Tyrrell is the fourth generation of his family to run this successful family-owned wine company. Maker Andrew Spinaze.
CURRENT RELEASE 1996   Quite a pale colour, and the nose is subdued. There is a little gas on the palate, together with plum, earth and cherry flavours. It's a plainer, lighter style which offers decent value at the price. Suits dips, such as taramasalata.

Tyrrell's Old Winery Shiraz

Quality	♟♟♟♟
Value	★★★★
Grapes	shiraz
Region	McLaren Vale, SA 50%; Coonawarra, SA 13%; Hunter Valley, NSW 37%
Cellar	🍷 5
Alc./Vol.	13.0%
RRP	$14.50 ⑤

Like so many products emanating from the Hunter, this was once all Hunter grapes, but is now an eclectic blend. It's aged in older barrels to emphasise fruit. Maker Andrew Thomas.
Previous outstanding vintages: '88, '91
CURRENT RELEASE 1995   A savoury style filled with earth, spice, dried herb and eucalypt/mint flavours. A good honest wine with a pleasingly dry finish and a refreshing lack of overt wood character. Serve with braised beef.

Tyrrell's Vat 9 Shiraz Aged Release

Quality	♟♟♟♟
Value	★★★
Grapes	shiraz
Region	Hunter Valley, NSW
Cellar	🍷 5+
Alc./Vol.	13.0%
RRP	$32.20 🍷

Vat 9 is based on the same old vines (planted 1879 and 1892) at Tyrrell's Ashmans vineyard near the winery every year. At less than four years old, this hardly qualifies as an aged release, but '93 will probably not be an especially long-living year.
Previous outstanding vintages: '79, '80, '81, '83, '85, '87, '90, '91, '92
CURRENT RELEASE 1993   Medium brick-red colour is showing some age, and the bouquet is earthy/dusty, slightly herbal and chestnutty. At best medium-bodied, it has dry, savoury, mellow Hunter flavour and a gentle finish. Try it with aged gruyère.

Vasse Felix Cabernet Merlot Classic Dry Red

The wording on the label is changing – could this mean they are doing away with the tired old Classic Dry Red nomenclature? We hope so.

CURRENT RELEASE 1995   This is Vasse's lighter, early-drinking red, but it's still a very credible wine. It has a slightly leafy, tobacco-like nose, bordering on mulberry. There is good depth of flavour and a nice touch of oak. The finish has some tannin and spine. Would go with a designer hamburger.

Quality	❛❛❛❛
Value	★★★❭
Grapes	cabernet sauvignon; merlot
Region	Margaret River, WA
Cellar	❘ 5
Alc./Vol.	13.6%
RRP	$17.50

Vasse Felix Cabernet Sauvignon

Why the falcon on the label? Founder Tom Cullity tried to train birds of prey to keep the little birds off his grapes – a major problem in the district.
Previous outstanding vintages: '85, '88, '90, '91, '94
CURRENT RELEASE 1995   A very fine wine displaying serious fruit concentration, plenty of weight, structure and tannin grip. There is sweet fruit on the palate but it's not a particularly fruity style. Classic Margaret River cabernet and should go the distance. Food: barbecued lamb.

Quality	❛❛❛❛❜
Value	★★★★
Grapes	cabernet sauvignon
Region	Margaret River, WA
Cellar	➙ 2–8+
Alc./Vol.	13.9%
RRP	$26.50 ❚

Vasse Felix Shiraz

At the winery, they impose a six-bottles-per-customer limit on this wine for the short period in which it's available. Maker Clive Otto.
Previous outstanding vintages: '83, '87, '88, '90, '91, '93, '94
CURRENT RELEASE 1995   Upturn the piggy bank and give it a shake: this is a must for your cellar! It's a sublime red of a kind all too rare in Margaret River. Powerful, rich, opulent flavour, masses of sweet plummy fruit that caress the palate. It's also well structured and will cellar superbly. Serve with seared kangaroo backstraps.

Quality	❛❛❛❛❛
Value	★★★★❭
Grapes	shiraz
Region	Margaret River, WA
Cellar	➙ 2–10+
Alc./Vol.	13.4%
RRP	$30.00 ❚

Virgin Hills

Quality	♟♟♟♟♟
Value	★★★╿
Grapes	cabernet sauvignon; shiraz; malbec; merlot
Region	Macedon, Vic.
Cellar	➥ 3–10+
Alc./Vol.	11.5%
RRP	$33.00

This small, cold-climate vineyard produces just one wine each year. Established in the early '70s, it acquired almost mythical status in the '80s. Maker (until 1996) Mark Sheppard.

Previous outstanding vintages: '74, '75, '76, '82, '85, '88, '91, '92

CURRENT RELEASE 1994   Always austere, tightly structured, fine-boned – even delicate – in youth. It's hard to judge, but the '94 looks like developing into a classic. The colour is not especially deep; the nose has some green-leafy and rhubarb characters, but also rose petals and a strange charm. The palate is lean and narrow (but not hollow); fine and very long. Cellar, then serve with cheese.

Water Wheel Cabernet Sauvignon

Quality	♟♟♟♟
Value	★★★★╿
Grapes	cabernet sauvignon
Region	Bendigo, Vic.
Cellar	♟ 6
Alc./Vol.	13.0%
RRP	$15.00 ▮

The Cumming family own Water Wheel and grow a veritable cornucopia of fruit. They are a breath of fresh air because of their inquiring minds that focus on growing techniques. They are the consummate farmers – that's high praise rather than a put-down. Maker Peter Cumming.

Previous outstanding vintages: '90, '91, '92, '94

CURRENT RELEASE 1995   Good effort for a supposedly duff vintage. It's a deep, dark style with plenty of concentration. The nose has cherry and spice aromas. Black cherry is the major flavour on the palate. The finish is tannic (as in black tea), and there is marked astringency. It may well throw a crust, so start decanting now. It's great with aged ox steaks.

Water Wheel Shiraz

A Bendigo beauty and made by one of the great lateral thinkers in the wine industry. The Cumming family are green thumbs in all types of growing endeavours, including tomatoes and cherries. What is really refreshing is their giant strides towards quality and an understanding of value for money. Maker Peter Cumming.

CURRENT RELEASE 1995 This is the first year the wine has been matured in seasoned American oak. The result is a very drinkable drop. The nose is a mixture of cherry and smoky wood aromas. The palate has a medium body with some spicy cherry flavours, which are matched by the oak on a dry finish. It needs a dish like osso bucco so it can really shine.

Quality	♥♥♥♥
Value	★★★★
Grapes	shiraz
Region	Bendigo, Vic.
Cellar	🍾 5
Alc./Vol.	13.0%
RRP	$14.40

Wetherall Cabernet Sauvignon

The Wetherall family has been growing fruit in the district for over 30 years, so the label is something of an afterthought. Maker Michael Wetherall.

CURRENT RELEASE 1995 A great effort from a less-than-bounteous vintage. The colour is a deep mulberry stain. The nose has berry and elegant oak aromas. The palate offers a medium body with blackberry fruit flavours. There are touches of vanilla and toasty wood to add to the complexity. The finish is quite firm. Try it with roast beef and Yorkshire pud.

Quality	♥♥♥♥
Value	★★★★
Grapes	cabernet sauvignon
Region	Coonawarra, SA
Cellar	🍾 5
Alc./Vol.	12.8%
RRP	$19.00

Wetherall Shiraz

Although the vineyards are long established, the winery and label date back to 1991. There are 35 hectares under vine.

CURRENT RELEASE 1993 The wine is on the cusp of bottle development. The colour is a youthful, deep ruby and the nose has some macerated plum aromas plus hints of wood. The medium-bodied palate is rich with sweet, ripe plum flavours, and there is plenty of grip on the astringent finish. It needs more time. Try it with oxtail stew.

Quality	♥♥♥♥
Value	★★★★
Grapes	shiraz
Region	Coonawarra, SA
Cellar	🍾 4
Alc./Vol.	12.5%
RRP	$18.00

Wendouree Cabernet Malbec

Quality	❦❦❦❦❦
Value	★★★★
Grapes	cabernet sauvignon; malbec
Region	Clare Valley, SA
Cellar	➤ 10–20+
Alc./Vol.	13.3%
RRP	$24.00 (cellar door)

Wendouree was the first winery in Clare to make a cabernet malbec. Leasingham followed suit in the '60s and, more recently, so have several others.
Previous outstanding vintages: '83, '86, '89, '90, '91, '92, '93, '94
CURRENT RELEASE 1995 This is one of the biggest Wendourees we can recall; it's simply massive. Penfolds would give their eyeteeth for fruit like this. The colour is very dark, the nose youthful and typically fruit-driven with blackcurranty, crushed-leaf cabernet and slightly stalky hints from malbec. The palate reflects the same fruit concentration and vibrancy, and chimes in with an extraordinary tannin grip – all of it natural. Any tougher and it would rust. Cellar, then serve with game meats.

Wendouree Cabernet Sauvignon

Quality	❦❦❦❦❦
Value	★★★★
Grapes	cabernet sauvignon
Region	Clare Valley, SA
Cellar	➤ 5–15+
Alc./Vol.	12.9%
RRP	$24.00 (cellar door)

This is an extraordinarily good wine, and being straight cabernet, winemaker Tony Brady and his consultant Steve George are these days using some new oak – but only a kiss.
Previous outstanding vintages: '83, '86, '89, '90, '91, '92, '93, '94
CURRENT RELEASE 1995 Majestic stuff indeed. Marvellously ripe, sweet blackberry/blackcurrant and faintly herby aromas, together with a touch of cedary oak – but understated. In the mouth it offers a lovely, rich, power-packed, full-blooded burst of flavour with masses of tannin, but in superb balance. Ripeness, concentration, length. It has stacks of everything but preserves a wonderful harmony. Cellar, then serve with aged cheeses.

Wendouree Shiraz

The straight shiraz is traditionally one of the most power-packed Wendouree reds. It's made from tiny yields of grapes off vines planted in 1919 on red loam over limestone.

Previous outstanding vintages: '90, '91, '92, '93

CURRENT RELEASE 1994 This is a monster and not really ready to approach. It has iron tonic and licorice characters, and is still a little closed up. The palate is very big and has a firm tannic grip. Oak is understated. A wine for heroes, which should be locked up in a safe place. Then serve with braised venison.

Quality	ΨΨΨΨΨ
Value	★★★★★
Grapes	shiraz
Region	Clare Valley, SA
Cellar	➙ 3–15+
Alc./Vol.	13.3%
RRP	$20.00 (cellar door)

CURRENT RELEASE 1995 This centenary vintage has yielded another crackerjack Wendouree shiraz. Sweet, classy blackberry aromas; ripe and gamy, not at all oaky. Palate is solid, full-bodied and tannic with an ironstone quality. Not ready for five years, then serve with hard cheeses.

Quality	ΨΨΨΨΨ
Value	★★★★ʕ
Grapes	shiraz
Region	Clare Valley, SA
Cellar	➙ 5–15+
Alc./Vol.	13.5%
RRP	$24.00 (cellar door)

Wendouree Shiraz Mataro

These days most trendy winemakers are calling mataro by its French handle, mourvèdre. But at Wendouree, few things ever change.

CURRENT RELEASE 1994 This is the drink-now Wendouree! A succulent young red, beautifully balanced and jam-packed with ripe plum, dark berry and spicy flavours. The nose shows marvellous complexity without any obvious oak character. It's typically full-bodied, but not at all overwrought or astringently tannic. Try it with pan-fried veal cutlets. ►

Quality	ΨΨΨΨΨ
Value	★★★★★
Grapes	shiraz; mataro
Region	Clare Valley, SA
Cellar	▮ 10
Alc./Vol.	12.8%
RRP	$18.00 (cellar door)

Quality	♟♟♟♟?
Value	★★★★
Grapes	shiraz; mataro
Region	Clare Valley, SA
Cellar	➥ 2–10+
Alc./Vol.	13.5%
RRP	$20.00 (cellar door) 🍾

CURRENT RELEASE 1995   This is a marvellous and relatively approachable Wendouree. It has the customary dense, dark colour, and concentration shows in every way. The nose is spicy with some meaty undercurrents. It's sweet and rich in the mouth with ripe but assertive tannins, and would be better served with some cellar time. Try it with cheddar.

West End Three Bridges Cabernet Sauvignon

Quality	♟♟♟♟
Value	★★★
Grapes	cabernet sauvignon
Region	Griffith, NSW
Cellar	🍷 4
Alc./Vol.	12.5%
RRP	$19.90

This is a premium label from the West End Winery. The winery was established in 1948 and this is their first foray into the premium area of the market. Maker William Calabria.

CURRENT RELEASE 1995   A very elegant and complex style that could be mistaken for a cool-climate wine. The nose has cassis and leaf aromas. The medium-bodied palate has blackberry flavours with hints of coffee and chocolate. There is plenty of fine-grained tannin on the finish, which supplies considerable grip. It would go well with kangaroo fillet.

Williams Rest Granite Flats Red

Quality	♟♟♟
Value	★★★
Grapes	not stated
Region	Mount Barker, WA
Cellar	🍷 2
Alc./Vol.	13.0%
RRP	$14.00

If our homework is correct (there is confusion between our reference sources) this is a new label from a vineyard of 4 hectares that was established in 1992. Crook label! CURRENT RELEASE 1996   The colour is a bright garnet and the nose has sweet berry aromas with a tinge of crushed leaf. The palate is light- to medium-bodied, and unyielding as far as fruit is concerned. There is a slight stalky character to the finish. It drinks now with a meat pie.

Willow Bend Shiraz Cabernet Merlot

This label was established in 1990 near Lyndoch in the Barossa Valley. It also has connections with the Forreston Vineyard in the Adelaide Hills. Maker Wayne Dutschke.

CURRENT RELEASE 1993 This is a very drinkable wine that has a degree of complexity. The nose offers blackberry and mulberry fruit aromas on a floral background. Berries dominate the palate and there is some attractive spice. The finish is dry with lingering tannins. It's a medium-bodied style that would go well with a veal casserole.

Quality	♥♥♥♡
Value	★★★ᚴ
Grapes	shiraz; cabernet sauvignon; merlot; cabernet franc
Region	Barossa Valley & Adelaide Hills, SA
Cellar	▮ 3
Alc./Vol.	13.5%
RRP	$14.95

Winstead Pinot Noir

Yet another new player from Tasmania that is adding to the swelling ranks of small vineyards from the Apple Isle.

CURRENT RELEASE 1995 There is more varietal character than in most. The nose is sappy with a background of cherries. The palate is medium-bodied with sweet, dark cherry flavour and there are some vegetal characters. The oak on the finish is soft and supportive. The waft of spice makes it fine with tandoori lamb.

Quality	♥♥♥♡
Value	★★★
Grapes	pinot noir
Region	Tasmania
Cellar	▮ 3
Alc./Vol.	12.9%
RRP	$22.50

Wirra Wirra Original Blend

Although it's billed as an 'original blend' this grenache shiraz has a new-age feel to its make-up. Clearly modern techniques have tamed tradition a tad.

CURRENT RELEASE 1996 A very drinkable wine that has plenty of fruit flavour and a warmth of alcohol. The nose has ripe raspberry fruit aromas. The palate is succulent with juicy raspberry flavours. It's a middleweight, and although the fruit is sweet it doesn't clog the palate. There is some discreet tannin on a gentle finish. It drinks well now with braised steak.

Quality	♥♥♥♥
Value	★★★ᚴ
Grapes	grenache 60%; shiraz 40%
Region	McLaren Vale, SA
Cellar	▮ 3
Alc./Vol.	14.5%
RRP	$18.00

Wolf Blass Bilyara Shiraz Grenache

Quality	♟♟♟៕
Value	★★★★
Grapes	shiraz; grenache
Region	not stated
Cellar	🍾 1
Alc./Vol.	13.0%
RRP	$11.00 Ⓢ

Grenache has become a fashion statement and in the process it's been transformed from a rusty tricycle into a Ferrari. But let's not get carried away: it's a good flavour, but it's not a classic.

CURRENT RELEASE 1996   Drink, don't think. There is plenty of berry flavour here. The colour is mid-ruby and the nose is bursting with berry smells. The palate is dominated by raspberry and bramble berry flavours. The finish is ever so gentle, making it a drink-now style. Dial a pizza and pull the cork.

Wolf Blass Black Label Cabernet Shiraz

Quality	♟♟♟៕
Value	★★
Grapes	cabernet sauvignon; shiraz
Region	Eden Valley, SA 90%; Langhorne Creek, SA 10%
Cellar	➥ 2–8+
Alc./Vol.	13.0%
RRP	$95.00 🍷

A controversial release this year: the price flew off the planet, the label was changed (for the worse) and the style is a bit of an aberration. It's based heavily on Eden Valley for a change. We liked the style, price and look of the '92 much better!

Previous outstanding vintages: '73, '74, '75, '78, '80, '82, '83, '84, '86, '87, '89, '91, '92

CURRENT RELEASE 1993   This 21st vintage of Black Label is a puzzle: it's enormously oaky and leaner than usual. There are red-berry flavours beneath the dominant wood flavour and woody tannins, and there is modest length to the palate. Perhaps time will bring the loose ends together?

Wolf Blass Brown Label Classic Shiraz

Quality	♟♟♟♟៕
Value	★★★★
Grapes	shiraz
Region	Eden Valley, McLaren Vale, Barossa Valley & Clare Valley, SA
Cellar	🍾 8
Alc./Vol.	13.0%
RRP	$25.00 Ⓢ 🍷

The force behind the Blass red-winemaking legend is John Glaetzer, and his ongoing presence at Bilyara is one of the keys to the consistency of style over the years.

Previous outstanding vintages: '83, '87, '90, '91, '92, '93

CURRENT RELEASE 1994   You could never accuse this of being a simple fruity style! It's a cleverly oak-infused red with a bouquet laden with forest-floor, earthy and dried-herb characters, and the mouth is dry and very savoury. As it airs, the mid-palate reveals some sweet fruit depths and spice towards the finish. Try it with a hamburger with the lot.

Wolf Blass Grey Label Cabernet Sauvignon

In the Blass lexicon the grey label was the original flagship. It preceded the black label, which was minted after Herr Blass won his first Jimmy Watson Memorial Trophy.

Previous outstanding vintages: '81, '84, '85, '88, '90, '93

CURRENT RELEASE 1993 There is a photo finish here between the wood and the fruit. The nose has strong berry aromas plus coconut oak and toasty wood. The palate is medium-bodied with cherry and blackberry flavours, and the finish is marked by vanilla, caramel and coconut oak. Typical of the Blass style, it drinks well now and is great fun with veal shanks in a reduction sauce.

Quality	♈♈♈♈♉
Value	★★★★
Grapes	cabernet sauvignon
Region	various, SA
Cellar	▯ 5
Alc./Vol.	13.0%
RRP	$32.00

CURRENT RELEASE 1994 The customary gumleaf Langhorne Creek regional character is quite green-leafy in this edition. It's not a very complex wine, but the palate has pleasing richness, smoothness, balance and quality. It could be drunk now, with beef satays.

Quality	♈♈♈♈
Value	★★☆
Grapes	cabernet sauvignon
Region	Langhorne Creek, SA
Cellar	▯ 5
Alc./Vol.	13.0%
RRP	$32.00 ⑤ ▮

Wolf Blass Pinot Noir

HIMMEL! Say it ain't so Joe . . . and all that. Herr Blass is on record as saying he would not have any truck with this grape variety. Mind you, he also said that about chardonnay and sparkling wine.

CURRENT RELEASE 1996 There can be no denying this is pinot noir. The nose has some ripe fruit aromas plus a hint of wood. It's a soft and drinkable style with a predominant ripe plum and cherry flavour, and the finish offers soft oak. It drinks well with chargrilled tuna.

Quality	♈♈♈
Value	★★★
Grapes	pinot noir
Region	Clare Valley, SA; Central Victoria; Padthaway SA
Cellar	▯ 3
Alc./Vol.	12.0%
RRP	$12.00

Woodstock Cabernet Sauvignon

Quality	▼▼▼▼
Value	★★★★
Grapes	cabernet sauvignon
Region	McLaren Vale, SA
Cellar	▮ 4
Alc./Vol.	12.5%
RRP	$15.00

This variety is the apple of this winemaker's eye. He likes to build them wines with boldness and precision.

CURRENT RELEASE 1995   While not exactly a shrinking violet this is a demure wine by Woodstock standards. The nose has berry, capsicum and spice aromas. The palate is full of sweet redcurrant fruit flavours, and these are matched by some black-tea-like tannins on a finish that displays gentle grip. It's a very good foil for tandoori lamb.

Woodstock Grenache

Quality	▼▼▼▼
Value	★★★★
Grapes	grenache
Region	McLaren Vale, SA
Cellar	▮ 3
Alc./Vol.	14.0%
RRP	$11.00

Come back grenache, all is forgiven. These days a winery simply must have a grenache on the books in order to have a smart red wine portfolio.

CURRENT RELEASE 1996   The colour is a perky scarlet and the nose is full of ripe raspberry on a background of spice and oak. The palate is bursting with sweet berry flavours and these are matched by some fine-grained tannins on a long, lingering finish. It drinks well now with a beef hotpot.

Woodstock Shiraz

Quality	▼▼▼▼
Value	★★★★▸
Grapes	shiraz
Region	McLaren Vale, SA
Cellar	▮ 8
Alc./Vol.	13.5%
RRP	$14.00

For some reason this wine recalls camp-fire cooking: hearty, robust, smoky and full of the great outdoors. It might lack frills, but it makes up by offering plenty of hearty flavour.

CURRENT RELEASE 1995   The colour is deep and the nose is complex with ripe plum, cherry and chocolate aromas. The palate is full of plums and vanilla flavours. These combine with some gentle wood characters. The finish is tinder-dry with tongue-coating tannins. It should cellar well and gain some finesse. It goes beautifully with a bunny stew.

Woodstock The Stocks Shiraz

This is winemaker's choice for the 'best wine of the vintage' and this year it falls to a shiraz. (Last year it was cabernet sauvignon.) Maker Scott Collett.

Previous outstanding vintages: '91, '93

CURRENT RELEASE 1994 A generous style that isn't without blemishes, but these add rather than detract from the whole. There is a slight acetone aroma on the nose but also lashings of plum and pepper smells. The palate is medium-bodied with rich shiraz flavours and sweet plums. The spices are wedded to some attractive oak on a long finish. It needs some venison in a reduction sauce.

Quality	♥♥♥♥
Value	★★★
Grapes	shiraz
Region	McLaren Vale, SA
Cellar	▮ 7
Alc./Vol.	13.5%
RRP	$24.00

Wyndham Estate Bin 888 Cabernet Merlot

This was a very successful label started by Brian Mc-Guigan in the early '80s. Then the company was sold to the Orlando group.

CURRENT RELEASE 1994 The colour is a brilliant cherry-red. The nose has strong berry aromas with raspberry to the fore. The palate is medium- to full-bodied with sweet raspberry flavours that are linked with some gentle tannins. It was made to drink rather than cellar. Try it with oxtail soup.

Quality	♥♥♥♥
Value	★★★★
Grapes	cabernet sauvignon; merlot
Region	Hunter Valley, NSW
Cellar	▮ 3
Alc./Vol.	12.5%
RRP	$13.00

Wynns Cabernet Shiraz Merlot

The handbrake on the Wynns steamroller must have been pulled out by the roots because sales are again a runaway success. This part of the portfolio represents value for money. Maker Peter Douglas.

CURRENT RELEASE 1994 A bit leafy this year, which expresses the nature of the vintage. The nose has briary and damp leaf aromas. There is blackberry on the palate and the leafy notes also register. The oak on the finish is discreet and soft. It's a drink-up style that goes great with Italian meatballs.

Quality	♥♥♥♥
Value	★★★★
Grapes	cabernet sauvignon; shiraz; merlot
Region	Coonawarra, SA
Cellar	▮ 3
Alc./Vol.	13.5%
RRP	$14.20 ⑤

Wynns Cabernet Sauvignon

Quality	筽筽筽筽筽
Value	★★★★★
Grapes	cabernet sauvignon
Region	Coonawarra, SA
Cellar	🍷 10
Alc./Vol.	13.5%
RRP	$20.00 Ⓢ

PENGUIN BEST RED WINE

One of the most loved commercial labels in the industry, and rightly so. It was a trailblazer from the start, and in many ways it's considered a barometer to the state of the vintage in the district.

Previous outstanding vintages: '62, '71, '76, '82, '85, '86, '88, '90, '91, '93

CURRENT RELEASE 1994   Textbook stuff! This is a very impressive vintage with loads of complexity from the start. The nose has blackberry and vanilla aromas. The palate is full of chocolate, vanilla and spices, which are dominated by blackberry fruit flavours. It's complex and entertaining. The wood works well; it adds balance and astringency. It's lovely to drink now because of the great balance. Have it with chargrilled eye fillet.

Wynns Michael Shiraz

Quality	筽筽筽筽
Value	★★★
Grapes	shiraz
Region	Coonawarra, SA
Cellar	⬥ 3–12
Alc./Vol.	13%
RRP	$54.00

Michael is a problem child and the authors won't agree on this one: MS finds the oak oppressive and excessive; HH thinks the fruit can carry the tall timber given some cellaring. It's a healthy debate, which means you should make up your own mind. Pay your money and find out for yourself.

Previous outstanding vintages: '55, '90, '91, '93

CURRENT RELEASE 1994   The wrestling match between oak and fruit continues. Oak seems to be winning this round with a full nelson on the fruit. The nose has coconut, vanilla and ripe berry aromas. The palate is intense with blackberry and cherry flavours, but oak is never very far away; the finish bristles with the stuff. It's concentrated and exerts a powerful tannin grip. The wine needs a dish that begs no pardons: let's settle for smoked kangaroo.

Wynns Shiraz

This is one of the most eagerly awaited releases in the wine calendar. The 1995 vintage in Coonawarra was rather arduous, so these results are interesting.

Previous outstanding vintages: '86, '88, '90, '91, '93, '94

CURRENT RELEASE 1995 The crosshairs are right on target: it might be a little lighter than usual but the flavours and structure are true to form. The nose has spicy, ripe plum fruit aromas. The palate is a mixture of mulberries and plums with some white pepper spice. The oak is perfectly matched to the volume of fruit. It drinks well now and is great with steak and eggs.

Quality	♟♟♟♟
Value	★★★★
Grapes	shiraz
Region	Coonawarra, SA
Cellar	▌ 4
Alc./Vol.	12.5%
RRP	$14.00 Ⓢ

Wynns John Riddoch Cabernet Sauvignon

This was a trendsetter in terms of Australian red wine. The first was made by John Wade (now of Howard Park fame). The mantle has been passed to Peter Douglas, who has assumed same without having to stoop.

Previous outstanding vintages: '82, '86, '87, '88, '90, '91, '93

CURRENT RELEASE 1994 Very classy wine with lots of regional and varietal definition. It packs a big whack of aroma and flavour. There are blackberries and mulberries and plenty of spice. Massive is the word, and there are lashings of oak tannins on an everlasting finish. Great stuff. It drinks well with a steak – no chaser.

Quality	♟♟♟♟♟
Value	★★★
Grapes	cabernet sauvignon
Region	Coonawarra, SA
Cellar	➥ 2–8
Alc./Vol.	13.5%
RRP	$54.00

Xanadu Cabernet Reserve

Quality	♆♆♆♆
Value	★★★
Grapes	cabernet sauvignon
Region	Margaret River, WA
Cellar	➤ 4–15+
Alc./Vol.	13.5%
RRP	$43.00 ▮

Conor Lagan and Jurg Muggli have forged an Irish–Swiss alliance, which continues the delightfully eccentric theme of this accomplished vineyard. Muggli makes the wines.

Previous outstanding vintages: '91

CURRENT RELEASE 1994   Margaret River is a chameleon and Xanadu displays one of its shades, the aroma of its cabernet usually being decidedly green/vegetal. There are redcurrant and oaky aromas along with the herbs. In the mouth it's big-boned, but lean and tightly structured with an angular ornery nature that may sort itself out with cellar time. The finish carries a big whack of grippy tannin. Cellar, then serve with roast leg of lamb with mint sauce.

Xanadu Cabernet Sauvignon

Quality	♆♆♆♆♆
Value	★★★★
Grapes	cabernet sauvignon
Region	Margaret River, WA
Cellar	➤ 1–7+
Alc./Vol.	13.5%
RRP	$25.00 ▮

This Margaret River winery is finally getting with it and dropping the 'chateau' prefix. Maker Jurg Muggli.

Previous outstanding vintages: '91

CURRENT RELEASE 1994   A year down the track and this is showing improvement over last year's review. Scented cedary French oak plus dark berries make a fine bouquet. The palate is solidly packed with flavour and has excellent structure, promising a long life. Puckering tannins are well matched by classy flavour. Serve with roast beef and demiglaze.

Quality	♆♆♆⟆
Value	★★⟋
Grapes	cabernet sauvignon
Region	Margaret River, WA
Cellar	➤ 3–10+
Alc./Vol.	13.5%
RRP	$25.00 ▮

CURRENT RELEASE 1995   A bit of a come-down from the '94, this one has shy, leafy, herbal and raspberry aromas. The mouth has a slight mid-palate dip, which is accentuated by typical cabernet firm tannin astringency on the finish. Tough at present, and needs time. Then serve with roast lamb and pesto sauce.

Xanadu Featherwhite

Two earlier vintages won gold medals at competitions in that well-known wine capital, Zurich. (Hint: winemaker Jurg Muggli is Swiss.)
CURRENT RELEASE 1996 The colour is a light salmon-pink, and the aroma and taste are all about green, dusty/leafy early-harvested cabernet. The palate is delicately structured, smooth and well balanced towards dryness. Give it a light chill and serve with antipasto.

Quality	♀♀♀
Value	★★★
Grapes	cabernet sauvignon
Region	Margaret River, WA
Cellar	▲ 1
Alc./Vol.	13.0%
RRP	$17.60

Yalumba Octavius

Think music rather than ancient Rome. Eight notes in a scale, and in this case the notes are small barrels made from well-seasoned (aged for over 6 years) American oak. The barrels call the tune. Maker Brian Walsh and team.
Previous outstanding vintages: '90, '91, '92
CURRENT RELEASE 1993 Lots of derring-do here in this boys'-own style. The colour is deep, and the nose strikes a major chord of resounding wood and ultra-ripe fruit. The depth is impressive, and there are ripe plums, red berries, vanilla and caramel flavours. That's before you get to the oak! It adds slabs of tannin and loads of grip. This wine needs time and then more time. Drink it now as a sparring partner for venison steaks.

Quality	♀♀♀♀♀
Value	★★★★
Grapes	shiraz
Region	Barossa Valley, SA 80%; Eden Valley, SA 20%
Cellar	� 3–8
Alc./Vol.	14.0%
RRP	$45.00

Yalumba Oxford Landing Merlot

This is what you'd expect from Riverland: merlot that has been made to drink now. Call it friendly quaffing.
CURRENT RELEASE 1996 The wine is very soft with a fruity nose and a lollipop aroma that could be a consequence of carbonic maceration. The palate is light with sweet berry flavours, and the finish is a tad short with a hint of tannin. It could be served chilled with chicken.

Quality	♀♀♀
Value	★★★
Grapes	merlot
Region	Riverland, SA
Cellar	▲
Alc./Vol.	12.5%
RRP	$8.00 Ⓢ

Yalumba Signature Blend

Quality	♟♟♟♟♟
Value	★★★★★
Grapes	cabernet sauvignon 70%; shiraz 30%
Region	Barossa Valley, SA 85%; McLaren Vale, SA 15%
Cellar	➥ 3–8
Alc./Vol.	13.0%
RRP	$24.00

A vertical tasting of this series, which started in 1962, is an interesting exercise. It's like looking at the various strata in sedimentary rock: you can chart the various changes in wine fashion as well as the vintage variation. *Previous outstanding vintages: '62, '63, '66, '67, '75, '76, '81, '88, '90, '91, '92*
CURRENT RELEASE 1993   A very formal wine that uses old-fashioned values as well as a modern oak treatment. The wine is all about structure. The colour shows no evidence of bottle-age, and the nose has briar patch and berry aromas. The palate is medium-bodied with sweet blackberry fruit, vanilla and oak spice. There are some lovely tannins on a grippy finish. It needs time, but try it now with a casserole of kid.

Yalumba The Menzies

Quality	♟♟♟♟
Value	★★★★
Grapes	cabernet sauvignon
Region	Coonawarra, SA
Cellar	↓ 5
Alc./Vol.	13.5%
RRP	$20.00

Prime Minister Menzies (King Ming, Lord Warden of the Cinque Ports) was a keen fan of Yalumba's Galway claret. This label was minted in memory of King Ming. *Previous outstanding vintages: '92*
CURRENT RELEASE 1994   A stylish wine that isn't exactly lordly but has great structure. The wine has a hint of leaves and blackberry fruit aromas. The palate has blackberry and raspberry flavours, and there is some dry oak which gives way to firm tannin on an astringent finish. It should age positively, but you can drink it now with a steak and kidney pie.

Yarra Burn Bastard Hill Pinot Noir

Quality	♟♟♟♟
Value	★★★★
Grapes	pinot noir
Region	Yarra Valley, Vic.
Cellar	↓ 4
Alc./Vol.	14.0%
RRP	$38.00

Having trudged up the hill at Hoddles Creek you can appreciate the name bestowed upon it by the pickers! It's too steep for a mechanical harvester.
CURRENT RELEASE 1994   Quite a big wine with lovely legs (streaks of glycerol on the inside of the glass). The nose has black cherry aromas with hints of mint. There are cherry and earthy flavours on the palate, and the finish is chalky and dry with plenty of grip. It's a sturdy style that goes well with field mushrooms on toast.

Yarra Burn Cabernets

This is part of the BRL Hardy conglomerate, and the access to winemaking technology has introduced a higher level of consistency. Maker David Fyffe.

CURRENT RELEASE 1993   The wine is an elegant style with a strong tobacco-leaf aroma on the nose. The light-to medium-bodied palate has blackberry fruit flavours and hints of tobacco and spice. There is fine-grained tannin on the finish and plenty of grip. It drinks well now with pink lamb fillets.

Quality	♥♥♥♥
Value	★★★★
Grapes	cabernet sauvignon; cabernet franc
Region	Yarra Valley, Vic.
Cellar	▮ 3
Alc./Vol.	12.5%
RRP	$22.00

CURRENT RELEASE 1994   Lovely nose with loads of class. There are berry and wood aromas plus a touch of cigar box. The palate is elegant, but it doesn't lack flesh or flavour. The blackberry shines through and it mingles with subtle oak on a sinuous finish. It's a poised wine that drinks well now, and is a treat teamed with pink lamb chops and mint sauce.

Quality	♥♥♥♥
Value	★★★★
Grapes	cabernet sauvignon; cabernet franc; merlot
Region	Yarra Valley, Vic.
Cellar	▮ 5
Alc./Vol.	13.0%
RRP	$22.00

Yarra Edge Cabernets

As the name suggests, the winery and vineyard are on the edge of the Yarra Valley. The proprietors are Susan and John Bingeman. Maker Michael Zitzlaff.

CURRENT RELEASE 1994   An elegant Bordeaux-style blend that presents something of a riddle. The alcohol is quite high but the fruit remains shy. The colour is a light cherry-red and the nose has berry aromas with a hint of marzipan. The palate is light-bodied with shy raspberry and cherry flavours, and there is plenty of acid on the finish. Decant and serve with pink roast lamb.

Quality	♥♥♥♥
Value	★★★
Grapes	cabernet sauvignon; merlot; cabernet franc; malbec
Region	Yarra Valley, Vic.
Cellar	▮ 3
Alc./Vol.	13.5%
RRP	$25.00 ▮

Yarra Ridge Merlot

Quality	♥♥♥♥⬝
Value	★★★★
Grapes	merlot
Region	Yarra Valley, Vic.
Cellar	▮ 2
Alc./Vol.	13.0%
RRP	$20.00 Ⓢ

Merlot is all talk, no action in Australia. There's very little planted, and disappointingly few of the wines are much good. This one's a beacon. Maker Rob Dolan.
CURRENT RELEASE 1996   A pretty wine, but very much a fly-now, pay-later style. In other words, we'd drink it without further ado. Aromatic green mint/leafy and mulberry/raspberry nose, then intense palate flavour, vivacious mouth-feel and good length. Enjoy it while it's fresh, with veal.

Yarra Ridge Pinot Noir

Quality	♥♥♥♥⬝
Value	★★★★
Grapes	pinot noir
Region	Yarra Valley, Vic.
Cellar	▮ 2
Alc./Vol.	13.0%
RRP	$20.00 Ⓢ

This variety looks like being the apple of the Yarra Valley's eye. It's evolving as one of the premier areas for pinot noir; however, there are strong political forces at play with regard to style. Watch this space.
CURRENT RELEASE 1996   A medium-bodied, sappy style that is easy to drink. The colour is deep red, and the nose has cherry and sap aromas. The palate is a mixture of plum and cherry flavours, which are attended by discreet oak. The finish is soft and the wine is ready to go. Try it with a flash pizza.

Yarrawonga Estate

Quality	♥♥♥⬝
Value	★★★⬝
Grapes	cabernet sauvignon, merlot, cabernet franc
Region	North East Victoria
Cellar	➥ 2–5
Alc./Vol.	13.5%
RRP	$16.00

Declaration of interest time: MS planned this vineyard for the Jane (as in Bob Jane T Marts) family. His involvement in the project has long ceased and he had no part in the making of this wine. His relationship with Bill and Bob Jane is one of friendship – not business.
CURRENT RELEASE 1994   The colour is a promising red–purple, and the nose is very attractive with berry and rose petal aromas. The palate is a slight pitfall: the berry flavours are contesting with some bitter tannins. Whether time in the bottle will change this remains to be seen, because this is a new area and a new vineyard with no recorded history. Try it with Peking duck.

Yering Station Cabernet Sauvignon Merlot

Victoria's first vineyard was planted on this site in 1838 and it came into Hubert de Castella's hands in 1850. The original vineyard did not survive, and this vineyard was re-established in 1988.

CURRENT RELEASE 1995 Great nose with lovely perfume and loads of berries. The palate is rather reserved and slightly forbidding in the manner of a young Bordeaux. The black-tea-like tannins have loads of grip and give the impression the wine will take time to soften. Drink it now with smoked kangaroo.

Quality	♥♥♥♥
Value	★★★★
Grapes	cabernet sauvignon; merlot; cabernet franc
Region	Yarra Valley, Vic.
Cellar	� 2–6
Alc./Vol.	13.0%
RRP	$17.00

Yering Station Pinot Noir

New, understated and handsome label from this vineyard planted on the site of de Castella's vineyard.

CURRENT RELEASE 1996 The light colour is deceptive; it has strength of flavour and backbone. The colour is pale pink and the nose has ripe strawberry aromas. The palate is wild strawberries, and the finish has acid and a slight stalky character. It drinks well now and is fine with a cassoulet.

Quality	♥♥♥
Value	★★★
Grapes	pinot noir
Region	Yarra Valley, Vic.
Cellar	▮ 3
Alc./Vol.	12.5%
RRP	$17.00

Zema Estate Cabernet Sauvignon

Zema Estate is truly a family affair, with Mum, Dad and the boys involved. Matt is the winemaker and Nick looks after viticulture. The vines are unirrigated and hand-pruned.

Previous outstanding vintages: '84, '86, '88, '90, '92, '94
CURRENT RELEASE 1995 A superb achievement from a difficult vintage in Coonawarra. Cedary, dark-berry aromas; sweet and ripe and fragrant. In the mouth it's refined and well-modulated with good concentration of sustained flavour. A classic Coonawarra cab. Serve with lamb satays.

Quality	♥♥♥♥♥
Value	★★★★★
Grapes	cabernet sauvignon
Region	Coonawarra, SA
Cellar	▮ 8
Alc./Vol.	12.9%
RRP	$17.60

Zema Estate Cluny

Quality	▮▮▮▮
Value	★★★
Grapes	cabernet sauvignon 65%; merlot 15%; cabernet franc 10%; malbec 10%
Region	Coonawarra, SA
Cellar	▮ 5
Alc./Vol.	13.2%
RRP	$17.60

The '95 is only the second release under this label from a new Zema vineyard. It's an attempt at a Bordeaux-style blend.

CURRENT RELEASE 1995   Youthful red-berry aromas with a sprinkling of toasty oak. Cassis and gunpowder smells. The profile is lean and somewhat austere, with a lingering tannin grip. Shows promise for the vineyard. Try it with meatballs.

Zema Estate Family Selection Cabernet Sauvignon

Quality	▮▮▮▮
Value	★★★
Grapes	cabernet sauvignon
Region	Coonawarra, SA
Cellar	▮ 8+
Alc./Vol.	13.1%
RRP	$25.75 ▮

This is a true reserve selection of the best Zema cabernet, with individually numbered labels. Only 8000 bottles were released.

CURRENT RELEASE 1994   Deep, rich, purple–red colour and a beefy, meat-stock, savoury, oak-influenced bouquet in which the cabernet blackcurrants come up with time in the glass. Sweet fruit of some richness on the palate, and going through a gangly phase as it starts to develop. Goes well with Italian pecorino.

Zema Estate Shiraz

Quality	▮▮▮
Value	★★★
Grapes	shiraz
Region	Coonawarra, SA
Cellar	▮ 3
Alc./Vol.	12.1%
RRP	$17.60

Zema's main Coonawarra vineyard is still hand-pruned and unirrigated. Winemaker Matt Zema.

Previous outstanding vintages: '84, '86, '88, '92, '94

CURRENT RELEASE 1995   More a product of the year than an accurate reflection of maker or vineyard, this has a cassisy/leafy nose with some underripe notes, and the palate lacks the usual Zema structure and oomph. A decent red to drink young, but falls well short of the good years. Serve with guinea fowl.

White Wines

Abbey Vale Chardonnay

The wood is missing in action in this chardonnay from the west. There are early signs of revolt in the minds of the press and some consumers about the nude chardonnay styles.

CURRENT RELEASE 1996 Melon and wintergreen aromas dominate the nose and the palate has a buttery texture. It's medium-bodied with melon and grapefruit flavours, and these are followed by a warmth of alcohol and some soft acid on the finish. It needs a big chill. Try it with pork chops.

Quality	???
Value	★★★★
Grapes	chardonnay
Region	Margaret River, WA
Cellar	2
Alc./Vol.	13.8%
RRP	$16.00

Abbey Vale Dry Verdelho

Western Australia seems to be intent on making this variety all their own. Don't tell them too loudly, but they're welcome to it!

CURRENT RELEASE 1996 Schizophrenic wine that takes elements from sauvignon blanc and semillon with tropical fruit tossed in for good measure. The palate is medium-bodied with passionfruit and gooseberry flavours. The finish is dry but devoid of oak. It has good balance and can take a big chill. Try it with chicken.

Quality	???
Value	★★★★
Grapes	verdelho
Region	Margaret River, WA
Cellar	3
Alc./Vol.	12.5%
RRP	$18.00

All Saints Chenin Blanc

Quality	🍷🍷🍷
Value	★★★
Grapes	chenin blanc
Region	North East Victoria
Cellar	2
Alc./Vol.	11.5%
RRP	$13.95

The label is part of the Brown Brothers empire. The variety is almost a lost cause, littering the ballroom steps with glass slippers.

CURRENT RELEASE 1996 The nose is nutty with a hint of green apples and honey. There is an impressive balance between sweetness and tartness on the palate, with Granny Smith apple flavour that is balanced by some strict acid on an astringent finish. It needs to be chilled to thrill. Try it with a chicken tikka.

All Saints Late Harvest Semillon

Quality	🍷🍷🍷🍷
Value	★★★★
Grapes	semillon
Region	North East Victoria
Cellar	3
Alc./Vol.	10.0%
RRP	$14.50 (375ml)

This is a much underrated bottle of botrytis dynamite. Great stuff, and an indicator of another style that should be encouraged in the region.

CURRENT RELEASE 1995 'A taste of honey, a taste that's much sweeter than wine . . . ' There are botrytis aromas mingled with typical macerated fruit aromas. The palate is mouthfilling, yet the alcohol is surprisingly low. There are sweet peach and gooseberry flavours, and there is firm acid on an acerbic finish. Try it with a summer pudding.

All Saints Marsanne

Quality	🍷🍷🍷½
Value	★★★½
Grapes	marsanne
Region	North East Victoria
Cellar	4
Alc./Vol.	13.0%
RRP	$13.95

This is quite an entertaining style with good varietal definition. Evidently there is more marsanne planted in Australia than there is in the Rhone Valley, France.

CURRENT RELEASE 1995 Quite complex with typical honeysuckle aroma on the nose. The palate is slightly honeyed and there are toasty notes on the gently oaked wine. The finish is dry and the wine can be served with a medium chill. Try it with roast pork and apple sauce.

Allandale Chardonnay

The vineyard and winery were established in 1977 and there are 7 hectares under vine. The cellar door is very welcoming and well worth a visit.

CURRENT RELEASE 1996 Big toasty nose but the fruit also passes muster. It has ripe peach and tropical fruit aromas. The palate is medium- to full-bodied with sweet, ripe peach flavours coupled with some toasty oak. The finish is long and satisfying. A medium chill and medallions of pork in a mango sauce will send you to heaven.

Quality	🍷🍷🍷🍷½
Value	★★★★½
Grapes	chardonnay
Region	Hunter Valley, NSW
Cellar	5
Alc./Vol.	12.5%
RRP	$16.00

Allandale Riesling

Riesling grown in the Hunter Valley was never successful; it was necessary to find grapes in cooler climates.

CURRENT RELEASE 1996 The nose is like lemon butter spread on fresh toast. The palate is limey and there is a hint of kero. The finish has crisp acid. It can take a big chill and goes well with oysters kilpatrick.

Quality	🍷🍷🍷½
Value	★★★½
Grapes	riesling
Region	Hilltops, NSW
Cellar	2
Alc./Vol.	11.5%
RRP	$12.00

Allandale Semillon

Like many small Hunter wineries, this one sells most of its wine to tourists at the front door.

CURRENT RELEASE 1996 The usual Hunter austerity applies to this wine. The nose is toasty with whispers of yeast. There are straw and gooseberry characters on the palate, and scorched wood and nutty flavours characterise the finish. It will cellar well, but drink now with a modest chill. Try it with prawns tempura.

Quality	🍷🍷🍷½
Value	★★★½
Grapes	semillon
Region	Hunter Valley, NSW
Cellar	2–6
Alc./Vol.	12.0%
RRP	$14.50

Allandale Hilltops Semillon

Quality	♟♟♟♟
Value	★★★★
Grapes	semillon
Region	Hilltops, NSW
Cellar	▮ 5
Alc./Vol.	12.5%
RRP	$14.50

This winery is sourcing fruit from different climes and it's interesting to note the flavour differences that result. In this case the grapes came from the Hilltops region of New South Wales.

CURRENT RELEASE 1996   The wine is crossing over into sauvignon blanc territory. Not exactly semillon with attitude, but there is a touch of aromatic herbs on the nose. There are citrus and gooseberry fruit flavours plus some dusty oak characters on the long, dry finish. It should develop more complexity with bottle-age. At the moment serve it well chilled with king prawns.

Andrew Garrett Chardonnay

Quality	♟♟♟
Value	★★★
Grapes	chardonnay
Region	McLaren Vale, SA
Cellar	▮ 2
Alc./Vol.	13.5%
RRP	$14.50 ⑤

The blurb tells us this has been fermented and aged in French and American oak barrels. It remains a fruit-driven style. Maker Phil Reschke.

CURRENT RELEASE 1996   Malt, honey and lanolin aromas greet the nose and there is little evidence of wood. The profile is lean and narrow and there's a touch of austerity to the wine. Starting to show some development, and will probably remain a leaner style. Try it with grilled baby octopus.

Angoves Butterfly Ridge Colombard Chardonnay

Quality	♟♟♟♟
Value	★★★★
Grapes	colombard; chardonnay
Region	Riverland, SA
Cellar	▮ 1
Alc./Vol.	12.5%
RRP	$8.95

It's becoming difficult to find a decent bottle of wine under ten bucks. Angoves have the solution. They have the huge Nanya vineyard, which provides good fruit at an economical price.

CURRENT RELEASE 1995   No bells and whistles, but a very good drink. There are passionfruit and peach aromas on the nose, and melon and tropical fruit aromas on the palate. The finish is dry and clean. It's a very quaffable style. Serve chilled with tandoori chicken wings.

Angoves Chardonnay

Angoves wines are a blessing to all of us who have limited pockets and a mighty thirst. Their wines are ever-reliable and fun to drink.
CURRENT RELEASE 1996   Straightforward and faithful to the varietal character. It has peach aromas on the nose, and the palate is fruity with sweet melon and peach flavours. The finish is soft and gentle. Serve well chilled with chicken from a picnic hamper.

Quality	♟♟♟
Value	★★★⯪
Grapes	chardonnay
Region	Riverland, SA
Cellar	▮ 2
Alc./Vol.	13.5%
RRP	$8.00

Annie's Lane Semillon

This is an on-premise (restaurant, bars and bistros only) line made at the old Quelltaler winery in the Clare Valley. Maker David O'Leary.
CURRENT RELEASE 1995   There is obvious barrel fermentation character on both the nose and palate. The nose is nutty and toasty, and the palate is soft with a lemon flavour and a hint of lanolin. There is also a mouthfilling buttery texture. The finish displays gentle oak. It's a very drinkable style that shouldn't be served too cold. Great with pan-fried veal in a cream-based sauce.

Quality	♟♟♟♟♟
Value	★★★★★
Grapes	semillon
Region	Clare Valley, SA
Cellar	▮ 3
Alc./Vol.	13.0%
RRP	$14.50

Antipodean

When it burst onto the scene, it was a powerful essay in packaging and flavour. Looks great and tastes great and is perfect for a trendy bistro. It's a clever fruit salad and a bit of fun.
Previous outstanding vintages: '94, '95
CURRENT RELEASE 1996   The wine is dominated by sauvignon blanc. It has a grassy, herbal nose. Tropical fruit does a fan dance on the palate, and there is a background of gooseberry. The acid on the finish is a tad soft, but a big chill adds a crisp aspect. It's perfect for a warm salad of smoked chicken.

Quality	♟♟♟♟
Value	★★★★
Grapes	semillon; sauvignon blanc; viognier
Region	Eden Valley, SA
Cellar	▮ 3
Alc./Vol.	12.5%
RRP	$14.50

Arlewood Semillon

Quality	♥♥♥♥
Value	★★★┝
Grapes	semillon
Region	Margaret River, WA
Cellar	↓ 5
Alc./Vol.	13.5%
RRP	$16.00

Aged Margaret River semillons can be curious beasties with a bit of careful cellaring. They seem to develop in an entirely different way from those in the Hunter Valley.

CURRENT RELEASE 1993   The nose has an incredible smell of ripe honeydew melon. The palate is mouthfilling in texture with more than a scant reference to honey. There are also some gooseberry flavours. French oak rides in over the top adding a tinder-dry, chalky element. It needs more time to soften and it goes well with kassler and sauerkraut.

Arlewood Semillon Sauvignon Blanc

Quality	♥♥♥♥
Value	★★★┝
Grapes	semillon; sauvignon blanc
Region	Margaret River, WA
Cellar	↓ 2
Alc./Vol.	12.5%
RRP	$16.00

A new label for the Margaret River district. The label design shows promise but the typography could use a little cleaning up.

CURRENT RELEASE 1996   All the elements are there. The nose is a mixture of pea, lychee and tropical fruit aromas. The palate is dominated by tropical fruit flavours with pineapple and mango. The finish shows plenty of crisp acid and impressive length. It can be served well chilled. Try it with Vietnamese rice paper rolls.

Arrowfield Chardonnay Show Reserve

Quality	♥♥♥♥
Value	★★★★
Grapes	chardonnay
Region	Hunter Valley, NSW
Cellar	⊸ 2–5
Alc./Vol.	13.0%
RRP	$20.00

This one gets the winemaking works, including new oak and extended lees contact. As a consequence it needs extra bottle-age.

CURRENT RELEASE 1995   The new wood is the major attraction and in this case there is a slightly resinous quality. The nose is toasty with hints of caramel and tropical fruit. The palate has a slightly creamy texture with peach and melon flavours. The oak on the finish is assertive, and the more the wine is chilled the more it stands out. Try it with smoked trout.

Arrowfield Cowra Chardonnay

There have been many changes at this winery and ever-shrinking vineyard. The most recent wines show they are getting to the nub of the matter. Don't take our word for it: call them toll free on 1800 64 2929. Maker Simon Gilbert.

CURRENT RELEASE 1995 This is a civilised, well-made wine that shows great balance. The colour is a bright yellow with a touch of green. The nose is a mixture of peach and oak aromas. The middleweight palate has peach, melon and citrus flavours that intermingle with integrated oak. It drinks well now and needs a medium chill. Try it with a warm salad of smoked turkey.

Quality	▼▼▼▼▽
Value	★★★★☆
Grapes	chardonnay
Region	Cowra, NSW
Cellar	4
Alc./Vol.	13.5%
RRP	$18.00

Ashton Hills Chardonnay

Ashton is an apple-growing area, high in the coolest part of the Adelaide Hills. Steve George makes the wines and his parents-in-law run the vineyard.

Previous outstanding vintages: '90, '91, '93

CURRENT RELEASE 1995 A refined style. The nose is dusty, minerally with a hint of vanilla; the taste is delicate, light-bodied, with fruit to the fore. There are peach and nectarine flavours. It seems to be ageing gently, and will probably retain its freshness for some years. Serve with yabbies.

Quality	▼▼▼▼▽
Value	★★★★
Grapes	chardonnay
Region	Adelaide Hills, SA
Cellar	5+
Alc./Vol.	13.0%
RRP	$21.60

Austin's Barrabool Riesling

Barrabool boasts some fabulous bluestone railway bridges. You didn't need to know that, but this book is big on trivia.

CURRENT RELEASE 1996 A very floral style with plenty of crushed violets. The palate has elementary lime flavours, and there is just a suggestion of coarseness on the finish. Acid rules the finish, and it can be served well chilled. Try it with oysters.

Quality	▼▼▼
Value	★★★
Grapes	riesling
Region	Geelong, Vic.
Cellar	3
Alc./Vol.	12.0%
RRP	$10.95

Azure Bay Sauvignon Blanc Semillon

Quality	♟♟♟
Value	★★★
Grapes	sauvignon blanc; semillon
Region	Gisborne, NZ
Cellar	▮ 1
Alc./Vol.	11.5%
RRP	$12.50

Can't get used to a wine in a blue bottle. Didn't blue bottles mean poison? This is a wine that has more hype than substance.

CURRENT RELEASE 1996   It's a light, fragrant style that is perfect for the ladies who lunch. The emphasis is on herbs and grassy aromas. The palate is lightweight with some tropical fruit and herb characters. The acid on the finish adds an element of crispness. It can be served well chilled, and it goes well with a chicken and rocket pesto salad.

Bannockburn Chardonnay

Quality	♟♟♟♟
Value	★★★
Grapes	chardonnay
Region	Geelong, Vic.
Cellar	▮ 5+
Alc./Vol.	13.5%
RRP	$37.80

Low-yielding vineyards and French methods are the key factors in the doggedly individualistic style of Bannockburn wines. Maker Gary Farr.

Previous outstanding vintages: '88, '90, '91, '92, '94

CURRENT RELEASE 1995   A somewhat austere vintage, which needs a little time to be coaxed out of its shell. There are toasty oak and creamy, nutty lees characters in a complex bouquet, and the palate is tight and firm and finishes very dry. Not your average Aussie chardonnay by a long shot. Could cellar well. Try it with pork and apple sauce.

Banrock Station Semillon Chardonnay

Quality	♟♟♟
Value	★★★★
Grapes	semillon; chardonnay
Region	Murray Valley, SA
Cellar	▮ 1
Alc./Vol.	12.0%
RRP	$7.25 Ⓢ

Judging by the appearance of the label and the sales spiel, this has been designed to appeal to nature lovers.

CURRENT RELEASE *non-vintage*   A remarkably tasty drop, considering the price. There are some spicy aromas, and the palate holds herbaceous and tropical flavours of surprising depth. A suspicion of wood adds to the palate length. Goes well with vegetarian terrines.

Banrock Station Unwooded Chardonnay

This is a very basic dry white, which makes a bit of a mockery of the label subscript: 'Show Release'. Perhaps they *showed* it to the marketer, who said '*Release* me from my employment'.
CURRENT RELEASE 1996 The aromas are pleasant enough with melon and a hint of citrus, but the palate is flat and has no length. The good news is the price: it's often heavily discounted. A clean, straightforward white that won't offend. Serve with caesar salad.

Quality	♛♛♜
Value	★★★⸙
Grapes	chardonnay
Region	Murray Valley, Vic.
Cellar	▮ 1
Alc./Vol.	13.0%
RRP	$11.00 Ⓢ

Barratt Chardonnay

Lindsay and Carolyn Barratt's vineyard is at Summertown in the beautiful Piccadilly Valley.
CURRENT RELEASE 1996 A highly refined chardonnay, which shows classic Adelaide Hills flavours albeit in a delicate framework. Honeydew melon, peach and cashew nut aromas; very lightly handled oak – it grows on you the more you drink. Try it with a vegetable terrine.

Quality	♛♛♛♛
Value	★★★⸙
Grapes	chardonnay
Region	Adelaide Hills, SA
Cellar	▮ 4
Alc./Vol.	13.5%
RRP	$24.00

Barwang Chardonnay

This vineyard has proved itself many times over with red wines from cabernet and shiraz, but it's still coming to terms with chardonnay. Maker Jim Brayne.
CURRENT RELEASE 1996 A fresh, delicate style that will probably show better after a year in the bottle. When tasted it had a very light colour and an undeveloped cashew nut and peach nose with little apparent wood. It also had a slightly sweet impression on the tongue – fruit-driven and somewhat straightforward. Keep for a year, then serve with fish balls.

Quality	♛♛♛♜
Value	★★★⸙
Grapes	chardonnay
Region	Hilltops, NSW
Cellar	➤ 1–4
Alc./Vol.	13.5%
RRP	$15.70 Ⓢ

Basedow Chardonnay

Quality	♥♥♥♪
Value	★★★
Grapes	chardonnay
Region	Barossa Valley, SA
Cellar	◊ 1
Alc./Vol.	13.5%
RRP	$16.90

This won the title of 'White Wine of the Year' at *WINE* magazine's International Challenge in the UK, and we can only assume it was better as a younger wine.
CURRENT RELEASE 1995   A decent but hardly spectacular chardonnay, which is ageing rather quickly. Deep yellow, heaps of toasty development plus wood, with a dry, acid and oak tannin finish, which coarsens it. Rather plain despite its toasty development. A decent drink to serve with roast chicken, but in its show career, a lucky wine.

Basedow Late Harvest White Frontignac

Quality	♥♥♥♪
Value	★★★★
Grapes	white frontignac
Region	Barossa Valley, SA
Cellar	◊ 1
Alc./Vol.	10.5%
RRP	$10.00

This is what's known in the trade as a cellar-door wine. People who arrive at the winery in tourist buses love it.
CURRENT RELEASE 1996   A captivating white wine that ensnares its victim with a pungently aromatic, muscaty bouquet. A lightly sweet, fresh, grapey taste adds the *coup de grâce*. Needs spicier foods, so take it to a Thai restaurant.

Basedow Riesling

Quality	♥♥♥♥♪
Value	★★★★
Grapes	riesling
Region	Barossa Valley, SA
Cellar	◊ 1
Alc./Vol.	12.0%
RRP	$32.00

This is a show reserve wine that hit the pot of gold at the Adelaide Show a couple of years ago.
CURRENT RELEASE 1988   Maturity shows in the deep golden-yellow colour and accompanying buttered-toast aged bouquet. Some citrus/lime fruit is still discernible. There is frisky acid holding the palate together, and the developed lemon/lime flavours are fully mature and quite delicious. Try it with crispy-skin chicken.

Best's Riesling

If vine maturity counts for anything, Best's should have a head start on most. Their riesling vines were planted in 1944 and 1978. Maker Simon Clayfield.
Previous outstanding vintages: '72, '81, '82, '85, '88, '90, '91, '92, '94
CURRENT RELEASE 1996 Bread-doughy yeast esters dominate the bouquet, and there are citrus and apricot flavours in the mouth with a little residual sugar. This could improve with a year or two's bottle-age. Try it with fried lamb's brains.

Quality	ΨΨΨΥ
Value	★★★★
Grapes	riesling
Region	Great Western, Vic.
Cellar	🍾 8+
Alc./Vol.	13.0%
RRP	$13.65

Bethany The Manse Dry White

The name sounds like a very sober, proper sort of wine, but in fact it tastes as though the Schrapel boys were in party mode when they made it.
CURRENT RELEASE 1996 Exaggerated tropical fruit aromas include mango and pineapple, lending an essence-like, fruit-juicy taste. It's not exactly vinous, but it's a competent white wine in a simple, softly fruity, non-woody style. Have it with a prawn cocktail at your local RSL club.

Quality	ΨΨΥ
Value	★★★
Grapes	riesling 40%; semillon 40%; chardonnay 20%
Region	Barossa Valley, SA
Cellar	🍾 1
Alc./Vol.	12.0%
RRP	$12.00

Bianchet Semillon

The Yarra Valley and this variety are not linked – perhaps they should be? This wine comes from a small winery that is not afraid to be individual.
CURRENT RELEASE 1993 Smells and tastes like there has been a bit of botrytis, although the result is a dry wine. The colour is a pale yellow and the nose has botrytis aromas plus a hint of lychee. The palate has gooseberry and apricot flavours, which are coupled with some dusty French oak on a dry finish. It drinks well now, and who knows what further cellaring will bring? Serve with a medium chill next to a bowl of Vietnamese soup.

Quality	ΨΨΨΥ
Value	★★★⋆
Grapes	semillon
Region	Yarra Valley, Vic.
Cellar	🍾 3
Alc./Vol.	12.5%
RRP	$13.50

Bindi Kostas Rind Chardonnay

Quality	♀♀♀♀♀
Value	★★★★
Grapes	chardonnay
Region	Macedon, Vic.
Cellar	🍾 4+
Alc./Vol.	12.5%
RRP	$20.00 (cellar door)

Kostas Rind, whose face is on the label, was a wine and food bon vivant and a mentor of owner Bill Dhillon. *Previous outstanding vintages: '94*
CURRENT RELEASE 1995   A very fine, restrained chardonnay from a cool year. Nectarine and peach fruit aromas underlined by gentle wood. A fine, complex style that's going slowly and that will benefit from cellaring. Could take a chill, then try serving it with Chinese fish balls.

Bloodwood Chardonnay

Quality	♀♀♀♀
Value	★★★
Grapes	chardonnay
Region	Orange, NSW
Cellar	🍾 4+
Alc./Vol.	13.0%
RRP	$20.00

Orange is showing a lot of potential for chardonnay, but perhaps they should rename the place. Orange wine has a slightly citrus ring to it.
CURRENT RELEASE 1996   There's nothing pithy about this Orange chardonnay! It's a shy, reserved style which is very fruit-driven and smells of herbs and a hint of pineapple. Not especially complex, but the finish has good length and harmony. Give it a few months to mellow, then serve with yabbies.

Bowen Estate Chardonnay

Quality	♀♀♀♀♀
Value	★★★★
Grapes	chardonnay
Region	Coonawarra, SA
Cellar	🍾 5
Alc./Vol.	12.5%
RRP	$21.00

Doug Bowen is closing in on The Great Australian Chardonnay Style. His reputation lies firmly with reds, but there's no reason why the chardonnay shouldn't be turning heads.
CURRENT RELEASE 1996   This is a fine, cashew nut peachy style, which is very much driven by fruit, with oak well in the background. It's smooth, rich and yet vibrant in the mouth, and the aftertaste lingers well, considering the modest alcohol. Serve with gratinéed scallops.

Brands Laira Chardonnay

This is often the most impressive wine in the Brands portfolio, built along extravagant lines with the full Burgundian treatment. Maker Jim Brand.

Previous outstanding vintages: '91, '94

CURRENT RELEASE 1995 Sleek and powerful, like a well-oiled weight-lifter; this has muscles that bulge! Intense peachy, buttery aromas, opulent flavour with some alcohol warmth, nice dry finish and good persistence. Crayfish is called for.

Quality	ΨΨΨΨ℘
Value	★★★★
Grapes	chardonnay
Region	Coonawarra, SA
Cellar	▮ 4+
Alc./Vol.	13.5%
RRP	$16.90 Ⓢ

Brands Laira Riesling

Nice to see some companies persisting with riesling in Coonawarra. It would be boring if all they grew was cabernet.

CURRENT RELEASE 1996 A delicate riesling with mineral and lime aromas, which is starting to show some richer, developed characters. It's very delicate in the mouth and perhaps lacks a little intensity, but on the other hand it's quite fine and easy to drink. Try it with yabbie salad.

Quality	ΨΨΨ℘
Value	★★★⊦
Grapes	riesling
Region	Coonawarra, SA
Cellar	▮ 5
Alc./Vol.	11.5%
RRP	$13.70 Ⓢ

Briagolong Estate Chardonnay

Gordon McIntosh is yet another winemaking doctor. His winery is in the East Gippsland region and he has specialised in the Burgundy varieties.

CURRENT RELEASE 1995 This is a 'Look Mum, no hands!' wine where nature seems to have been given a free rein. The colour is light yellow, and the bouquet is somewhat mawkish with rampant malolactic character. The palate is sweetish and somewhat flabby, again a result of vigorous malolactic fermentation, and despite a slight bitterness, the wine has good depth and length. A rich fish pie would be in order.

Quality	ΨΨΨ
Value	★★⊦
Grapes	chardonnay
Region	East Gippsland, Vic.
Cellar	▮ 2
Alc./Vol.	13.3%
RRP	$31.40

Bridgewater Mill Chardonnay

Quality	♀♀♀♀
Value	★★★
Grapes	chardonnay
Region	Adelaide Hills & Clare Valley, SA
Cellar	▮ 3+
Alc./Vol.	13.5%
RRP	$19.30

The second label of Petaluma is named after the company's sparkling wine cellar/restaurant/ tourist facility in the Adelaide Hills.

CURRENT RELEASE 1995   A shy, slightly rubbery nose leads into a dry, savoury palate, which has good fruit–oak balance and lingering aftertaste. A few steps behind the *grand vin* but a decent drink with veal sweetbreads.

Brindabella Hills Riesling

Quality	♀♀♀♀♀
Value	★★★★⊾
Grapes	riesling
Region	Canberra district, NSW
Cellar	▮ 6+
Alc./Vol.	12.5%
RRP	$13.50 (cellar door)

Beautiful name, Brindabella, with all its evocations of Miles Franklin's novel and the glorious country of the upper reaches of the Murrumbidgee River. Maker Roger Harris.

CURRENT RELEASE 1996   Intense lime fragrance, and the lifted aromatics continue throughout the wine. It's a delicate style with intense, pristine, cool-grown riesling fruit threaded with steely acidity. The finish is balanced to dryness. Serve with larb (minted Thai salad).

Brokenwood Cricket Pitch

Quality	♀♀♀♀
Value	★★★⊾
Grapes	sauvignon blanc; semillon
Region	McLaren Vale & Padthaway, SA; Cowra, NSW
Cellar	▮ 2
Alc./Vol.	13.0%
RRP	$16.00

This winery has grown from humble 'weekend hobbyist' origins into one of the most professional and successful wine companies in the country.

CURRENT RELEASE 1997   A cheerful, early-drinking white with dominant herbal, grassy aromas. There's a fragrant estery, bread-dough yeast overtone. The palate is lively and delicate but smooth, without being too dry. It's up-front and somewhat lollyish, and will fill out to positive effect over the first nine months of its life. Food: waldorf salad.

Brokenwood Gewurztraminer Jelka Vineyard

There's a story here: the grapes were not botrytis-affected, but encouraged to raisin on the vine by cutting the sapwood and starving them of nutrients – a common method known as 'cut-cane'. The difference is, these vines were chopped off at ground level for grafting, so this is an unrepeatable wine!

CURRENT RELEASE 1996 Golden colour; lifted spicy/lychee gewurz varietal fruit coupled with vanilla, creating a lovely fragrance. The palate is sweet and rich with loads of everything, including pleasing structure. Complex, semi-luscious and lingering. Yum-yum! Serve with summer pudding.

Quality	🍷🍷🍷🍷🍷
Value	★★★★
Grapes	gewurztraminer
Region	McLaren Vale, SA
Cellar	🍾 2
Alc./Vol.	11.0%
RRP	$14.50 (375ml)

Brokenwood Graveyard Chardonnay

The crème de la crème of this maker's wines are released from the Graveyard vineyard, which is next-door to the winery at Pokolbin.

CURRENT RELEASE 1995 A more marked contrast to the unwooded chardonnay is hard to imagine. There is a stack of toasty, slightly resiny oak that pervades the nose and mouth. It's quite powerful and has excellent persistence, although the finish carries some astringency from the wood. A style that polarises. Food: smoked chicken.

Quality	🍷🍷🍷🍷
Value	★★★
Grapes	chardonnay
Region	Hunter Valley, NSW
Cellar	🍾 3+
Alc./Vol.	13.0%
RRP	$25.00 (cellar door)

Brokenwood Semillon

Brokenwood has moved away from the herbaceous style of semillon because they found it didn't age as well as the more trad, lemony style. Maker Iain Riggs.

Previous outstanding vintages: '83, '85, '86, '91, '92, '94, '95

CURRENT RELEASE 1996 The '97 wasn't quite ready to taste at the time of going to press, but the '96 was still about. It has toned down in the aromatic department since last year's review, and is now more a matter of freshly shelled nuts, lemons and a hint of toast. The acid is prominent and it will certainly age well. While young, it needs food. Try it with sushi.

Quality	🍷🍷🍷🍷
Value	★★★★
Grapes	semillon
Region	Hunter Valley, NSW
Cellar	🍾 7+
Alc./Vol.	11.0%
RRP	$18.50

Brokenwood Unwooded Chardonnay

Quality	▼▼▼▼
Value	★★★★
Grapes	chardonnay
Region	Hunter Valley, NSW
Cellar	▮ 2+
Alc./Vol.	12.5%
RRP	$17.00

The Brokenwood gang are always among the first to get their new-vintage light whites onto the market. Maker Iain Riggs.

CURRENT RELEASE 1997   A most appealing unwooded in a sea of dross. There are smooth cashew nut aromas, and the palate has some richness, with fig and peach flavours that are quite delicious. It has a rounded structure, is well balanced and finishes dry. Try it with sushi.

Brookland Valley Chardonnay

Quality	▼▼▼▼▼
Value	★★★☆
Grapes	chardonnay
Region	Margaret River, WA
Cellar	▮ 4
Alc./Vol.	14.5%
RRP	$28.00

This winery is yet another excellent Margaret River chardonnay maker. So good that BRL Hardy bought 50% of it in May 1997.

CURRENT RELEASE 1996   A complex, lifted wine with richness and typical concentrated flavour of the region. The bouquet has plenty of smoky, slightly sweaty fruit wedded to liberal French oak; the palate is full-bodied and complex, again with no shortage of oak but very nicely done. Try it with veal sweetbreads.

Brown Brothers Family Reserve Chardonnay

Quality	▼▼▼▼
Value	★★★
Grapes	chardonnay
Region	King Valley, Vic.
Cellar	▮ 1
Alc./Vol.	13.5%
RRP	$28.70

This label signifies wines that have been held back for further bottle-ageing. Maker Roland Wahlquist and team.

CURRENT RELEASE 1994   Three years of age have mellowed this wine and given it a deep golden/buttercup-yellow colour with some matured characters, but time has not conferred any real complexity. There are soft, mellow, mature flavours and it drinks well with roast chicken.

Brown Brothers Family Reserve Riesling

Not only is this selection of outstanding grapes given some bottle-age, it also has a slight botrytis influence, which sets it further apart from Browns' standard King Valley riesling. Maker Terry Barnett.

CURRENT RELEASE 1994 Browns have given this just enough bottle-age to let it reveal its talent. The bouquet is full of toasty, honey and earthy/mineral development. In the mouth it's lost its floral youth and has rich, complex, aged flavours with a slight phenolic grip that is countered by a little sweetness. Juicy and long; very appealing drink. Try it with a rich, buttery scallop dish.

Quality	♟♟♟♟♟
Value	★★★★
Grapes	Riesling
Region	King Valley, Vic.
Cellar	🍾 3
Alc./Vol.	13.0%
RRP	$22.50

Brown Brothers Gewurztraminer

The '95 edition won a Penguin award last year. It's an underrated grape variety and deserves a bigger audience. Maker Terry Barnett.

CURRENT RELEASE 1996 Very pungent varietal spiciness pole-vaults out of the glass. The bath soap, lychee perfume also permeates the mouth flavour. It's light-bodied, fine and lively, ending with some alcohol warmth. Serve with Thai fish cakes.

Quality	♟♟♟♟♟
Value	★★★★
Grapes	gewurztraminer
Region	King Valley, Vic.
Cellar	🍾 2
Alc./Vol.	13.5%
RRP	$13.50

Brown Brothers King Valley Chardonnay

In the next century they might have to rename the company Brown Sisters, as the next generation is nearly all girls.

CURRENT RELEASE 1995 This is a pretty smart chardonnay and if we sound surprised, we are. There are rich and complex oak/fruit harmonies throughout, with smoky and tropical notes. It could use a little more length, but the overall impression is stylish. Team it with crispy-skin chicken.

Quality	♟♟♟♟
Value	★★★⯪
Grapes	chardonnay
Region	King Valley, Vic.
Cellar	🍾 2
Alc./Vol.	14.0%
RRP	$17.00

Brown Brothers King Valley Riesling

Quality	♍♍♍
Value	★★★
Grapes	riesling
Region	King Valley, Vic.
Cellar	▲ 2
Alc./Vol.	12.5%
RRP	$13.00

The King Valley is quickly gaining importance: it has 50 vineyards and nearly all were planted since the early '80s.

CURRENT RELEASE 1996 Destined for early drinking, this is a soft, up-front style, which is tending towards blowsy. It has a broad, soft flavour of something like peach and apricot, and while it's perfectly decent drinking, it lacks a little harmony and length. Try it with onion quiche.

Brown Brothers Late Harvest Orange Muscat & Flora

Quality	♍♍♍⟨
Value	★★★
Grapes	orange muscat; flora
Region	North East Victoria
Cellar	▲ 2
Alc./Vol.	9.5%
RRP	$16.40

Trust the Brown brethren to come up with a left-field blend like this! Most ordinary mortals wouldn't have heard of either of these grapes.

CURRENT RELEASE 1996 Candied, honey and spice aromas without botrytis character. The taste is very sweet and somewhat straightforward, with crisp acid to finish. A crowd-pleaser. Try it with fresh fruit salad.

Brown Brothers Semillon

Quality	♍♍♍♍
Value	★★★★
Grapes	semillon
Region	North East Victoria
Cellar	▲ 2
Alc./Vol.	13.5%
RRP	$15.00

North East Victoria is hardly famous for semillon, but this is a cleverly made style that makes good use of toasted oak barrels. Maker Terry Barnett.

CURRENT RELEASE 1996 Nothing adds flavour to semillon like wood, and this has plenty, but the result is a good drink rather than a mouthful of splinters. It's a rich, full-bodied semillon with dominant toasty oak flavours and smooth, lingering aftertaste. Serve with smoked chicken.

Brown Brothers Whitlands Sauvignon Blanc

This scored a gold medal at the Victorian Wines Show in Seymour, in 1996. It comes from one of the country's highest-altitude vineyards – Whitlands – at over 800 metres. The standard '96 King Valley release ($15.30 retail) is not far behind it. Maker Terry Barnett.

CURRENT RELEASE 1996 Benchmark sauvignon blanc with citrus, grassy aromas and tangy acidity that lingers on the finish; it betrays its cool-climate origins. Very intense and a fine partner for fresh Sydney Rock oysters.

Quality	♥♥♥♥⟲
Value	★★★★⟩
Grapes	sauvignon blanc
Region	King Valley, Vic.
Cellar	⬦ 3
Alc./Vol.	11.5%
RRP	$14.30 (cellar door)

Bulletin Place Chardonnay

Another Len Evans label, this one featuring the facade of the old building at 16–18 Bulletin Place, Sydney, which used to house Len Evans Wines. The oldest commercial premises still in use in Australia, it was built by emancipated transportee Mary Reiby in 1816.

CURRENT RELEASE 1996 A touch of earthiness together with peach and nectarine on the nose, which is subtle in the wood department. The taste is straightforward, light-bodied, and offers good value at the price. A partner for pumpkin risotto.

Quality	♥♥♥
Value	★★★⟩
Grapes	chardonnay
Region	not stated
Cellar	⬦ 2
Alc./Vol.	12.5%
RRP	$11.10

Cambewarra Estate Chardonnay

Cambewarra does two chardonnays and you need to read the back label to identify them. One is lightly wooded, the other unwooded. They taste remarkably similar. Winemaking is at Tamburlaine.

CURRENT RELEASE 1996 Light yellow–green colour indicates a well-looked-after white wine. The subtle nose has grapefruit aromas and a hint of oak. It's a reserved style of some delicacy, but it's not really complex. Serve it with salads.

Quality	♥♥♥⟲
Value	★★⟩
Grapes	chardonnay
Region	South Coast, NSW
Cellar	⬦ 3+
Alc./Vol.	12.8%
RRP	$24.00

Canobolas-Smith Chardonnay

Quality	???????
Value	★★★★★
Grapes	chardonnay
Region	Orange, NSW
Cellar	4+
Alc./Vol.	13.5%
RRP	$18.00 (cellar door)

Orange is emerging as one of New South Wales's most exciting regions, with its high-altitude, continental climate. Murray Smith makes wine from his unirrigated vineyard at 850 metres.

Previous outstanding vintages: '93, '94

CURRENT RELEASE 1995   This has really come into its own since last year's review, winning two trophies at the February '97 Canberra Wine Show. An intense, restrained yet complex Chablis style, smelling of butter-scotch and melon with well-integrated oak character. Powerful, rich and long with a steely spine of fine acidity. Drink with crayfish.

Quality	?????
Value	★★★★
Grapes	chardonnay
Region	Orange, NSW
Cellar	1–6
Alc./Vol.	13.8%
RRP	$18.00 (cellar door)

CURRENT RELEASE 1996   What a difference a year makes. This is a nutty, lively style with oak calling the tune. The nose is smoky and there are some stone-fruit aromas. The middleweight palate has peach and grapefruit flavours, and these are matched with some youthful oak that adds a strong tang. The finish is firm. It should be served near room temperature.

Cape Jaffa Unwooded Chardonnay

Quality	?????
Value	★★★★
Grapes	chardonnay
Region	Mount Benson, SA
Cellar	2
Alc./Vol.	13.0%
RRP	$16.00

Cape Jaffa sounds like something you roll down the aisle at the movies. It's a new and promising district north of Robe on the south coast of South Australia. The vineyard is on terra rossa soil. Maker Ralph Fowler.

CURRENT RELEASE 1996   The nose is slightly smoky, and there are clear melon and peach aromas. It has a distinct sauvignon blanc character because of the herbal aspect. The palate has citrus and peach flavours, and there is crisp acid on the finish. It can be served well chilled, and it cries out for a crayfish.

Cape Mentelle Chardonnay

The sample came with a label designed for the UK. It's interesting to note there was no mention of preservatives or alcohol by volume. Maybe the Poms have got it right: drink and the devil take the hindmost. Maker David Hohnen.

CURRENT RELEASE 1995 A cultured style that shows great integration between fruit and wood. The nose is a mixture of melon, grapefruit and oak aromas. It's a creamy-textured wine, thanks to the barrel treatment, and peach and melon are the major flavours. The finish is dry and it doesn't need to be over-chilled. Have it with stirfried pork and vegetables.

Quality	????
Value	★★★★
Grapes	chardonnay
Region	Margaret River, WA
Cellar	4
Alc./Vol.	not stated
RRP	$26.50

Cape Mentelle Semillon Sauvignon Blanc

This marque makes faultless wines, their reputation hinging around red wines. The white wines are ever so refined; sometimes a bit more grunge would be appreciated.

CURRENT RELEASE 1996 As ever, this is a blanched and refined wine. The herbal nose has a strong goose-berry element with hints of fennel and tinned peas. The sauvignon blanc provides the tropical fruit flavours. There is also evidence of barrel fermentation in the texture. Discreet wood adorns the finish. Don't get us wrong: it's a beautifully crafted, complex wine, but where's the grunt? Serve with a medium to deep chill, and try it with tripe in a black bean sauce.

Quality	????
Value	★★★★
Grapes	sauvignon blanc 50%; semillon 50%
Region	Margaret River, WA
Cellar	2
Alc./Vol.	13.5%
RRP	$18.50

Carlyle Estate Chardonnay

A new label on the block from North East Victoria. The emphasis seems to be on the production of fine table wines.

CURRENT RELEASE 1994 The nose is peachy with a trace of wood aroma. The palate is medium-bodied, with peach flavour dominant. The finish is ruled by oak. It can cope with a medium chill, and it goes well with smoked turkey.

Quality	???
Value	★★★★
Grapes	chardonnay
Region	North East Victoria
Cellar	2
Alc./Vol.	13.5%
RRP	$14.00

Cassegrain Hastings River Chardonnay

Quality	????
Value	★★★★
Grapes	chardonnay
Region	Hastings Valley, NSW
Cellar	↓ 5
Alc./Vol.	12.2%
RRP	$16.95

A pox on Tom Wolfe's excellent book *The Right Stuff* because it exposed the aviation term 'envelope' and turned it into common currency. The Cassegrains went beyond the envelope when they planted their Hastings Vineyard in 1981.

CURRENT RELEASE 1996   The wood gets in the way a bit, but there is excellent chardonnay character. The nose has peach and wood aromas. There are peach and melon flavours on the palate, and these are seasoned with some exuberant oak with a slightly raw edge. Time may soften the equation. Don't over-chill, and serve with smoked trout.

Cathcart Ridge Rhymney Reef Chardonnay

Quality	????
Value	★★★
Grapes	chardonnay
Region	Grampians, other Vic.
Cellar	↓ 4
Alc./Vol.	12.5%
RRP	$17.00

This winery has joined the wooded-versus-unwooded chardonnay debate. They believe the public want the unwooded style.

CURRENT RELEASE 1996   This has been given the full treatment including malolactic fermentation on lees. The only thing missing is the oak treatment. It has a peachy nose, and the palate is broad with a buttery texture and a soft peach flavour. The acid on the finish is equally soft, almost cuddly. It can be served well chilled. Try it with a warm salad of smoked chicken.

Cathcart Ridge Rhymney Reef Colombard Chenin Blanc

Quality	???
Value	★★★
Grapes	colombard; chenin blanc
Region	Grampians, other Vic.
Cellar	↓ 2
Alc./Vol.	12.5%
RRP	$13.00

Rhymney Reef is a goldfield and when it appears on the Cathcart Ridge label, it means estate-grown fruit had been augmented by fruit from the district.

CURRENT RELEASE 1996   This is a big, soft drink-now style with some apple qualities. The nose is fresh and spicy, and the palate has green apple flavours and a lively tartness. The acid on the finish is crisp. It can be served well chilled. Try it with roast pork.

Chain of Ponds Riesling

Chain of Ponds took the Sydney market by storm in 1996, with a bevy of lovely wines from their Adelaide Hills and Kangaroo Island vineyards. Proprietors are Caj and Ginny Amadio.
CURRENT RELEASE 1996   Minerally and slightly floral aromas; lime and peach in the mouth, soft and up-front with a hint of sweetness that's balanced by firmness on the finish. A promising wine from an excellent riesling region. Try it with pan-fried bream.

Quality	?????
Value	★★★★⊦
Grapes	riesling
Region	Adelaide Hills, SA
Cellar	▮ 5
Alc./Vol.	13.0%
RRP	$15.30

Chain of Ponds Sauvignon Blanc Semillon

Adelaide Hills sauvignon blanc triumphs again! What with the Weavers, Shaws & Smiths, Leland Estates, and so on, it's proving a deadly combination.
Previous outstanding vintages: '96
CURRENT RELEASE 1997   A very aromatic, vivacious wine that really sings on the palate and has an impressively long aftertaste. Crisp, fresh, crushed gooseberry and green-leafy aromas, together with pepper and grass/hay. The use of oak is so subtle it's barely discernible. Food: oven-baked Kangaroo Island marron.

Quality	?????
Value	★★★★★
Grapes	sauvignon blanc; semillon
Region	Adelaide Hills, SA
Cellar	▮ 3
Alc./Vol.	13.0%
RRP	$17.70

PENGUIN BEST WHITE BLEND/OTHER VARIETY

Chapel Hill Eden Valley Riesling

Chapel Hill might be located in the Southern Vales but it has to admit defeat and source riesling from Eden Valley. Needs must: the outcome is an attractive wine. Maker Pam Dunsford.
CURRENT RELEASE 1995   There is evidence of bottle-age on the nose, but fresh citrus is still dominant. The palate has a zesty, sherbet-like quality and the finish retains fresh acid that goes well with the lime flavours on the palate. Give it a big chill and it will thrill with pan-fried whiting in beer batter.

Quality	????
Value	★★★⊦
Grapes	riesling
Region	Eden Valley, SA
Cellar	▮ 2
Alc./Vol.	12.0%
RRP	$14.50

Chapel Hill Reserve Chardonnay

Quality	ㅜㅜㅜㅜ℉
Value	★★★★⊦
Grapes	chardonnay
Region	McLaren Vale, SA
Cellar	➡ 2–6
Alc./Vol.	13.5%
RRP	$16.50

There is a real chapel on the hill and it also doubled as a primary school. It's charming, albeit a little kitsch. The winery is super-high-tech, and a winemaker couldn't want for more.

CURRENT RELEASE 1995 A wood-driven style, but time should liberate the fruit. There are peach and melon aromas and tinges of spice. The palate is full-bodied, with peach and melon flavours. There is a sting of oak on the finish that time in the bottle should tame. Don't over-chill, and try it with smoked trout.

Chateau Tahbilk Chardonnay

Quality	ㅜㅜㅜㅜ
Value	★★★★
Grapes	chardonnay
Region	Goulburn, Vic.
Cellar	▮ 4
Alc./Vol.	14.0%
RRP	$17.00

This variety is a late arrival at this historic vineyard. In fact, the first commercial Australian chardonnay came from Mudgee in 1971.

CURRENT RELEASE 1995 This is a substantial white that has plenty of flavour and body. The nose has citrus and peach aromas plus a background of oak (both American and French). The palate is mouthfilling with a glycerol texture. There are lemon and peach flavours and a tickle of vanilla. The wood adds a dry aspect to the finish. It should cellar well. Don't over-chill, and try it with whitebait fritters.

Chestnut Grove Verdelho

Quality	ㅜㅜㅜ
Value	★★★
Grapes	verdelho
Region	Manjimup, WA
Cellar	▮ 2
Alc./Vol.	13.0%
RRP	$16.50

The winery was established in 1991 and planted to 16 hectares under vine. The wines are made by various contract winemakers.

CURRENT RELEASE 1996 In a masked line-up you could be forgiven for thinking this is a sav. blanc. The nose is grassy and herbal with a smoky background. The palate is light with passionfruit and other tropical elements, and there is crisp acid on the finish. It can be served well chilled. Try it with a pasta carbonara.

Cleveland Chardonnay

This is a wine with attitude, just like the proprietor of the estate, Keith Brien, who makes no bones about not making 'commercial styles'. The vineyard was founded in 1984 and there are 4 hectares under vine. Maker Keith Brien.

CURRENT RELEASE 1996 This is a flinty style that needs time in the bottle. The nose is rich and there is abundant toasty oak with underlying peach aromas. The palate is medium-bodied with a complex fruit structure and yeasty lees qualities. The finish is ruled by oak. It should be served with a little chill. Try it with smoked cod.

Quality	♥♥♥♥
Value	★★★★
Grapes	chardonnay
Region	Macedon, Vic.
Cellar	➦ 2–6
Alc./Vol.	12.5%
RRP	$18.00

Clonakilla Rhine Riesling

Normally anything that comes out of the Canberra district ends up being a pain in the posterior, but when it comes to wine there are some promising drinks to be had.

CURRENT RELEASE 1996 This is a fresh, crisp riesling with a hint of sugar and plenty of acid. There are pinpoint bubbles, which prove the wine was bottled under a head of CO_2 (they bleed off quickly). The nose is aromatic with citrus aromas. The palate includes a shock of lime and the aforementioned sugar. The acid is zesty and mouth-trilling. Serve it very well chilled with pan-fried whiting.

Quality	♥♥♥♥
Value	★★★★
Grapes	riesling
Region	Canberra region, NSW
Cellar	➦ 4
Alc./Vol.	11.3%
RRP	$14.00 (cellar door)

Clonakilla Semillon Sauvignon Blanc

The symbol on the label has certain significance in Irish history. According to MS it would make a great sign for a mosquito coil factory. Maker John Kirk.

CURRENT RELEASE 1996 A well-made wine with plenty of flavour. The nose has a herb and newly mown paddock aroma. The palate introduces a tinned pea element to the gooseberry flavours, and there is fresh acid on the finish. It can be served with a full chill. Try spaghetti marinara.

Quality	♥♥♥♥
Value	★★★★
Grapes	semillon; sauvignon blanc
Region	Canberra region, NSW
Cellar	▮ 2
Alc./Vol.	13.0%
RRP	$14.00 (cellar door)

Cloudy Bay Chardonnay

Quality	ΥΥΥΥΫ́
Value	★★★★
Grapes	chardonnay
Region	Marlborough, NZ
Cellar	▮ 4
Alc./Vol.	13.5%
RRP	$26.50

It's big and bold but it also shows restraint and masterful winemaking. Cloudy Bay was established in 1985 and set the scene for civilised New Zealand white wine styles. There are 50 hectares under vine. Maker Kevin Judd.

Previous outstanding vintages: '92, '93, '94

CURRENT RELEASE 1995   All the bells, lights and whistles are working in this wine. It has received every winemaking treatment to ensure maximum complexity. The nose has a mixture of aromas from tropical fruit through to nuts and flinty smoke. The palate is an exotic bowl of fruit including guava and figs, and the oak adds licorice and nutty characters. The finish is dry and balanced. It goes well with a medium chill and a warm salad of quail.

Cloudy Bay Sauvignon Blanc

Quality	ΥΥΥΥ
Value	★★★★
Grapes	sauvignon blanc
Region	Marlborough, NZ
Cellar	▮ 2
Alc./Vol.	13.5%
RRP	$18.00

This has been a nice little earner for the makers. When first released there was a buying frenzy, and stocks lasted only a matter of weeks. These days it sells out each year but the pace is more stately. Maker Kevin Judd.

CURRENT RELEASE 1996   More buxom than usual, but it remains restrained by early New Zealand standards. The nose is grassy, with tropical fruit and herb aromas. The same translates as far as the flavours on the palate go. There is also a hint of sweetness, and the finish is soft and clean. The wine can be well chilled, and it's great with goat's cheese.

Coldstream Hills Chardonnay

This is the cooking chardonnay from Coldstream Hills. The reserve gets all the guts and glory, but quite often in a good year the lower ranks have loads of promise. *Previous outstanding vintages: '90, '91, '92, '94, '95* CURRENT RELEASE 1996 A solid citizen with power and complexity. The colour is a bright lemon–yellow with tinges of green. The nose has melon, peach and wood aromas. There is a reasonably complex palate with peach, melon and a hint of nuts. There is abundant French oak on the finish. Don't over-chill, and serve with flounder in a lemon sauce.

Quality	♟♟♟♟
Value	★★★⯪
Grapes	chardonnay
Region	Yarra Valley, Vic.
Cellar	▮ 4
Alc./Vol.	13.0%
RRP	$22.00

Coldstream Hills Reserve Chardonnay

Since the last edition of this book, the company has been absorbed by the Southcorp group. James Halliday remains as winemaker, but where his new company allegiance leaves him in terms of writing remains to be seen. *Previous outstanding vintages: '86, '88, '90, '91, '92, '94* CURRENT RELEASE 1995 This wine is more reserved than usual (pardon the play on words). French oak dominates the nose with a smoky bacon character. The colour is a pale lemon–yellow, and the palate is a mixture of grapefruit and stone-fruit flavours. The finish brings out the tall timbers with great length and toasty flavours. Don't over-chill, and serve it with turkey.

Quality	♟♟♟♟
Value	★★★⯪
Grapes	chardonnay
Region	Yarra Valley, Vic.
Cellar	▮ 5
Alc./Vol.	13.0%
RRP	$30.00

Coldstream Hills Semillon Sauvignon Blanc

Quality	♥♥♥♥
Value	★★★★
Grapes	semillon; sauvignon blanc
Region	Yarra Valley, Vic.
Cellar	🍷 2
Alc./Vol.	12.0%
RRP	$19.00

'Say it isn't so, Joe' . . . Why this blend from one of the best vineyards in the region? Not that it's a bad wine, it's just that this marriage of convenience usually means that sauvignon blanc comes to dictate the flavour. HH approves; MS doesn't. Maker James Halliday.

CURRENT RELEASE 1996   Although it's the minority of the blend, the sauvignon blanc seems to be in seven league boots and strides ahead of the semillon. The nose is full of crushed-pea-pod and herb aromas. The palate is grassy and lean, with fresh herbs and citrus flavours. These are backed up by crisp acid on a clean finish. Chill well and trot out the white asparagus.

Coolangatta Estate Alexander Berry Chardonnay

Quality	♥♥♥
Value	★★★
Grapes	chardonnay
Region	South Coast, NSW
Cellar	🍷 2
Alc./Vol.	13.0%
RRP	$16.00

Coolangatta Estate is in the Shoalhaven district and the wines are made at Tyrrell's. There is also a resort at the vineyard.

CURRENT RELEASE 1996   This is a straightforward chardonnay with light oak treatment and good body-weight. The nose is subdued with a hint of pineapple and dusty wood; the palate is dry with prominent acid and a slight grip. It would go well with oysters mornay.

Coriole Semillon

Quality	♥♥♥♥
Value	★★★★
Grapes	semillon
Region	McLaren Vale, SA
Cellar	🍷 4
Alc./Vol.	13.5%
RRP	$18.50

Unlike the Hunter Valley there is no definitive McLaren Vale semillon style. Could this be a blueprint? While it's hardly a svelte super model, it's a voluptuous full-on style.

CURRENT RELEASE 1996   Big wine with loads of character, thanks to the wood treatment. The nose has gooseberry and lanolin aromas. The palate is full-bodied with a creamy texture. Gooseberry is the major flavour and there is also a nutty character. The oak builds a raft for the fruit with a long, dry finish. It should be served with a medium chill. Try it with a quail and mushroom risotto.

Cowra Estate Cool Classic Chardonnay

Blue wine bottles pose many questions. Isn't blue glass reserved for poisons? How will a wine age in blue glass? Why put it in blue in the first place? We guess because it's supposed to look cool.

CURRENT RELEASE 1996 It comes as quite a shock to see the wine pour and reveal a normal, yellow–gold colour. The nose is peachy and there is a toasty background. Peach and melon flavours seem to be haunted by ever-present oak. The finish shows plenty of wood. It should not be served too cold. Try it with pan-fried veal.

Quality	🍷🍷🍷½
Value	★★★½
Grapes	chardonnay
Region	Cowra, NSW
Cellar	🍾 3
Alc./Vol.	13.5%
RRP	$10.00

Craig Avon Vineyard Chardonnay

Cool-climate viticulture and a dedicated, intense maker (in terms of wine goals), Ken Lang, has developed a distinctive style with chardonnay.

CURRENT RELEASE 1995 It's a flinty style in the Chablis definition. The nose has distinctive varietal aromas of grapefruit and melon. There is also some smoky oak lurking. The palate is flinty with grapefruit flavours, which dovetail with the wood, adding to a very dry finish. It can be served with a medium chill, and it goes well with scallops in a black bean sauce.

Quality	🍷🍷🍷🍷
Value	★★★★
Grapes	chardonnay
Region	Mornington Peninsula, Vic.
Cellar	🍾 5
Alc./Vol.	13.0%
RRP	$26.00

Craiglee Chardonnay

This pioneering vineyard is the labour of love (and sometimes fear and loathing) of Patrick Carmody. He has endured and triumphed, making a distinctive style with great finesse.

CURRENT RELEASE 1995 The nose has citrus and stone-fruit aromas, and the colour is a sparkling lemon–yellow with hints of green. The palate is steely and slightly reserved at this point of development. There is a hint of lees character and plenty of grapefruit flavours. The finish is well tailored and elegant, with sympathetic oak. Serve it with a medium chill beside some smoked trout.

Quality	🍷🍷🍷🍷½
Value	★★★★½
Grapes	chardonnay
Region	Macedon, Vic.
Cellar	🍾 8
Alc./Vol.	13.0%
RRP	$22.00

Craigmoor Mudgee Chardonnay

Quality	♥♥♥
Value	★★★
Grapes	chardonnay
Region	Mudgee, NSW
Cellar	▮ 3
Alc./Vol.	12.5%
RRP	$13.50

Craigmoor is the birthplace of chardonnay in Australia, and that goes back over 100 years (look up the history books). The winery can boast the first modern release in 1971.

CURRENT RELEASE 1996 A softer style with the emphasis on fruit. The nose has melon, apricot and peach smells. These are the flavours encountered on the palate as well as a dash of toasty wood spices. The finish has more toast character and adds support to the fruit. It can tolerate a medium to full chill. Try it with lightly curried prawns.

Craigmoor Mudgee Semillon

Quality	♥♥♥♥
Value	★★★★
Grapes	semillon
Region	Mudgee, NSW
Cellar	▮ 6
Alc./Vol.	12.5%
RRP	$12.00

If the Hunter Valley does well with the variety, why not the neighbouring district of Mudgee, which is higher and therefore cooler?

CURRENT RELEASE 1996 Big perfumed nose with lanolin, honeysuckle and gooseberry aromas. The palate has tart gooseberry fruit and a medium body. There is evidence of oak and high acid on the finish. It should cellar well, but you can drink it now with a reasonable chill. Try it with crab mousse.

Cranswick Estate Autumn Gold Botrytis Semillon

Quality	♥♥♥♥↓
Value	★★★★
Grapes	semillon
Region	Griffith, NSW
Cellar	▮ 3
Alc./Vol.	11.0%
RRP	$22.00 (375ml)

Yet another Griffith super-sweetie. Cranswick are trying really hard with their presentation and marketing under the direction of CEO Graham Cranswick-Smith. Maker Ian Hongell.

CURRENT RELEASE 1994 A developing style with a bright gold/green colour and a honeyed complex nose. The palate is equally complex with a honeyed texture, and marmalade and toffee flavours. There is also some underlying citrus, which adds to the sensation of acid on the finish. The coda is crisp and refreshing, so the wine can be served well chilled. Try it with smoked salmon.

Crawford River Riesling

John Thomson is a farmer who turned his hand to winemaking in 1975, and judging by his last few vintages he's mastered the art with startling ease. All the wines are estate-grown.

CURRENT RELEASE 1996   A drum roll, please, for one of the best rieslings we've seen from this corner of Australia. It's an impressively aromatic, pungent cool-climate style with slightly herbaceous, green-tinged floral aromas and concentrated palate flavour. The floral/citrus flavours are fresh and very long on the aftertaste. It's bonzer with a full chill, and we'd recommend it with a scallop and leek gratin.

Quality	🍷🍷🍷🍷🍷
Value	★★★★★
Grapes	riesling
Region	Portland, Vic.
Cellar	🍷 6+
Alc./Vol.	13.0%
RRP	$19.00

PENGUIN BEST RIESLING

Dalfarras Sauvignon Blanc

Alister Purbrick is an active chap: he's involved in wine industry politics, has branched out into contract grape-growing for major wine companies, and together with wife Rosa he's launched this new brand.

CURRENT RELEASE 1996 Passionfruit, pineapple, nectarine – a very tropical style with touches of green herbs, and a palate that's stacked full of soft fruit heightened by a tickle of sweetness. A fine sauvignon to serve with a vegetable terrine.

Quality	🍷🍷🍷🍷🍷
Value	★★★★★
Grapes	sauvignon blanc
Region	Goulburn Valley, Vic.; McLaren Vale, SA
Cellar	🍷 2
Alc./Vol.	12.5%
RRP	$14.50

Dalfarras Unoaked Chardonnay

Rosa Purbrick, Alister (Chateau Tahbilk) Purbrick's wife, was a Dalfarra before marriage. He makes the wine, she paints the labels.

CURRENT RELEASE 1996 Tropical fruit, melon and grapefruit aromas greet the nose, and there's some freshly fermented banana esteriness, too. Clean, vibrant, fruity – not bone-dry but very much the current vogue in unwooded chardonnay. Serve with crudités.

Quality	🍷🍷🍷🍷
Value	★★★★
Grapes	chardonnay
Region	Central Vic.
Cellar	🍷 2
Alc./Vol.	13.0%
RRP	$14.50

Dalwhinnie Chardonnay

Quality	♟♟♟♟♟
Value	★★★¢
Grapes	chardonnay
Region	Pyrenees, Vic.
Cellar	▮ 5
Alc./Vol.	13.0%
RRP	$27.40

Dalwhinnie is the Jones family vineyard, adjacent to Taltarni. Trivia buffs will know it's also the name of a very fine single-malt whisky from Scotland.

CURRENT RELEASE 1996   A captivating, multi-faceted wine with deep tropical fruit aromas and a hint of butterscotch. The fruit salad character reappears in the mouth and the wood is lightly handled. It has real finesse and sustains interest to the last drop. Try it with snapper quenelles.

d'Arenberg The Noble Riesling

Quality	♟♟♟♟
Value	★★★
Grapes	riesling
Region	McLaren Vale, SA
Cellar	▮ 2
Alc./Vol.	14.5%
RRP	$25.75 (375ml)

The folks at d'Arenberg have struck a flash new range of labels and every wine has a grand title: The Olive Grove, The Old Vine, The Peppermint Paddock, and so on.

CURRENT RELEASE 1995   This maker's sticky riesling is always a marriage of major sweetness and major alcohol, so handle with care. The colour is deep yellow to gold, the nose has a slightly left-field chemical overtone together with sweet fruit aromas, while the taste is tremendously unctuous, syrupy, concentrated and alcoholic, with a nectar-like quality. Try crème brûlée.

d'Arenberg The Olive Grove Chardonnay

Quality	♟♟♟
Value	★★★
Grapes	chardonnay
Region	McLaren Vale, SA
Cellar	▮ 2
Alc./Vol.	13.5%
RRP	$14.50

It's 'The' this and 'The' that at d'Arenberg (and many other wineries) these days. It sounds very singular and authoritative, but too many 'The's are just a pain in the The neck.

CURRENT RELEASE 1996   Pineapple and nectarine feature on the nose. The wine is lightly wooded and has a slight alcohol lift. It's a straightforward, decent drink that falls away a little on the finish. Serve with lemon chicken.

d'Arenberg White Ochre

You don't often see crouchen in a quality wine these days, which puts this in the 'blast from the past' category. Maker Chester Osborn.
CURRENT RELEASE 1996   Dusty, powder-puff aromas, light and essence-like, with slight spiciness. Lightweight and somewhat wispy, it has herbal flavours on the palate and is a decent dry-finishing, soft, quaffing white to serve with whitebait fritters.

Quality	♟♟♟
Value	★★★★
Grapes	riesling 68%; crouchen 20%; chardonnay 12%
Region	McLaren Vale, SA
Cellar	▮ 1
Alc./Vol.	13.0%
RRP	$9.65

David Traeger Verdelho

This is probably only the second verdelho from the King Valley, and is something of a benchmark wine for ex-Mitchelton winemaker Traeger. (The other is by Brown Brothers, natch.)
CURRENT RELEASE 1996   Simple nectarine/stone-fruit aroma, clean and well made, with a trace of sweetness filling out the soft, rounded palate. Fruit-salad-like in the mouth and very drinkable if well chilled. One of the better verdelhos around. Try it with duck and lychee salad.

Quality	♟♟♟♟
Value	★★★
Grapes	verdelho
Region	King Valley, Vic.
Cellar	▮ 2
Alc./Vol.	12.5%
RRP	$16.75

De Bortoli Gulf Station Chardonnay

We get to read lots of back labels, but few with poetry supplied. The marketers have tried to weave a spell here, but the wine stands up perfectly well by itself. Maker Steve Webber.
CURRENT RELEASE 1995   A complex style featuring charred oak and butterscotch aromas, added to honey and lemon flavours, which are very seductive. The palate is tightly structured and fine, with a dry finish and good length. A most impressive debut. Serve with cheese soufflé. ►

Quality	♟♟♟♟♟
Value	★★★★
Grapes	chardonnay
Region	Yarra Valley, Vic.
Cellar	▮ 4
Alc./Vol.	13.0%
RRP	$17.40

Quality	♈♈♈♉
Value	★★★
Grapes	chardonnay
Region	Yarra Valley, Vic.
Cellar	🍷 2
Alc./Vol.	13.0%
RRP	$18.00 ⑤

CURRENT RELEASE 1996   This vintage has a touch of 'gymnasium'. There's a sweaty, herbal aroma overlying pineapple fruit and there's also a smoky overtone. The palate has good flavour with a little richness, and it finishes agreeably smooth. The wood is lightly handled. Try it with asparagus quiche.

De Bortoli Noble One Botrytis Semillon

Quality	♈♈♈♈♈
Value	★★★★★
Grapes	semillon
Region	Riverina, NSW
Cellar	🍷 4+
Alc./Vol.	11.0%
RRP	$25.00 (375ml)

This is *the* one – the one that turned the Riverina's reputation around. It's amazing what one wine can achieve if it's good enough. Maker Darren De Bortoli and team.
Previous outstanding vintages: '82, '83, '84, '87, '90, '91, '92, '93
CURRENT RELEASE 1994   What? Only two trophies and 11 golds? They're slipping! But seriously, this is a marvellous drop of sticky wine. It has a deep golden/amber colour, a bouquet that's a cacophony of marmalade, mixed peel, honey and vanilla, and a mouthfilling unctuous sweetness and intensity. Rich and powerful; this is the marque on song. Drink with crème brûlée.

De Bortoli Windy Peak Rhine Riesling

Quality	♈♈♈♈♉
Value	★★★★★
Grapes	riesling
Region	King & Yarra Valleys, Vic.
Cellar	🍷 4
Alc./Vol.	11.5%
RRP	$13.65 ⑤

Riesling is still one of the great under-valued Australian wines. It comes into its own with a little bottle-age.
CURRENT RELEASE 1995   This is ageing gracefully, and while the bouquet has had time to evolve, the delicacy on the palate remains. The aromas are of peach blossom and small flowers, and the taste reveals more as you drink. It's light-bodied and very fine, and should not be served too cold. Good with scallops à la nage.

De Bortoli Windy Peak Spatlese Riesling

This is a brilliant wine but its genius will probably never be appreciated. Spatlese is the dodo of the wine world. CURRENT RELEASE 1996 A complex medium–sweet white, this smells spicy and floral. There is also a light hint of botrytis in the tea-leafy/sweaty aspects. It's quite sweet but also soft and deliciously flavoured. Just the thing for foie gras, or failing that, pâté.

Quality	♀♀♀♀⦶
Value	★★★★
Grapes	riesling
Region	King Valley, Vic.
Cellar	▮ 5+
Alc./Vol.	11.0%
RRP	$13.65 Ⓢ

De Bortoli Yarra Valley Chardonnay

The De Bortoli motto is *Semper ad Majora*, which means always striving for better. Their Yarra wines do just that. Maker Steve Webber.
Previous outstanding vintages: '91, '92, '93, '94, '95
CURRENT RELEASE 1996 True to form, this is a subtle, refined style with restrained oak. The colour is a brilliant mid-yellow and the bouquet offers subdued butter-scotch, melon and pear scents. It's tight and focused on the palate with good intensity, and it promises much more if kept a year or so. Try it with sautéed Balmain bug tails.

Quality	♀♀♀♀⦶
Value	★★★★
Grapes	chardonnay
Region	Yarra Valley, Vic.
Cellar	▮ 4
Alc./Vol.	13.5%
RRP	$24.00 Ⓢ

De Bortoli Yarra Valley Semillon

The restaurant at the De Bortoli Yarra Valley winery has been voted the best tourism restaurant (whatever that means) twice running at the Victorian Tourism Awards. CURRENT RELEASE 1996 An impressive debut for this new varietal. The aromas are of cut-grass, basil and assorted herbs; the taste is soft, fruity and dry. It has crispness and fragrance and is quite up-front. Probably best drunk young. Try it with vegetarian foods.

Quality	♀♀♀♀
Value	★★★⯪
Grapes	semillon
Region	Yarra Valley, Vic.
Cellar	▮ 4
Alc./Vol.	11.0%
RRP	$18.60 Ⓢ

Deakin Estate Alfred Chardonnay

Quality	♟♟♟♟♟
Value	★★★★★
Grapes	chardonnay
Region	Murray Valley, Vic.
Cellar	🍷 2
Alc./Vol.	13.5%
RRP	$12.00 Ⓢ

Alfred Deakin did a stint as prime minister of Australia. He was instrumental in bringing irrigation to the Murray Valley and hence creating the wine industry there.

Previous outstanding vintages: '95

CURRENT RELEASE 1996   Fruit aromas of peach, melon and nectarine overlaid with a gentle kiss of oak. There is some richness on the palate and the finish is long and properly dry. A stylish, restrained chardonnay and a triumph considering its origins and price. Serve with scallop mousseline.

Deakin Estate Chardonnay

Quality	♟♟♟♟
Value	★★★★★
Grapes	chardonnay
Region	Murray Valley, Vic.
Cellar	🍷 2
Alc./Vol.	14.0%
RRP	$9.95 Ⓢ

This Riverland maker has come close to disproving the old adage that you can't make a silk purse out of a sow's ear, by proving that the Murray River regions can grow some excellent grapes. This won a gold medal in Perth.

CURRENT RELEASE 1996   Superbly stylish wine for a chardonnay with so little apparent wood. The nose is melon and cashew nuts with a very subtle veneer of oak and malolactic influence. The palate has great delicacy, yet lovely flavour and length. Hard-to-beat value. Try it with asparagus gratin.

Deakin Estate Colombard

Quality	♟♟♟♟♟
Value	★★★★★
Grapes	colombard
Region	Murray Valley, Vic.
Cellar	🍷 1
Alc./Vol.	12.5%
RRP	$9.35

Winemaker Mark Zeppel is one of the quiet achievers of the wine industry. He was a Roseworthy contemporary of one of the authors, where he was a hard worker and as quiet as a dormouse.

CURRENT RELEASE 1996   An excellent dry white that transcends its lowly Riverland origins. Sandalwood and ripe, tropical fruit aromas, which are estery and inviting. It's fresh and lively in the mouth, with intense yet balanced flavour. The richness and length hint at a subtle use of wood. Delicious wine, skilfully made. Food: seafood cocktail.

Deakin Estate Semillon Chardonnay

This wine appears under a new Qantas Australian Grand Prix label and continues the amazing quality this company produces from Riverland grapes.
CURRENT RELEASE 1996   Fresh, bracing lime and lemongrass aromas, delicate and fine in the mouth with no hot-climate phenolic coarseness at all. There's a deft touch of wood in the background that's barely noticeable. Superior stuff – worthy of a great race. Try it with Vietnamese salad.

Quality	▼▼▼▼?
Value	★★★★★
Grapes	semillon; chardonnay
Region	Murray River, Vic.
Cellar	⬦ 1
Alc./Vol.	13.0%
RRP	$12.00

Delatite Chardonnay

The first Delatite wines to see the light of the glass were under a special vineyard label from Brown Brothers. Since then the family have taken over the wine chores.
CURRENT RELEASE 1996   This is an engaging style that has some aromatic qualities as well as the traditional chardonnay elements. The nose is quite floral and the palate weighs in with peach, melon and lemon flavours. There is also some supportive oak on a long finish. A medium chill and sweetbreads in white wine sauce will thrill.

Quality	▼▼▼▼
Value	★★★★
Grapes	chardonnay
Region	Mansfield, Vic.
Cellar	⬦ 4
Alc./Vol.	12.5%
RRP	$21.00

Demondrille The Dove Semillon Sauvignon Blanc

This wine won a silver medal and trophy at the '97 Canberra District Wine Show for the best semillon, sauvignon blanc or blend.
CURRENT RELEASE 1996   A light, fresh, crisp wine with apple and herbaceous aromas, and semillon-dominant, straw/hay and lemony flavours that linger well. A promising start for a new producer.

Quality	▼▼▼▼
Value	★★★☆
Grapes	semillon 50%; sauvignon blanc 50%
Region	Hilltops, NSW
Cellar	⬦ 2
Alc./Vol.	11.9%
RRP	$15.00

Devil's Lair Fifth Leg

Quality	♥♥♥♥❦
Value	★★★❦
Grapes	chardonnay 60%; sauvignon blanc 20%; semillon 20%
Region	Margaret River, WA
Cellar	▮ 4
Alc./Vol.	13.0%
RRP	$20.00

This wine, released in late 1996, is a masterpiece of modern marketing. It must have impressed 'Big Brother' Southcorp, because they bought the place. Maker Janice McDonald.

CURRENT RELEASE 1996   Startling for its labelling as much as its flavour, this new blend of chardonnay, sauvignon blanc and semillon bursts from the glass with riveting tropical fruit and lime/citrus aromas. It owes nothing to oak, and the flavour is tangy and intense with richness and length to burn. Food: sushi.

Diamond Valley Blue Label Chardonnay

Quality	♥♥♥♥♥
Value	★★★★★
Grapes	chardonnay
Region	Yarra Valley, Vic.
Cellar	▮ 4
Alc./Vol.	13.0%
RRP	$18.50

This wine, made from bought-in Yarra grapes, upstaged its silver-medal-winning big sister, the estate-grown chardonnay, by winning gold at the '96 Victorian Wines Show. The Blue Label shows better young; the other's built for a longer haul.

CURRENT RELEASE 1996   A more fruit-accented style than the estate chardonnay, and it encapsulates the essence of Yarra Valley chardonnay. A very fine, understated, seamless and long-finishing chardonnay with oodles of class. Try it with grilled blue-eye steaks.

Diamond Valley Estate Chardonnay

Quality	♥♥♥♥❦
Value	★★★★
Grapes	chardonnay
Region	Yarra Valley, Vic.
Cellar	▮ 4+
Alc./Vol.	13.2%
RRP	$29.50

David Lance has succeeded in crafting a distinctive and highly attractive style. It's very delicately wooded.
Previous outstanding vintages: '90, '92, '94, '95
CURRENT RELEASE 1996   A brilliant fruit-driven style, still with green tints in the colour, and smelling of fresh melon, white peach and a hint of basil. Tropical flavours burst in the mouth: passionfruit, guava and grapefruit flavours abound, beautifully harmonised. Try it with smoked salmon.

Domaine Chandon Colonnade Chardonnay

This is fashioned from the premier tailles of sparkling wine grapes. It's very lightly oaked.

CURRENT RELEASE 1995   The nose is simple but has hi-fi lemon essence aromas. The taste is soft, light, straightforward and fruity, again with pervading lemon flavours. It's adaptable with food. Try shellfish.

Quality	♟♟♟
Value	★★★
Grapes	chardonnay
Region	various
Cellar	▮ 2
Alc./Vol.	12.5%
RRP	$12.90

Drayton's Verdelho

This is one of the most popular verdelhos in the Hunter. The somewhat garish labelling makes it hard to miss on the bottle-shop shelf. Maker Trevor Drayton.

CURRENT RELEASE 1997   From what winemakers like to term a 'difficult' vintage (read 'nightmare') this is a very acceptable verdelho, which has plenty of flavour and promises to settle down with a few more months in the bottle. It has a grapey nose with hints of sandalwood over typical verdelho musky spice. The texture is quite viscous with plenty of weight and mouth-feel. Try it with tandoori chicken.

Quality	♟♟♟♟
Value	★★★★
Grapes	verdelho
Region	Hunter Valley, NSW
Cellar	▮ 2
Alc./Vol.	13.0%
RRP	$14.80 ⑤

Eaglehawk Rhine Riesling

A Wolf Blass brand that recalls the period when Blass's Clare Valley winery – Quelltaler – was briefly renamed. We much prefer the historic Quelltaler.

CURRENT RELEASE 1995   Starting to develop the beginnings of toastiness, this riesling still has some dusty and slightly green, tangy fruit aromas. The palate has some fruit sweetness, and the finish comes on strong and dry with a classic minerally Clare aftertaste. Try it with whitebait fritters.

Quality	♟♟♟♟
Value	★★★★
Grapes	riesling
Region	Clare Valley, SA
Cellar	▮ 3
Alc./Vol.	11.5%
RRP	$11.20 ⑤

Edencrest Eden Valley Chardonnay

Quality	ΨΨΨ℟
Value	★★★↟
Grapes	chardonnay
Region	Eden Valley, SA
Cellar	⏺ 3
Alc./Vol.	13.3%
RRP	$16.00

Sounds like a TV soapie but it's a label (and superannuation package) belonging to Jim Irvine. Trivia buffs will note Jim invented Siegersdorf riesling for Hardys using fruit from a vineyard of the same name.

CURRENT RELEASE 1996   This is a straightforward and sunny style with a strong nose of peach and melon fruits. The palate is medium- to full-bodied with melon and peach flavours, and the finish has plenty of acid to keep things lively and balanced. It can take a reasonable chill. Try it with Thai fish cakes.

Ermes Estate Riesling

Quality	ΨΨΨ℟
Value	★★★
Grapes	riesling; malvasia
Region	Mornington
	Peninsula, Vic.
Cellar	⏺ 3
Alc./Vol.	12.0%
RRP	$16.00

There is a slight twist to this wine, which is a blend of two varieties. Not that the ring-in makes much difference to the end result, but it would drive the participants at masked tastings nuts.

CURRENT RELEASE 1996   There is a hint that something extra has been added, but it's only a hint. The usual lime aroma has wintergreen accompaniments. The palate has lime and tropical fruit flavours, and there is plenty of acid to make for a crisp finish. Serve well chilled with mirror dory in a beer batter.

Evans & Tate Chardonnay

Quality	ΨΨΨ℟
Value	★★★↟
Grapes	chardonnay
Region	Margaret River, WA
Cellar	⏺ 4
Alc./Vol.	13.0%
RRP	$18.00

E&T are a dynamic force in the West and are spreading East (plus North and South) with a will. The driving force in the promotion is Frank Tate, but the key is quality and that is directly attributed to the winemaker. Maker Brian Fletcher.

CURRENT RELEASE 1995   A robust style that gives plenty of bangs for your bucks. The nose is peachy with a background of nutty wood. The palate continues the peach theme and there are also some melon flavours. The wood on the finish is toasty and it should develop well. A medium chill and a plate of poached scallops will thrill.

Evans Family Pinchem Chardonnay

Len Evans' Loggerheads vineyard is divided by grape variety into blocks, and he now puts the name of the block on the label. Hence the Pinchem.

Previous outstanding vintages: '88, '91, '93

CURRENT RELEASE 1996 A complex wine with the customary Hunter richness and sweet fruit. The secondary characters of butterscotch and honey flirt with the herbal, fig-like fruit aromas; the oak is well harmonised and the palate soft and round. Would team well with prosciutto melone.

Quality	♟♟♟♟♟
Value	★★★★
Grapes	chardonnay
Region	Hunter Valley, NSW
Cellar	♦ 5
Alc./Vol.	12.4%
RRP	$26.50

Evans Wine Company Chardonnay

This brand, owned by the Welsh-born Len Evans, features a gryphon motif. In mythology, the gryphon was smaller but fiercer than the English dragon. A bit like the man himself.

CURRENT RELEASE 1995 Burnt wood aromas dominate the nose with a charred, toasted smell. The palate offers respectable weight of flavour and good length. It's a singular style – the toasty oak will probably polarise people as either lovers or haters. Try serving with char-grilled chicken.

Quality	♟♟♟
Value	★★★
Grapes	chardonnay
Region	Hunter Valley, NSW
Cellar	♦ 2
Alc./Vol.	12.5%
RRP	$16.10

Eyton on Yarra Chardonnay

This wine is under the old (or is it the new?) label, and bottle-age gives a clue to the potential of the estate-grown fruit. The vineyard was established in 1970 and there are 10 hectares under vine.

CURRENT RELEASE 1994 Things are coming together well. The nose has peach and melon aromas plus some tropical fruit and yeast notes. The palate has a mouth-filling texture with peaches and cream flavours. The oak integration on the finish makes for a complete wine. A moderate chill and some Thai fish cakes will make a pleasant diversion. ▸

Quality	♟♟♟♟
Value	★★★★
Grapes	chardonnay
Region	Yarra Valley, Vic.
Cellar	♦ 3
Alc./Vol.	12.9%
RRP	$19.00

Quality	♟♟♟♟
Value	★★★★
Grapes	chardonnay
Region	Yarra Valley, Vic.
Cellar	🍷 4
Alc./Vol.	13.2%
RRP	$19.00

CURRENT RELEASE 1995   Two years down the track and it remains a fresh, lively style. The colour is a pale lemon–yellow. The nose is a dead heat between oak and varietal fruit aromas. There are melon and fig flavours on the palate. The wood tastes fresh and new, and the finish means it doesn't need much more chilling than a brief spell in the fridge. Try it with pan-fried sardines.

Eyton on Yarra Sauvignon Blanc

Quality	♟♟♟
Value	★★★
Grapes	sauvignon blanc
Region	Yarra Valley, Vic.
Cellar	🍷 3
Alc./Vol.	13.0%
RRP	$16.00

You get a crick in your neck trying to read this label, especially after you've pulled the cork. Don't bother – you won't discover anything you don't already know. Why does the label design remind MS of a Year 12 textbook?
CURRENT RELEASE 1996   On a curious nose that smells like recently baked cookies, there are toast and caramel aromas. The palate is a mixture of peas, tropical fruit and gooseberry flavours. There is plenty of acid to refresh the palate. Serve well chilled with a wintergreen salad.

Fermoy Estate Chardonnay

Quality	♟♟♟♟
Value	★★★⊹
Grapes	chardonnay
Region	Margaret River, WA
Cellar	🍷 3
Alc./Vol.	13.6%
RRP	$20.30

Fermoy sells 45% of its wine in New South Wales, thanks to a vigorous sales force in the person of Karen Hunter. Maker Michael Kelly.
CURRENT RELEASE 1996   A lighter style of chardonnay, pale yellow in colour and delicately wooded (despite 100% barrel fermentation). Refined cashew nut and grapefruit characters. Easy to drink with seafood salads.

Fermoy Estate Reserve Chardonnay

Quality	♟♟♟♟⸵
Value	★★★⊹
Grapes	chardonnay
Region	Margaret River, WA
Cellar	🍷 5+
Alc./Vol.	13.8%
RRP	$25.00

A tiny 300-case bottling. It's interesting to compare this with the standard bottling as they started off as the same wine. Difference is, this was worked and stirred a lot more. (Tasted as a barrel sample.)
CURRENT RELEASE 1996   A sumptuous wine: very rich and powerful, with intense grapefruit flavour, well-harmonised oak and extraordinary length. Serve with lobster.

Fermoy Estate Semillon

Fermoy is a relatively new winery in Margaret River, with 30 producing acres of vineyards and 10 more coming on. This wine won an SGIO award in 1996.
CURRENT RELEASE 1996 A very big wine, one-third barrel fermented, which has power and strength, but to lovers of traditional semillon it's somewhat overpowering. It's rich but dry with some alcohol warmth and a finish that echoes for ages. Try it with roast chicken.

Quality	♥♥♥♥?
Value	★★★➤
Grapes	semillon
Region	Margaret River, WA
Cellar	▮ 3
Alc./Vol.	13.3%
RRP	$17.40

Fern Hill Estate Chardonnay

Fern Hill was begun by Wayne Thomas, who sold it to Sydney wine-marketer and owner of Marienberg and Basedows, Terry Hill.
CURRENT RELEASE 1995 A very forward wine, showing more age than we'd expect for a '95. Deep golden colour, fig-jam aged bouquet with greener herbal aromas underneath. The palate is soft and slightly dull, with lots of maturity but not a lot of life. Drink soon, with roast chicken.

Quality	♥♥♥
Value	★★➤
Grapes	chardonnay
Region	McLaren Vale, SA
Cellar	▮
Alc./Vol.	12.6%
RRP	$19.00

Fleurieu Heritage Semillon Sauvignon Blanc

This is made in McLaren Vale by Jacques Lurton, a 'flying winemaker' and member of a well-known Bordeaux wine family.
CURRENT RELEASE 1995 Wood, wood and more wood! There's not much of the Old World here. The nose is all toasty oak and the beginning carries searing acid. It does have length, thanks to oak and acid. Perhaps it's intended as a style to age, but right now you need to have a fondness for wood to get pleasure from it.

Quality	♥♥♥
Value	★★➤
Grapes	semillon, sauvignon blanc
Region	McLaren Vale, SA
Cellar	➤ 2+
Alc./Vol.	12.5%
RRP	$17.00

Forrest Marlborough Riesling

Quality	♥♥♥♥
Value	★★★★
Grapes	riesling
Region	Marlborough, NZ
Cellar	▮ 5
Alc./Vol.	12.0%
RRP	$13.00

John and Brigid Forrest established their 21-hectare vineyard at Renwick in the Marlborough region in 1989. CURRENT RELEASE 1996 The colour is pale and reflects the tight, restrained, reserved style of the wine. There are mineral, slatey, limey aromas and the palate is soft, full and dry. Good flavour without a lot of verve. It could age well. Try a Thai chicken salad.

Forrest Sauvignon Blanc

Quality	♥♥♥♥
Value	★★★★
Grapes	sauvignon blanc
Region	Marlborough, NZ
Cellar	▮ 2
Alc./Vol.	12.5%
RRP	$15.00

Yet another new (to these shores) name from Marlborough, New Zealand. We'd love to know how many Marlborough sauvignon blancs are on the market. The style is one of the most successful new regional varietals in the entire history of wine.

CURRENT RELEASE 1996   Freshly cut grass, parsley and basil aromas airing to have a suggestion of honey. Intense, balanced, attractive. The palate is typically Marlborough: fresh and zesty with lantana-like flavour and a little sweetness, adding a juicy softness. Admirable depth and length too. Try it with greenlip mussels.

Fox Creek Sauvignon Blanc

Quality	♥♥♥
Value	★★★
Grapes	sauvignon blanc
Region	McLaren Vale, SA
Cellar	▮ 1
Alc./Vol.	13.2%
RRP	$15.70

Fox Creek hit the headlines when its blockbuster shiraz won the McLaren Vale Bushing Trophy. Maker Sparky Marquis.

CURRENT RELEASE 1996   Stalky green herbal aromas; no doubt about its freshness. The green-leafy flavours turn bitter towards the finish, which has a sprinkle of counterbalancing sweetness. A simple wine that may improve with a few months in the bottle. Take it to a vegan restaurant.

Frankland Estate Rhine Riesling

This must be one of the most remote vineyards in the whole country. But it's a beautiful spot and Barrie Smith runs a model vineyard.
Previous outstanding vintages: '92, '93, '94, '95
CURRENT RELEASE 1996 Very aromatic, forceful, pungent citrus nose; a lighter-bodied, more delicate style than the two previous vintages, still with some doughy hints and very fine, soft palate. Excellent wine, although a drop more acid might have made it even better. Great with fish and chips.

Quality	♀♀♀♀
Value	★★★↾
Grapes	riesling
Region	Lower Great Southern, WA
Cellar	↓ 5+
Alc./Vol.	12.8%
RRP	$17.60

Freycinet Chardonnay

Tasmanian chardonnays are some of the few in this country that actually improve with age. They start out quite austere and need a year or two in the bottle to reveal their true colours. Maker Claudio Radenti.
CURRENT RELEASE 1995 Twelve months after last year's review and it's still very reserved. Despite barrel fermentation and ageing on lees in oak for 10 months, it's very fruit-driven and delicate. Very fine nectarine and honeydew melon aromas, with oak well disguised. It's clean and technically A1, with real length and finesse. Try it with prosciutto melone.

Quality	♀♀♀♀↾
Value	★★★★
Grapes	chardonnay
Region	East Coast, Tasmania
Cellar	↓ 5
Alc./Vol.	13.5%
RRP	$29.00

Freycinet Riesling Muller Thurgau

Muller thurgau was developed by the Germans as an early-ripening grape to plant in colder sites. Hence what little there is in Australia tends to be in Tassie. Maker Claudio Radenti.
CURRENT RELEASE 1996 Powder-puff, flowery aromatics and lightly grassy, cool-edged but not unripe notes. Tart lemony flavours, crisp and juicy with a little sweetness; superb flavour and finesse. Great with trout and a creamy sorrel sauce.

Quality	♀♀♀♀↾
Value	★★★↾
Grapes	riesling; muller thurgau
Region	East Coast, Tasmania
Cellar	↓ 4+
Alc./Vol.	12.5%
RRP	$19.30

Galafrey Rhine Riesling

Quality	🍷🍷🍷
Value	★★★
Grapes	riesling
Region	Great Southern, WA
Cellar	🍷 3
Alc./Vol.	12.0%
RRP	$13.50

Galafrey was the galaxy of the time lords in the long-running TV series *Dr Who*. MS thinks Tom Baker was the definitive Dr Who, but others will argue for the late Jon Pertwee. What's that got to do with wine? Put it down to one of the quirks of this book, which was never meant to be boring. Bring back Dr Who! Maker Ian Tyrer.

CURRENT RELEASE 1995   The nose is fruity with a strong citrus aroma, and the palate has a hint of sweetness plus plenty of lemon flavour. The finish is soft with discreet acid, so chill it down and serve it with a chicken pie.

Garry Crittenden Bianco

Quality	🍷🍷🍷🍷
Value	★★★★
Grapes	trebbiano; sauvignon blanc
Region	not stated
Cellar	🍷 1
Alc./Vol.	12.5%
RRP	$14.50

The proprietor/winemaker seems to have experienced an Italian conversion. He is not alone, as sales of Italian-style wines climb in Australia. Maker Garry Crittenden.

CURRENT RELEASE 1996   This is a lively wine with lots of brio. It has a lively nose with fruity grape aromas and hints of citrus. The palate is medium-bodied with herbal flavours and a gooseberry background. There is plenty of tart, crisp acid on the finish that makes it a very refreshing drop. It can be served well chilled with an antipasto platter.

Geoff Weaver Chardonnay

Quality	🍷🍷🍷🍷🍷
Value	★★★★★
Grapes	chardonnay
Region	Adelaide Hills, SA
Cellar	🍷 6+
Alc./Vol.	13.0%
RRP	$24.00

Geoff Weaver keeps his chardonnay back a year longer than most people, because Adelaide Hills wines need time to develop. All his grapes come from his own small vineyard at Lenswood.

Previous outstanding vintages: '90, '91, '93, '94

CURRENT RELEASE 1995   A more reserved wine than the splendid '94, with lighter colour and less overt oak. HH thinks this is Weaver's best yet: it's very refined and subtle, and the underlying complexity is outstanding. The structure is tight and it will age well. This would make a fascinating pair with its almost-neighbour, the great '95 Petaluma. Drink with veal sweetbreads.

Geoff Weaver Riesling

Riesling is still the best value in Australian white wine. This is Weaver's cheapest wine but its quality and style are right up with the others.

Previous outstanding vintages: '88, '90, '91, '92, '93, '94

CURRENT RELEASE 1995   Still has a very light yellow colour, restrained aromatics, and minerally rather than overtly flowery varietal fruit. It's a very refined riesling, which will age slowly. The palate is juicy but dry, soft and delicate. A real gem. Try it with crumbed lamb's brains.

Quality	🍷🍷🍷🍷
Value	★★★★
Grapes	riesling
Region	Adelaide Hills, SA
Cellar	🍾 7+
Alc./Vol.	12.0%
RRP	$14.50

Geoff Weaver Sauvignon Blanc

Weaver has dropped the Stafford Ridge vineyard name off his labels, for simplicity's sake. Unlike lesser sauvignons, this ages superbly: witness the first-vintage 1989, which is delicious today.

Previous outstanding vintages: '89, '90, '91, '93, '94, '95

CURRENT RELEASE 1996   No sign of grassy green aromas here: lemon and passionfruit scents predominate. The taste is at the fuller end of the sauvignon blanc spectrum with crisp, lively mouth-feel and just a trace of bitterness on the finish, which doesn't hold the wine back. A serious sauvignon with real strength. Try it with salmon gravlax.

Quality	🍷🍷🍷🍷
Value	★★★★
Grapes	sauvignon blanc
Region	Adelaide Hills, SA
Cellar	🍾 5
Alc./Vol.	12.0%
RRP	$20.00

Gilbert Mount Barker Riesling

No points for guessing that this wine is named after the family who planted the vineyard. Bev and Jim Gilbert are a pioneering family in the Great Southern region in Western Australia.

Previous outstanding vintages: '90, '93, '94

CURRENT RELEASE 1996   The wine is fine, albeit a tad predictable. The nose is full of crushed violets and citrus notes. The palate is medium-bodied with a shock of lime flavour, which is followed by some zesty acid on a crisp finish. It can be served well chilled and goes well with whiting.

Quality	🍷🍷🍷🍷
Value	★★★★
Grapes	riesling
Region	Mount Barker, WA
Cellar	🍾 3
Alc./Vol.	11.0%
RRP	$16.00

Glenara Riesling

Quality	🍷🍷🍷🍷½
Value	★★★★★
Grapes	riesling
Region	Adelaide Hills, SA
Cellar	6+
Alc./Vol.	12.3%
RRP	$14.00

This is one of the very few wineries in Australia that market their wines as organically grown. Riesling runner-up in the '97 Boutique Wines of Australia Awards. Maker Trevor Jones.

CURRENT RELEASE 1996 Exaggerated citrus and herbaceous aromas are the feature of this arresting wine. It has herbal, tangy, slightly green accents, and in the mouth there are delicate, light-bodied lemon/slatey flavours and a classically dry finish. Goes well with whiting quenelles.

Glenguin Chardonnay

Quality	🍷🍷🍷🍷
Value	★★★½
Grapes	chardonnay
Region	Hunter Valley, NSW
Cellar	2–6
Alc./Vol.	12.5%
RRP	$20.00

This is the other side of the equation (to the unwooded version) showing what a full-blooded wood treatment can do for a wine.

CURRENT RELEASE 1996 Wood is very obvious, both on the nose and on the palate. The nose has a strong nutty aroma as well as peach and melon smells. The palate also shows an obvious impact of wood. The peach, melon and fig are found on the palate, and there is a creamy barrel-ferment character. The finish is dry, and guess what – there is plenty of wood. Don't over-chill, and serve it with a warm salad of smoked chicken.

Glenguin Semillon

Quality	🍷🍷🍷½
Value	★★★
Grapes	semillon
Region	Hunter Valley, NSW
Cellar	8
Alc./Vol.	11.0%
RRP	$16.00

A new brand started by ex–merchant banker Robin Tedder in the Broke region of the Hunter Valley.

CURRENT RELEASE 1996 Pristine, fresh, youthful, unwooded Hunter semillon aromas of lanolin and lemon, with straw and slight toast in the background. The palate is dry, tangy and rather acidic when drunk solo, so we recommend having it with a meal. Try fresh oysters.

Glenguin Unwooded Chardonnay

Sounds like a single-malt whisky from the highlands of Scotland, but this is a new label from the Hunter Valley.
CURRENT RELEASE 1996 There is already evidence of bottle development in the green–gold colour. The nose has peach and melon aromas, and there is a hint of sweetness on the palate, which is dominated by peach flavours. The finish is firm, so it can be served well chilled. It's a good pizza style.

Quality	🍷🍷🍷
Value	★★★
Grapes	chardonnay
Region	Hunter Valley, NSW
Cellar	2
Alc./Vol.	12.5%
RRP	$15.50

Goodchild Rhine Riesling

Not-so-new kids on the block. This is a recently introduced label from a family of established growers who sell their grapes to other wine companies. Obviously they think some of their fruit is good enough to keep.
CURRENT RELEASE 1996 Very typical of the region, with plenty of powerful varietal character. The nose is floral with lime and citrus aromas. The palate offers keen lime flavours, which are backed by abundant acid on a very fresh finish. It can take plenty of cold and it's sublime with fresh oysters.

Quality	🍷🍷🍷🍷½
Value	★★★★½
Grapes	riesling
Region	Eden Valley, SA
Cellar	5
Alc./Vol.	11.0%
RRP	$14.50

Goona Warra Chardonnay

As with Coonawarra, there is a black swan connection in the Aboriginal name. This is a historic site with 5 hectares under vine very close to Melbourne's Tullamarine airport. Maker John Barnier.
CURRENT RELEASE 1995 The wine is wood-driven, and the nose has biscuit and toast aromas. The fruit on the palate is slightly subdued with gentle peach and melon flavours. The finish is powerful with dry oak flavours. Serve it near room temperature with a smoked chicken salad.

Quality	🍷🍷½
Value	★★★★
Grapes	chardonnay
Region	Sunbury, Vic.
Cellar	3
Alc./Vol.	13.0%
RRP	$19.90

Gramp's Botrytis Semillon

Quality	🍷🍷🍷🍷
Value	★★★★
Grapes	semillon
Region	Riverina, NSW
Cellar	🍾 4
Alc./Vol.	11.0%
RRP	$13.00 (375ml)

This is a useful half-bottle which should also offer a prize for those who can read the alcohol by volume on the label. Double the points for dim lighting in the average bistro.

CURRENT RELEASE 1996 Plenty of botrytis character in this wine. There is an attractive combination of aromas and flavours in a well-made wine. There are honeysuckle and dried-fruit aromas on the nose, and the palate has dried apricot, marmalade and ginger flavours that are matched by some zesty acid. It has to be super-cold. Try it with a rich dessert.

Gramp's Chardonnay

Quality	🍷🍷🍷
Value	★★★
Grapes	chardonnay
Region	not stated
Cellar	🍾 3
Alc./Vol.	13.0%
RRP	$12.50

This is a very reliable budget label that seems to sit in solitude in the Orlando portfolio. No point pondering the Orlando meaning of life – just drink up.

CURRENT RELEASE 1996 You knock on a solid oak door to get into this one. The nose bristles with toasted oak aromas. The palate is a straightforward peach flavour, and the finish shows some tough wood tannins and great length. It's not the kind of wine you would cellar, but you could well be surprised. Give it a medium chill and try it with tripe in a white sauce.

Grant Burge Kraft Sauvignon Blanc

Quality	🍷🍷🍷½
Value	★★★½
Grapes	sauvignon blanc
Region	Barossa Valley, SA
Cellar	🍾 2
Alc./Vol.	11.5%
RRP	$15.50

Burge has not become a multinational (although he is trying hard): Kraft is the name of one of his vineyards in the Barossa Valley.

CURRENT RELEASE 1996 A predictable wine with refreshing qualities, making it great summer drinking. The nose has cut-grass, herb and gooseberry aromas. The palate offers tropical fruit and gooseberry flavours. There is crisp acid on the finish. It goes well with scallops in a light lemon sauce.

Grant Burge Virtuoso

A big packaging exercise and great presentation from the burgeoning Burge dynasty. Helen and Grant Burge are movers and shakers in the Barossa – perhaps around the globe as well.

CURRENT RELEASE 1996 It looms very handsome sticking out of an ice bucket. The nose has tropical fruit aromas. The medium-weight palate has gooseberry and straw flavours with hints of cut grass. There is refreshing acid on the finish, and the wine can be served well chilled. It's a great wine for yum cha.

Quality	♟♟♟♟
Value	★★★★
Grapes	sauvignon blanc 60%; semillon 40%
Region	Barossa Valley, SA
Cellar	▲ 4
Alc./Vol.	13.0%
RRP	$15.00

Green Point Chardonnay

This could be considered the plaything of the winemakers at Domaine Chandon when they get bored with putting bubbles into things. Not so – it's a serious wine in its own right. Maker Wayne Donaldson and Maryann Egan.

CURRENT RELEASE 1996 There has been a bit of barrel flexing here and it's been through malolactic fermentation (what would you expect from bored fizz-makers?). It's a buttery, toasty style with honey and peaches on both nose and palate. The wood on the finish adds a dry quality. Good balance and some ageing potential, and it's brilliant with a goose liver pâté.

Quality	♟♟♟♟⸮
Value	★★★★⼲
Grapes	chardonnay
Region	various
Cellar	▲ 5
Alc./Vol.	13.5%
RRP	$20.00

Grevillea Estate Gewurztraminer

This vineyard was established in 1985 and there are 7.5 hectares under vine. Yes, there are flowers on the label.

CURRENT RELEASE 1996 This is a pungent style with loads of spice, lychee and crushed flowers. The palate has tropical fruit flavours and hints of citrus, and there is crisp acid on the finish. It can be served well chilled. Try it with an asparagus quiche.

Quality	♟♟♟
Value	★★★
Grapes	gewurztraminer
Region	Bega, NSW
Cellar	▲ 1
Alc./Vol.	11.5%
RRP	$12.50

Grevillea Estate Rhine Riesling

Quality	???
Value	★★★
Grapes	riesling
Region	Bega, NSW
Cellar	◊ 1
Alc./Vol.	11.5%
RRP	$12.50

Help! There is a little packaging confusion here. The riesling comes in a white burgundy bottle and the gewurztraminer is in a riesling/hock bottle. Conventions were meant to be broken. Maker Nicola Collins.

CURRENT RELEASE 1996   The nose is a bit of a problem: it's sappy and musty without an indication of fruit. (The sample wasn't corked). The palate straightens up and flies right with crisp lime and lemon flavours, and there is crisp acid on the finish. Serve it with spaghetti marinara.

Grevillea Estate Sauvignon Blanc

Quality	???
Value	★★★
Grapes	sauvignon blanc
Region	Bega, NSW
Cellar	◊ 2
Alc./Vol.	12.0%
RRP	$12.50

Most small wineries have a broad spectrum of wine styles. This company is no exception.

CURRENT RELEASE 1996   It's a big style with all the pungent attributes of the variety. The nose is grassy and herbal, and there is a tinned-pea character. The palate shows a hint of sweetness with tropical fruit flavours, and this is matched by some strong acid on the finish. The wine can be served well chilled. Try it with a leafy green salad.

Grevillea Estate Unwooded Chardonnay

Quality	????
Value	★★★★
Grapes	chardonnay
Region	Bega, NSW
Cellar	◊ 2
Alc./Vol.	12.2%
RRP	$12.50

The storm clouds of doubt are gathering over unwooded chardonnay styles. They are starting to attractive negative press.

CURRENT RELEASE 1996   The nose has lychee, citrus and peach aromas. The palate has some mouthfilling traits and a lemon and grapefruit mix dominates. The finish has plenty of acid and the wine can take a reasonable chill. Try it with calamari poached in white wine.

Hanging Rock The Jim Jim Sauvignon Blanc

The Jim Jim is the traditional name for the hill behind the Hanging Rock winery on which John and Annie Ellis planted their vineyard. Maker John Ellis.

CURRENT RELEASE 1996 Pungent pea and capsicum aromas point to a very cool year in a very cool meso-climate. It follows that the acid is a tad prominent and the finish is somewhat hard. Tight green and lemony flavours. This must be served with food! Try asparagus and a creamy cheese sauce.

Quality	♥♥♥♥
Value	★★★
Grapes	sauvignon blanc
Region	Macedon Ranges, Vic.
Cellar	▮ 5
Alc./Vol.	11.0%
RRP	$21.00

Hardys Adelaide Hills Sauvignon Blanc

BRL Hardy have started a new line of regional varietals to tap into the specialty side of the business. The Hills are certainly putting a lot of runs on the board with sauvignon blanc. This was grown at Hahndorf.

CURRENT RELEASE 1996 Very pale lemon–green colour. The nose is more like soft drink than wine, with a passionfruit pop smell. It's very light in the mouth and has that same exaggerated guava/mango/passionfruit tropical character. Frisky, zesty and juicy with a clean acid finish. Serve with seafood.

Quality	♥♥♥◗
Value	★★★
Grapes	sauvignon blanc
Region	Adelaide Hills, SA
Cellar	▮ 1
Alc./Vol.	11.5%
RRP	$18.00

Hardys Eileen Hardy Chardonnay

The '94 won our major chardonnay gong two years ago. This is the top of the totem for Hardys whites. Maker Tom Newton.

Previous outstanding vintages: '86, '89, '90, '92, '94

CURRENT RELEASE 1995 Obvious toasty, fresh-sawn oak aromas dominate the fruit. While the wine has weight and richness underneath, it's hard to see at this stage how it will develop. It should have been given more time to mature in the bottle before release. Cellar, then serve with crayfish.

Quality	♥♥♥♥
Value	★★★
Grapes	chardonnay
Region	Padthaway & Adelaide Hills, SA; Yarra Valley, Vic.
Cellar	▬ 1–5+
Alc./Vol.	13.5%
RRP	$29.50 Ⓢ

Hardys Hunter Ridge Chardonnay

Quality	♟♟♟
Value	★★★
Grapes	chardonnay
Region	Hunter Valley, NSW
Cellar	▮ 1
Alc./Vol.	13.0%
RRP	$12.00 Ⓢ

This new Hardys range should appeal to those who don't appreciate subtlety. If there's a label with a bigger range of bright, bold colours on it, we haven't seen it.
CURRENT RELEASE 1995 The subscript proclaims 'Vintners Reserve', which is drawing a long bow as this is a fairly basic chardonnay. Intense herbal, parsley-like aroma; broad, developed and soft. The oak is barely there, and it's a decent mouthful of simple flavour. It's appropriately priced. Try it with crab cakes.

Hardys Sir James Chardonnay

Quality	♟♟♟♟
Value	★★★⊁
Grapes	chardonnay
Region	Padthaway, SA; Yarra Valley, Vic.; and others
Cellar	▮ 3
Alc./Vol.	13.5%
RRP	$15.00 Ⓢ

Sir James 'Gentleman Jim' Hardy is one of the god-fathers of the wine industry. The marketers have recently turned his name into a promotional tool.
CURRENT RELEASE 1996 A remarkably fine wine, showing cool-climate delicacy and understated oak treatment. There are toasty hints and lemony fruit accents, lively peach/butter flavours and frisky acidity. It pulls up slightly short, but the flavours are fine and appealing. Serve with scallops.

Hay Shed Hill Chardonnay

Quality	♟♟♟♟⊁
Value	★★★⊁
Grapes	chardonnay
Region	Margaret River, WA
Cellar	▮ 4+
Alc./Vol.	13.5%
RRP	$22.40

Owner Barry Morrison is a Perth orthodontist. Wine-maker is Peter Stanlake.
CURRENT RELEASE 1995 Tropical fruits, honey and butter feature in this classic Margaret River chardonnay. It was in oak (50% new) nearly a year but you wouldn't know it. Very stylish palate with nicely restrained oak and impeccable balance. Serve with lobster.

Hay Shed Hill Semillon

All sounds very homespun and hicksville, but check out the cellar door and it's a slick operation, with some excellent sculpture and metalwork about the place.
CURRENT RELEASE 1996   This is 35% barrel-fermented and the oak's commendably subtle. Fine, tinder-dry finish, long aftertaste and precision balance. Stylish wine to serve with shellfish.

Quality	♟♟♟♟
Value	★★★
Grapes	semillon
Region	Margaret River, WA
Cellar	🍷 4
Alc./Vol.	13.5%
RRP	$19.65

Heemskerk Chardonnay

Heemskerk is now part of Joe Chromy's enterprising Tamar Vineyards group and things are looking up. They've built a swish new winery at Rochecombe, where the group will focus its winemaking. Maker Garry Ford.
CURRENT RELEASE 1995   Ultra-complex, cool-climate stuff, and just starting to mature into a splendid drink at two years of age. Hazelnuts, lightly browned toast with hints of butterscotch and honey, are features of this stylish chardonnay. It's rich and full in the mouth with a very long carry, although still within the relatively refined cool-climate context. Food: Tassie abalone.

Quality	♟♟♟♟
Value	★★★
Grapes	chardonnay
Region	Pipers River, Tas.
Cellar	🍷 4+
Alc./Vol.	13.5%
RRP	$28.00

Heggies Chardonnay

Colin Heggie, a friend of the Hill Smiths of Yalumba, sold them the land on which they planted this vineyard. Maker Simon Adams and team.
CURRENT RELEASE 1995   A restrained style that's progressed nicely from last year's review. It's a lean and serious style with certain feral French characters that give an exotic persona. It's tightly structured, with a nice dry finish and long, complex flavours. Intriguing stuff! Try it with a scallop and leek gratin.

Quality	♟♟♟♟
Value	★★★★
Grapes	chardonnay
Region	Eden Valley, SA
Cellar	🍷 5
Alc./Vol.	13.5%
RRP	$21.00 Ⓢ

Heggies Viognier

Quality	ΨΨΨΨ
Value	★★★★
Grapes	viognier
Region	Eden Valley, SA
Cellar	🍷 3
Alc./Vol.	14.5%
RRP	$19.00 Ⓢ

This is a rare grape variety in Australia. It's the famous grape of France's Condrieu and Chateau Grillet. It seems to demand very low yields and high ripeness, as the Heggies winemakers have discovered over the years. *Previous outstanding vintages: '95*
CURRENT RELEASE 1996 The bouquet has dusty, bracken aromas over the top of spicy, almost pinot-gris-like fruit. The palate is rich and seems slightly sweet, although the high alcohol can play tricks in this department. It has a big finish and excellent length, and the wine's personality is quite individual. This is different!

Helm's Non-oaked Chardonnay

Quality	ΨΨΨⱣ
Value	★★★
Grapes	chardonnay
Region	Canberra district, NSW
Cellar	🍷 1
Alc./Vol.	12.0%
RRP	$16.00 (cellar door)

Helm's is one of the senior Canberra district wineries, established at Murrumbateman in 1974. Maker Ken Helm no longer bothers with a wooded chardonnay.
CURRENT RELEASE 1995 Has aged quite gracefully since last year's review: the nose is of dry grass/hay, and the lean, narrow palate has life and zest. It's a decent everyday-drinking white wine and goes well with crab cakes.

Helm's Rhine Riesling Classic Dry

Quality	ΨΨΨ
Value	★★★
Grapes	riesling
Region	Canberra district, NSW
Cellar	🍷 4
Alc./Vol.	12.0%
RRP	$14.00 (cellar door)

The back label says 'Drink wine in moderation to promote joy, never anger', which seems to be a case of begging the question.
CURRENT RELEASE 1996 Pale colour and a very fresh, youthful aroma of bread dough and dusty, slightly grassy cool-climate characters. The palate has good intensity and a fruit juice flavour, but doesn't quite sing. Goes well with waldorf salad.

Henschke Lenswood Croft Chardonnay

Mr Croft was an early owner of a fruit-growing block next door to the one the Henschkes own today. Maker Stephen Henschke.

Previous outstanding vintages: '94, '95

CURRENT RELEASE 1996 A full-throttle style, which shows off the full repertoire of the winemaker. The nose reveals toasty oak and butterscotch with a hint of rubber; the flavour is powerful, oaky and incredibly long in the mouth. A classy wine with major impact and the potential to mature gracefully in the cellar. Serve with cheese soufflé.

Quality	ΨΨΨΨΨ
Value	★★★★
Grapes	chardonnay
Region	Adelaide Hills, SA
Cellar	🍶 4+
Alc./Vol.	14.3%
RRP	$33.00

Heritage Estate Semillon

Heritage is the labour of sweat of Christine and Steve Hoff. When not doing his day job, Steve does yeoman's service winemaking at Saltram. Christine is a local medico.

CURRENT RELEASE 1996 Typical regional style with a blast of American oak. The nose has gooseberry and wet wool aromas. The palate is medium-bodied with gooseberry and grassy herbs. Oak adds a touch of vanilla and the finish is long. It should be served with a modest chill. Try it with grilled flake.

Quality	ΨΨΨΨ
Value	★★★★
Grapes	semillon
Region	Barossa Valley, SA
Cellar	🍶 3
Alc./Vol.	12.0%
RRP	$14.50

Hermit's Brook Chardonnay

Western Australia isn't the only place where the creeks are brooks – for example, Moondah, Piesse, Marri, Boyup, Willyabrup, Red, Smith; the Hunter has a few as well.

CURRENT RELEASE 1996 The nose is straightforward ripe pineapple, and the palate is soft to the point of being floppy. It's very plain but has ample ripe fruit flavour, which is starting to show some development. Serve with ham steak and pineapple.

Quality	ΨΨΨ
Value	★★★
Grapes	chardonnay
Region	Hunter Valley, NSW
Cellar	🍶 1
Alc./Vol.	12.0%
RRP	$15.30 Ⓢ

Hermit's Brook Semillon

Quality	♟♟♟
Value	★★★
Grapes	semillon
Region	Hunter Valley, NSW
Cellar	◊ 4
Alc./Vol.	11.5%
RRP	$12.00

There's a new wine producer springing up every week these days. True! In 1996, 50 new producers, not all of them wineries, opened for business. This is one.

CURRENT RELEASE 1996   A typically restrained Hunter semillon in its youth, early harvesting resulting in a delicate style which makes for an adaptable food wine. It's fresh and light, with doughy, lemony aromas and respectable flavour and balance in the mouth. Goes well with cold seafood.

Highfield Marlborough Chardonnay

Quality	♟♟♟♟
Value	★★★⊦
Grapes	chardonnay
Region	Marlborough, NZ
Cellar	◊ 2
Alc./Vol.	12.5%
RRP	$20.00

San Gimignano comes to the Wairau! The owners of Highfield have built a Tuscan-style tower on their property. You can see it on their label.

CURRENT RELEASE 1995   This is a good effort considering the vintage, and it bears some telltale signs of the year. The nose has powdered milk aromas from a vigorous malolactic fermentation, and the palate is quite tart, although not out of balance. There are toasty, smoky hints, good freshness, and the volume of flavour is pleasing.

Hill Smith Estate Chardonnay

Quality	♟♟♟♟
Value	★★★⊦
Grapes	chardonnay
Region	Eden Valley, SA
Cellar	◊ 4
Alc./Vol.	13.5%
RRP	$16.00 ⓢ

Grown on the airstrip block at the Hill Smith Estate vineyard, which is in the hills behind Angaston.

CURRENT RELEASE 1995 Nutty, peachy and fig aromas; a smooth, soft style with a trace of sweetness. Needs more time for the wood, lively acid and fruit flavours to come into harmony. Plenty of flavour and good value. Try it with gravlax.

Hollick Chardonnay

Winemaker Pat Tocaciu has left the partnership here to set up a contract winemaking facility in Coonawarra.
CURRENT RELEASE 1995 This is an unusual beastie: the nose shows salami sausage aromas early on, which could be the toasty oak and malolactic characters interacting in a slightly uncouth way. Whatever, it airs to reveal complex oaky flavours and an unctuous, buttery/honeyed palate. There's no denying it's a wine of character. Try it with honey prawns.

Quality	▼▼▼▼
Value	★★★ど
Grapes	chardonnay
Region	Coonawarra, SA
Cellar	▮ 2
Alc./Vol.	13.5%
RRP	$18.00

Hollick Unwooded Chardonnay

Everybody's stripping off and scampering about naked. Sadly, when the veneer is peeled away from many unoaked chardonnays there's not much worth looking at underneath.
CURRENT RELEASE 1996 Subdued aroma of melon and stone fruits. A rather slight wine with clean, well-made although simple character. Try it with caesar salad.

Quality	▼▼▼
Value	★★★
Grapes	chardonnay
Region	Coonawarra, SA
Cellar	▮ 1
Alc./Vol.	13.0%
RRP	$14.50

Houghton Chablis

This wine's days are surely numbered. The brains trust at BRL Hardy need to have their thinking caps on for a replacement name for chablis.
CURRENT RELEASE 1996 Not a bad imitation of French Chablis, if only for the sulfuric nose and light-bodied, angular profile. A basic, simple dry white that would partner a lot of foods. Try shellfish.

Quality	▼▼ど
Value	★★★
Grapes	not stated
Region	various, WA
Cellar	▮ 1
Alc./Vol.	11.5%
RRP	$12.85 Ⓢ

Houghton Chardonnay Verdelho

Quality	♟♟♟
Value	★★★
Grapes	chardonnay; verdelho
Region	various, WA
Cellar	♦ 1
Alc./Vol.	12.5%
RRP	$12.85 ⓢ

Judging by their ad campaign, Houghton view this as expanding the market for the chardonnay franchise – or some such gobbledegook.

CURRENT RELEASE 1996 A sweaty, herbaceous, passionfruit nose marks this immediately as a Houghton house-style. It's a soft, simple, light commercial wine, not completely dry on the finish, which makes it a crowd-pleaser. Closes with slight coarseness. An FAQ (that's fair average quality) white. Goes with vegetable terrine.

Houghton Show Reserve Riesling

Quality	♟♟♟♟♟
Value	★★★★¼
Grapes	riesling
Region	Frankland River, WA
Cellar	♦ 2
Alc./Vol.	12.0%
RRP	$25.00

Great Australian riesling needs several years in the bottle to develop its full glory. Alas, few are probably given the chance. Maker Paul Lapsley.

CURRENT RELEASE 1991 Its three trophies and six gold medals were well earned. This is a superb aged riesling, which is full of buttered-toast character yet which still retains a smidgin of varietal identity. The flavour has become smooth, rich and round; it's mouthfilling and despite the aged complexity it has life and finesse in the mouth. Serve with pan-fried swordfish.

Houghton Show Reserve Verdelho

Quality	♟♟♟♟¼
Value	★★★★
Grapes	verdelho
Region	various, WA
Cellar	♦ 2
Alc./Vol.	13.0%
RRP	$25.00

If it hadn't been for Houghton, verdelho probably would have died a cold and lonely death in Australia. Now it's quite a happening thing. Maker Paul Lapsley.

CURRENT RELEASE 1990 This is loaded with rich, complex, aged flavour but still retains some primary fruit. Full yellow colour, and toasty development, but also nut, pineapple, and grassy/herbal aromas. The aged flavours are quite rich on the tongue and the finish has a light tannin grip. Ready to drink with stuffed, grilled calamari.

Houghton Show Reserve White Burgundy

Most years, Houghton releases two white burgundies: the current vintage, plus an older wine that has been through the show system. The Show Reserve is the same wine with bottle-age. Makers Peter Dawson and Paul Lapsley.

Previous outstanding vintages: '82, '83, '86, '87, '88

CURRENT RELEASE 1990   Not very different from an old Hunter semillon, this has a very deep yellow colour and a bouquet of toasted bread, straw/hay and nuts. The palate is full, round, mellow-flavoured and fully mature – there is a stack of flavour. Goes well with stuffed roast chicken.

Quality	♥♥♥♥♥
Value	★★★★
Grapes	chenin blanc; muscadelle; verdelho; chardonnay; and others
Region	various, WA
Cellar	🍾 1
Alc./Vol.	12.5%
RRP	$25.00

Houghton White Burgundy

Considering the vast quantities Houghton produces of this wine (it's one of the three-top selling white wines in bottles in Australia) the quality is remarkable. The line commenced with Jack Mann in 1937.

CURRENT RELEASE 1996   A party wine with real style. It has a light aroma of cashew nut and tropical fruits with a subtle hint of oak. The flavour is simple, but soft and ample. It has good length and fills the back palate nicely. Good with fresh asparagus.

Quality	♥♥♥♥
Value	★★★★✦
Grapes	chenin blanc; verdelho; muscadelle; semillon; chardonnay; and others
Region	various, WA
Cellar	🍾 5+
Alc./Vol.	12.5%
RRP	$12.80 Ⓢ

Howard Park Riesling

Quality	♛♛♛♛
Value	★★★★
Grapes	riesling
Region	Lower Great Southern, WA
Cellar	➥ 2–7+
Alc./Vol.	12.0%
RRP	$19.00

John Wade has built this brand into one of the most consistently excellent rieslings in the country. He gets to pick and choose from some of south-west Western Australia's best grapes.

Previous outstanding vintages: '86, '90, '91, '92, '93, '94, '95

CURRENT RELEASE 1996   More herbal than usual for this marque, and possibly not showing as well as it might with some bottle-age. It's very soft and easy on the tongue, light-bodied with seamless fruit and not the slightest hint of harshness that's so often seen when acid is added in warmer climes. Cellar it, then serve with pan-fried fish.

Hungerford Hill Tumbarumba Sauvignon Blanc

Quality	♛♛♛♛
Value	★★★⊢
Grapes	sauvignon blanc
Region	Tumbarumba, NSW
Cellar	▮ 2+
Alc./Vol.	12.0%
RRP	$15.65 Ⓢ

Southcorp's Tumbarumba vineyards are located in the foothills of the Snowy Mountains at 580 metres. Maker Ian Walsh.

CURRENT RELEASE 1996   Dusty green capsicum, nettle-like and herbaceous aromas coupled with bracing acidity put this very strongly in the cool-climate pigeon-hole. It's got a tangy presence in the mouth that's typical of the variety. Needs food: try it with mussels.

Hunter's Sauvignon Blanc

Quality	♛♛♛♛♛
Value	★★★★⊢
Grapes	sauvignon blanc
Region	Marlborough, NZ
Cellar	▮ 3+
Alc./Vol.	13.0%
RRP	$20.00

Proprietor Jane Hunter is a viticulturalist first and foremost, and we all know you can't make fine wine without top grapes. Maker Gary Duke.

Previous outstanding vintages: '94, '95

CURRENT RELEASE 1996   Hunter's is consistently one of the leading New Zealand sauvignons, and this is a top vintage. The aromas are gooseberry and lime, with no hint of vegetal cabbage or asparagus tones. The flavour is very intense and lively without excess acidity, finishing with clean vibrancy and great length. Serve with spanner crab.

Jamiesons Run Chardonnay

The label tells us Jamieson's Run is named after the original property where Mildara was established in 1888. CURRENT RELEASE 1996 This used to be a Coonawarra but it's now a multi-region blend. The pressures of grape supply and wine demand not meeting in the middle . . . It's a simple, uncomplicated quaffer, which is very light on wood but which has some authentic melon, peach chardonnay fruit flavours. Try it with Chinese fish balls.

Quality	ΨΨΨ
Value	★★★
Grapes	chardonnay
Region	McLaren Vale & Barossa Valley, SA; King Valley, Vic.; Cowra, NSW
Cellar	🍷 1
Alc./Vol.	12.0%
RRP	$15.60 Ⓢ

Jeanneret Riesling

This is a newish brand from the Sevenhill sub-region of Clare, where riesling is king. It topped the riesling class at the '97 Boutique Wines of Australia Awards. Maker Ben Jeanneret.
CURRENT RELEASE 1996 This is a classic Watervale riesling, which is developing nicely in the bottle. The nose is all limes and slate, with flowery and lightly toasty complexities. It's soft in the mouth with a tinge of mixed spice. The finish is properly dry and lingers well, and it's lively on the tongue. Goes well with most white-fleshed fish.

Quality	ΨΨΨΨΨ
Value	★★★★★
Grapes	riesling
Region	Clare Valley, SA
Cellar	🍷 6+
Alc./Vol.	11.5%
RRP	$12.00 (cellar door)

Jim Barry Lavender Hill

Never let it be said we are wine snobs: some of our best friends are moselles and although the style is out of vogue, there are a few decent wines under the banner. CURRENT RELEASE 1996 A delicate wine that is slightly sweet. The nose is floral (you might fancy you detect lavender) but there are tropical fruit smells. The palate has some residual sugar and there is a zap of acid on the finish. It goes well with a dim sum platter.

Quality	ΨΨΨ
Value	★★★
Grapes	not stated
Region	Clare Valley, SA
Cellar	🍷
Alc./Vol.	10.5%
RRP	$9.90

Jim Barry Semillon

Quality	♟♟♟♟
Value	★★★★
Grapes	semillon
Region	Clare Valley, SA
Cellar	▮ 5
Alc./Vol.	11.7%
RRP	$14.50

The Barry boys can do good labels. This is a good example of arresting packaging. Peter Barry ('Fast' – see below) does the labelling.

CURRENT RELEASE 1996 The wine is quite pungent and begs the question about how it will be after a few years in the cellar. (Should be good!) The nose is toasty and there are elements of cut hay. The palate has gooseberry flavours and there is some attractive wood that makes the transition to the finish, which is long and dry. It goes well with a warm salad of chicken.

Jim Barry Watervale Riesling

Quality	♟♟♟♟
Value	★★★★ｒ
Grapes	Riesling
Region	Clare Valley, SA
Cellar	▮ 3
Alc./Vol.	11.5%
RRP	$9.90

Shake any bush in the Clare Valley and a Barry will fall out of it. Wine writer Phillip White aptly named the three Barry boys 'Fast, Medium and Slow'. Mark ('Medium') makes the wine.

CURRENT RELEASE 1996 This is a regulation Clare Valley riesling with a floral/citrus smell. The palate is chock-full of lime flavours and there is crisp acid. A drink-now wine with a big chill. It's brilliant with oysters natural.

Jimmy Watson's Chardonnay

Quality	♟♟♟
Value	★★★
Grapes	chardonnay
Region	not stated
Cellar	▮ 2
Alc./Vol.	13.0%
RRP	$13.85 Ⓢ

The label is signed by Allan Watson, Jimmy's son, who owns the wine bar of the same name today. The wine is produced by Mildara Blass.

CURRENT RELEASE 1996 A light, straightforward, rather neutral style of chardonnay with little apparent oak and some sweetness lending an oily viscosity. There are lemon flavours on a rich, open-knit palate. Could be served well chilled, with chicken schnitzel.

Karina Vineyard Chardonnay

Another Mornington Glory, this 3-hectare vineyard is small, but that doesn't diminish the importance of the product. Maker Graeme Pinney.

Previous outstanding vintages: '95

CURRENT RELEASE 1996 The colour is bright lemon–yellow and the nose has obvious wood, peach and tropical fruit. The palate is medium- to full-bodied with pineapple and peach flavours, and there is a nutty wood-derived element. The wood fills out the finish and there is a smoky/toasty quality. The wine should not be over-chilled, and it goes well with a crab mousse.

Quality	▼▼▼▼▼
Value	★★★★⯪
Grapes	chardonnay
Region	Mornington Peninsula, Vic.
Cellar	▮ 6
Alc./Vol.	13.0%
RRP	$20.00

Katnook Botrytised Riesling

English as she is spoke, this label comes down on the formal side of the term *botrytis cinerea*, which might not be a good marketing ploy but it looks refreshingly correct to the eyes of jaded wine scribes. So does the wine, by the way.

CURRENT RELEASE 1996 Although the botrytis is evident the variety shines through. There are apricot jam, lime and marmalade aromas on the nose. The palate is medium-bodied with lime, lemon and pineapple-flavoured fruit. This is followed by some zesty, crisp acid on a refreshing finish. It has far to go in the cellar. It can be served well chilled and the food to go with it is a citrus sorbet.

Quality	▼▼▼▼▼
Value	★★★★
Grapes	riesling
Region	Coonawarra, SA
Cellar	▮ 6
Alc./Vol.	12.0%
RRP	$18.90

Katnook Chardonnay

Quality	🍷🍷🍷🍷
Value	★★★
Grapes	chardonnay
Region	Coonawarra, SA
Cellar	🍾 4
Alc./Vol.	13.5%
RRP	$29.00

This variety in Coonawarra can be disappointing – it's seldom voluptuous or naturally complex; winemakers have to work hard to achieve spectacular results. At Katnook they work very hard.

Previous outstanding vintages: '90, '92, '93

CURRENT RELEASE 1995 A refined style that hides its full quota of alcohol. The nose has citrus and melon aromas. Ditto the palate, in terms of flavour, and it could be regarded as lean. The finish is a mixture of wood and acid. It has been put together well and it can be served with a full chill. Try it with yabbies.

Katnook Riesling

Quality	🍷🍷🍷🍷
Value	★★★
Grapes	riesling
Region	Coonawarra, SA
Cellar	🍾 4
Alc./Vol.	12.0%
RRP	$16.00

The fortunes of this variety ebb and flow in Coonawarra. Katnook have long been its champions and tend to release their wine with a bit of bottle-age.

CURRENT RELEASE 1995 Limes on toast: that's the aroma on the nose. The palate is intense and has plenty of body. It's starting to show a touch of bottle-age but it also remains very crisp and fresh. The acid on the finish is what you would expect from the region. It can be served well chilled. Try it with yabbies.

Katnook Sauvignon Blanc

Quality	🍷🍷🍷🍷
Value	★★★
Grapes	sauvignon blanc
Region	Coonawarra, SA
Cellar	🍾 3
Alc./Vol.	13.5%
RRP	$22.00

This winery put Coonawarra on the map as one of the regions capable of producing premium sauvignon. At first the asking price seemed audacious, but other marques are catching up fast. Maker Wayne Stehbens.

Previous outstanding vintages: too numerous to mention

CURRENT RELEASE 1996 While not exactly an elephant in a tutu, this is a big wine. It's cloaked in tropical fruit aromas on the nose, but underneath there are herb and tinned-pea aromas. The palate is almost chewy with passionfruit, lychee and tropical fruit flavours, plus herbs and wintergreen. The finish adds a footnote of acid. It needs to be very cold, and it goes with a pesto pasta.

Kay's Amery Vineyards Sauvignon Blanc

If you stand at the cellar door and look to the east you'll see a vineyard with sauvignon blanc grown from cuttings that were transported from Chateau d'Yquem, pre-phylloxera. What's that got do with anything? Trot it out at dinner parties.

CURRENT RELEASE 1995   The development is slow and the colour is pale. The nose is herbal with tropical fruit and green leaf aromas. The medium-bodied palate offers mango, pineapple and gooseberry flavours. There is plenty of acid on the finish and it can be served well chilled. The wine goes well with mussels in a light chilli sauce.

Quality	♟♟♟
Value	★★★
Grapes	sauvignon blanc
Region	McLaren Vale, SA
Cellar	♦ 3
Alc./Vol.	12.5%
RRP	$12.90

Killerby Semillon

Semillon from the west seems like a different breed from its east-coast cousin. In the east the alcohol tends to be low and development is slow. In the west they are much more forward.

CURRENT RELEASE 1996   This is the full chorus line with barrel fermentation and plenty of alcohol. The nose smells of lanolin and gooseberry. The palate has a mouthfilling texture with gooseberry and hints of tropical fruit. The palate is tinder-dry, with a numbing French oak. It should not be over-chilled. Try it with a kedgeree.

Quality	♟♟♟♟
Value	★★★★
Grapes	semillon
Region	Capel, WA
Cellar	♦ 3
Alc./Vol.	13.5%
RRP	$18.00

Kingston Estate Chardonnay

Quality	🍷🍷🍷🍷
Value	★★★★
Grapes	chardonnay
Region	Kingston (on Murray), SA
Cellar	2
Alc./Vol.	12.5%
RRP	$12.00

The winery was established in 1979 and there are 50 hectares on the banks of the Murray. The wine is made on site and there is a storage capacity of 10 000 000 litres. Maker David Nelson.

CURRENT RELEASE 1996 A portion of the wine was barrel-fermented and it shows in the finished wine. The nose has peach and loquat aromas with a smoky oak character. The medium-bodied palate has peach and citrus flavours that add zest. The finish has a mouth-coating wood quality that is tinder-dry. It can be served with a medium chill. Have it with pork fillet in a mango sauce.

Kingston Estate Semillon Sauvignon Blanc

Quality	🍷🍷🍷
Value	★★★
Grapes	semillon; sauvignon blanc
Region	Kingston (on Murray), SA
Cellar	1
Alc./Vol.	11.0%
RRP	$11.00

The background of the label recalls the decor of many an Adelaide fish caff in Gouger Street. (Some of us actually yearn for green laminex!)

CURRENT RELEASE 1996 This is a fresh and fruity style that has a frivolous drink-now feel. The colour is pale and the nose has strong tropical fruit aromas. The palate is light and fruity with sweet tropical fruit flavours. The finish has some soft acid. It can be served well chilled as a pre-dinner drink.

Knight Granite Hills Riesling

Quality	🍷🍷🍷🍷
Value	★★★★
Grapes	riesling
Region	Macedon, Vic.
Cellar	3
Alc./Vol.	12.0%
RRP	$14.95

This was one of the pioneers of the Macedon District that was started by Gordon Knight (aka 'Silent Knight' because he is forever on the telephone). Maker Lew Knight.

CURRENT RELEASE 1995 The fruit is a prisoner of the weather and in tough years quality can suffer. Not the greatest year, but good winemaking has rendered a zesty style with a citrus nose. The palate is lean with crisp, lime flavours. The finish is marked by tingling acid on a crisp finish.

Knight Granite Hills Chardonnay

The vineyard was originally established by Gordon Knight in 1970. Son Lew carries on the project. This release bears their new label design.

CURRENT RELEASE 1995   A flinty style that reflects the nature of the climate. The nose has citrus and peach aromas. The medium-bodied palate has grapefruit and peach flavours. The finish is quite forceful with lots of acid. The wine can be served with a medium chill. The relatively high alcohol is not apparent and it can handle chilli calamari.

Quality	♥♥♥♥
Value	★★★★
Grapes	chardonnay
Region	Macedon, Vic.
Cellar	🍾 5
Alc./Vol.	14.0%
RRP	$19.00

Koppamurra Botrytis Riesling

This is the original vineyard in the district north of Coonawarra and east of Naracoorte, known loosely as Koppamurra. But the proprietors of the vineyard understandably want the name to themselves, and prefer the regional name Naracoorte Ranges.

CURRENT RELEASE 1995   Absolutely delicious wine: medium–light yellow, and lovely fragrant, floral riesling aroma with traces of honey from restrained botrytis infection. It's medium-sweet only, and the palate features fresh, lively acid and fine citrus riesling fruit. Goes with fresh fruit salad.

Quality	♥♥♥♥♥
Value	★★★★★
Grapes	riesling
Region	Naracoorte Ranges, SA
Cellar	🍾 3+
Alc./Vol.	11.5%
RRP	$11.00 (375ml)

Koppamurra Riesling

The vineyard was founded in 1972 and although it's somewhat stateless, being halfway between Naracoorte and Coonawarra, it can claim terra rossa soil over limestone.

CURRENT RELEASE 1996   The wine is pale and the nose has citrus and lime aromas. The palate is medium-bodied with lime and other citrus flavours, which are backed by crisp acid. A little extra bottle-age won't hurt and it can be served well chilled. Try it with oysters.

Quality	♥♥♥♥
Value	★★★★
Grapes	riesling
Region	Naracoorte Ranges, SA
Cellar	🍾 3
Alc./Vol.	11.3%
RRP	$9.50

Krondorf Family Reserve Chardonnay

Quality	♟♟♟♟
Value	★★★★
Grapes	chardonnay
Region	McLaren Vale, Eden & Barossa Valleys, SA
Cellar	♦ 2
Alc./Vol.	13.0%
RRP	$17.00 ⑤

The 'family reserve' is indeed puzzling. Do they mean winemaker Nick Walker's family? We've scratched our greying heads but we can't remember it ever being a family winery.

Previous outstanding vintages: '90, '91, '92, '93, '94

CURRENT RELEASE 1995   This is a generous, ripe-fruit style with plenty of toasty oak and bottle-age starting to pay handsome dividends. There are lots of savoury oak-influenced flavours in the mouth, with some peach and nut primary fruit still discernible. Try it with grilled crayfish.

Krondorf Semillon

Quality	♟♟♟♟
Value	★★★★
Grapes	semillon
Region	various, SA
Cellar	♦ 5
Alc./Vol.	12.0%
RRP	$11.30 ⑤

This is a barrel-fermented style which bagged a gold medal at the '96 Brisbane Show. Maker Nick Walker.

CURRENT RELEASE 1996   Greenish, stalky aromas with the barest trace of oak. It's a clean, easy-to-like young semillon, which has depth of flavour plus subtlety. The palate has the beginnings of toast and the finish shows lemony acid. Try it with deep-fried calamari.

Lalla Gully Sauvignon Blanc

Quality	♟♟♟
Value	★★★
Grapes	sauvignon blanc
Region	Pipers River, Tas.
Cellar	♦ 2
Alc./Vol.	11.6%
RRP	$19.00

Lalla Gully is the small northern Tasmanian vineyard of Rod Ascui and Kim Seagram (yes, she's one of those Seagrams!).

CURRENT RELEASE 1996   This is about as pungent and racy as sauvignon blanc gets. The nose has high-toned greenery plus cabbage-like low notes, which combine for a most unusual aroma. The wine has a little sweetness and searingly high acidity; it's rather unbalanced, so it demands to be drunk with food. Try it with oysters, perhaps.

Lamonts Chenin Blanc

The new Lamonts white wines, made by young Mark Warren, are a departure from the traditional Jack Mann style of this producer. They're a prime example of what can be achieved with quality Swan grapes in the hands of a good modern winemaker.
CURRENT RELEASE 1996   A big, bouncy wine packed with flavour. It's softly fruity, well-endowed with smooth generous flavour, and well balanced, finishing fairly dry. It won a silver medal at the Perth Wine Show and is a beacon for the region. Serve with West Australian marron.

Quality	?????
Value	★★★★
Grapes	chenin blanc
Region	Swan Valley, WA
Cellar	1
Alc./Vol.	12.7%
RRP	$10.00 (cellar door)

Lark Hill Chardonnay

Lark Hill is located at an altitude of 860 metres on the Lake George Escarpment, near Canberra. Maker Sue Carpenter.
Previous outstanding vintages: '87, '88, '90, '91, '93, '95
CURRENT RELEASE 1996   A fuller wine than the fine '95, with intense tropical-fruit, fine oak perfumes and hints of apricot on the nose. It has great impact and length in the mouth as well as subtlety, and thoroughly deserved its trophy for best Canberra chardonnay at the '97 Canberra District Wine Show. Try it with a ripe brie.

Quality	?????
Value	★★★★
Grapes	chardonnay
Region	Canberra district, NSW
Cellar	5+
Alc./Vol.	13.5%
RRP	$20.00 (cellar door)

Leasingham Bin 37 Chardonnay

Chardonnay, normally a great traveller, has had a chequered career in Clare. Leasingham is an outpost of the BRL Hardy empire.
CURRENT RELEASE 1996   American oak has imparted a lifted, confectionery aspect to the nose, which also has pawpaw-like fruit. The palate has some sweetness coupled with lively acid, resulting in a slightly hard finish. It could fill out with a few months in the bottle. Try with crumbed lamb's brains.

Quality	???
Value	★★★
Grapes	chardonnay
Region	Clare Valley, SA
Cellar	3
Alc./Vol.	13.5%
RRP	$14.50 Ⓢ

Leasingham Bin 7 Rhine Riesling

Quality	???????
Value	★★★★★
Grapes	riesling
Region	Clare Valley, SA
Cellar	➥ 1–6+
Alc./Vol.	12.0%
RRP	$14.50 ⑤

For reasons best known to themselves, the BRL Hardy marketers stick to the old rhine riesling nomenclature for this wine. The '95 won the Penguin Best Bargain White Award last year.

CURRENT RELEASE 1996 This is a classic style and although it's made to drink now, it would be much better in a year or three. There is a little free sulfur, which breathes off to reveal a distinctive lemon–lime aroma and a hint of slate. The palate is sprightly and finishes with an appealing tang. A lovely drink to serve with grilled whiting fillets.

Leconfield Chardonnay

Quality	???
Value	★★★
Grapes	chardonnay
Region	Coonawarra, SA
Cellar	▮ 2
Alc./Vol.	12.7%
RRP	$16.90

Leconfield is part of the Richard Hamilton operation, which is based in McLaren Vale and Coonawarra. Maker Ralph Fowler.

CURRENT RELEASE 1996   This is a pleasant fruit-driven wine, but it's just a bit too light. There are passionfruit and tropical aromas, and a subtle kiss of dusty oak. It almost tastes like an unwooded chardonnay with simplistic, rather shallow flavour and fairly short finish. Bottle-age may help fill it out a little. Try it with taramasalata.

Leconfield Twelve Rows Riesling

Quality	?????
Value	★★★★★
Grapes	riesling
Region	Coonawarra, SA
Cellar	▮ 5+
Alc./Vol.	11.5%
RRP	$18.00

This is a commemorative bottling. The original 12 rows of riesling in the Leconfield vineyard, planted by founder Sydney Hamilton in 1974, were pulled up after the '96 vintage to make way for cabernet. Maker Ralph Fowler.

CURRENT RELEASE 1996 Marvellous riesling. Fresh, estery bread-dough and flower aromas fill the senses, and rich, powerful flavours flood the mouth. This is right at the biggest end of the riesling spectrum, but it isn't at all heavy. Great persistence; a true reserve selection and worth cellaring. Try it with grilled whiting.

Leeuwin Estate Art Series Chardonnay

This is the large-calibre cannon from Leeuwin. It's regarded by many as the best chardonnay in the country. Maker Bob Cartwright.

Previous outstanding vintages: '80, '81, '82, '83, '85, '86, '87, '90, '91, '92, '93

CURRENT RELEASE 1994 By Leeuwin standards a subdued, tame wine without the usual pungent fruit intensity. There is some richness on the palate, with underlying concentration, but it doesn't sing – at least not yet; it may need more time to unfurl its charms. Seems to be a good, but not great, chardonnay – in other words, a lesser Leeuwin. Serve with marron.

Quality	♥♥♥♥
Value	★★★
Grapes	chardonnay
Region	Margaret River, WA
Cellar	🍷 3+
Alc./Vol.	13.5%
RRP	$52.00

Leeuwin Prelude Chardonnay

This is the quaffing chardonnay from Leeuwin, if a $24 wine could be described thus. The musical theme links up nicely with the famous annual concert on the winery lawns.

CURRENT RELEASE 1996 This is more like fruit juice than wine. Passionfruit esters galore! Typically tropical, it's all about primary fruit rather than oak or winemaking embellishment, and the finish is all alcohol warmth and lively acid. Hard to mate with food, but try quail and lychee salad.

Quality	♥♥♥
Value	★★★
Grapes	chardonnay
Region	Margaret River, WA
Cellar	🍷 2
Alc./Vol.	14.0%
RRP	$24.00

Lenswood Vineyards Chardonnay

Tim Knappstein's Lenswood chardonnays have consistently vindicated his decision to sell up the Clare business and head for the hills.

Previous outstanding vintages: '93, '94

CURRENT RELEASE 1995 This is a superb chardonnay and we'd like to see it in a taste-off with the Petaluma, Geoff Weaver and Henschke '95s. The nose is a riot of smoky, butterscotch and slightly herbaceous scents; in the mouth there's concentrated tropical flavour, tight structure with frisky acid, great complexity and tremendous length. Most impressive! Food: truffled pheasant.

Quality	♥♥♥♥♥
Value	★★★★★
Grapes	chardonnay
Region	Adelaide Hills, SA
Cellar	🍷 4
Alc./Vol.	14.0%
RRP	$28.70

Lenton Brae Chardonnay

Quality	ŸŸŸŸ
Value	★★★⭒
Grapes	chardonnay
Region	Margaret River, WA
Cellar	▬ 4
Alc./Vol.	13.5%
RRP	$19.75

This is the Margaret River winery of Bruce Tomlinson, who has stirred a few people up since he got involved in wine industry politics. He is a former architect, and his rammed earth winery is quite superb.

CURRENT RELEASE 1996 A full-bodied chardonnay with typical Margaret River richness. The nose is smoky oak, lemons, earth and minerals. The palate has good depth and richness, with a long, dry aftertaste, and it features plenty of good oak. Try it with a very soft, ripe brie.

Leo Buring Clare Valley Chardonnay

Quality	ŸŸŸŸ
Value	★★★★★
Grapes	chardonnay
Region	Clare Valley, SA
Cellar	▬ 2
Alc./Vol.	13.5%
RRP	$12.00 Ⓢ

With their new packaging, the Leo Buring varietals have also hit new heights in quality. Maker Geoff Henriks.

CURRENT RELEASE 1996 This is more than just a pretty face: it has attractive fruit but also some wine-making complexities, such as butterscotch and slight oak characters, into the bargain. The palate has peach and honey flavours, which sustain the interest. A soft, round, not terribly refined but generous flavour, and great value. Try it with scallops.

Leo Buring Clare Valley Riesling

Quality	ŸŸŸŸ⸮
Value	★★★★★
Grapes	riesling
Region	Clare Valley, SA
Cellar	▬ 6+
Alc./Vol.	12.0%
RRP	$11.30 Ⓢ

It's only a matter of time before the world wakes up to the fact that Clare Valley riesling is a great wine. Then the price will go up, so enjoy it cheap while ye may.

CURRENT RELEASE 1996 Classic stuff: restrained, backward aromas of flowers, limes and lemons. Subtle wine all round, and there's plenty of zip in the palate. It's crisp and jumpy, with perhaps a touch of CO_2, and the finish is dry but not austere, smooth and very drinkable. Cellarable, too. Serve with pan-fried john dory.

Leo Buring Clare Valley Semillon

The Buring standard labels have been simplified and now even we can understand them! Gone and unlamented are the arcane bin numbers of yore. Maker Geoff Henriks.

CURRENT RELEASE 1996 Delicious young semillon with all the straw/dry-grass character and crisp, dry flavour that you might expect to find in a good young Hunter. It has delicacy and just enough firmness on the finish. Should cellar well. Goes well with poached sole.

Quality	♥♥♥♥
Value	★★★★★
Grapes	semillon
Region	Clare Valley, SA
Cellar	🍾 5+
Alc./Vol.	12.0%
RRP	$11.30 Ⓢ

Leo Buring Late Picked Riesling

This is the sort of wine that people who come to visit wineries in buses love, yet it's dead as a dodo in retail shops. This one has a percentage of botrytis-affected grapes.

CURRENT RELEASE 1996 Full, flowery nose with some tighter, minerally overtones – a typical riesling nose. There is sweetness galore on the palate, together with some late-picked richness and good length. Would be good with some bottle-age. Serve well chilled with pâté.

Quality	♥♥♥♥
Value	★★★★
Grapes	riesling
Region	Clare Valley, SA
Cellar	🍾 5
Alc./Vol.	12.0%
RRP	$10.00 Ⓢ

Leo Buring Leonay Eden Valley Riesling

The old Buring Show Reserve Bin-numbered rieslings were true Australian classics. They continue, but the label's been smartened up and the bin numbers have been given the heave-ho.

Previous outstanding vintages: '70, '71, '72, '73, '75, '76, '79, '84, '86, '87, '90

CURRENT RELEASE 1991 As good as they come. For all its gently bottle-aged, buttered-toast complexities, this still has typical Eden Valley herbal, lemon and floral primary aromas, and a crisp citrus palate. When most rieslings would be peaking, this still has a big future. Try it with lemon sole.

Quality	♥♥♥♥♥
Value	★★★★★
Grapes	riesling
Region	Eden Valley, SA
Cellar	🍾 10
Alc./Vol.	11.5%
RRP	$20.00

Leo Buring Leonay Watervale Riesling

Quality	♥♥♥♥♥
Value	★★★★★
Grapes	riesling
Region	Clare Valley, SA
Cellar	🍶 5+
Alc./Vol.	12.5%
RRP	$21.00

The new Leo Buring labels are a godsend: anyone can understand them. You felt like you had to belong to some secret society to understand the old bin numbers and show bottlings. Maker Geoff Henriks.
Previous outstanding vintages: '71, '73, '75, '79, '84, '86, '87, '90, '91, '92, '93, '94
CURRENT RELEASE 1992   Perhaps not a blinder like the '91 Eden Valley, but certainly up to speed. A little more forward than previous Leonays, but still a delicate, restrained style in the context of Aussie riesling. The nose is a mixture of minerals and citrus, with slatey and lime-zesty characters to the fore. It's classically dry but not austere, and the concentration of fruit sets it apart. The flavour builds on the mid-palate and lingers long on the aftertaste. Serve with grilled flounder.

Leydens Vale Riesling

Quality	♥♥♥♥
Value	★★★★
Grapes	riesling
Region	Mt Barker, WA; Yarra Valley, Vic.
Cellar	🍶 3
Alc./Vol.	11.0%
RRP	$15.00 ⑤

Mr Leyden was a pioneer in the Pyrenees region. This is made by French-born Vincent Gere, under whose guidance Blue Pyrenees Estate has made much progress.
CURRENT RELEASE 1994   This had a few buckets of traminer thrown in to jazz up the bouquet, and it shows. Candied, lychee-like traminer aromas, and the taste is very spicy with the richness and weight that come from both traminer and bottle-age. Try it with a warm duck salad. Good value.

Lillydale Vineyards Chardonnay

Quality	♥♥♥
Value	★★★
Grapes	chardonnay
Region	Yarra Valley, Vic.
Cellar	🍶 3
Alc./Vol.	13.0%
RRP	$15.30 ⑤

Lillydale was started by Alex and Judith White with a vineyard in the rich, red fertile soils of the Yarra Valley's Seville sub-region. It's now part of McWilliams.
CURRENT RELEASE 1996   A rather delicate style with a light yellow colour, an aromatic bouquet of fresh, fruit-driven melon-like aromas, and hints of toast and butterscotch complexity. The palate is lean, highly acidic and slightly austere. Try it with oysters.

Lillydale Vineyards Classic Dry White

If ever there was a misnomer, 'classic dry white' is it. Many wines are anything but classic, and some aren't even dry!
CURRENT RELEASE 1996 Dusty, sweaty, tinned-pea vegetable aromas and pale colour suggest vigorous vines and shaded bunches. There's a touch of New Zealand about this wine. The palate is a tad flimsy, but it does have some flavour and balance. Very drinkable, as long as you don't try to keep it. Food: caesar salad.

Quality	♟♟♟
Value	★★★
Grapes	not stated
Region	Yarra Valley, Vic.
Cellar	▮ 1
Alc./Vol.	12.5%
RRP	$13.00 Ⓢ

Lillydale Vineyards Gewurztraminer

Gewurz is a much overlooked grape these days, but how many of us cut our teeth on it? And it does go well with Vietnamese food.
CURRENT RELEASE 1995 This is a typically pungent cool-climate gewurz, and the bouquet has developed honey, almost raisin overtones. There are fig and spice flavours aplenty. In the mouth it's very light and somewhat short. Clean, simple, easy to like. Try it with Vietnamese salad.

Quality	♟♟♟
Value	★★★
Grapes	gewurztraminer
Region	Yarra Valley, Vic.
Cellar	▮ 2
Alc./Vol.	10.5%
RRP	$15.30 Ⓢ

Lillydale Vineyards Sauvignon Blanc

The white wines from this vineyard are always restrained – some would say light; kinder souls would say delicate.
CURRENT RELEASE 1996 Fragrant cool-climate aromas of herbs and citrus fruits greet the nose. It's an attractive wine of subtlety and good balance: you can drink more than one glass. There are some vegetable and herb flavours, and it's smooth and harmonised in the mouth. Try it with scallops.

Quality	♟♟♟?
Value	★★★⊦
Grapes	sauvignon blanc
Region	Yarra Valley, Vic.
Cellar	▮ 1
Alc./Vol.	11.0%
RRP	$15.30 Ⓢ

Lillypilly Sauvignon Blanc

Quality	♥♥♥♥♥
Value	★★★★★
Grapes	sauvignon blanc
Region	Riverina, NSW
Cellar	1
Alc./Vol.	12.6%
RRP	$8.70 (cellar door)

Lillypilly's Robert Fiumara bottled some '96 whites, including tramillon, with Stelvin screw caps instead of corks because he was so disillusioned with cork quality. He calls his wines 'unplugged'. Eric Clapton eat your heart out.

CURRENT RELEASE 1996 Sauvignon blanc doesn't usually yield great results when grown in hot climates such as that of the Riverina, but this is a triumph. A quite delicious sauvignon with restrained varietal pungency and a lively, intense, fresh nectarine-like flavour, which finishes balanced and nicely dry. Try it with goat's cheese tartlets.

Lillypilly Tramillon

Quality	♥♥♥♥
Value	★★★★
Grapes	gewurztraminer; semillon
Region	Riverina, NSW
Cellar	1
Alc./Vol.	12.5%
RRP	$8.70 (cellar door)

HH tasted both the cork-sealed and screw-capped tramillon and sauvignon blanc, and found the screw-capped bottlings slightly fresher, even at less than a year old. It's an indictment of the quality of imported cork.

CURRENT RELEASE 1996 Fragrantly aromatic, moderately sweet, beautifully spicy blend of traminer and semillon. Technically A1, although some may find the sweetness too high for their taste. Try it with a ripe peach.

Lindemans Bin 65 Chardonnay

Quality	♥♥♥
Value	★★★★
Grapes	chardonnay
Region	Murray Valley, Vic.
Cellar	2
Alc./Vol.	13.0%
RRP	$9.80 ⑤

'Dontcha gimme no lip now.' This is one of Australia's biggest selling export wines, but Lindemans is not resting on its laurels: it's relaunched the wine in a trendy flange-lipped bottle.

CURRENT RELEASE 1996 Peachy, cashew nut fruit and shavings-like oak aromas, with a certain suggestion of toasted chips. This wine has become more wood-accented with successive vintages. It has decent flavour and style for the price. Serve with BBQ prawns.

Lindemans Cawarra Classic Dry White

Lindemans has taken the bull by the horns and committed its entire Cawarra range to synthetic corks. These are designed to beat the winemaker's scourge – cork taint.

CURRENT RELEASE 1996 Smells a bit like lemonade: estery, lollyish and essence-like. It's sweet on entry but dries a little towards the finish. There's a sherbet taste of peppermint Lifesavers on a short-and-sweet palate. It's technically A1, and perfectly acceptable at the price. Try it with larb (minted Thai salad).

Quality	🍷🍷🍷
Value	★★★★
Grapes	not stated
Region	not stated
Cellar	1
Alc./Vol.	11.5%
RRP	$7.30 (S)

Lindemans Hunter River Chardonnay

The Lindemans Hunter wines are all bin-numbered: this one is Bin 8681. Maker Patrick Auld.

CURRENT RELEASE 1995 The deep yellow colour shows that this has some bottle-age as well as a lot of oak, and is developing quickly. The bouquet has smoky, toasty and resinous nuances, and the palate relies on wood and bottle-age, giving caramel and vanilla flavours. The finish has a touch of astringency. Drink soon, with roast chicken.

Quality	🍷🍷🍷
Value	★★★
Grapes	chardonnay
Region	Hunter Valley, NSW
Cellar	
Alc./Vol.	13.0%
RRP	$13.50 (S)

Lindemans Hunter River Semillon

Some fabulous wines have appeared under this name in the past. With age, the best young semillons transform into tremendously flavoursome, complex wines. Maker Pat Auld.

Previous outstanding vintages: '65, '68, '70, '79, '80, '86, '87, '91, '93, '94

CURRENT RELEASE 1995 Bin 8655. Pronounced lanolin and herbal aromas, with parsley/basil overtones. Light-bodied, simple fruit flavour with a trace of apparent sweetness. A good, fruity young semillon that drinks well young with salads.

Quality	🍷🍷🍷🍷
Value	★★★★
Grapes	semillon
Region	Hunter Valley, NSW
Cellar	10+
Alc./Vol.	11.5%
RRP	$13.50 (S)

Lindemans Padthaway Chardonnay

Quality	YYYY?
Value	★★★★★
Grapes	chardonnay
Region	Padthaway, SA
Cellar	▮ 4
Alc./Vol.	13.5%
RRP	$14.00 $

Earlier vintages of this wine have come in for high praise in certain American magazines of late. They probably won't like this vintage: it's not woody enough.
Previous outstanding vintages: '85, '90, '94
CURRENT RELEASE 1996 A change in style here: the wine is much less oaky and more delicate all round. Light yellow colour, restrained melon–peach aromas, lightly toasty oak well married, and impeccable balance. It can be found discounted as low as $10 and is one of the great bargains in white wine. Food: Chinese chicken and cashew nuts.

Lindemans Padthaway Classic Release Botrytis Riesling

Quality	YYYY?
Value	★★★★
Grapes	riesling
Region	Padthaway, SA
Cellar	▮ 1
Alc./Vol.	11.0%
RRP	$50.00

This was part of the 1996 Lindemans Classic Release program, a praiseworthy scheme to cellar-age and re-release selected top Lindemans wines at full maturity.
CURRENT RELEASE 1985 This exceptional sweetie is remarkably Germanic in style. It's deep golden in colour, and has inviting fragrances of vanilla and mixed peel. The palate is only medium-sweet and has a hint of Padthaway saltiness, which doesn't mar it. With a drying finish, it's more suited to cheese than dessert. Try it with washed-rind cheeses.

Lindemans Reserve Hunter River Semillon

Quality	YYYY?
Value	★★★★
Grapes	semillon
Region	Hunter Valley, NSW
Cellar	➥ 5–15+
Alc./Vol.	11.5%
RRP	$20.00 $

Lindemans has selected this Bin 8650 as a top bet for the cellar. Hence it's released as a two-year-old with bells and whistles and a higher price. Maker Pat Auld.
CURRENT RELEASE 1995 If you want a classic Hunter semillon to put down, this is the one. Very herbal to sniff, with notes of parsley and basil. It's classically unwooded, fresh and fruity and seems to be ageing slowly, which is desirable. It has fine flavour, well-harmonised acid and real delicacy. It should repay at least 10 years in a cool cellar.

Macedon Ridge Chardonnay

This ultra-cool-climate vineyard was planted by multi-media personality Derryn Hinch when he was enjoying better days. The wine is made under contract by John Ellis.

CURRENT RELEASE 1993 Time seems to be standing still in this bottle. The only clue of age is the colour, which is a yellow green–gold. The nose is slightly smoky, with peach and melon dominating. The palate is lean with citrus flavour as the major attraction. There is also an underscore of peach flavour. The finish is very dry and lingers long. Don't over-chill, and try it with smoked chicken.

Quality	♥♥♥♥
Value	★★★★
Grapes	chardonnay
Region	Macedon, Vic.
Cellar	↓ 4
Alc./Vol.	12.5%
RRP	$21.00

Madew Riesling

David Madew had to quit his Queanbeyan vineyard in lieu of a housing estate, but he now sources his grapes from the former Westering vineyard at Lake George.

CURRENT RELEASE 1996 A little free sulfur dioxide needs time to breathe off, but a few months in the bottle should rectify that. There is cool, limey riesling fragrance, and the palate has soft, gentle floral flavour. The finish is dry, thanks partly to a little phenolic grip. Withal, a good wine. Serve with grilled fish.

Quality	♥♥♥♥
Value	★★★★
Grapes	riesling
Region	Canberra district, NSW
Cellar	↓ 4+
Alc./Vol.	12.5%
RRP	$15.00 (cellar door)

Madfish Bay Western Australian Premium Dry White

There is a bay in Western Australia populated by mad fish. The fish are herded into the bay by predatory dolphins that want to turn them into lunch.

CURRENT RELEASE 1996 This is a soft, drinkable style dominated by chardonnay varietal flavours. The nose has ripe pawpaw, peach and citrus aromas. The palate is full of soft peach flavours and these are balanced by some gentle acid on a dry finish. It can handle a fair chill. Try it with stuffed calamari.

Quality	♥♥♥♡
Value	★★★
Grapes	chardonnay; semillon; sauvignon blanc
Region	Great Southern, WA
Cellar	↓ 2
Alc./Vol.	13.5%
RRP	$16.00

Marienberg Reserve Chardonnay

Quality	♟♟♟♟
Value	★★★
Grapes	chardonnay
Region	McLaren Vale, SA
Cellar	▪ 3
Alc./Vol.	13.5%
RRP	$15.50

There has been considerable effort expended on revamping the packaging. The vineyards and winery are now owned by Marienberg Wine Company Pty Ltd. Maker John Loxton.

CURRENT RELEASE 1996 Well-made wine with impressive integration of all components. The nose has varietal elements plus savoury oak smells. The palate has a creamy texture and a mouthfilling palate. The major flavour is peach and the oak assimilates with the fruit. The finish is dry and soft. It can take a medium chill and is great served with chilli prawns.

Marienberg Riesling

Quality	♟♟♟♟
Value	★★★★
Grapes	riesling
Region	Adelaide Hills, SA
Cellar	▪ 2
Alc./Vol.	12.0%
RRP	$14.00

This label was started by Ursula Pridham, who used to be a bit of a curio as 'Australia's first female winemaker'. It was a little big deal at the time and these days not much has changed. Winemaking is still a bloke's sport.

CURRENT RELEASE 1996 Regulation riesling with no vices. The colour is a pale, sparkling lemon–yellow. The nose has lemon and various citrus aromas. The palate is full-bodied (for a riesling) with straightforward lemon flavours, and there is sufficient acid to carry the fruit. It can be served well chilled and it can handle a spaghetti marinara.

Marienberg Sauvignon Blanc Semillon Riesling

Quality	♟♟♟
Value	★★★
Grapes	sauvignon blanc; semillon; riesling
Region	Adelaide Hills, SA
Cellar	▪
Alc./Vol.	12.0%
RRP	$12.00

Any artist will tell you that if you mix all the colours together you'll always end up with neutral grey. Is that the same with grape varieties?

CURRENT RELEASE 1996 This one is difficult to describe. It has sauvignon blanc grassy aromas on the nose. The palate has semillon gooseberry flavours and there is acid from the riesling on the finish. It can be served well chilled. Have it with a designer salad and chicken and sage sausages.

Maritime Estate Chardonnay

The enterprise was established in 1988 with 4.6 hectares under vine. If the proprietors have their way you'll be hearing much more about it. Maker Quealy & McCarthy (contract).

CURRENT RELEASE 1995 Typical of the region with some malolactic fermentation thrown in for extra complexity. The colour is pale straw and the nose has peach aromas. There is a buttery texture on the middleweight palate, which has stone fruit and rockmelon flavours. French oak adds to a dry finish. It should be gently chilled and is superb with a feed of smoked cod.

Quality	♛♛♛♛
Value	★★★★
Grapes	chardonnay
Region	Mornington Peninsula, Vic.
Cellar	🍷 4
Alc./Vol.	13.6%
RRP	$19.00

McWilliams Eden Valley Rhine Riesling

This is something of a show-stopper; that is, it was made for wine shows. It also shows the confusion that lurks in the McWilliams portfolio. The wines seem to come from everywhere.

CURRENT RELEASE 1988 Plenty of development here but the wine is still lively. The colour is a bright gold and the nose has a hint of kero as well as citrus aromas. The palate is rich and mellow and it's balanced by lingering acid that keeps the wine young and alive. It can and should be served with a decent chill. Try it with a smoked salmon quiche.

Quality	♛♛♛♛♛
Value	★★★★★
Grapes	riesling
Region	Eden Valley, SA
Cellar	🍷 2
Alc./Vol.	12.0%
RRP	$15.50

McWilliams Maurice O'Shea Chardonnay

Quality	♟♟♟♟
Value	★★★★
Grapes	chardonnay
Region	Hunter Valley, NSW
Cellar	▮ 4
Alc./Vol.	12.5%
RRP	$20.00

Younger readers will probably ask, 'Who was Maurice O'Shea?' He is a winemaking legend who pioneered modern winemaking in the Hunter Valley in the '40s. In his private life he was evidently a very enigmatic man with an impish sense of humour.

CURRENT RELEASE 1994   This is a well-rounded wine with no vices. The nose is peachy with French oak aromas. The palate is full-bodied with a mouthfilling texture. Peach is the major flavour, and this is attended by a hint of melon. The oak is a perfect fit, adding to a substantial finish. It's a model of balance and should not be served too cold. Try it with veal in a light cream sauce.

McWilliams Mount Pleasant Verdelho

Quality	♟♟♟♟
Value	★★★★
Grapes	verdelho
Region	Hunter Valley, NSW
Cellar	▮ 6
Alc./Vol.	13.0%
RRP	$14.90

The Hunter Valley is one of the original abodes (Western Australia is the other) of this capricious variety. In the Hunter the makers put much store on bottle-age to produce complexity.

CURRENT RELEASE 1996   This wine seems like a chardonnay and semillon cross. There are melon and tropical fruit aromas and these are also the major flavours on the palate. The medium-bodied fruit flavours are balanced by crisp acid on the finish. The wine can be served well chilled and it goes nicely with chicken casserole.

Meadowbank Chardonnay

This is a landlocked vineyard north of Hobart. It was established in 1974. There are 10 hectares under vine. Maker Greg O'Keefe.

CURRENT RELEASE 1995   Although the grapes obviously got fairly ripe, the wine remains in a flinty and austere mood. The nose has grapefruit and melon aromas. The palate continues this melon and grapefruit score, and there is also a flinty, mineral quality. New French oak fills out the finish. It can be served with a medium chill, and it ain't bad with smoked cod in a white sauce.

Quality	♀♀♀⚲
Value	★★★⚬
Grapes	chardonnay
Region	southern Tasmania
Cellar	▮ 5
Alc./Vol.	13.1%
RRP	$20.00

Merrebee Estate Chardonnay

Brand new label that isn't in the *Wine Industry Journal* yet. It comes from Mount Barker, Western Australia, and this is an impressive debut.

CURRENT RELEASE 1995   Big, full-on and begging no pardons. This is a lavish wine with nutty, toasty aromas on the nose plus some tropical fruit. The palate floods the mouth with tropical and melon flavours, which are garnished by roasted nuts. The finish has plenty of robust wood flavours so don't over-chill, and serve with pan-fried quail.

Quality	♀♀♀♀
Value	★★★★
Grapes	chardonnay
Region	Mount Barker, WA
Cellar	➡ 2–6
Alc./Vol.	14.0%
RRP	$24.50

Merrivale Semillon Chardonnay

Trivia buffs will revel in the knowledge that this label was founded by the late Jack Starr and the place is now owned by the Light family who founded Coolawin. Confused? Just drink the stuff. Maker Brian Light.

CURRENT RELEASE 1996   This is a very soft style that can take a big chill. The nose is a mixture of peach, gooseberry and wood aromas. The palate has soft peach and melon flavours and the wood coats the tongue during the finish. It's a good tripe in white sauce style.

Quality	♀♀♀
Value	★★★
Grapes	semillon;
	chardonnay
Region	McLaren Vale, SA
Cellar	▮ 2
Alc./Vol.	12.0%
RRP	$13.00

Milburn Park Reserve Chardonnay

Quality	♟♟♟♟
Value	★★★★
Grapes	chardonnay
Region	Mildura, Vic.
Cellar	♦ 3
Alc./Vol.	13.0%
RRP	$11.00

This vineyard at Irymple is not afraid to test viticultural theories like deficit watering and various forms of trellising. The objective is to improve the quality of the wines.

CURRENT RELEASE 1996 A very civilised style that shows synergy of fruit and oak. The colour is a pale yellow and the nose has peach, melon and oak aromas. The palate is full-bodied with peach, melon and fig flavours, and these are adorned by elegant oak on a long, dry finish. It can be served well chilled and it's great with three-cheese gnocchi.

Milburn Park Reserve Sauvignon Blanc

Quality	♟♟♟
Value	★★★
Grapes	sauvignon blanc
Region	Mildura, Vic.
Cellar	♦ 1
Alc./Vol.	12.5%
RRP	$11.00

What happened to the old rule about table wine being bottled in coloured glass to regulate the ingress of light? This wine comes in a clear claret bottle and perhaps it suffers in the process.

CURRENT RELEASE 1995 The wine shows some premature bottle development. The nose is slightly musty with a background of herbs. The palate has a slightly oily texture and the herb flavours are muted. The finish shows some soft acid. It can be served well chilled. Try it with a seafood pizza.

Mildara Vintage Reserve Chardonnay

Quality	♟♟♟
Value	★★★★
Grapes	chardonnay
Region	not stated
Cellar	♦ 2
Alc./Vol.	11.5%
RRP	$10.50 ⓢ

This is the basic Mildara chardonnay, although one wonders with a subtitle like Vintage Reserve. In fact, it's not so much a true reserve wine as a case of gilding the lily.

CURRENT RELEASE 1996 A fruit-driven style without obvious oak. There are inviting fruit aromas of nectarine, fresh cashew nuts and honey, and a slight herbal edge. The taste is soft and slightly broad with a hint of sweetness, and the finish is firmed by a whisper of tannin. Good value. Serve with antipasto.

Miranda Golden Botrytis

They've spent a lot of time on label design. It suits the style, which is slowly gaining recognition and extended use by consumers.
CURRENT RELEASE 1994   The colour is a deep yellow–gold and the nose is pungent, marmalade, dried-fruit, botrytis smells. The palate is complex and mouthfilling. There are many flavours including fig, nectarine, peach and lime. These are followed by a tinder-dry finish. The wine can easily cope with a big chill. It's great with pork in a mango sauce.

Quality	??????
Value	★★★★↑
Grapes	rhine riesling 53%; semillon 47%
Region	King Valley, Vic.; Griffith, NSW
Cellar	▮ 4
Alc./Vol.	11.0%
RRP	$16.90 (375ml)

Miranda High Country Chardonnay

This is a mid-range wine with attractive packaging. The grapes come from growers in the district.
CURRENT RELEASE 1996   There is a big charge of toasty oak on the nose. Peach and stone-fruit aromas are also present. The palate is full-bodied with ripe varietal flavours but the oak is lurking. To misquote Churchill: 'A wooden curtain has fallen across the palate'. The finish is very macho. Don't chill, and try it with smoked salmon.

Quality	????
Value	★★★↑
Grapes	chardonnay
Region	King Valley, Vic.
Cellar	▮ 4
Alc./Vol.	13.5%
RRP	$12.00

Miranda High Country Sauvignon Blanc

This is another arm of the Grey Label Series that draws fruit from high-altitude vineyards in other regions.
CURRENT RELEASE 1996   The colour is a pale green/lemon–yellow. The nose has pea-pod, herbs and cut-grass aromas. The palate has some tropical fruit flavours and there is a pleasant zap of acid on a lively finish. It drinks well with a big chill. Try it with a caesar salad.

Quality	????
Value	★★★↑
Grapes	sauvignon blanc
Region	King Valley, Vic.
Cellar	▮ 3
Alc./Vol.	10.5%
RRP	$12.00

Miranda Rovalley Ridge Grey Series Chardonnay

Quality	♟♟♟♟
Value	★★★★ﾚ
Grapes	chardonnay
Region	Barossa Valley, SA
Cellar	▮ 3
Alc./Vol.	13.0%
RRP	$13.00

If the title gets any longer we'll need a wide-screen book. The portfolio from the Griffith/Barossa-based company is large and somewhat confusing.

CURRENT RELEASE 1995　All the devices have been used to produce a complex wine. The nose has peach and melon aromas plus some smoky wood. The palate has creamy textures with peach and melon flavours, and the oak has been well integrated. The finish has a smooth quality and the wine should be served with a gentle chill. Try it with prawns in a light lemon sauce.

Miranda Show Reserve Chardonnay

Quality	♟♟♟♟
Value	★★★ﾚ
Grapes	chardonnay
Region	Eden Valley, SA
Cellar	▮ 4
Alc./Vol.	13.5%
RRP	$19.00

This wines comes with an 'exclusive money-back quality guarantee'. It's tempting to send a bottle back to see what happens. Who determines the quality?

CURRENT RELEASE 1995　The colour has a youthful appearance and the nose gives an indication of the wood that is to follow. There are toasty, sappy aromas that almost swamp the peach fruit. The palate is medium-bodied with peach and apricot flavours. These are soon joined by oak on a bold finish. Don't over-chill, and try it with smoked cod.

Mirrool Creek Rhine Riesling

Quality	♟♟♟
Value	★★★
Grapes	riesling
Region	Griffith, NSW
Cellar	▮ 1
Alc./Vol.	12.0%
RRP	$9.80

The label is about as Aussie as corks dangling from the brim of an Akubra. Corny, but it kinda works.

CURRENT RELEASE 1996　This wine says riesling. The nose is limey with a hint of kero. The palate has a slight oily citrus flavour and there is soft acid on the finish. It can be served well chilled, and a seafood platter is the go.

Mitchell The Growers Semillon Sauvignon Blanc

The 'Growers' range seems to be a burgeoning part of this label. It pays tribute to the independent growers in the Clare Valley. Maker Andrew Mitchell.

CURRENT RELEASE 1996   The nose has lemon and citrus aromas and the respective parts play their role flawlessly. Sauvignon blanc leads the dance on the nose with grassy aromas. There is mellow citrus flavour on the palate, which has a creamy texture, and there is discreet wood on the finish. It's loaded, so be ready to pull the trigger (cork). Try it with chicken pie.

Quality	▼▼▼▼▼
Value	★★★★
Grapes	semillon; sauvignon blanc
Region	Clare Valley, SA
Cellar	2
Alc./Vol.	13.0%
RRP	$13.50

Mitchelton Chardonnay

It's not often you find chardonnay playing second fiddle in a white wine portfolio, but here marsanne is king and chardonnay is regarded as a latecomer.

CURRENT RELEASE 1994   The door has opened just a chink since last year. It's still a buttoned-down wine, but there has been progress towards realising its full potential. The nose is a fruit–wood mix with peach dominating. The palate remains austere but there are melon and stone-fruit flavours, which are matched by an austere, almost astringent, finish. It can be served lightly chilled with some trippa – Italian style.

Quality	▼▼▼▼▼
Value	★★★★
Grapes	chardonnay
Region	Yarra Valley & Strathbogie Ranges, Vic.
Cellar	5
Alc./Vol.	13.9%
RRP	$24.00

Mitchelton Marsanne

Mitchelton added a new dimension to this rather pallid variety by giving it an oak treatment. Traditionalists had a fit, but the consumer and show judges reacted favourably and a star was born. Maker Don Lewis.

Previous outstanding vintages: too numerous to mention

CURRENT RELEASE 1993   As ever, this is a handsome mixture of fruit and oak. The nose has strong honeysuckle and oak aromas. The palate continues the honey theme with strong mouthfilling gooseberry flavours that are adorned by vanilla and caramel in the oak treatment. Too much chill is a turn-off. It's great with pasta carbonara.

Quality	▼▼▼▼
Value	★★★★
Grapes	marsanne
Region	Goulburn Valley, Vic.
Cellar	4
Alc./Vol.	13.0%
RRP	$19.00

Molly Morgan Chardonnay

Quality	♀♀♀⁊
Value	★★★
Grapes	chardonnay
Region	Hunter Valley, NSW
Cellar	▮ 2
Alc./Vol.	12.6%
RRP	$13.50 (cellar door)

This is named after a pioneer of the Hunter Valley, who ran a pub there and owned land. She had a colourful career as a transportee who befriended the ship's captain, returning as his mistress to England, where she (bigamously) married and was re-transported for burning down hubbie's house.

CURRENT RELEASE 1996 This has a dusty, toasty, slightly sawdust-like oak-dominant aroma, which may integrate better with time. There is a degree of richness to the palate and liberal acid adds zing to the finish. Freshness appeals. Try it with braised calamari.

Montana Gisborne Chardonnay

Quality	♀♀♀⁊
Value	★★★★
Grapes	chardonnay
Region	Gisborne, NZ
Cellar	▮ 4
Alc./Vol.	13.0%
RRP	$12.95

The Gisborne vineyard was planted in 1960, which makes it one of the pioneers of the modern New Zealand wine industry.

CURRENT RELEASE 1996 The nose is dominated by fruit and there is also a whisper of oak aroma. The middleweight palate has attractive peach and melon flavours, which are supported by some smoky oak. The finish is dry with a hint of tannin and the wine is best with a slight chill. Try it with smoked chicken.

Montana Sauvignon Blanc

Quality	♀♀♀⁊
Value	★★★★
Grapes	sauvignon blanc
Region	Marlborough, NZ
Cellar	▮ 3
Alc./Vol.	12.0%
RRP	$12.95

There are Montana vineyards scattered across and around New Zealand. This one is located at Marlborough and was established in 1977. Maker Andy Frost.

CURRENT RELEASE 1996 This is full-on Enzed style. It takes no prisoners with an over-the-top herbal, cut-grass nose. The palate pulls back a little with a hint of tropical fruit and loads of gooseberry. There is fresh acid on the finish. It can be served well chilled. Try it with greenlip mussels.

Montara Chasselas

It might sound like a new grape variety but it has been a stalwart in the Grampians region for over 100 years. Its origin is Switzerland. Maker Mike McRae.

CURRENT RELEASE 1995 A work-person-like style with a sappy, aromatic nose. The palate has unusual caramel and butterscotch flavours and the finish is soft with some gentle acid. Serve well chilled with a pizza with some claim to elegance.

Quality	♟♟♟
Value	★★★
Grapes	chasselas
Region	Grampians, Vic.
Cellar	♟ 1
Alc./Vol.	12.0%
RRP	$12.95

Montara Riesling

Riesling from this neck of the woods is relatively unknown, but there are promising examples on the market. Given the popularity of the variety, it's a bit like tilting at winemills (err sorry windmills).

CURRENT RELEASE 1995 The nose is smoky with underlying citrus aromas. There is an attractive lemon essence flavour on the palate, which is matched by some crisp acid. It's a substantial wine that can take plenty of chilling. Try it with sweet chilli calamari.

Quality	♟♟♟♟
Value	★★★★
Grapes	riesling
Region	Grampians, Vic.
Cellar	♟ 3
Alc./Vol.	13.0%
RRP	$11.00

Montrose Chardonnay

In Mudgee they obviously aren't afraid of the tall timber: this wine has seen plenty of wood. It's part of the Orlando/Wyndham group. Maker Robert Paul.

CURRENT RELEASE 1995 Plenty of wood makes this wine bristle with oak. The nose has toasted oak, caramel, plus tropical fruit and melon aromas. The palate is medium-bodied with peach adding to the melon and tropical fruit flavours. The finish is firm with assertive toasty oak influence. The more you chill, the more the wood dominates. Try it with oysters kilpatrick.

Quality	♟♟♟♟
Value	★★★★
Grapes	chardonnay
Region	Mudgee, NSW
Cellar	♟ 2
Alc./Vol.	12.5%
RRP	$12.00

Moondah Brook Chardonnay

Quality	YYYY
Value	★★★⯧
Grapes	chardonnay
Region	Moondah Brook, WA
Cellar	▮ 4
Alc./Vol.	13.5%
RRP	$15.30 ⑤

If you were a young marketing wunderkind and you were given the Moondah Brook portfolio you could well wonder what you have done to offend the powers that be. Not that there is anything wrong with the wines, it's just that the marketing is a real challenge.

CURRENT RELEASE 1996   Plenty of oak here and it jousts with some attractive fruit. The nose has nutmeg, cinnamon, vanilla, peach and melon aromas. The palate has a mouthfilling texture and peach flavours, but these are quickly vanquished by oak with a slightly raw edge. The finish is lively and long. It can be served near room temperature with roast pork.

Moondah Brook Chenin Blanc

Quality	YYY
Value	★★★
Grapes	chenin blanc; quercus alba
Region	Darling Ranges, WA
Cellar	▮ 1
Alc./Vol.	13.5%
RRP	$15.30 ⑤

Chenin is a stone motherless variety these days, so it was interesting to see this one take home a gold medal from the '96 Brisbane Show. Maker Paul Lapsley.

CURRENT RELEASE 1995   Have to disagree with the judges here: the aroma and flavour are more about oak than anything else. Confectionery, peppermint oak and a hint of caramel on the nose; vanilla flavour dominates delicate fruit in the mouth. There is a hint of richness, and the toasty bottle-age is conspiring with the oak against the fruit. Smoked chicken here.

Moondah Brook Verdelho

Quality	YYY
Value	★★★
Grapes	verdelho
Region	Darling Ranges, WA
Cellar	▮ 1
Alc./Vol.	13.5%
RRP	$15.30 ⑤

Moondah is a vineyard in the Darling Ranges north of Perth. A babbling brook does indeed wend its way through the picturesque property.

CURRENT RELEASE 1996   Delicate powder-puff aroma, which is one of the many guises of the chameleon verdelho. The taste is very delicate – a tad wispy – and falls away at the finish. It may build on the palate with a little more bottle-age. Try it with caesar salad.

Moorilla Estate Chardonnay

Here's a wine that dares to be different, from one of the Tasmanian pioneers that started in 1958.

CURRENT RELEASE 1995   This wine comes down on the citrus end of the flavour spectrum. There are strong lemon and lychee aromas on the nose. The palate is light and slightly tart, with lemon and grapefruit mixing with a green apple character. The wood on the finish is subdued but adds balance. Serve lightly chilled with scallops.

Quality	▼▼▼▼
Value	★★★
Grapes	chardonnay
Region	Southern Tasmania
Cellar	🍾 4
Alc./Vol.	13.1%
RRP	$25.00

Mornington Vineyards Chardonnay

The Peninsula is proving a fine place to make chardonnay, but the names are confusing. There is also a Peninsula Estate down there.

CURRENT RELEASE 1995   The nose makes an introduction featuring vanilla, caramel, burnt sugar and varietal fruit aromas. You name it, the palate has got it: fig, melon, peach and citrus with a hint of cashew nut. The oak is well integrated and the finish is dry and long, with a refreshing quality. Don't over-chill, and enjoy it beside Atlantic salmon.

Quality	▼▼▼▼▼
Value	★★★★
Grapes	chardonnay
Region	Mornington Peninsula, Vic.
Cellar	🍾 5
Alc./Vol.	13.2%
RRP	$19.00

CURRENT RELEASE 1996   Youthful wine with a fresh, frisky nature. The nose has citrus and melon aromas, and the middleweight palate offers a melon, grapefruit and peach mixture. The wood offers a dry influence on the finish. The wine needs only a minor chill and it goes well with Thai fish cakes.

Quality	▼▼▼▼
Value	★★★★
Grapes	chardonnay
Region	Mornington Peninsula, Vic.
Cellar	🍾 4
Alc./Vol.	13.0%
RRP	$20.00

Morris Chardonnay

Quality	🍷🍷🍷
Value	★★★↑
Grapes	chardonnay
Region	Rutherglen, Vic.
Cellar	↓ 4
Alc./Vol.	13.0%
RRP	$13.50

Nothing this winery produces lacks flavour – even the whites. Although not totally for heroes only, the whites have no beg-pardons in the power game.

CURRENT RELEASE 1996 The colour is a vibrant lemon–yellow with green tinges, and the nose has peach and melon aromas on a smoky wood background. The medium-bodied palate has peach and cumquat flavours. The oak on the finish integrates well and has a powdery/dusty quality on the finish. The fridge should be kind to it. Try it with pan-fried veal.

Morris Semillon

Quality	🍷🍷🍷
Value	★★★↑
Grapes	semillon
Region	Rutherglen, Vic.
Cellar	↓ 4
Alc./Vol.	12.0%
RRP	$13.00

What would fortified semillon taste like? You don't equate the Morris stamping grounds with white table wines – perhaps one should. Maker David Morris.

CURRENT RELEASE 1996 Big style with lots of lanolin and gooseberry, not to mention wood. The colour is a bright lemon–yellow and the nose has a lanolin aroma. The palate is full-bodied with rich gooseberry flavours and hints of straw. There is plenty of vibrant wood on the finish. It doesn't need to be super-cold. Try it with smoked trout.

Moss Brothers Sauvignon Blanc

Quality	🍷🍷🍷🍷
Value	★★★★
Grapes	sauvignon blanc
Region	Margaret River, WA
Cellar	↓ 2
Alc./Vol.	13.0%
RRP	$16.00

The Brothers Moss have 6.8 hectares of various varieties under vine. While the marketing and labelling is not exactly dynamic, the wines are honest and usually good value.

CURRENT RELEASE 1996 It's all 'rain drops on roses' and the things that come with sauvignon blanc. Herbs and grass on the nose and a palate dominated by tropical fruit flavours, with passionfruit and pineapple to the fore. The finish is dry with plenty of fresh acid. It can be served well chilled with pipis in a black bean sauce.

Moss Brothers Semillon

Semillon from this region has an entirely different character when compared to the stuff from the Hunter Valley. It's an interesting facet to this underrated grape variety. Maker David and Jane Moss.

CURRENT RELEASE 1996 The colour is pale straw and the nose is grassy with a hint of green leaf. The palate is generous and mouthfilling with obvious gooseberry flavours, and the finish is clean and dry. It can handle the big chill and it's great with mussels.

Quality	♆♆♆♆
Value	★★★★
Grapes	semillon
Region	Margaret River, WA
Cellar	🍷 4
Alc./Vol.	13.0%
RRP	$16.00

Mountadam Chardonnay

Can there be too much alcohol? In this case it gets in the way, adding a warmth to the wine that tends to mask the complexity. Maker Adam Wynn.

Previous outstanding vintages: '90, '91, '92, '94

CURRENT RELEASE 1995 Behold a youthful monster. The nose has oak and varietal aromas with peach, melon and figs dominant. The palate is slightly disjointed with many flavours scrambling for a piece of the action: melon, peach, grapefruit, figs and cashew nuts, to name but a few. Wood adds to the score but the warmth of alcohol tends to flood the mouth. Give it a medium chill and serve it with roast turkey.

Quality	♆♆♆♆
Value	★★★☆
Grapes	chardonnay
Region	Eden Hills, SA
Cellar	🍷 5
Alc./Vol.	14.5%
RRP	$29.00

Mount Avoca Classic Dry White

Yet another fruit salad cloaked under the 'classic' classification. Never mind, at least it's a drinkable style.

CURRENT RELEASE 1996 There are plenty of tropical fruit flavours and the same aromas can be found on the pert nose. The palate is quite intense and there is crisp acid on the finish, which is highly refreshing. It can be served well chilled. Try it with a chicken schnitzel.

Quality	♆♆♆♆
Value	★★★☆
Grapes	sauvignon blanc; trebbiano; semillon
Region	Pyrenees, Vic.
Cellar	🍷 1
Alc./Vol.	13.5%
RRP	$14.50

Mount Avoca Sauvignon Blanc

Quality	♥♥♥♥
Value	★★★★
Grapes	sauvignon blanc
Region	Pyrenees, Vic.
Cellar	▮ 2
Alc./Vol.	14.4%
RRP	$16.50

What happens when white grapes get a bit willing in the sugar department? Plenty of alcohol and a struggle to maintain acid balance. Maker Rod Morrish.

CURRENT RELEASE 1996 The high alcohol really doesn't register in the mouth. The nose consists of lantana, pea pod and passionfruit smells. The palate has strong pineapple and other tropical fruit flavours, as well as gooseberry. There is enough acid on the finish to bestow a semblance of balance. It's hard to believe the alcohol is so high. Chill well and serve with soft goat's cheese.

Mount Horrocks Semillon Sauvignon Blanc

Quality	♥♥♥♥
Value	★★★★
Grapes	semillon 75%;
	sauvignon blanc 25%
Region	Clare Valley, SA
Cellar	▮ 3
Alc./Vol.	12.5%
RRP	$14.00

Although this blend makes sense in terms of flavour and style, it's a very different wine compared to the benchmark, white Bordeaux.

CURRENT RELEASE 1996 A fair bit of woodwork went into this wine. The nose has herb and gooseberry smells. The palate offers sweet fruit flavours with gooseberry and tropical fruit plus a hint of vanilla, thanks to the oak. The finish is dominated by oak. The wine should not be served over-chilled. Try it with a warm salad of chicken.

Mount Horrocks Unwooded Chardonnay

Quality	♥♥♥♥
Value	★★★★
Grapes	chardonnay
Region	Clare Valley, SA
Cellar	▮ 2
Alc./Vol.	13.0%
RRP	$14.00

One of the more satisfying examples of the trend towards de facto rieslings. Can't help wondering what this wine would have been like with a bit of wood treatment.

CURRENT RELEASE 1996 Varietal aromas shine through on the nose. There are overt melon and peach smells and these are also the major flavours on the palate. The acid on the finish is clean and bracing. It can be served well chilled. Try it with whitebait fritters.

Mount Hurtle Sauvignon Blanc

Globetrotting proprietor Geoff Merrill is going from strength to strength. We watched his appearances on the Jancis Robinson TV program with a degree of mirth: it seems the only time he'll pick up a hose in a winery is when you point a Beta cam at him. Maker Joe DeFabio. **CURRENT RELEASE 1996** Early picked to capture the freshness. Herbs and tropical fruit aromas greet you on the nose. The palate is medium-bodied with strong tropical fruit flavours, and acid on the finish keeps things lively and entertaining to the tongue. It can take the big chill and it's great with beer-battered whiting.

Quality	ҮҮҮҮ?
Value	★★★★
Grapes	sauvignon blanc
Region	McLaren Vale, SA
Cellar	▲ 2
Alc./Vol.	12.0%
RRP	$18.00

Murray Robson Wines Semillon

Murray was one of the colourful pioneers of the new wave of vineyards in the Hunter Valley. This new venture is his third incarnation.
CURRENT RELEASE 1996 A typical regional style with a wet hay aroma on the nose. The palate is light- to medium-bodied with gooseberry fruit flavours, and there is crisp acid on the finish. It can be served with a medium chill and goes well with calamari.

Quality	ҮҮҮ?
Value	★★★★
Grapes	semillon
Region	Hunter Valley, NSW
Cellar	▲ 5
Alc./Vol.	11.8%
RRP	$18.00

Murray Robson Wines Traminer

Perhaps a 120-case production isn't large enough to include in this tome but cynics might say the wine will certainly still be in stock at the time of publication as traminer is not the flavour of the moment.
CURRENT RELEASE 1996 Big nose with full-on traminer aroma. It comes close to a muscat aroma, but there are also crushed violet and lavender smells. The palate has delicate lychee flavours as well as gooseberry, and fresh acid makes the wine fun to drink. Try it with an asparagus quiche.

Quality	ҮҮҮҮ
Value	★★★★
Grapes	gewurztraminer
Region	Hunter Valley, NSW
Cellar	▲ 1
Alc./Vol.	11.3%
RRP	$19.00

Murrindindi Chardonnay

Quality	⟡⟡⟡⟡⟡
Value	★★★★★
Grapes	chardonnay
Region	Murrindindi, Vic.
Cellar	🍷 6
Alc./Vol.	13.0%
RRP	$20.00

It would be safe to say this is one of our pets. It's great to watch a vineyard develop a consistent style and market following, and the Cuthbertson family are delightful folk.

Previous outstanding vintages: '95

CURRENT RELEASE 1996 A fine wine indeed; cool-climate breeding and stylish oak combine to make this a joy. The colour is a bright lemon–yellow with tinges of gold. The nose has wood, citrus and peach aromas. The medium-bodied palate is already complex with peach, grapefruit, melon and cashew nut flavours that are attended by savoury oak. It should age well. Chill lightly and try it with spaghetti marinara.

Nepenthe Vineyards Chardonnay

Quality	⟡⟡⟡⟡
Value	★★★
Grapes	chardonnay
Region	Adelaide Hills, SA
Cellar	🍷 2
Alc./Vol.	13.5%
RRP	$20.00

Nepenthe is a promising new Adelaide Hills vineyard, with vines yet to come into production. Till then the grapes come from other growers in the area. Roman Bratasiuk made the '96.

CURRENT RELEASE 1996 Lovely nose, but a pity it's short and lacks strength on the palate. Interesting honey, vanilla, buttery, Burgundy-like complexities with a suggestion of botrytis. Good peachy intensity early, then nosedives towards the finish. Serve with cheese soufflé.

Nobilo White Cloud Medium Dry White

Quality	⟡⟡⟡
Value	★★★
Grapes	not stated
Region	various, NZ
Cellar	🍷 1
Alc./Vol.	11.0%
RRP	$10.00 ⑤

The observant among us may think they notice some similarities between this wine and Seaview's Glass Mountain. Nah, it's just your fertile imaginations!

CURRENT RELEASE 1996 Might well be the 'number-one-selling premium dry white in New Zealand', but numbers ain't everything. The nose has a sulfur whiff and some sweet, slightly muscaty aromas of ripe fruit. The taste is light, simple, again fruity in a spicy muscat sort of way, and there's only a hint of sweetness. A clean, well-made quaffer.

Normans Bin C207 Chardonnay

This partially barrel-fermented wine won a gold medal in Adelaide in 1996. Maker Brian Light.

CURRENT RELEASE 1996 Essentially straightforward and toasty oak–driven, this is nevertheless a very appealing current drinker. There are still green tints to the colour and the nose has caramel and vanilla nuances. It has a trace of sweetness in the mouth together with some richness and length. Very good value. Goes well with honey prawns.

Quality	🍷🍷🍷🍷
Value	★★★★½
Grapes	chardonnay
Region	not stated
Cellar	3
Alc./Vol.	14.0%
RRP	$13.70 (S)

Normans Lone Gum Chardonnay

This is a new series of budget table wines from Normans. No prizes for guessing what's depicted on the label.

CURRENT RELEASE 1996 A simple peach/nectarine style without apparent oak. It won't make the earth move but neither will it offend. The taste is peachy with some grape sweetness adding to its soft quaffability. Try it with fish and chips.

Quality	🍷🍷🍷
Value	★★★
Grapes	chardonnay
Region	not stated
Cellar	1
Alc./Vol.	13.0%
RRP	$10.45 (S)

Normans Unwooded Chardonnay

What can we say about unwooded chardonnay, other than it continues to swell while the riesling market contracts. Unwooded chardonnay is the de facto riesling of the '90s.

CURRENT RELEASE 1996 This is one of the better examples of the style and is very good value. Attractive fruit aromas of lime/citrus and melon; a trace of sweetness on entry then nicely weighted mouthfilling flavour and decent length. While it's not complex, it's more than adequate at the price. Serve with cold meats and salads.

Quality	🍷🍷🍷½
Value	★★★★
Grapes	chardonnay
Region	not stated
Cellar	1
Alc./Vol.	12.5%
RRP	$13.30 (S)

Oakland Semillon Sauvignon Blanc

Quality	♀♀♀♀
Value	★★★⯪
Grapes	semillon 50%; sauvignon blanc 50%
Region	Barossa Valley, SA
Cellar	▮ 1
Alc./Vol.	13.0%
RRP	$13.00

This is a second or drink-now label from the Grant Burge stable. As ever, it has its roots firmly in the Barossa Valley.

CURRENT RELEASE 1996   A crisp, dry white style with a cut-grass/herbal nose and tropical fruit and gooseberry on the palate. There is plenty of zesty acid on the finish. It can be served with a deep chill and is fine with Asian food.

Oakvale Peach Tree Semillon

Quality	♀♀♀
Value	★★★
Grapes	semillon
Region	Hunter Valley, NSW
Cellar	▮ 4
Alc./Vol.	11.8%
RRP	$16.00 (cellar door)

This is a small, 5000-case winery in the Pokolbin district owned by ex–legal eagle Barry Shields.

CURRENT RELEASE 1996   A well-made but rather light wine, lacking a little in the deep aroma and flavour departments. Soft, round and slightly bland, but clean; it may grow a little in the bottle with short-term cellaring.

Orlando Jacobs Creek Chardonnay

Quality	♀♀♀♀
Value	★★★★⯪
Grapes	chardonnay
Region	various
Cellar	▮
Alc./Vol.	13.0%
RRP	$9.00 Ⓢ

Orlando has been putting a lot of effort into raising the standard of its big-production numbers, and the '96 of this is truly an excellent wine for the quantity and price. Maker Phil Laffer and team.

CURRENT RELEASE 1996   Attractive peach and melon fruit aromas without apparent oak. The taste is similar with smooth, round structure softened by a little subliminal sweetness. A generously flavoured fruity white – although we have noted some batch variation. Serve it with Nicoise salad.

Orlando St Hillary Chardonnay

At one stage this wine looked like it would become the white wine spear carrier for the Orlando Wyndham group but it's now a solid mid-range campaigner.
CURRENT RELEASE 1995   There has been little change since the last review; this remains one of the best examples of the style yet. A melon and peach nose, and a middleweight palate with melon and grapefruit flavours. The finish shows some understated wood making it easy to drink now. Don't over-chill, and serve it with pâté.

Quality	▼▼▼▼
Value	★★★★
Grapes	chardonnay
Region	Padthaway, SA
Cellar	🍾 1
Alc./Vol.	13.5%
RRP	$15.30 Ⓢ

CURRENT RELEASE 1996   Even though it's a very youthful wine it drinks well because it has been carefully put together. The nose has melon and oak aromas. The palate is lively with lemon, melon and toasty oak flavours. There is attractive wood on the finish, which is tinder-dry almost to the point of being gritty. It should be given a gentle chill. Serve it with pâté.

Quality	▼▼▼▼
Value	★★★★
Grapes	chardonnay
Region	Padthaway, SA
Cellar	🍾 4
Alc./Vol.	13.0%
RRP	$18.00

Palmers Chardonnay

These wines have enjoyed considerable show success, not unrelated perhaps to their strong wood characters. Made by Eddie Price of Amberley Estate.
Previous outstanding vintages: '91, '94
CURRENT RELEASE 1995   This is a big, rather ungainly wine which is very strong on both alcohol and oak. It's very rich, full-bodied and somewhat heavy, with an impression of sweetness. Needs more Margaret River acid cut to enliven it. Serve with roast turkey.

Quality	▼▼▼⸮
Value	★★⸸
Grapes	chardonnay
Region	Margaret River, WA
Cellar	🍾 2
Alc./Vol.	14.5%
RRP	$22.00

Paradise Enough Reserve Chardonnay

Quality	🍷🍷🍷🍷🍷
Value	★★★★
Grapes	chardonnay
Region	South Gippsland, Vic.
Cellar	🍷 4
Alc./Vol.	13.5%
RRP	$20.00 (ex-winery)

Where is Paradise Enough? Why, Kongwak Victoria, of course. Maker John Bell.

Previous outstanding vintages: '94

CURRENT RELEASE 1995   This emerging South Gippslander is both subtle and multi-faceted. The aromas are of pear, cashew nut, and citrus with some tropical echoes. It has marvellous intensity and length in the mouth, as well as cool-area refinement. Sheer nirvana. Food: yabbies.

Paringa Estate Chardonnay

Quality	🍷🍷🍷🍷🍷
Value	★★★★
Grapes	chardonnay
Region	Mornington Peninsula, Vic.
Cellar	🍷 4+
Alc./Vol.	12.5%
RRP	$25.00 (cellar door)

Leading Mornington vineyard, which first turned heads with its pinot, then shiraz, and now tickling our fancy with chardonnay too. Maker Lindsay McCall.

Previous outstanding vintages: '93, '94

CURRENT RELEASE 1995   Cool-year herbaceous and honeyed aromas have a slightly feral edge, which adds extra interest. A refined style in the mouth, with light-bodied delicacy and refreshing acidity. Deliciously moreish. Suits pasta with clams.

Pattersons Unwooded Chardonnay

Quality	🍷🍷🍷🍷
Value	★★★★
Grapes	chardonnay
Region	Lower Great Southern, WA
Cellar	🍷 2
Alc./Vol.	14.0%
RRP	$17.25

Pattersons is a tiny vineyard near Mt Barker which has recently installed a rammed earth tasting/sales outlet. The wines are made at Plantagenet.

CURRENT RELEASE 1996   Pungent herbaceous/tropical fruit, typical southern West Australia aroma. It's a pretty wine to sniff, but the palate has real strength and intensity, which is more than can be said for most unwoodeds. It has lively pineapple-dominant flavours and good length. Serve with asparagus quiche.

Pauletts Sauvignon Blanc

Neil Paulett's white wines tend to be crisp and fine, typical of the Polish Hill River sub-district. His winery is a must-visit when you're in the Clare Valley: it has a spectacular view.

CURRENT RELEASE 1996   A delicate, racy style with intense tropical fruit character, restrained aromatics and the merest suggestion of grassiness. Ripe, fragrant and tangy. The crisp, dry finish makes it a good food-style. Try it with a crab salad.

Quality	♟♟♟♟
Value	★★★★
Grapes	sauvignon blanc
Region	Clare Valley, SA
Cellar	▲ 3
Alc./Vol.	12.5%
RRP	$15.30

CURRENT RELEASE 1997   If only they could stay as fresh as this! The nose is bursting with tropical fruit aromas. The palate is zesty and intense with passionfruit, pineapple and pawpaw, and the acid is super-fresh and tingling. It's excitement in the mouth and should be served well chilled. Try it with mud crab.

Quality	♟♟♟♟♟
Value	★★★★★
Grapes	sauvignon blanc
Region	Clare Valley, SA
Cellar	▲ 2
Alc./Vol.	12.5%
RRP	$15.30

Penfolds Adelaide Hills Trial Bin Chardonnay

Penfolds has long hungered for a white wine reputation to match its red. So, in 1992 the winemakers were ordered to develop 'the ultimate Australian white wine'. God help 'em if they fail.

CURRENT RELEASE 1995   The 'White Grange' quest is off to a flying start here. It's a lovely wine with typical Adelaide Hills finesse, and they've restrained themselves in the oak department. Aromas of butter, toast and cream indicate efforts to make a complex wine, and it is full-bodied, richly concentrated and lingering on the tongue. The acid gives a lively cut to the palate. Delicious stuff to serve with scallops.

Quality	♟♟♟♟♟
Value	★★★★
Grapes	chardonnay
Region	Adelaide Hills, SA
Cellar	▲ 3+
Alc./Vol.	13.0%
RRP	$24.00

Penfolds Bottle Aged Riesling

Quality	▼▼▼▼
Value	★★★★
Grapes	riesling
Region	Eden Valley, SA
Cellar	🍾 3
Alc./Vol.	12.0%
RRP	$15.00

It's good to see more wine companies releasing mature rieslings in order to encourage people to drink and enjoy them this way.

CURRENT RELEASE 1992 This has a medium-yellow colour which shows age, and the aromas are of lemons and limes – quite fresh for its age. The palate flavour is soft and broadening out a little. A good mature riesling at an attractive price. Serve with pan-fried whiting.

Quality	▼▼▼▼▼
Value	★★★★★
Grapes	riesling
Region	Clare Valley, SA
Cellar	🍾 4
Alc./Vol.	13.0%
RRP	$15.00

CURRENT RELEASE 1993 Three years cellaring at a constant 15 degrees C have resulted in a toasty, aged bouquet with a sweaty overtone, and the fresh fruit is still showing through. It's juicy and drinking at its peak, and retains a crisp acid finish. Serve with grilled flounder.

Penfolds Clare Estate Chardonnay

Quality	▼▼▼
Value	★★★
Grapes	chardonnay
Region	Clare Valley, SA
Cellar	🍾 1
Alc./Vol.	12.0%
RRP	$15.50 Ⓢ

Mick Knappstein originally spotted the piece of land on which this vineyard was planted for his colleague Max Schubert.

CURRENT RELEASE 1995 Slightly resiny, toasty bottle-aged bouquet overlying herbal/melon fruit. The wine is ageing fairly quickly but not gaining much complexity, so it's best drunk soon. A pleasant, mature mouthful of chardonnay to serve with smoked chicken.

Penfolds Koonunga Hill Chardonnay

Like so many mid-market brands, Koonunga Hill moved up in price and a new brand (in Penfolds' case it was Rawson's Retreat) came in to plug the gap.
CURRENT RELEASE 1996   A fresh, simple fruit style that has flavour but not a great deal of finesse. It's designed to drink young and will probably only coarsen with age. There are peach and tropical aromas, and a trace of sweetness adds to the fruity appeal in the mouth. Goes well with asparagus quiche.

Quality	♀♀♀
Value	★★★
Grapes	chardonnay
Region	various, SA
Cellar	▮ 1
Alc./Vol.	13.0%
RRP	$11.65 Ⓢ

Penfolds Koonunga Hill Semillon Sauvignon Blanc

Koonunga Hill is the name of a Penfolds vineyard at the northern end of the Barossa. It was developed by the late Max Schubert.
CURRENT RELEASE 1996   A quality full-flavoured dry white, which has depth and length of flavour above its lowly station. The colour is mid-yellow, and there's a hint of wood in the nutty, toasty bouquet, which is starting to show some age development. It manages to be smooth and fruity without resorting to sweetness. Try it with Chinese wontons.

Quality	♀♀♀⸮
Value	★★★★
Grapes	semillon; sauvignon blanc
Region	not stated
Cellar	▮ 2
Alc./Vol.	12.0%
RRP	$11.65 Ⓢ

Penfolds Old Vine Barossa Semillon

Did someone mention bandwagon? Penfolds never used to mention the Barossa, nor old vines, until both became fashionable. 'Old Vine' in this case means over 30 years.
CURRENT RELEASE 1995   Deep yellow colour and trademark Penfolds oak lead the performance on nose and palate. Lovely toasty nose from oak plus development, with fruit still discernible under it all. The taste is very full and rich, smooth and long – a real mouthful – and the antithesis of the restrained classic Hunter style. Very powerful finish. Drink with chicken chasseur.

Quality	♀♀♀♀⸮
Value	★★★★
Grapes	semillon
Region	Barossa Valley, SA
Cellar	▮ 3
Alc./Vol.	12.5%
RRP	$17.00 Ⓢ

Penfolds The Valleys Chardonnay

Quality	🍷🍷🍷
Value	★★★
Grapes	chardonnay
Region	Clare & Eden Valleys, SA
Cellar	🍾 3
Alc./Vol.	13.0%
RRP	$15.00 Ⓢ

This is the former Barrel Fermented Chardonnay repackaged. Penfolds were concerned people might assume it was an unfashionably woody wine!

CURRENT RELEASE 1996   The oak has been throttled back with this vintage, so the nose shows fig and hints of butter, probably from malolactic fermentation. There is good mouth-feel due to the wine's viscosity. A little bottle-age should give it some complexity. Try it with salmon pie.

Pepper Tree Semillon Sauvignon Blanc

Quality	🍷🍷
Value	★★★
Grapes	semillon; sauvignon blanc
Region	Hunter Valley, NSW; McLaren Vale, SA
Cellar	🍾 1
Alc./Vol.	11.9%
RRP	$17.50

Pepper Tree is another Lower Hunter Valley winery to venture further afield for fruit to blend with its Hunter grapes. Maker Chris Cameron.

CURRENT RELEASE 1996   The nose is not at all grassy or herbaceous, but is slightly flat with a yeast lees aspect. There is decent fruit flavour in the mouth and a fairly extravagant measure of sweetness. Give it a big chill, and serve with asparagus quiche.

Pepper Tree Traminer

Quality	🍷🍷🍷
Value	★★★
Grapes	gewurztraminer
Region	Hunter Valley, NSW
Cellar	🍾 1
Alc./Vol.	12.2%
RRP	$15.80

This comes in a blue bottle with a canary yellow synthetic cork. Don't laugh: the cork at least does a seriously good job.

CURRENT RELEASE 1996   Subdued nose that doesn't have a lot of traminer aromatics, but there is a hint of spice in the mouth. It's a spatlese style, very sweet on the palate, and is hard to treat as a serious food wine. Try it with chicken liver pâté.

Pepper Tree Verdelho Reserve

This is one for the adventurous: it comes in a tall riesling-shaped bottle in purple glass. Maker Chris Cameron.
CURRENT RELEASE 1996   This starts off winning hearts with a captivating nose that shows heaps of spicy fruit. But then the sweetness chips in, rendering the palate syrupy and thick, and masking the fruit flavour. Will have its fans, but not us.

Quality	♈♈♈
Value	★★⊱
Grapes	verdelho
Region	Hunter Valley, NSW
Cellar	▮ 1
Alc./Vol.	13.6%
RRP	$15.80

Petaluma Chardonnay

The subscript Piccadilly Valley has crept onto the front label of this vintage, underlining the maker Brian Croser's commitment to promoting his vineyards as 'distinguished sites'.
Previous outstanding vintages: '90, '91, '92, '93, '94
CURRENT RELEASE 1995   This is a peak year for this label. The wine has enormous class and manages to combine understatement and finesse with power. Toasty oak and grapefruit/melon fruit give both a complex bouquet that translates to a full-bodied palate of great length, and a rich but not heavy mouth-feel. Serve with crayfish.

Quality	♈♈♈♈♈
Value	★★★★⊱
Grapes	chardonnay
Region	Adelaide Hills, SA
Cellar	▮ 5+
Alc./Vol.	13.5%
RRP	$34.60

CURRENT RELEASE 1996   **Brian Croser reckons this will be as good as the great '95, and we wholeheartedly agree. We wouldn't mind a case under the bed. Like the '95, this is tight and a tad austere upon release and will improve enormously over the coming 12 months. Fine melon and cashew nut aromas with notes of cedar and peach. Great finesse, structure and length. Really resonates on the finish with brilliant clarity and harmony. This is Oistrakh playing Paganini in splendid isolation. Try it with scampi.**

Quality	♈♈♈♈♈
Value	★★★★⊱
Grapes	chardonnay
Region	Adelaide Hills, SA
Cellar	➤ 1–5+
Alc./Vol.	13.8%
RRP	$39.00

PENGUIN WINE OF THE YEAR AND BEST WHITE WINE

Peter Lehmann Chardonnay

Quality	♟♟♟
Value	★★★
Grapes	chardonnay
Region	Barossa Valley, SA
Cellar	🍷 2+
Alc./Vol.	12.5%
RRP	$13.70 ⓢ

Lehmann is not noted for chardonnay: most of his star performers are either reds or whites made from other varieties.

CURRENT RELEASE 1996 Unusual lemon-essence aroma and flavour, which reminds us more of semillon than chardonnay. Some herbal hints complete the nose, and the palate is light and lean with some oak astringency bringing up the rear. Try it with whitebait fritters and lemon juice.

Peter Lehmann Riesling

Quality	♟♟♟
Value	★★★⊩
Grapes	riesling
Region	Eden Valley, SA
Cellar	🍷 4
Alc./Vol.	11.5%
RRP	$11.30 ⓢ

Lehmann's wines are all from Barossa Valley grapes, although this comes from the nearby Eden Valley, which grows superior riesling. Maker Andrew Wigan.

CURRENT RELEASE 1996 Slate and earth characters mingle with the lemon and vanilla nuances on the bouquet. A soft, fuller-flavoured riesling which drinks well young with trout.

Peter Lehmann Semillon

Quality	♟♟♟⅃
Value	★★★★
Grapes	semillon
Region	Barossa Valley, SA
Cellar	⬤ 1–6
Alc./Vol.	12.0%
RRP	$11.30 ⓢ

This is a barrel-fermented style, which won a gold medal in Melbourne. What would they know about semillon down there? Maker Andrew Wigan.

CURRENT RELEASE 1996 A little sulfur to open, but when it cleared the bouquet was very shy with delicate wood influence uppermost. The taste is smooth, juicy, and slightly simple in its youth, but it should build more interesting character with a year or so in the bottle. Try it with braised calamari.

Peter Lehmann Semillon Chardonnay

In the early days of chardonnay in Australia, winemakers used to stretch their limited supply with semillon, and often improved the wine! Maker Andrew Wigan.

CURRENT RELEASE 1996 Straw/dry-grass nose with lemon and a hint of toastiness creeping in. A dry white of some finesse; tight and dry on the palate with that semillon leanness dictating the structure of the wine. Serve with baked snapper.

Quality	♥♥♥♪
Value	★★★★
Grapes	semillon; chardonnay
Region	Barossa Valley, SA
Cellar	🍷 5
Alc./Vol.	12.5%
RRP	$11.30 Ⓢ

Pewsey Vale Riesling

Pewsey is an individual vineyard owned by Yalumba in the Eden Valley region. In a previous life it was one of the Barossa district's very first vineyards. Maker Brian Walsh and team.

CURRENT RELEASE 1996 Shy, restrained aromas of lemon and confectionery rise from the glass. The wine has plenty of body and a hint of sweetness, balancing a soft, rich, mouthfilling flavour that seems quite up-front for this marque. Goes well with sole meunière.

Quality	♥♥♥♪
Value	★★★★
Grapes	riesling
Region	Eden Valley, SA
Cellar	🍷 5+
Alc./Vol.	12.0%
RRP	$11.20 Ⓢ

Pewsey Vale Sauvignon Blanc

Joseph Gilbert was the first to plant vines at Pewsey Vale – in 1847. We doubt if sauvignon blanc was among his vines: it's a Johnny-come-lately.

CURRENT RELEASE 1996 A greener style of sauvignon with nettle and cut-capsicum notes: very herbal aromas coupled with almond scents. The profile is light and lean, a little straightforward but undoubtedly refreshing. Try it with mussel soup.

Quality	♥♥♥♪
Value	★★★
Grapes	sauvignon blanc
Region	Eden Valley, SA
Cellar	🍷 1
Alc./Vol.	12.0%
RRP	$13.50 Ⓢ

Pierro Chardonnay

Quality	♟♟♟♟♟
Value	★★★★
Grapes	chardonnay
Region	Margaret River, WA
Cellar	▮ 5
Alc./Vol.	14.5%
RRP	$37.00

For years this has been one of our favourite Aussie chardonnays and the '95 is a top vintage. There's also a rare unfiltered bottling, which has even more power and length. Maker Mike Peterkin.

Previous outstanding vintages: '90, '91, '92, '93, '94

CURRENT RELEASE 1995 A titan of a wine, with amazing power and concentration from obviously low-yielding vines. Toasted nuts, butterscotch ... a multitude of inviting aromas none of which really sticks out, and that's our idea of good balance. A real red-wine-drinker's white, with impressive richness and weight, and an endless aftertaste. Serve with crayfish.

Pierro Semillon Sauvignon Blanc

Quality	♟♟♟♟
Value	★★★
Grapes	semillon; sauvignon blanc
Region	Margaret River, WA
Cellar	▮ 4+
Alc./Vol.	13.0%
RRP	$20.00

Mike Peterkin uses Scott Henry trellising and other measures to avoid excessive herbaceous flavours in his wines. The payoff is greater palate depth and weight in these vigorous varieties.

CURRENT RELEASE 1996 The aromas are of dry grass and twigs rather than rank vegetable smells. There is good concentration of flavour, structure and length. It's soft but dry, round and easy to enjoy. A serious SSB-style. Try it with pan-fried swordfish.

Pikes Riesling

Quality	♟♟♟♟♟
Value	★★★★★
Grapes	riesling
Region	Clare Valley, SA
Cellar	▮ 8+
Alc./Vol.	11.5%
RRP	$13.70

Aside from making wine, the Pikes resurrected a 19th-century family tradition of brewing beer. It's not a bad drop either. Maker Neil Pike.

Previous outstanding vintages: '86, '90, '91, '94, '95

CURRENT RELEASE 1996 This brash, frisky youngster will be better for a few months in the cellar. The nose is shy and pepperminty, and the palate has some fiery youthful vigour. There are lemons and limes galore and a well-judged grip on the finish. Expect this to cellar well – for at least a decade. Food: Singapore crab.

Pipers Brook Gewurztraminer

This is simply one of the best traminers available anywhere in Australia. But does anyone actually care? Seriously, it's great to see there is a niche market for serious gewurz.
Previous outstanding vintages: '84, '88, '90, '91, '92, '93, '94
CURRENT RELEASE 1996 This is pungent, as you'd expect from the variety, but there's also a suspicion of botrytis in the quince/honey/somewhat-Germanic overtones. The palate is restrained with subtle spiciness, and finishes soft, yet dry. A fine traminer; you can drink more than a glass of this. Try it with smoked chicken and lychee salad.

Quality	?????
Value	★★★ɼ
Grapes	gewurztraminer
Region	Pipers Brook, Tas.
Cellar	◊ 4
Alc./Vol.	13.3%
RRP	$20.15

Pipers Brook Pinot Gris

Pinot gris is the name given to pinot grigio in Alsace, where the wines are richer and riper than in Italy. Maker Dr Andrew Pirie.
CURRENT RELEASE 1996 From a 'difficult' vintage, this is an odd wine. The nose has a peppermint toothpaste aroma that recalls American oak, and is not what we expected. The entry is oddly salty, followed by asparagus and cabbage flavours with just a glimmer of spicy, varietal character. The finish is high in acid and has respectable length. Try it with gado gado.

Quality	???
Value	★★ɼ
Grapes	pinot gris
Region	Pipers River, Tas.
Cellar	◊ 2
Alc./Vol.	13.4%
RRP	$20.00

Pipers Brook Riesling

With a climate like northern Tasmania's, you might expect that there should be some kinship with Germany or at least Alsace. But no: Tassie has its own terroir and its own style. Maker Andrew Pirie.
Previous outstanding vintages: '82, '84, '85, '90, '91, '92, '93, '94, '95
CURRENT RELEASE 1996 Oh well, when you tread the cold-climate tightrope you have to be prepared for some years when things don't go according to Hoyle. 1996 was a difficult year, as they say in the winery press releases. The green flavours dominate this one, with herb and boiled potato aromas. It lacks delicacy, and although it may improve in the bottle, we wouldn't hold our breath.

Quality	???
Value	★★ɼ
Grapes	riesling
Region	Pipers Brook, Tas.
Cellar	◊ 3
Alc./Vol.	13.0%
RRP	$20.15

Plantagenet Omrah Unoaked Chardonnay

Quality	♟♟♟
Value	★★★⸰
Grapes	chardonnay
Region	Lower Great Southern, WA
Cellar	◊ 2
Alc./Vol.	13.5%
RRP	$16.40

This was one of the first unwooded chardonnays to make a splash. The vineyard has since been bought by BRL Hardy, but the brand remains. Maker Gavin Berry.
CURRENT RELEASE 1996   Pale yellow colour and passionfruit/tropical aromas are typical of this label. It's a very pretty wine with moderate depth of soft, fruity flavour, finishing with more length than most unwoodeds. Try it with prosciutto melone.

Plantagenet Riesling

Quality	♟♟♟
Value	★★★⸰
Grapes	riesling
Region	Mount Barker, WA
Cellar	◊ 3
Alc./Vol.	11.5%
RRP	$14.00

Mount Barker – indeed the whole of the Lower Great Southern – has emerged as a charmed spot for riesling. This won a gold medal at the Sheraton Perth Wine Awards. Maker Gavin Berry.
CURRENT RELEASE 1996   The pale yellow colour and slightly sweaty, herbaceous aroma are indicative of a cooler year. It's a pleasant wine, fresh and lively, but at this point it doesn't have a lot of varietal character. Serve with salads.

Plantagenet Sauvignon Blanc

Quality	♟♟♟
Value	★★★
Grapes	sauvignon blanc
Region	Lower Great Southern, WA
Cellar	◊ 1
Alc./Vol.	12.5%
RRP	$16.00

The winegrowing area of Mount Barker is in the Plantagenet Shire, hence the name of the winery. Maker Gavin Berry.
CURRENT RELEASE 1996   A delicate, restrained, pale-coloured sauvignon with a light dusty/herbaceous nose and subtle palate that finishes with slightly green acid. Could use a little more strength, but okay to drink young. Serve with goat's cheese tartlets.

Poole's Rock Chardonnay

The Macquarie Bank's David Clarke is making major inroads into the wine business these days, what with his involvement in McGuigan Brothers, Pousse d'Or, Smithbrook, Cockfighter's Ghost and Poole's Rock. Maker Iain Riggs.

CURRENT RELEASE 1996 Charred oak, passionfruit and peach characters. The nose is subdued, and the palate is lean and has a little astringency. A pleasant enough wine, but not cheap. Try it with chicken schnitzel.

Quality	▼▼▼▼
Value	★★★
Grapes	chardonnay
Region	Hunter Valley, NSW
Cellar	🍾 4
Alc./Vol.	13.5%
RRP	$21.25

Preece Chardonnay

Colin Preece was a crusty old wine industry denizen who acted as consultant when Mitchelton was being established in the early '70s. Preece worked all his life for Seppelt, so we bet Seppelt is cranky that Mitchelton beat them to a Preece label.

CURRENT RELEASE 1996 A slightly dull, dusty nose and a straightforward, wispy palate. Tea-leaf and vanilla flavours. Rather undistinguished after the lovely '95, no doubt due to the less than auspicious season.

Quality	▼▼▼
Value	★★★
Grapes	chardonnay
Region	King & Goulburn Valleys, Vic.
Cellar	🍾
Alc./Vol.	13.5%
RRP	$14.65 $

Renmano Chairmans Selection Show Reserve Chardonnay

This is going through a change of name. In the past it has been the definitive Dolly Parton style. These days it's less outrageous.

CURRENT RELEASE 1996 HH saw this when it won two gold medals at the Griffith Show. It didn't go into bottle terribly well, and has been a slight disappointment thereafter. Dusty, slightly acrid oaky aroma, lacking fruit, and somewhat meagre in the mouth as well. It has considerable sweetness and a broad, slightly flabby palate. At $12–$14, it's not bad value. Serve with chicken maryland.

Quality	▼▼▼
Value	★★★
Grapes	chardonnay
Region	Murray Valley, SA
Cellar	🍾 2
Alc./Vol.	14.0%
RRP	$14.00 $

Reynolds Yarraman Semillon

Quality	🏆🏆🏆
Value	★★★
Grapes	semillon
Region	Hunter Valley, NSW
Cellar	🍷 4+
Alc./Vol.	12.5%
RRP	$17.00

Jon Reynolds has vast experience as a winemaker, at Houghton and then Wyndham Estate. This property is the former Horderns Wybong Estate.

Previous outstanding vintages: '91, '92, '95

CURRENT RELEASE 1996   There's a touch of sulfur and a lot of straw/hay herbal character on the nose. The taste is dry and lean – typically angular young Hunter. But it's soft and easy enough to enjoy now. Try it with fish patties.

Richard Hamilton Synergy Unwooded Chardonnay

Quality	🏆🏆🏆
Value	★★★
Grapes	chardonnay
Region	McLaren Vale, SA
Cellar	🍷 1
Alc./Vol.	12.5%
RRP	$12.90 Ⓢ

The label says synergy is 'the combination of two things working together to exceed the sum of their individual parts'. But this is a single varietal isn't it, not a blend?

CURRENT RELEASE 1996   A slight wine with some residual sweetness. No faults; slightly herbal and not especially chardonnay-like, with a sherbet acidity on the finish. A pleasant, simple, light white that makes no demands on the drinker. Take it to a vegetarian restaurant.

Richmond Grove Traminer Riesling

Quality	🏆🏆🏆
Value	★★★
Grapes	gewurztraminer; riesling
Region	Eden Valley, SA
Cellar	🍷 2
Alc./Vol.	11.0%
RRP	$11.00

According to the marketing suits, this blend is a Sydney and Brisbane style. Does that mean sunshine, hedonism and no brains?

CURRENT RELEASE 1996   A light, fresh style with aromatic lychee and violet aromas from the gewurztraminer and a backbone from the early-picked riesling. It was made for drinking rather than thinking, and can be served well chilled. Try it with a Greek salad.

Riddoch Chardonnay

This is the second label of Katnook Estate, one of Coonawarra's leading wineries. They've recently jazzed up the
label, which plays up the 'fine wines from unique soils'
angle. Maker Wayne Stehbens.
CURRENT RELEASE 1995 A straightforward, lightly
oaked chardonnay with rather slight fruit and some
astringency in the finish. Clean peach and nectarine
aromas are attractive, and it finishes a little short. Serve
with cold cooked prawns.

Quality	♟♟♟
Value	★★★
Grapes	chardonnay
Region	Coonawarra, SA
Cellar	▯ 1
Alc./Vol.	13.5%
RRP	$15.30

Riddoch Sauvignon Blanc

The snappy new Riddoch label won an award for label
design. The saying goes 'Beware of things in pretty pack-
ages', but this one really does taste as good as it looks.
CURRENT RELEASE 1996 A vibrant, youthful, very
intense sauvignon which is well endowed with fruit.
Crushed leaves and gooseberries on the nose; tangy and
flowing with charm. Impressive depth of flavour for this
grape, and everything's in perfect harmony. Serve with
warm goat's cheese on toast.

Quality	♟♟♟♟♟
Value	★★★★★
Grapes	sauvignon blanc
Region	Coonawarra, SA
Cellar	▯ 3+
Alc./Vol.	13.0%
RRP	$16.00

Robertson's Well Chardonnay

Who the heck was Robertson? Why, one of South Australia's most illustrious and colourful pioneers, says the
producer, Mildara. His property, near Coonawarra, is
now a Mildara vineyard, but none of the grapes for this
wine come from it. Puzzling?
CURRENT RELEASE 1995 Last year we said this would
be better given more time, and so it is. Fine bouquet of
peach, nectarine and cedary, toasty aromas. Plenty of
character and length; a stylish wine with some richness
and complexity. Drinks well with Chinese lemon
chicken.

Quality	♟♟♟♟♟
Value	★★★★
Grapes	chardonnay
Region	Yarra Valley &
	Strathbogie Ranges,
	Vic.; Adelaide Hills,
	SA
Cellar	▯ 3
Alc./Vol.	13.0%
RRP	$18.80 ⓢ

Rochecombe Sauvignon Blanc

Quality	🍷🍷🍷🍷
Value	★★★⯪
Grapes	sauvignon blanc
Region	northern Tasmania
Cellar	🍷 2
Alc./Vol.	11.0%
RRP	$17.40

Is the platypus on the label in extreme agony or delirious with pleasure? It's hard to tell. Maker Gary Ford.
CURRENT RELEASE 1995 Ageing very gracefully, thanks no doubt to well-exposed vine canopy and consequent lack of green, asparagus flavours. Fresh, tangy, gooseberry aromas; very fine, crisp palate with a smidgin of sweetness, which is all in perfect balance. Great with goat's cheese.

Rosabrook Estate Semillon Sauvignon Blanc

Quality	🍷🍷🍷🍷🍷
Value	★★★★★
Grapes	semillon; sauvignon blanc
Region	Margaret River, WA
Cellar	🍷 2
Alc./Vol.	13.2%
RRP	$15.30 🍷

This vineyard is down the southern end of the Margaret River region. The winery is a former abattoir, but don't let that put you off the wines, which are superb.
CURRENT RELEASE 1996 This really improved as it sat in the glass. The nose started out subdued and vaguely herbal, the taste quite astringent with acid and alcohol. Later, it sported lovely minerally, pebbly, non-green sauvignon aromas, and the superior ripeness and concentration of fruit was apparent. Very long aftertaste: an outstanding example of a popular blend. Try it with paella.

Rosemount Giant's Creek Noble Semillon

Quality	🍷🍷🍷
Value	★★★
Grapes	semillon
Region	Hunter Valley, NSW
Cellar	🍷 1
Alc./Vol.	16.5%
RRP	$19.30

We're not sure how they can make a sticky with 16.5% alcohol that retains as much sweetness as this!
CURRENT RELEASE 1990 A most unusual style of sweetie. Why did they keep it so long? Because it was over-oaked? Maybe: it still shows a power of wood on the nose, while the palate is rather hard and oaky with orange-peel type bitterness galore. The colour is deep amber–gold, and the nose has fully mature vanilla and flyspray botrytis and oak characters. Try it with a citrus flan.

Rosemount Roxburgh Chardonnay

Remove your hat and bow your head in the presence of one of the icons of Australian wine. This is Philip Shaw's pièce de résistance.

Previous outstanding vintages: '84, '87, '89, '90, '92, '93

CURRENT RELEASE 1994 A year after last year's review and this is still a puzzle. All the pieces are there but the jigsaw doesn't quite fit. Wood, wood and more wood. It's a huge and clumsy wine, but many will love its full-on style. This is the Dolly Parton of the late '90s. Serve it with veal – and a pair of tweezers.

Quality	🍷🍷🍷🍷½
Value	★★★½
Grapes	chardonnay
Region	Hunter Valley, NSW
Cellar	🍾 5
Alc./Vol.	13.5%
RRP	$45.00

Rosemount Semillon Chardonnay

The split-label blended varietals generally give super value for money. This one is Exhibit A. It won gold medals in Perth and Brisbane, which might be stretching it, but we'd give it at least silver.

CURRENT RELEASE 1996 Very quaffable vino, this. Sappy, leafy, herbal nose; pineapple-like and nutty in the mouth. Softly fruity, rich and generously flavoured with the merest hint of sweetness. Deserves to be the house dry white. Goes with a wide range of foods, but try prawn cocktail.

Quality	🍷🍷🍷🍷
Value	★★★★★
Grapes	semillon; chardonnay
Region	not stated
Cellar	🍾 2
Alc./Vol.	12.5%
RRP	$12.60 ($)

Rosemount Show Reserve Chardonnay

HH has noticed some bottle variation with the '95, but the good bottles are simply stellar. The grapes are drawn from several of Rosemount's own Upper Hunter Valley vineyards. Maker Philip Shaw.

Previous outstanding vintages: '87, '90, '92, '93

CURRENT RELEASE 1995 A complex wine that shows more finesse and reserve than is usual in Hunter chardonnay. Smoky bacon, toasty oak, toasted nut aromas and a rich yet dry palate. The flavour is well focused with a keenly calculated grip that helps dry and extend the finish. Should age well, too. Try it with BBQ octopus. ►

Quality	🍷🍷🍷🍷🍷
Value	★★★★★
Grapes	chardonnay
Region	Hunter Valley, NSW
Cellar	🍾 5
Alc./Vol.	13.5%
RRP	$25.00

Quality	♟♟♟♟♟
Value	★★★★★
Grapes	chardonnay
Region	Hunter Valley, NSW
Cellar	🍷 4+
Alc./Vol.	13.5%
RRP	$25.00

CURRENT RELEASE 1996 This new release has come out fighting. It tasted great from the moment it hit the shops. Marvellous smoky, creamy, peachy complexities and the oak melts into the wine beautifully. The taste is superbly intense and fine, with a seamless harmony that lingers on and on. The finish is endless. Perhaps they should rename it 'Where The Dreams Have No End'. Only joking.

PENGUIN BEST CHARDONNAY

Rosemount Yarra Valley Chardonnay

Quality	♟♟♟♟
Value	★★★
Grapes	chardonnay
Region	Yarra Valley, Vic.
Cellar	🍷 4
Alc./Vol.	13.5%
RRP	$20.00

Every Tom, Dick and Harry is pushing out a Yarra chardonnay, and why not? It's a distinguished place for this fashionable grape. Maker Philip Shaw.

CURRENT RELEASE 1996 Smoky, malolactic-influenced nose, plenty of sweet oak and typical Yarra delicacy of fruit. There is good texture and mouth-feel – very much a Rosemount trademark. The palate has a hint of sweetness and modest length. It's fine with Nicoise salad.

Rothbury Estate Cowra Chardonnay

Quality	♟♟♟♟
Value	★★★★
Grapes	chardonnay
Region	Cowra, NSW
Cellar	🍷 1
Alc./Vol.	13.0%
RRP	$14.50 Ⓢ

Rothbury is now part of the Fosters conglomerate along with Mildara Blass. Its Cowra chardonnay has been a model of consistency. Maker Peter Hall.

CURRENT RELEASE 1996 A touch of sweetness and lightly handled oak are the Hall-marks here. The colour is light and the nose is all pear-like chardonnay fruit: straightforward, grapey and easy to enjoy. It has no pretence to greatness, but goes well with warehou and leek sauce.

Rouge Homme Chardonnay

We've been continually amazed at the ever-rising quality of the Rouge Homme wines, especially the reds. But then along comes this chardonnay, which really knocked our socks off. Maker Paul Gordon.

CURRENT RELEASE 1996 Great style and finesse for the price! This is a delicate, restrained chardonnay, which has more goodies the closer you look. The bouquet hides smoky, butterscotch and toasty aromas among the pear and melon fruit scents. The palate is properly dry and very fine, with a crisp, tangy freshness and a long, balanced finish. Discounted below $13 at times, which makes it a total steal. Try it with agedashi tofu.

Quality	♟♟♟♟♟
Value	★★★★★
Grapes	chardonnay
Region	Coonawarra, SA
Cellar	🍷 5
Alc./Vol.	12.5%
RRP	$14.00 ⑤

PENGUIN BEST BARGAIN WHITE

Rouge Homme Unoaked Chardonnay

Is it just our feverish imaginations, or are unwooded chardonnays becoming more and more like a new form of confectionery?

CURRENT RELEASE 1996 Green tints in the colour and lightly herbaceous, tropical-fruit aroma. The taste is very big, peach-fruity, soft and up-front, with no subtlety or finesse. Sweetish and round, it leaves a mawkish taste that's a bit overpowering. It's not a food wine, nor can we drink much of it. No doubt thousands will. A big chill helps tame it.

Quality	♟♟♟♟
Value	★★★
Grapes	chardonnay
Region	Coonawarra, SA
Cellar	🍷 2
Alc./Vol.	12.5%
RRP	$14.00 ⑤

Rymill June Traminer

This was made from grapes harvested in June, which is very late indeed. Most of the Coonawarra harvest is in March–April. Maker John Innes left the grapes out in the hope of attracting botrytis mould, which is exactly what happened.

CURRENT RELEASE 1996 Deep golden/amber colour and a developed tea-leafy, toasty bouquet mark this as a fast-ageing wine. It has dried apricot, marmalade and vanilla flavours with plenty of sweetness, balanced by a slightly extractive bitter-peel finish. Goes well with citrus tarts.

Quality	♟♟♟♟
Value	★★★★
Grapes	gewurztraminer
Region	Coonawarra, SA
Cellar	🍷 1
Alc./Vol.	14.5%
RRP	$10.50 (375ml)

Rymill March Traminer

Quality	▼▼▼▽
Value	★★★
Grapes	gewurztraminer
Region	Coonawarra, SA
Cellar	▮ 2
Alc./Vol.	14.0%
RRP	$14.00

Although it's over 14% alcohol, this is classed as the early pick. Rymill also makes a late-picked June Traminer from botrytis-affected grapes.

CURRENT RELEASE 1996 The alcohol adds heat and a volatile lift to the nose, and oddly enough it lacks traminer aromatics. There are some bath-soapy traminer flavours on the palate, which is appropriately oily. The finish is hot and somewhat hard. Needs food: try it with boudin blanc.

Sacred Hill Rhine Riesling

Quality	▼▼▼▽
Value	★★★★
Grapes	riesling
Region	not stated
Cellar	▮ 2
Alc./Vol.	11.5%
RRP	$6.50 Ⓢ

This won a silver medal in Canberra, which must have shocked a few of the judges. It's the cheapie range from De Bortoli.

CURRENT RELEASE 1996 A delicate, retiring little number, with pale colour and light, flowery and spicy aromas. The taste is light and soft with a hint of fruity sweetness, but to all intents and purposes, it's dry. Good balance and freshness. Suits dim sims.

Salitage Chardonnay

Quality	▼▼▼▼▼
Value	★★★★
Grapes	chardonnay
Region	Pemberton, WA
Cellar	▮ 3+
Alc./Vol.	13.8%
RRP	$26.60

Salitage is the Pemberton vineyard of Leeuwin Estate co-founder John Horgan. He's aiming to give his brother Denis a bit of competition. Maker Patrick Coutts.

Previous outstanding vintages: '93, '94

CURRENT RELEASE 1995 An amazing and challenging wine! There's enough charred oak to sink a battleship, but it has the flavour concentration and complexity to carry it. There are pungent toasty, smoky, breathy and sweaty aromas, which come over as somewhat bizarre. A very full-bodied, indeed colossal wine, loaded with buttery, sweaty, tropical fruit and vegetable flavours, the whole thing enlivened by vital acidity. A white for red lovers. Try it with strongly flavoured chicken dishes.

Sandalford Mount Barker Margaret River Chardonnay

The vineyard was founded in 1840 and today it has three vineyards: Swan Valley 20 hectares, Margaret River 120 hectares and Mount Barker 64 hectares. Maker Bill Crappsley.

Previous outstanding vintages: '95

CURRENT RELEASE 1996   A complex style that has a good balance between fruit and oak. There are smoky characters on the nose as well as varietal fruit aromas. The peach and melon win, but only just. The medium-bodied palate has melon, grapefruit and peach flavours. The finish is tinder-dry with dusty wood characters. It can be served with a medium chill. Try it with pork fillet stuffed with prawns.

Quality	▼▼▼▼
Value	★★★★
Grapes	chardonnay
Region	Mount Barker, Margaret River, WA
Cellar	🍾 3
Alc./Vol.	13.0%
RRP	$19.00

Scarpantoni Botrytis Riesling

These days there are more wineries chancing their arm with this style. It's not something that can be turned on and off: noble rot has to make a visit first.

CURRENT RELEASE 1992   There is evidence of bottle development with a deep gold colour with orange tinges. The nose is powerful with dried fruit and almond aromas. The palate has a butterscotch texture and flavour, and there are marmalade and dried apricot flavours. The finish is slightly dusty and very dry. It should be given a stern chilling and served with soft blue cheese.

Quality	▼▼▼▼
Value	★★★★
Grapes	riesling
Region	McLaren Vale, SA
Cellar	🍾 2
Alc./Vol.	12.5%
RRP	$20.00

Scarpantoni Chardonnay

It's hard to believe that this rather sleepy winery is sponsoring a very exciting form of rubber surfboat racing. They obviously have a need for speed.

CURRENT RELEASE 1996   The nose is pure melon liqueur; if ever you want to smell melons here they are. Melon also dominates the palate and there are hints of peach. There are strong oak influences with a sweet vanilla flavour. It doesn't need much chilling to bring out the best. Serve it with pasta.

Quality	▼▼▼▼
Value	★★★★
Grapes	chardonnay
Region	McLaren Vale, SA
Cellar	🍾 4
Alc./Vol.	13.0%
RRP	$12.50

Scotchmans Hill Chardonnay

Quality	♥♥♥♥◗
Value	★★★★★
Grapes	chardonnay
Region	Geelong, Vic.
Cellar	◖ 5
Alc./Vol.	13.8%
RRP	$20.00

This label is gathering force and accolades as the vines mature and the winemaking techniques are honed. It appears to have a very bright, and hopefully long, future ahead.

Previous outstanding vintages: '95

CURRENT RELEASE 1996 Already quite complex and satisfying. The colour is a bright lemon–yellow. The nose has grapefruit, cashew nut and melon smells. The medium-bodied palate has a hint of honey as well as citrus and melon flavours. There is tinder-dry oak on the finish, which has great length. It's well balanced and can be served at room temperature. Try it with crayfish salad.

Scotchmans Hill Sauvignon Blanc

Quality	♥♥♥♥
Value	★★★★
Grapes	sauvignon blanc
Region	Geelong, Vic.
Cellar	◖ 2
Alc./Vol.	12.8%
RRP	$18.50

They seldom set a foot wrong on this vineyard. To date all the results in the bottle have been very impressive. Long may they prosper.

CURRENT RELEASE 1996 The colour is a bright green lemon–yellow, and there are strong tropical fruit aromas on the nose. The palate has a discreet hint of sweetness in the pineapple and passionfruit flavours. There are also herbs and grassy flavours. The finish is crisp and balanced. It can be chilled to thrill. Try it with stir-fried chicken in a black bean sauce.

Seaview Chardonnay

Quality	♥♥♥◗
Value	★★★★
Grapes	chardonnay
Region	McLaren Vale, SA
Cellar	◖ 2
Alc./Vol.	13.5%
RRP	$10.30 Ⓢ

Seaview is the quiet achiever in the Southcorp group. While the emphasis is on sparkling wines, the table wines should not be neglected because they represent great value for money. Maker Mike Farmilo.

CURRENT RELEASE 1996 Simple and sunny, yet not without charm. The nose has a nutty/toasty character with varietal peach aroma underneath. The palate offers a slight hint of creamy character but the major flavour is peach. The finish has an overt woody character. Don't over-chill, and try it with some well-seasoned chicken.

Seaview Edwards & Chaffey Chardonnay

Famous pioneering names in the Southern Vales; Chaffey was very influential in the establishment of the Riverland, thanks to his irrigation expertise. These days Southcorp use their names as the flagship for the Seaview label.

CURRENT RELEASE 1995   This style is unfiltered, which means minimal loss of flavour at bottling. The wine is full-on chardonnay with a peachy nose adorned by toasty oak aromas. The palate has a buttery texture and strong peach flavours. These are quickly followed by toasty, savoury oak on a dry and penetrating finish. Don't over-chill, and serve with a cold ham salad.

Quality	♥♥♥♥
Value	★★★★
Grapes	chardonnay
Region	McLaren Vale, SA
Cellar	▮ 3
Alc./Vol.	13.0%
RRP	$25.00

Seaview Riesling

Seaview should be considered a marketing thorn in the side of nearly every competing wine company: the quality is consistently high and the prices are better than reasonable.

CURRENT RELEASE 1996   Lime-fresh and very aromatic with keen acid and plenty of zest. The nose is floral and the palate is dominated by lime flavours. If you want to be picky you'll find a touch of coarseness on the finish, but you don't notice it when well chilled. Have it with oysters natural.

Quality	♥♥♥♥
Value	★★★★
Grapes	riesling
Region	McLaren Vale, SA
Cellar	▮ 1
Alc./Vol.	12.0%
RRP	$9.00 Ⓢ

Selaks Marlborough Sauvignon Blanc

When the concept of New Zealand sauvignon blanc was thrust upon the world it was with fanfare that amounted to 'It doesn't get any better than this'. The problem was you couldn't drink more than one glass. These days the age of reason has dawned.

CURRENT RELEASE 1996   The nose has hints of lantana and plenty of herbal notes. The palate is full-bodied with gooseberry and tropical fruit flavours. The finish is long and dignified by crisp acid. A big chill and a steaming plate of white asparagus, and New Zealand sauvignon blanc becomes very tolerable.

Quality	♥♥♥♥
Value	★★★★⋆
Grapes	sauvignon blanc
Region	Marlborough, NZ
Cellar	▮ 2
Alc./Vol.	12.0%
RRP	$16.75

Seppelt Chardonnay

Quality	♟♟♟¿
Value	★★★★
Grapes	chardonnay
Region	Yarra Valley & Strathbogie Ranges, Vic; Coonawarra, SA
Cellar	▮ 2
Alc./Vol.	12.5%
RRP	$10.00

The brand managers seem to have staged a palace coup and are dashing up the marble stairs to try out the gold taps in the executive washroom. In short, yet another label for this longstanding line.

CURRENT RELEASE 1996   These days the fruit is from up-market origins. It's a very stylish wine with peach and melon on the nose. There are peach, melon and fig flavours on the palate plus a touch of lychee. The oak is very discreet but its presence is there; a bit like salad dressing: you'd notice the absence. Serve with a medium chill and try it with tripe in a white sauce.

Seppelt Drumborg Riesling

Quality	♟♟♟
Value	★★★ǃ
Grapes	riesling
Region	Drumborg, Vic.
Cellar	➥ 2–5
Alc./Vol.	13.5%
RRP	$18.00

This vineyard was a ground-breaking exercise in the Western District of Victoria. It was messy right from the start with several unwanted (by consumers) varieties. There were great expectations for riesling; they have yet to be realised.

CURRENT RELEASE 1996   This is a pungent style that could almost be off-putting because of its intensity. It has a scented bath-powder nose. There are citrus flavours on the slightly oily palate, and the acid on the finish helps retain freshness. It can be served well chilled. Prawn dumplings are just about right.

Seppelt Moyston Unoaked Chardonnay

Quality	♟♟♟
Value	★★★
Grapes	chardonnay
Region	not stated
Cellar	▮ 1
Alc./Vol.	13%
RRP	$9.90

How far can the once-mighty fall? This was once a celebrated red wine label of the legendary winemaker Colin Preece. These days it's the home of cross-dressing chardonnay.

CURRENT RELEASE 1996   Not a bad summer style with plenty of melon fragrance. The palate is fruity with melon and citrus and hints of tropical fruits. The acid on the finish is soft and undemanding. Chill it well and slurp it with a pizza.

Seppelt Sheoak Spring Riesling

Where the hell is Sheoak Spring? The same place as Happy Meadow, Sandy Vales, Coonawarra Alps and other such bogus marketing place names. Leave us out of the marketing crap that is set to confuse consumers.
CURRENT RELEASE 1996 The nose has lime and citrus aromas with floral notes. The palate is full of lime and this is matched by snapping fresh acid on the finish, which is long and refreshing. It drinks well now and can take a deep chill. Try it with a mild curry.

Quality	🍷🍷🍷🍷
Value	★★★★
Grapes	riesling
Region	Strathbogie, Vic.
Cellar	2
Alc./Vol.	12.0%
RRP	$12.50

Seville Estate Chardonnay

There is no dispute about the worth of this variety. It has developed an international reputation and this estate is one of the pioneers that built this reputation.
CURRENT RELEASE 1996 All you could want from this style. The complexity is already obvious with a bouquet of honey, nuts and peaches. The mouthfilling palate has a rich peach and melon flavour that is adorned by some classy oak on a long finish. Too much cold will play it false and deaden the flavour. Serve near room temperature with chicken and chives sausages.

Quality	🍷🍷🍷🍷½
Value	★★★★½
Grapes	chardonnay
Region	Yarra Valley, Vic.
Cellar	5
Alc./Vol.	13.2%
RRP	$30.00

Shaw & Smith Reserve Chardonnay

Michael Hill Smith is proprietor of one of Australia's best wine bars, Adelaide's The Universal. This chardonnay is one of a bevy of beauties asserting themselves in the Hills.
Previous outstanding vintages: '92, '94
CURRENT RELEASE 1995 Bottle variation has bedevilled this vintage, but the best ones are excellent and almost up to the rarefied heights of the '94. It will benefit from more time in the cellar, but drinks well now. The nose is tropical with creamy barrel-ferment characters and the oak is still evident on the finish. Good concentration and length. Goes well with roast chicken.

Quality	🍷🍷🍷🍷½
Value	★★★½
Grapes	chardonnay
Region	Adelaide Hills, SA
Cellar	4+
Alc./Vol.	13.5%
RRP	$25.75

Shaw & Smith Sauvignon Blanc

Quality	ᵀᵀᵀᵀꝊ
Value	★★★★
Grapes	sauvignon blanc
Region	Adelaide Hills, SA
Cellar	🍾 2
Alc./Vol.	12.5%
RRP	$18.50

Kissin' cousins? Well, not exactly. First-cousins Michael Hill Smith and Martin Shaw are both married with kids, so we're not casting aspersions. Maker Martin Shaw.
Previous outstanding vintages: '94, '95
CURRENT RELEASE 1996 These guys haven't missed a beat with sauvignon blanc, and the '96 is right up to speed. Perhaps it's a tad softer and rounder than usual, without quite the green tang of some, and there's generous smooth ripe lime/citrus and gooseberry varietal character throughout. Drink it now, with a vegetable terrine.

Shingle Peak Pinot Gris

Quality	ᵀᵀᵀᵀ
Value	★★★★
Grapes	pinot gris
Region	Marlborough, NZ
Cellar	🍾 3
Alc./Vol.	12.0%
RRP	$16.00

On paper there is a good case for this variety in New Zealand and this wine adds weight to the argument. No doubt the shingle in the peak refers to a scree slope, but it does have unfortunate medical connotations.
CURRENT RELEASE 1995 A solid style with some interesting flavours. The nose has a hint of musk (as advertised on the label) as well as some tropical fruit smells. The medium-bodied palate has a hint of sweetness and peach flavours. The acid on the finish is brisk, so the wine can be served well chilled. Try it with some poached mussels.

Shingle Peak Sauvignon Blanc

Quality	ᵀᵀᵀꝊ
Value	★★★ᵏ
Grapes	sauvignon blanc
Region	Marlborough, NZ
Cellar	🍾 2
Alc./Vol.	12.0%
RRP	$19.00

This is a restrained style in terms of New Zealand sauvignon blanc. It comes from the top of the South Island.
CURRENT RELEASE 1996 Loads of tropical fruit here, and tinned peas and herbs are kept until late in the palate. The nose has strong tropical fruit aromas including pineapple and star fruit. The palate is passionfruit, pineapple and tamarillo followed by wintergreen herbs. The finish is crisp and clean.

Shottesbrooke McLaren Vale Chardonnay

The presentation is becoming as elegant as the contents of the bottle. This is a very well-made style that offers value not usually expected from a small winemaking concern. Maker Nick Holmes.

CURRENT RELEASE 1996   This is not a blockbuster but it has plenty of complexity. The nose has strong melon aromas with a hint of stone fruits. The medium-bodied, barrel-ferment-textured palate is complex with melon, citrus and peach flavours adorned by some discreet oak on a dry finish. Bowl it up with a medium chill and yabbies straight from the kero tin.

Quality	ŶŶŶŶ
Value	★★★★
Grapes	chardonnay
Region	McLaren Vale, SA
Cellar	🍶 4
Alc./Vol.	12.5%
RRP	$14.50

Smithbrook Chardonnay

Yet another vineyard in the burgeoning Great Southern region of Western Australia. This vineyard is adjacent to a karri nature reserve. Maker John Wade (consultant).

CURRENT RELEASE 1995   Delightful nose with exotic tropical fruit and peach aromas. The palate is medium-bodied with peach, figs and a hint of honey. Barrel fermentation adds to the complexity with a mouthfilling quality. The wood is still very lively on the finish, so it needs more time. Try it with a medium chill, and pork in a mango sauce.

Quality	ŶŶŶŶ
Value	★★★
Grapes	chardonnay
Region	Pemberton, WA
Cellar	➡ 2–6
Alc./Vol.	13.5%
RRP	$27.50

Spencer Hill Chardonnay

Another presence from Marlborough country and this one isn't a coffin nail. In fact, this wine will be very beneficial – if you drink in moderation, of course.

CURRENT RELEASE 1995   Very wholesome chardonnay, brothers and sisters. It has grapefruit and lychee aromas on the nose. The palate is medium-bodied with attractive mouth-feel. The flavours are lemon, lychee and grapefruit and these are framed by some discreet oak and underlying acid. Give it a chill and try it with kassler sans sauerkraut.

Quality	ŶŶŶŶ
Value	★★★
Grapes	chardonnay
Region	Marlborough, NZ
Cellar	🍶 3
Alc./Vol.	13.0%
RRP	$22.00

St Francis Chardonnay

Quality	🍷🍷🍷½
Value	★★★½
Grapes	chardonnay
Region	McLaren Vale, SA
Cellar	3
Alc./Vol.	13.0%
RRP	$14.00

This historic old winery is now part of a complex at the start of the Southern Vales. It's also now part of suburban Adelaide.

CURRENT RELEASE 1996 Bright, fresh lemon–yellow colour and there are peach aromas on the nose. The palate offers the almost requisite peach and also a layer of grapefruit. There is powder-dry oak on a firm finish. It should be served near room temperature and it goes well with lightly curried prawns.

St Hallett Semillon Sauvignon Blanc

Quality	🍷🍷🍷½
Value	★★★½
Grapes	semillon; sauvignon blanc
Region	Barossa Valley, SA
Cellar	1
Alc./Vol.	13.0%
RRP	$16.00

No mention of St Hallett would be complete without a small sketch of larger-than-life partner and promoter, Bob McLean. Big bad Bob roams the world beating the St Hallett drum. He is agreeable, albeit dangerous, company. Maker Stuart Blackwell.

CURRENT RELEASE 1996 The sauvignon blanc is very herbal and the semillon is quite rich. The palate is medium-bodied with a hint of tinned peas and lots of lemon flavour. The finish is crisp and clean, and it can take a big chill. Try it with butterfish in a light lemon sauce.

St Hallett Semillon Select

Quality	🍷🍷🍷🍷
Value	★★★★
Grapes	semillon
Region	Barossa valley, SA
Cellar	4
Alc./Vol.	12.5%
RRP	$16.00

St Hallett was established in 1944 (what did you do in the war, Grandpa) and can now claim 50 hectares under vine and a storage capacity of 1 000 000 litres. It processes fruit for many wineries as well as maintaining a growing house label.

CURRENT RELEASE 1995 Clever use of the variety, which in this region can become overly fulsome. The nose has gooseberry and damp straw aromas. The palate is a mixture of citrus and gooseberry flavours and there is plenty of acid on the finish, which is a refreshing change for Barossa semillon. Chill it down and try it with a chicken pie.

Stanley Brothers Full Sister Semillon

The brothers Stanley are Ray and Lindsay. The latter has experienced a multi-faceted winemaking career for longer than he cares to remember. Maker Lindsay Stanley.
CURRENT RELEASE 1996   This semillon has been given the full oak treatment usually reserved for chardonnay. The result is a red-drinker's white. It has oak and gooseberry aromas on the nose and the palate is full-bodied with a smooth peanut butter texture. It clings to the mouth, imparting gooseberry and citrus flavours. The finish is dry and dusty. It should not be served too cold. Try it with smoked turkey.

Quality	YYYY
Value	★★★
Grapes	semillon
Region	Barossa Valley, SA
Cellar	🍷 4
Alc./Vol.	13.0%
RRP	$18.00

Stefano Lubiana Riesling

This is an interesting labelling concept: minimalist on the front and maximum on the back. But which is the front and which is the back?
CURRENT RELEASE 1996   The nose has a strong tropical fruit aroma with a citrus underlay. The palate is quite intense with some residual sugar to add some padding, and the major flavours are lime and pineapple. Crisp acid on the finish contributes a zesty note. It can be served well chilled. Try crayfish.

Quality	YYYY
Value	★★★★
Grapes	riesling
Region	Granton, Tas.
Cellar	🍷 4
Alc./Vol.	12.2%
RRP	$17.95

Stephen John Pedro Ximinez

Pedro 'ham and eggs' is usually used to make sherry. In this case it has been cast as a table wine. The fruit comes from 70-year-old vines.
CURRENT RELEASE 1996   This is an interesting diversion. The nose has a whiff of geraniums and the palate offers a slightly oily texture. There are also some lychee and gooseberry flavours, which are balanced by some subtle oak on a lingering finish. Serve well chilled with whitebait fritters.

Quality	YYY
Value	★★★
Grapes	pedro ximinez
Region	Clare Valley, SA
Cellar	🍷 1
Alc./Vol.	11.5%
RRP	$11.00

Stephen John Riesling

Quality	▼▼▼▼
Value	★★★★
Grapes	riesling
Region	Clare Valley, SA
Cellar	▮ 3
Alc./Vol.	11.5%
RRP	$12.00

This might be a new label from a new company but few can boast a more experienced winemaker than this one. Stephen John has a distinguished career working for the man in the form of the large wine companies; now he is winging it on his own.

CURRENT RELEASE 1996   The nose is extremely floral with lime aromas. The palate is medium- to full-bodied with a slight sherbet texture. The fresh fruit flavours include lime and tropical varieties. There is crisp acid on the finish so the wine can be served well chilled. Try oysters natural.

Stonier's Chardonnay

Quality	▼▼▼▼▼
Value	★★★★★
Grapes	chardonnay
Region	Mornington Peninsula, Vic.
Cellar	▮ 4
Alc./Vol.	13.0%
RRP	$22.00

Brian Stonier was head of Sun Books which sold to Macmillan which became Pan Macmillan. Brian started a vineyard at his country retreat, and by taking on partners became one of the biggest endeavours on the Mornington Peninsula. And you thought wine was complicated.

CURRENT RELEASE 1996   The colour is a pale yellow and the powerful nose offers peach and citrus aromas. Wood lurks in the background. The palate is intense, but not obese. There is a generosity of fruit flavour that gives way to some flinty characters on a long finish. The oak adds a smoky quality. Don't over-chill, and try it with crab salad.

Stonier's Reserve Chardonnay

Quality	▼▼▼▼▼
Value	★★★★
Grapes	chardonnay
Region	Mornington Peninsula, Vic.
Cellar	▮ 5
Alc./Vol.	14.0%
RRP	$30.00

The biggest and the best fruit gets the Roller treatment in this winery. The result is always a wine of extra dimensions. *Previous outstanding vintages: '91, '93*

CURRENT RELEASE 1995   Not a lot has changed since the last review, if anything it's more complex. Dare we say Burgundian in style, it's rich and chewy but with a flinty element. The nose is complex with citrus, stone fruit, blanched vegetables and spicy wood aromas. The palate has a broad barrel-ferment character and the finish adds that flinty component. It should not be served too cold. Try it with warm salad of turkey.

Taltarni Sauvignon Blanc

Taltarni is one of the quiet success stories of the modern wine industry in Victoria, with a wide range of wines and an output of 60 000 cases a year.
CURRENT RELEASE 1996 Don't look for canned peas or capsicum pungency: this is a subtle, ripe wine that avoids the outrageous characters of many sauvignons. It's a good drink and well made, but it lacks distinctive personality. Good length and balance on the palate. Serve with asparagus hollandaise.

Quality	♥♥♥♡
Value	★★★
Grapes	sauvignon blanc
Region	Pyrenees, Vic.
Cellar	▮ 2
Alc./Vol.	13.5%
RRP	$17.60

Tapestry McLaren Vale Chardonnay

This is part of the Merrivale portfolio, which has its roots in the Southern Vales district. They typify reliable quality for not a lot of money.
CURRENT RELEASE 1996 Quite elegant for a Southern Vales style and further bottle-age should enhance the complexity. There is an attractive mixture of wood and fruit. The major flavour is peach and there are some ripe melon flavours. The wood adds a graceful note and dry elements to the finish. It drinks well with a medium chill.

Quality	♥♥♥♥
Value	★★★★
Grapes	chardonnay
Region	McLaren Vale, SA
Cellar	▮ 3
Alc./Vol.	13.0%
RRP	$16.00

Tarrawarra Chardonnay

Owner Marc 'Sussan' Besen's aim was to make an Australian Corton Charlemagne when he established Tarrawarra in 1983. Only 2050 dozen produced. Maker Michael Kluczko.
Previous outstanding vintages: '87, '88, '90, '91, '92, '94
CURRENT RELEASE 1995 This is a spellbinder! Intense, almost searing, acidity and exceptional length are the hallmarks here. The nose is a riot of hazelnut, toast and mineral characters. Powerful fruit soars above the many intriguing layers of winemaker-induced characters. Simply marvellous complexity. Serve with lobster.

Quality	♥♥♥♥♥
Value	★★★★⊢
Grapes	chardonnay
Region	Yarra Valley, Vic.
Cellar	▮ 6
Alc./Vol.	13.0%
RRP	$31.50

Tatachilla Clarendon Vineyard Riesling

Quality	🍷🍷🍷🍷
Value	★★★★½
Grapes	riesling
Region	McLaren Vale, SA
Cellar	🍾 3
Alc./Vol.	12.5%
RRP	$12.90

Tatachilla is a name with a past. It was one of the famous brands in McLaren Vale last century. The new Tatachilla has nothing to do with the old one, though. Maker Michael Fragos.

CURRENT RELEASE 1996 A remarkably forward riesling, but also a good one. The colour remains light yellow, the bouquet flows with floral and herbal/grassy aromas, and there are tart limes on the palate. Juicy and balanced with fresh acid. It makes a delicious early-drinking white with crab cakes.

Tatachilla Keystone Semillon Chardonnay

Quality	🍷🍷🍷🍷½
Value	★★★★½
Grapes	semillon 80%; chardonnay 20%
Region	McLaren Vale, SA
Cellar	🍾 3
Alc./Vol.	13.5%
RRP	$15.30

A keystone is a piece of rock that sits above a doorway and holds the arch from crashing down on your scone. It's also a classic McLaren Vale wine of last century, which Tatachilla resurrected. Maker Michael Fragos.

CURRENT RELEASE 1996 A delicious general-purpose wine, adaptable to a range of foods and situations. It also drinks well solo, being soft and fruity with richness and length. It has the herbal and straw/hay aromas of semillon, and the cashew nut characters from chardonnay. Despite eight months in oak, it's very gently wooded. Try it with spaghetti carbonara.

Tatachilla Sauvignon Blanc

Quality	🍷🍷🍷🍷
Value	★★★★
Grapes	sauvignon blanc
Region	McLaren Vale, SA
Cellar	🍾 3
Alc./Vol.	12.5%
RRP	$15.30

Tatachilla is a proud old name in the Vales with a distinguished history, but the new Tatachilla has nothing much to do with the old.

CURRENT RELEASE 1996 A reserved wine showing a little sulfur at first then warming up to reveal aromas of nectarine and green herbs. A shy wine that at least has some refinement. The palate has very good length and even a hint of richness. Try it with crab.

Taylors Chardonnay

The Taylors wines are proud to be 100% varietal and 100% Clare Valley, and their labels shout it to the world.
CURRENT RELEASE 1995 Typical of the maker's style, this is a lighter-bodied, fruit-driven style with gently handled wood. At two years, the colour is still a light shade of yellow. The bouquet holds shy peach aromas that continue onto the palate, which finishes with modest persistence. Try vegetarian lasagne.

Quality	▼▼▼▽
Value	★★★▸
Grapes	chardonnay
Region	Clare Valley, SA
Cellar	▮ 3
Alc./Vol.	13.5%
RRP	$15.30 Ⓢ

Taylors Clare Valley Riesling

Taylors' vineyard in the Auburn district of the Clare Valley has 550 hectares of vines; a truly large spread.
CURRENT RELEASE 1996 Pretty smart stuff for a second label. Earthy, minerally Clare aromas, gentle toasty/bready development just beginning to creep in, lime/citrus undertones and a tickle of sweetness enhancing its commercial appeal. A real crowd-pleaser. Serve with mussel soup.

Quality	▼▼▼▼
Value	★★★★★
Grapes	riesling
Region	Clare Valley, SA
Cellar	▮ 4
Alc./Vol.	12.0%
RRP	$8.85 Ⓢ

Taylors Riesling

This is the dearer of the two Taylors rieslings, and even then, its full price is only $12. Taylors was started in 1969 and is still family-owned. Maker Andrew Tolley.
CURRENT RELEASE 1996 This is a trophy and championship winner at the Melbourne Wine Show. It's a drier and richer wine than its cheaper sister, scented with slate/mineral aromas, and the taste is concentrated, refined and very long in the mouth. Lovely now, but it could be cellared for up to a decade. Serve with Alsatian onion tart.

Quality	▼▼▼▼▽
Value	★★★★★
Grapes	riesling
Region	Clare Valley, SA
Cellar	▮ 10
Alc./Vol.	12.0%
RRP	$12.00 Ⓢ

Taylors White Clare

Quality	♟♟♟
Value	★★★
Grapes	chardonnay; crouchen
Region	Clare Valley, SA
Cellar	▮ 1
Alc./Vol.	12.5%
RRP	$12.90 Ⓢ

The subscript still declares this to be a blend of chardonnay and crouchen – it must be the only wine left on the market that admits to including the unfashionable crouchen.

CURRENT RELEASE 1995   This has a herbal, fruity nose with a suggestion of toasted oak. In the mouth it's light-bodied, simple and basic. It's respectably soft and balanced, albeit rather light on flavour, and the cashew nut character of chardonnay shows through. Serve with fish balls.

The Willows Semillon

Quality	♟♟♟♟
Value	★★★★
Grapes	semillon
Region	Barossa Valley, SA
Cellar	▮ 2
Alc./Vol.	13.0%
RRP	$14.50

This is the night-time job of Peter Scholz, one of Peter Lehmann's hardworking winemakers.
Previous outstanding vintages: '92, '93, '94
CURRENT RELEASE 1995   Has built a little more toasty bottle-aged character since last year, and the nose shows masses of toast, straw and oak. The palate is soft and rich, with good weight and breadth. There is richness aplenty and it's properly dry, with a long wood-assisted finish. Probably best drunk young, with roast chicken.

Tim Gramp Watervale Riesling

Quality	♟♟♟♟
Value	★★★★▸
Grapes	riesling
Region	Clare Valley, SA
Cellar	� 2–7+
Alc./Vol.	12.0%
RRP	$14.00

As a descendant of the Gramp family, founders of Orlando, Tim Gramp should know a thing or two about making riesling.
CURRENT RELEASE 1996   A delicate, almost austere, classically dry riesling with tingling high acidity, which needs time and which promises to age well. Shy apple aroma and attenuated flavour; comes up given time in the glass. One for the cellar but, while young, try it with oysters.

Tisdall Mount Helen Chardonnay

This brand is part of the Mildara Blass group, although the vineyard is not. Made at Echuca by Tisdall winemaker Toni Stockhausen.
CURRENT RELEASE 1996 A fruit-driven style, this has peach and nectarine aromas and a warmth of alcohol on the finish. It has some richness in its full-bodied palate, as well as a pleasing liveliness. Could reveal more with a few months in the cellar. Food: braised calamari.

Quality	▼▼▼▼
Value	★★★★
Grapes	chardonnay
Region	Strathbogie Ranges, Vic.
Cellar	▮ 4+
Alc./Vol.	13.0%
RRP	$21.75 ⑤

Tollana Botrytis Riesling

Tollana has consistently turned out a smart botrytis wine, but the market is apparently very limited as they often turn up later on special under retailers' own labels.
CURRENT RELEASE 1994 Typical forward development shows here. The colour is a deep orange/amber and the mature bouquet shows toasty, marmalade and vanilla aged characters. The palate is sweet but lively, and there's a trace of acid hardness that doesn't bother it. Good with a citrus tart.

Quality	▼▼▼▼
Value	★★★★
Grapes	riesling
Region	Coonawarra & Eden Valley, SA
Cellar	▮ 1
Alc./Vol.	11.0%
RRP	$13.00 (375ml) ⑤

Trentham Estate Chardonnay

Trentham Estate is the Murphy family's 35-hectare vineyard in the New South Wales Murray Valley. Their advantage is that they manage their own vineyards and irrigate less than the average grower. Maker Tony Murphy.
CURRENT RELEASE 1996 A very smart wine, especially considering its provenance. The slightly subdued nose has nutty and peachy aromas, with good oak subtly employed. The palate has style and complexity, with just the right degree of mouth-feel or viscosity. Excellent chardonnay: serve with a hot yabbie dish.

Quality	▼▼▼▼?
Value	★★★★★
Grapes	chardonnay
Region	Murray Valley, NSW
Cellar	▮ 2+
Alc./Vol.	13.5%
RRP	$12.90

Trentham Estate Noble Taminga

Quality	♥♥♥
Value	★★★
Grapes	taminga
Region	Murray Valley, NSW
Cellar	▮ 1
Alc./Vol.	13.0%
RRP	$9.70 (375ml)

Taminga is a dinky-di Australian grape variety, bred for the hot climates by the CSIRO's Allan Antcliff from riesling, traminer and farana.
Previous outstanding vintages: '94
CURRENT RELEASE 1995 Deep golden/amber colour prepares the senses for a flood of honeyed richness and sticky sweetness. Flowers, citrus, vanilla, honey and spices mingle in the bouquet. There's a 'mixed peel' bitterness on the finish and plenty of sugar, although it perhaps lacks the finesse of some earlier vintages. Serve with orange tart.

Tulloch Verdelho

Quality	♥♥♥
Value	★★★★
Grapes	verdelho
Region	Hunter Valley, NSW
Cellar	▮ 2
Alc./Vol.	12.5%
RRP	$13.00 Ⓢ

The 1996 vintage was one of the Hunter's best in recent years for whites. As usual with verdelho, this hasn't been aged in oak. Maker Patrick Auld.
CURRENT RELEASE 1996 An honest wine, very much in the Hunter mould with dry grass/straw aromas and a lingering, dry, savoury taste. A wine of substance and a refreshing change from the estery, sweet, lollyish verdelhos which have been proliferating. Food: chicken broth with dumplings.

Quality	♥♥♥
Value	★★★★
Grapes	verdelho
Region	Hunter Valley, NSW
Cellar	▮ 2
Alc./Vol.	13.0%
RRP	$13.00 Ⓢ

CURRENT RELEASE 1997 Why do so many wineries make verdelho sweet? It would be better drier. The nose has attractively spicy, musky fruit, which still has a freshly fermented doughy character. It's soft and easy on the palate and undemanding on the senses. A well-made commercial style.

Twin Islands Sauvignon Blanc

This Enzedder is a new kid in town. At least the wines are cheap. 1996 was a very successful vintage in Marlborough.

CURRENT RELEASE 1996   The range of green fruit flavours possible in New Zealand white wines is cause for endless fascination. This one has a scent like freshly-cut sapwood. The taste is medium- to lightweight with abundant grassy/leafy flavour and a trace of firmness on the finish. Take it to a vegetarian restaurant.

Quality	♟♟♟♟
Value	★★★★
Grapes	sauvignon blanc
Region	Marlborough, NZ
Cellar	▮ 1
Alc./Vol.	12.0%
RRP	$13.00

Twin Valley Estate St Beth Rhine Riesling

Hands up all those who remember Karrawirra or maybe Red Gum? These were the previous names of these cellars near Lyndoch.

CURRENT RELEASE 1993   The bottle-age is obvious with a developed toasty nose and a whiff of kero. The palate has a slightly oily texture and a lemon flavour. There is soft acid on the finish. It can be served well chilled. Try it with chicken.

Quality	♟♟♟
Value	★★★
Grapes	riesling
Region	Barossa Valley, SA
Cellar	▮
Alc./Vol.	11.45%
RRP	$12.00

Tyrrell's Lost Block Semillon

The name of this wine could be turned into a fun guessing game. Was it Murray Tyrrell's legendary temper, or did Bruce drop some of his cuisenaire in the fermenter? *Previous outstanding vintages: '95*

CURRENT RELEASE 1996   Fresh herbaceous and tropical aromas; almost a hint of sauvignon blanc. The flavour is soft and has some richness. There is sherbet acid on the finish and while pretty straightforward now, it will improve with age. Try sardines.

Quality	♟♟♟♟
Value	★★★
Grapes	semillon
Region	Hunter Valley, NSW
Cellar	▮ 5+
Alc./Vol.	10.4%
RRP	$19.30 Ⓢ

Tyrrell's Moon Mountain Chardonnay

Quality	♟♟♟♟
Value	★★★
Grapes	chardonnay
Region	Hunter Valley, NSW
Cellar	🍾 4+
Alc./Vol.	13.0%
RRP	$22.50 Ⓢ

This won a trophy at the Hunter Wine Show. It's based on grapes from a vineyard of the same name.
CURRENT RELEASE 1996   A bouquet of singed coconuts, which could be due to toasted oak. There are pungent aromatics and tropical, mango, passionfruit and peach flavours. It's an unusual style for the Hunter. There is some sweetness on the palate, and the fruit triumphs over the wood. Good with mango chicken.

Tyrrell's Old Winery Chardonnay

Quality	♟♟♟
Value	★★★
Grapes	chardonnay
Region	Hunter Valley & Liverpool Plains, NSW 90%; SA 10%
Cellar	🍾 2
Alc./Vol.	13.0%
RRP	$14.50 Ⓢ

The old winery on the label is the original part of the Tyrrell's winery, built by the founder of the Tyrrell marque, Edward Tyrrell, more than 120 years ago.
CURRENT RELEASE 1996   Shy herbal, melon aroma; very much a fruit wine with minimal oak involvement, and a soft, round commercial palate that has a trace of sweetness balanced by fresh acid. A fairly simple but very agreeable style to have with antipasto.

Tyrrell's Vat 1 Semillon

Quality	♟♟♟♟♟
Value	★★★★⊦
Grapes	semillon
Region	Hunter Valley, NSW
Cellar	🍾 10+
Alc./Vol.	11.9%
RRP	$32.00

Aged, unwooded Hunter semillon is one of the great wine styles of Australia. Tyrrell's release Vat 1 as a young wine, then again several years later, bless their hearts. Maker Andrew Spinaze.
Previous outstanding vintages: '65, '77, '79, '83, '84, '85, '86, '87, '90, '91, '93, '94, '95
CURRENT RELEASE 1992   **Mid-yellow colour; ageing slowly and still shy and reserved on the nose. Palate is very refined: soft yet delicate; lemony and under-developed, indicating a long life ahead. This is an Aged Release, and Tyrrell's expect it to equal the great '86 in time. Serve with lemon chicken. ▶**

CURRENT RELEASE 1996 A very good Vat 1 and one that's built for the long haul. Delicate lemony herbal nose, a touch of passionfruit, very lively acid on the palate and great potential. Cellar, then drink with fish.

Quality	♥♥♥♥♥
Value	★★★★★
Grapes	semillon
Region	Hunter Valley, NSW
Cellar	➥ 4–15
Alc./Vol.	10.6%
RRP	$20.00

Vasse Felix Classic Dry White

Vasse Felix is the Janet Holmes à Court ranch. It has come on since the early days, and now boasts beautifully kept landscaped grounds, ponds, an elegant entrance drive and restaurant.
CURRENT RELEASE 1996 One of the few CDWs that lives up to the much misused name. Soft cashew nut aromas, gentle fruity taste that doesn't overdo the residual sweetness, good balance and smooth finish. Goes well with Nicoise salad.

Quality	♥♥♥?
Value	★★★
Grapes	semillon; sauvignon blanc; chardonnay
Region	Margaret River, WA
Cellar	▮ 2
Alc./Vol.	13.0%
RRP	$17.30

Vasse Felix Semillon

Margaret River is certainly a great place for semillon, fully justifying those who argue the maritime climate best suits Bordeaux grape varieties. (But where does that leave chardonnay?) Maker Clive Otto.
CURRENT RELEASE 1996 Crushed green leaves and snapped twigs . . . how to describe the distinctive aroma of semillon from this district? The taste is delicate and classically dry; the flavour is tight and firm with a well-judged trace of grip to the finish. Excellent with fresh oysters.

Quality	♥♥♥♥♥
Value	★★★★
Grapes	semillon
Region	Margaret River, WA
Cellar	▮ 5+
Alc./Vol.	12.5%
RRP	$22.50

Voyager Estate Semillon

Quality	????
Value	★★★
Grapes	semillon
Region	Margaret River, WA
Cellar	↓ 5
Alc./Vol.	13.5%
RRP	$22.50

Odd name for a winery, but the handle comes from a company that owner Michael Wright had before he entered the wine biz, which he did by buying the former Freycinet vineyard. Maker Stuart Pym.

CURRENT RELEASE 1996   Very Margaret River: it's a crisp, tangy, green-herby style with marvellous zesty freshness that dances on the tongue. The dusty, peppery, capsicum aromas are confronting, but the mouth flavour is intense and long. Good with salads and vegetable terrines.

Wa De Lock Chardonnay

Quality	???
Value	★★★★
Grapes	chardonnay
Region	Gippsland, Vic.
Cellar	↓ 3
Alc./Vol.	12.5%
RRP	$16.95

Give us a break! It might be a parish name but it doesn't exactly roll off the tongue, and the labelling is a little lurid. In a perverse way, both might work very well. Maker Graeme Little.

CURRENT RELEASE 1995   Bottle-age has played its part in this developed style. There are nutty oak aromas and peach smells on the nose. The palate is medium-bodied and there is synergy between fruit and wood. The finish is dominated by oak, which adds nuts and spices. Don't over-chill. Try it with a pasta dish that uses chicken and cream.

Water Wheel Chardonnay

Quality	????
Value	★★★★
Grapes	chardonnay
Region	Bendigo, Vic.
Cellar	↓ 3
Alc./Vol.	13.0%
RRP	$ 14.00

The Cumming family who own the vineyard and winery are the proverbial green thumbs of Victoria. They grow tomatoes (25% of the Victorian crop) and cherries, which are some of the best in the land. Maker Peter Cumming.

CURRENT RELEASE 1995   This is a sunny and open wine, just like its maker. It's an open book with a peach and melon nose. The palate is dominated by overt peach flavours, and the finish has some discreet wood that adds to this homely but handsome package. Don't over-chill, and try it with veal in a cream sauce. ►

CURRENT RELEASE 1996 Some seasoned American oak has played a part in this wine. The nose has a smoky character with peach and melon aromas. The palate has a creamy peach, buttery texture. The wood is a neat fit, making for a very dry finish. A nice drink that doesn't have to be too cold. Try it with smoked cod in a white sauce.

Quality	🍷🍷🍷🍷
Value	★★★★½
Grapes	chardonnay
Region	Bendigo, Vic.
Cellar	🍾 4
Alc./Vol.	13.0%
RRP	$14.50

Water Wheel Sauvignon Blanc

According to MS (with Len Evans as a supporting act, or should that be the other way round?), sauvignon blanc should be pruned with extreme prejudice. That means chopped off at the roots; but sometimes a wine comes along to change the point of view.

CURRENT RELEASE 1996 A very clean style that offers abundant tropical fruit aromas and characters. The nose has a hint of herbs and pineapple. The palate is fresh and frisky with rich tropical fruit flavours that almost demand wearing a pith helmet. The finish offers lively acid and another zing. To thrill, give it a big chill and try it with a deep-fried flounder.

Quality	🍷🍷🍷🍷
Value	★★★★½
Grapes	sauvignon blanc
Region	Bendigo, Vic.
Cellar	🍾 3
Alc./Vol.	12.5%
RRP	$12.50

West End Golden Mist Botrytis Semillon

This is yet another sweet white style that comes from the Griffith region. There is no doubt the breakthrough changed the image of the district from that of bulk wine producer to quality wine region.

CURRENT RELEASE 1995 A more delicate style that keeps the botrytis characters in check. There is a strong hint of honey on the nose and the background is mixed citrus with some peel qualities. The palate is medium-bodied, with sweet honey flavours interlaced with some lime and other citrus. The finish features crisp acid. Only a medium chill is required if the wine is served as a pre-dinner drink.

Quality	🍷🍷🍷🍷
Value	★★★
Grapes	semillon
Region	Griffith, NSW
Cellar	🍾 3
Alc./Vol.	10.5%
RRP	$17.20 (375ml)

West End Three Bridges Chardonnay

Quality	▼▼▼◗
Value	★★★
Grapes	chardonnay
Region	Griffith, NSW
Cellar	◗ 3
Alc./Vol.	13.0%
RRP	$19.90

A new label that is making a tilt at the premium end of the market. The winery was established in 1948 to make bulk wine styles. Maker William Calabria.

CURRENT RELEASE 1996   Loads of timber in the wine. The nose has a smoky, nutty aroma plus some varietal peach. The palate is medium-bodied with peach flavour assuming the role of a serf. The oak is tyrannical and holds sway over the finish, which is long and bold. Don't over-chill, and serve with pâté.

Westfield Bronzewing Estate Chardonnay

Quality	▼▼▼▼
Value	★★★⯪
Grapes	chardonnay
Region	Pemberton, WA
Cellar	◗ 3
Alc./Vol.	13.0%
RRP	$20.00

Westfield is based in the Swan Valley, but Bronzewing Estate is a new vineyard that's developed in the southerly Pemberton region. Maker John Kosovich.

CURRENT RELEASE 1995   A delicate, refined style that reveals its cool-climate origins. It's won two gold medals to date but as much as it appeals, it's quite a light and not especially complex wine. The flavours are herbal and peachy with a very gentle wood treatment, and it's ageing gracefully. Try it with braised calamari.

Quality	▼▼▼▼▼
Value	★★★★⯪
Grapes	chardonnay
Region	Pemberton, WA
Cellar	◗ 6
Alc./Vol.	13.0%
RRP	$26.50

CURRENT RELEASE 1996   A remarkable wine, especially as it has no barrel- or malolactic fermentation. Fine, fruit-dominant aromas of honeydew melon and faintly tropical fruits. The oak is subtle, and there is marvellous delicacy and refinement. Good underlying concentration with none of the shortness that afflicts some wines from this area. Superb! Try it with yabbie salad.

Westfield Bronzewing Estate Verdelho

Quality	▼▼▼◗
Value	★★★
Grapes	verdelho
Region	Pemberton, WA
Cellar	◗ 2
Alc./Vol.	12.0%
RRP	$17.00

John Kosovich's Westfield is a leading winery in the Swan Valley, but his new vineyard in the cool Pemberton region is upping the ante for quality.

CURRENT RELEASE 1996   Slightly sweaty, typical West Australian herbaceous aromas tinged with estery hints of peppermint. A fine, delicate taste with lemon/citrus undertones. Good with duck and lychee salad.

Wignalls Sauvignon Blanc

This company is focused on excellence. It was established in 1982 and has 10 hectares under vine. Bill Wignall is the proprietor. Maker John Wade (consultant).
CURRENT RELEASE 1996 Very classy wine that manages to avoid the pitfalls that can bedevil the variety. Lots of passionfruit aromas on the nose, and the palate gives an impression of sweetness with liberal tropical fruit flavours. There is plenty of crisp acid on the finish. It can take the big chill, and it's great with spaghetti pesto.

Quality	♀♀♀♀
Value	★★★
Grapes	sauvignon blanc
Region	Great Southern, WA
Cellar	🍷 3
Alc./Vol.	12.5%
RRP	$19.50

Willow Bend Chardonnay

This is a new label from Lyndoch in the Barossa Valley, although the fruit is not tied to a vineyard and is sourced from various regions. Maker Wayne Dutschke.
CURRENT RELEASE 1995 A big fruity style with loads of ripe peaches bursting from the glass. The palate is full of varietal flavours, peach, melon and quince, and these joust with a lively wood treatment. It can take a medium chill, and it teams well with smoked trout.

Quality	♀♀♀♀
Value	★★★★
Grapes	chardonnay
Region	Adelaide Hills, SA
Cellar	🍷 4
Alc./Vol.	13.0%
RRP	$15.00

Wirra Wirra Chardonnay

Getting fruit to ripen has never been a problem in McLaren Vale. High alcohol wines are the norm rather than the exception. Thus the art in winemaking in this district is retaining finesse.
CURRENT RELEASE 1996 The wine remains light on its feet but it's dominated by the three tenors (Vosges, Allier and Troncais) oak. The nose is peachy and nutty. The palate shows some full-flavoured fruit, which is offset by some yeasty ferment characters plus oak. The finish has plenty of grip and the wine should only be lightly chilled. Try it with chargrilled chicken.

Quality	♀♀♀♀
Value	★★★★
Grapes	chardonnay
Region	McLaren Vale, SA
Cellar	🍷 4
Alc./Vol.	14.0%
RRP	$20.00

Wirra Wirra Late Picked Riesling

Quality	▼▼▼▼
Value	★★★★
Grapes	riesling
Region	McLaren Vale, SA
Cellar	▮ 4
Alc./Vol.	11.5%
RRP	$15.00 (375ml)

This wine only comes into being when the conditions are right for the infection of *botrytis cinerea*. In this vintage all the elements came together.

CURRENT RELEASE 1995   A typical botrytis riesling with a nose that is a dead give-away. The nose has dried fruit, smoke and marmalade aromas. The palate is complex with dried apricot, lime and nectarine flavours, plus a hint of dried fruit. The finish adds a zap of acid and plenty of length. It's a refreshing style that can be served with soft blue cheese.

Wirra Wirra Sauvignon Blanc

Quality	▼▼▼▼
Value	★★★★
Grapes	sauvignon blanc
Region	McLaren Vale, SA
Cellar	▮ 3
Alc./Vol.	13.0%
RRP	$19.00

Proprietor Greg Trott is one of the unsung heroes in the Southern Vales, and the scope of his quiet influence has also helped shape the national wine industry. He is a legend not necessarily in his own lunchtime. Maker Ben Riggs.

CURRENT RELEASE 1996   There is a heavy emphasis on tropical fruit aromas and flavours: pineapple, passionfruit and mangoes mingled with fresh herbs. There is plenty of fresh acid on the tingling finish, which has commendable length. A big chill will not deaden the flavour, and it goes well with pan-fried scallops.

Wolf Blass Classic Dry White

Quality	▼▼▼▼
Value	★★★▸
Grapes	chardonnay;
	semillon; colombard
Region	various
Cellar	▮ 3
Alc./Vol.	12.5%
RRP	$15.00 Ⓢ

What a change of style this wine has seen. It used to be a cooper's delight, stacked with oak. Now, fruit is the main event. Maker Wendy Stuckey.

CURRENT RELEASE 1996   The semillon component seems to be riding high at this point, with high-toned lemony aromas, lean structure and reserved palate flavour. The oak is well in the background and there is admirable delicacy. Good with crab cakes.

Wolf Blass Oak Matured Chardonnay

This won a gold medal at the Adelaide Show in 1996, which surprises HH. Did the judges see a tank sample, perchance? Maker Wendy Stuckey.

CURRENT RELEASE 1996   Straightforward but attractive smoky, nutty and peachy chardonnay aromas, and the palate has toasty oak and pineapple flavours with a touch of broadness. Not a wine of finesse, but keen value for money. Try it with cold seafood salad.

Quality	♀♀♀♀
Value	★★★★
Grapes	chardonnay
Region	various
Cellar	🍾 2
Alc./Vol.	13.0%
RRP	$13.00 Ⓢ

Wolf Blass Show Reserve Chardonnay

Adelaide Hills, either solo or in a blend, is emerging as one of the very greatest regions in Australia for chardonnay. Here's further proof. If you treat yourself to one expensive, great Aussie chardonnay for a special occasion this year, try this. Maker Chris Hatcher.

CURRENT RELEASE 1994   A blinder of a chardonnay! The three years of age is a bonus, and we'd happily pay more for such quality. A quite magnificent wine, fully mature and with a swag of awards under its belt. Tremendously complex butterscotch, toasty/charry oak and fine melon/grapefruit nuances. It's incredibly powerful and long. Food: chargrilled lobster.

Quality	♀♀♀♀♀
Value	★★★★★
Grapes	chardonnay
Region	McLaren Vale & Adelaide Hills, SA
Cellar	🍾 2
Alc./Vol.	13.0%
RRP	$28.00

Woodstock Botrytis Sweet White

The wine is a peculiar fruit salad that got in the way of some botrytis. Although it's a small segment of the market, the sweet white category is growing as the consumer begins to understand how to use the style.

CURRENT RELEASE 1996   The perfume from the frontignac manages to dominate the nose. There is an amalgam of flavours with some honey, ripe grapes and butterscotch. There is a hint of lime marmalade on the finish. It should be served well chilled. Try it with fruitcake.

Quality	♀♀♀♀
Value	★★★
Grapes	chenin blanc; riesling; white frontignac
Region	McLaren Vale, SA
Cellar	🍾 3
Alc./Vol.	11.0%
RRP	$13.00 (375 ml)

Woodstock Chardonnay

Quality	♥♥♥♥
Value	★★★★
Grapes	chardonnay
Region	McLaren Vale, SA
Cellar	▮ 3
Alc./Vol.	13.0%
RRP	$14.00

These days the letterhead says 'Woodstock Winery & Coterie'. Proprietor Scott Collett has a reputation for being an ageing boy wonder tearaway, but look closer and you'll find an astute businessman.

CURRENT RELEASE 1996 If you add up the flavour, scores are level for both wood and fruit. There are strong peach and melon aromas that translate as flavours on the palate. There is toasty oak on the finish, which adds to the texture and length. It should be served with a light chill. Have it with some pan-fried sardines.

Woodstock Semillon Sauvignon Blanc

Quality	♥♥♥♥
Value	★★★★
Grapes	semillon; sauvignon blanc
Region	McLaren Vale, SA
Cellar	▮ 2
Alc./Vol.	12.0%
RRP	$11.00

This winery was established in 1973 and now boasts 20 hectares under vine as well as a function centre and stocks at the front gate. Maker Scott Collett.

CURRENT RELEASE 1996 A fresh fruity style that is great summer drinking. The sauvignon blanc component has a strong pea-pod character, and there are straw and gooseberry smells. The medium-bodied palate has a hint of sweetness in the tropical fruit mix. The finish is dominated by some crisp acid. It can be served well chilled and is great with chargrilled tuna.

Wyndham Estate Bin 222 Chardonnay

Quality	♥♥♥
Value	★★★
Grapes	chardonnay
Region	not stated
Cellar	▮ 2
Alc./Vol.	13.0%
RRP	$14.00

This is a successful commercial style that enjoys wide distribution. It makes a virtue of drinkability at an affordable price. Maker John Baruzzi.

CURRENT RELEASE 1996 A sunny, fresh style with a minimal use of wood. The nose has peach aromas and a slight nutty wood component. The palate has sweet varietal fruit flavours, and the finish is a bit of a pussy cat with soft oak and acid. It can be served well chilled. Try it with smoked trout.

Wynns Coonawarra Chardonnay

Coonawarra has never been noted for premium chardonnays. Wynns soldiers on, making credible wines that
always represent value for money. Maker Peter Douglas.
CURRENT RELEASE 1996   This is a little more delicate
than the usual style. It's been to Weight Watchers, with
the emphasis on balance. The nose is toasty with citrus
aromas. The palate has grapefruit flavours and there is
plenty of wood on the finish. It can be served with a
medium chill, then roll up a crayfish.

Quality	♟♟♟♟
Value	★★★★
Grapes	chardonnay
Region	Coonawarra, SA
Cellar	🍷 3
Alc./Vol.	13.0%
RRP	$14.50 Ⓢ

Wynns Coonawarra Riesling

Coonawarra riesling is always something of a wallflower.
In most cases the bottles are sitting there with just cause,
but the Wynns model is always quite winsome and
should have a full dance card.
CURRENT RELEASE 1996   You could do worse for your
dollar if you want a crisp, dry white. The nose has floral
citrus aromas. The palate is a crunch in the mouth of
lemon and lime flavours, and there is sassy acid on a
crisp finish. Give it a big chill, and get yourself a mud
crab that has been killed in a humane manner.

Quality	♟♟♟♟
Value	★★★★★
Grapes	riesling
Region	Coonawarra, SA
Cellar	🍷 2
Alc./Vol.	12.5%
RRP	$12.00 Ⓢ

Xanadu Semillon

Xanadu want you to know that this was made from the
fruit of 20-year-old vines, and it underwent wood maturation as well as a malolactic fermentation. Psst: it also
tastes pretty good. Maker Jurg Muggli.
Previous outstanding vintages: '95
CURRENT RELEASE 1996   The '95 won our best semillon award last year. The '96 continues the tradition in
fine style, if a little lighter weight. The nose has dusty
capsicum herbal fruit, and there is delicacy as well as a
fresh grassy tang on the palate. Good depth and length
of flavour and a nice dry finish. Goes well with salads.

Quality	♟♟♟♟
Value	★★★
Grapes	semillon
Region	Margaret River, WA
Cellar	🍷 4
Alc./Vol.	13.5%
RRP	$21.00

Yalumba Christobel's

Quality	♛♛♛♛
Value	★★★¼
Grapes	semillon; sauvignon blanc; marsanne
Region	Barossa Valley, SA
Cellar	🍷 1
Alc./Vol.	11.7%
RRP	$11.00

Hands up all those who remember the S. T. Coleridge poem and the lovely lady Christabel? Never mind, here endeth the literary reference. This is a very enjoyable commercial style.

CURRENT RELEASE 1996   The nose is fruity with loquat and tropical fruit aromas. The medium-bodied palate continues the loquat and throws in some gooseberry as well as a dash of herbs. There is well-defined acid on a crisp finish. It can be well chilled and suits flathead in beer batter.

Yalumba Eden Valley Family Reserve Riesling

Quality	♛♛♛♛
Value	★★★★
Grapes	riesling
Region	Eden Valley, SA
Cellar	🍷 2
Alc./Vol.	11.5%
RRP	$11.00

Yet another unsung bargain that captures authentic regional character. It drinks well now and exceeds its humble price.

CURRENT RELEASE 1996   The nose is very floral with an underscore of lime and citrus aromas. The palate is full of fresh lime and there are some crisp acids on a lingering finish. Serve it well chilled. Try it with pan-fried whiting.

Yalumba Family Reserve Chardonnay

Quality	♛♛♛♛
Value	★★★¼
Grapes	chardonnay
Region	not stated
Cellar	🍷 2
Alc./Vol.	13.0%
RRP	$13.00 Ⓢ

If this was a car the badge would read something like 'GL' instead of a simple 'L'. That's a complicated way of saying it's a step up from the baseline. Maker Simon Adams.

CURRENT RELEASE 1995   A full-on style with a peach and apricot nose with hints of other stone fruit. There are peach and apricot flavours in good measure on the palate, and the finish shows a deft use of oak. It's ready to drink now. Don't over-chill, and try it with smoked chicken. ▶

CURRENT RELEASE 1996   This is the utility model sans bells and whistles. The nose is peachy and the palate is medium-bodied, with stone-fruit flavours and drying oak. The finish is well balanced with soft oak tannins. It drinks well with a medium chill and pipis in a black bean sauce.

Quality	♥♥♥♥
Value	★★★↓
Grapes	chardonnay
Region	Barossa Valley, SA
Cellar	▮ 2
Alc./Vol.	13.0%
RRP	$13.00 Ⓢ

Yalumba Oxford Landing Chardonnay

No doubt this company wishes to emulate the success of wines like Lindemans Bin 65 or Jacobs Creek Chardonnay in the UK market.
CURRENT RELEASE 1996   A likeable wine that drinks easily. The nose has peach aromas and the palate offers melon and peach flavours. There is a suggestion of wood on the finish. It can be served with a severe chill. Try it with calamari.

Quality	♥♥♥♥
Value	★★★↓
Grapes	chardonnay
Region	Murray Valley, SA
Cellar	▮
Alc./Vol.	12.5%
RRP	$9.00

Yalumba Oxford Landing Sauvignon Blanc

Oxford Landing is a very large vineyard on the banks of the Murray. The landing itself is a beautiful spot for a picnic, but you need company permission before you boil the billy.
CURRENT RELEASE 1996   This is a wine that drinks well at a modest price. The nose has gentle herb aromas plus a hint of sap. The palate is light- to medium-bodied with a touch of sweetness. There are also tropical fruit flavours, and these are balanced by some crisp acid. It can be served well chilled. Try it with soda and ice.

Quality	♥♥♥♥
Value	★★★★
Grapes	sauvignon blanc
Region	Riverland, SA
Cellar	▮
Alc./Vol.	11.5%
RRP	$8.00

Yalumba Reserve Verdelho

Quality	♟♟♟
Value	★★★
Grapes	verdelho
Region	Barossa Valley, SA
Cellar	♦
Alc./Vol.	12.5%
RRP	$12.00

Reserve it all they like, we bet they want to sell it in the end. Yalumba have always been interested in expanding their varietal portfolio. Who can remember the melon saga? That's another story . . .

CURRENT RELEASE 1996   Not a lot happens here. It doesn't burst with varietal character (whatever that is) but it's a clean, well-made wine. The nose has tropical fruit aromas. The palate is medium-bodied with pineapple and passionfruit flavours and there is soft acid on the finish. Serve it well chilled with fish and chips

Yalumba Reserve Viognier

Quality	♟♟♟♟
Value	★★★★
Grapes	viognier
Region	Barossa Valley, SA
Cellar	♦ 3
Alc./Vol.	12.5%
RRP	$12.00

Yalumba are pioneers of the propagation of this variety in Australia. Where it will fit in the scheme of things has yet to be determined.

CURRENT RELEASE 1996   This is a fresh style that is hard to put into a category. The nose is dominated by tropical fruit. The palate has lime and passionfruit flavours and there is crisp acid on the finish. It's a very refreshing style that can be served well chilled. Try it with yabbies.

Yarra Burn Bastard Hill Chardonnay

Quality	♟♟♟♟
Value	★★★★
Grapes	chardonnay
Region	Yarra Valley, SA
Cellar	♦ 4
Alc./Vol.	13.5%
RRP	$42.00

Named by the pickers and pruners. If you ever walk up this hill at Hoddles Creek (MS and HH have) you'll realise it's very aptly named. You almost need pitons and belays to get to the top.

CURRENT RELEASE 1994   This wine shows some bottle development with a green–gold colour. There are peach, toast and honey aromas on the nose. The palate is full-bodied with some well-rounded peach and melon flavours, which show toasty elements. The finish shows a lavish oak that is softening with time. It should not be served too cold. Try it with a salmon pâté.

Yarra Burn Sauvignon Blanc Semillon

Since September 1995 this has been part of BRL Hardys' holding in the Yarra Valley. The founders David and Christine Fyffe remain to make the wines.

CURRENT RELEASE 1996 Roll out the fruit bowl: this is full of mango, passionfruit, kiwi fruit and tamarillo. In this blend sauvignon blanc does all the legwork while semillon adds the structure. The nose is tropical and herbal, and the palate is a cocktail with gooseberry added to the mix. There is plenty of fresh acid on the finish. It's a good hot-weather style that can be served well chilled. Try it with chilli calamari.

Quality	♈♈♈♈
Value	★★★★
Grapes	sauvignon blanc; semillon
Region	Yarra Valley, Vic.
Cellar	🍶 2
Alc./Vol.	12.0%
RRP	$14.50

Yarra Ridge Chardonnay

The trick to this distinctive style of Yarra chardonnay is brief maturation in American oak, and no malolactic fermentation. Hence the fruit is given full expression. Maker Rob Dolan.

Previous outstanding vintages: '91, '93, '94

CURRENT RELEASE 1995 The nose is a mixture of peach and melon with a touch of vanilla. The palate is all about peach and melon, and there is an attractive mouth-feel. The finish has a distinct vanilla lift with some toasty characters. Serve with a medium chill. Try it with a veal marsala.

Quality	♈♈♈♈
Value	★★★★
Grapes	chardonnay
Region	Yarra Valley, Vic.
Cellar	🍶 3
Alc./Vol.	12.7%
RRP	$19.00

CURRENT RELEASE 1996 Intense grapefruit and lemon aromas come rocketing out of the glass. The same flavours reappear in the mouth, augmented by subtle oak. A fruit-driven chardonnay with lovely finesse and length. Serve with king prawns.

Quality	♈♈♈♈♈
Value	★★★★↑
Grapes	chardonnay
Region	Yarra Valley, Vic.
Cellar	🍶 5+
Alc./Vol.	12.5%
RRP	$20.00 Ⓢ

Yarra Ridge Reserve Chardonnay

Quality	YYYY?
Value	★★★
Grapes	chardonnay
Region	Yarra Valley, Vic.
Cellar	▮ 4
Alc./Vol.	12.7%
RRP	$24.00 Ⓢ

Very sexy packaging: it makes the wine look like a million dollars. Small makers could well take a leaf out of this book and spend time and money on good label design.

CURRENT RELEASE 1995   Complex wine but oak rules, okay! There is plenty of wood evident on the nose. There are also caramel, vanilla, toast and peach aromas. The palate is rich with some developed fruit, peach and pawpaw being the major flavours. Oak is never far away, dominating the finish with a savoury character and an intense vanilla character. The length is impressive. It needs a medium chill, and it could be served with Thai pork with rice noodles.

Sparkling Wines

All Saints St Leonards Cabernet Sauvignon

Both All Saints and St Leonards are part of the growing Brown Brothers empire. This fizzy cabernet is one more brick in their ever-expanding walls.

CURRENT RELEASE *non-vintage* Cabernet sauvignon is never totally convincing in this role. This is an attractive fizz with a fruity, ripe berry nose. The palate has sweet raspberry and cherry flavours, and there are oak and tannin on the finish. The bubbles come to the party. Serve well chilled with smoked turkey.

Quality	🍷🍷🍷
Value	★★★
Grapes	cabernet sauvignon
Region	North East Victoria
Cellar	🍾 1
Alc./Vol.	13.5%
RRP	$19.00

Andrew Garrett Chardonnay Pinot Noir Vintage

This is a new label for Andrew Garrett, added to the non-vintage blend. It scored well in the Sydney International Top 100.

CURRENT RELEASE 1994 The colour is light yellow, the aroma rather delicate with slight herbaceousness and tropical fruit hints. The mousse is very brisk and fluffy, and the palate has finesse and some length. It's smooth and slips down easily. Fine with cucumber sandwiches.

Quality	🍷🍷🍷🍷
Value	★★★★
Grapes	chardonnay; pinot noir
Region	not stated
Cellar	🍾 3
Alc./Vol.	11.5%
RRP	$17.50 ⑤

Andrew Garrett Sparkling Burgundy

Quality	♟♟♟♟
Value	★★★★
Grapes	shiraz
Region	McLaren Vale, SA
Cellar	🍷 2
Alc./Vol.	12.5%
RRP	$14.00 Ⓢ

Plotting the progress of this company requires a cine-mascopic presentation. It's now part of the Mildara/Blass group, but it's a sure bet the wine was started by Warren Randall, thanks to his experience at Seppelt Great Western. He now owns Tinlins winery down the road. Confused? Just sit back and enjoy the wine.

CURRENT RELEASE *non-vintage* Lovely colour, and the aroma of McLaren Vale shiraz wafts through. The nose has ripe cherry aromas and hints of spice. The palate is quite sweet, and the rich cherry and plum flavours are spruced up by some oak and a lively mousse. It should be served well chilled. Try it with smoked turkey.

Ashton Hills Salmon Brut

Quality	♟♟♟♟♟
Value	★★★★
Grapes	chardonnay 75%; pinot noir 25%
Region	Adelaide Hills, SA
Cellar	🍷 2
Alc./Vol.	12.2%
RRP	$28.00

It's pink in colour, it goes great with smoked salmon . . . what other connection can we make? I think you get the picture. Maker Steve George.

CURRENT RELEASE 1994 Youthful deep hot pink in colour, this is a rosé of real substance. The nose shows cherry and strawberry pinot notes with hints of vanilla and candy. Lots of fruit; very pinot-led flavour although it's mostly chardonnay. A delicious bubbly with style and balance. Serve with gravlax.

Bleasdale Sparkling Shiraz

Quality	♟♟♟
Value	★★★
Grapes	shiraz
Region	Langhorne Creek, SA
Cellar	🍷 5+
Alc./Vol.	13.0%
RRP	$17.00

This is a newly fashionable style of wine. According to Ian Loftus, creator of National Sparkling Red Day, the number of wineries with a sparkling red on the market jumped from five in 1991 to 57 in 1996.

CURRENT RELEASE *non-vintage* Vivid, youthful purple–red colour, stacks of coconut oak and licorice shiraz fruit. Lots of sweetness: too much for our tastes, but chill well and serve with BBQ pork ribs in plum sauce.

Blue Pyrenees Midnight Cuvée

Winemaker Vincent Gere has actually proved that if he picks the grapes at night the acid content is higher than it was earlier that day, or the following day. Mystery abounds.

CURRENT RELEASE *non-vintage* The chardonnay aromas dominate, with herbal and straw/hay characters plus a little resinous bready character and the merest suggestion of oak. The palate is lively and fresh with energetic bubbles and a tangy aftertaste. Good as an aperitif, with oysters.

Quality	ᵀᵀᵀᵀ
Value	★★★★
Grapes	chardonnay; pinot noir
Region	Pyrenees, Vic.
Cellar	🍾 3
Alc./Vol.	12.3%
RRP	$31.40

Bowen Estate Sanderson

Sanderson was Joy Bowen's maiden name. What was once the house bubbly at Bowen's has grown into a commercial item with this vintage.

CURRENT RELEASE 1990 Very developed colour and bouquet, the latter being vanilla, smoke and candy. The palate is very high in acid and perhaps there is some variation in the liqueuring levels. Best taken with food. Try gravlax with crème fraiche.

Quality	ᵀᵀᵀᵀ
Value	★★★
Grapes	not stated
Region	Coonawarra, SA
Cellar	🍾 2
Alc./Vol.	11.5%
RRP	$21.00

Brown Brothers Pinot Chardonnay Brut NV

The higher parts of the King Valley are proving to be an excellent source of sparkling wine grapes. Maker Terry Barnett.

CURRENT RELEASE *non-vintage* Peach and pastry-like aromas greet the nose and there are some gamy developed pinot overtones. The palate is smooth and agreeable with a trace of sweetness from *liqueur d'expédition*. It has more character and finesse than usual at its price. Serve with hors d'oeuvres.

Quality	ᵀᵀᵀᵀ
Value	★★★★
Grapes	pinot noir; chardonnay
Region	King Valley, Vic.
Cellar	🍾 1
Alc./Vol.	11.5%
RRP	$16.00

Brown Brothers Whitlands Pinot Chardonnay Brut

Quality	ио́ио́ио́
Value	★★★★
Grapes	pinot noir; chardonnay
Region	King Valley, Vic.
Cellar	2
Alc./Vol.	12.0%
RRP	$29.80

Whitlands is a chilly, high-altitude place and therefore well suited to growing the finest base wines for bubbly. Maker Terry Barnett.

CURRENT RELEASE 1993 A rich, full-throttle sparkler that's brimful of bready, yeast-derived flavours and toasty richness from age and pinot noir grapes. The palate is enlivened by a vigorous mousse and is full-bodied yet refined; rich in multi-faceted complexities. Serve with smoked trout.

Cleveland Brut 94er

Quality	ио́ио́ио́
Value	★★★★⋆
Grapes	chardonnay 70%; pinot noir 30%
Region	Macedon, Vic.
Cellar	3
Alc./Vol.	12.0%
RRP	$26.50

This is the fizzy side of a small but not insignificant shaker in the Macedon region. The estate features a historic homestead, function room and underground cellars. Maker Keith Brien.

CURRENT RELEASE 1994 The nose makes an impressive introduction to a complex style. It has yeast and cooked bread aromas. The palate is medium-bodied with some fresh citrus characters and meaty elements from the pinot noir. The finish has strong, crisp acid and cleansing bubbles. It should be served well chilled as a pre-dinner drink.

Clover Hill

This is the Tasmanian venture for Taltarni, which is stealing the show from the mainland fizz. The textbooks would have it no other way because Tasmania should be ideal for the production of quality sparkling wine.

Previous outstanding vintages: '92, '93
CURRENT RELEASE 1994 They've changed the blend but the character remains the same. Complexity finds a new high – it's outstanding! The nose has yeast and green apple aromas. The palate is steely but this is tempered by some fluffy bubbles. Apples are the major fruit flavour, and this is balanced by some crisp acid on a clean, dry finish. It should be served well chilled as a pre-dinner drink.

Quality	?????
Value	★★★★⟩
Grapes	chardonnay 50%; pinot noir 50%
Region	Pipers River, Tas.
Cellar	▮ 4
Alc./Vol.	13.0%
RRP	$29.75

PENGUIN BEST SPARKLING WINE

Craigmoor Vintage Chardonnay Sparkling Brut

This was made in Craigmoor's 136th vintage year. It can claim to be the birthplace of chardonnay in Australia.

CURRENT RELEASE 1994 It's a light, lean style with plenty of acid. It has a refreshing quality and should be served well chilled. It has lemon and yeast aromas, and the palate is flinty with lemon and grapefruit flavours that are matched by crisp acid.

Quality	???
Value	★★★
Grapes	chardonnay
Region	Mudgee, NSW
Cellar	▮
Alc./Vol.	12.0%
RRP	$13.00 Ⓢ

De Bortoli Emeri Pinot Noir Brut

Emeri De Bortoli is the wife of chairman Deen De Bortoli and mother of Darren and Leanne, who both work for the company.

CURRENT RELEASE *non-vintage* This has spent over 12 months on lees. It has a broad, resiny, candy nose with some caramel aromas. The taste is very light and not especially fine, but at the price, who's complaining? It's good value. Mix with orange juice as a Bucks Fizz.

Quality	???
Value	★★★⟩
Grapes	pinot noir
Region	Riverina, NSW
Cellar	▮
Alc./Vol.	11.0%
RRP	$10.00 Ⓢ

De Bortoli Windy Peak Prestige

Quality	▾▾▾⁊
Value	★★★⋆
Grapes	pinot noir
Region	Yarra Valley, Vic.
Cellar	▮
Alc./Vol.	11.5%
RRP	$13.65 ⑤

Darren De Bortoli's main priority in moving to the Yarra was to make bubbly. The emphasis has shifted somewhat since those days.

CURRENT RELEASE *non-vintage*   Don't be put off by the pale pink colour: it's just an indication of the red (pinot) grapes. Smoky, strawberry and vanilla pinot scents dominate the aroma, and the palate is very flavoursome, soft and creamy with a slight grip to the finish and appealing balance. It goes well with delicate smoked salmon.

Deakin Estate Brut

Quality	▾▾▾⁊
Value	★★★★⋆
Grapes	chardonnay 40%; colombard 40%; chenin blanc 20%
Region	Murray Valley, Vic.
Cellar	▮ 1
Alc./Vol.	13.5%
RRP	$9.35 ⑤

This won the Penguin Award for Best Bargain Sparkling Wine last year, and the current bottling is every bit as good. These people are making a mockery of the Riverland's critics. Maker Mark Zeppel.

CURRENT RELEASE 1996   The colour is a bright, light yellow and everything about the wine points to white grapes with a strong chardonnay component. There are fresh peach, nectarine and lightly herbal aromas without age or yeast-derived characters. It's soft and round in the mouth; a youthful, fruit style – a 'chardonnay with bubbles'. Good party sipping.

Deakin Estate Grand Prix Brut

Quality	▾▾⁊
Value	★★★
Grapes	pinot noir; chardonnay
Region	Murray Valley, Vic.
Cellar	▮
Alc./Vol.	13.0%
RRP	$12.00

The folks at Deakin never let an opportunity go begging. They named their brand after a former prime minister and now they're heralding a range of wines for the Melbourne Formula One Grand Prix.

CURRENT RELEASE 1996   It hasn't had much time to build yeast-aged character, but it's a pleasant, soft, round, fruity style with a somewhat beery, leesy nose. Chill well and it'll taste okay amid the petrol fumes.

Domaine Chandon Blanc de Noirs

A *blanc de noirs* is a white-coloured bubbly made from 100% red – or as they call them in Champagne, black – grapes. Maker Wayne Donaldson and team.
CURRENT RELEASE 1992   The colour is a slightly pink-stained mid-yellow. The nose reveals smoky, caramel and vanilla notes, with pinot noir showing its personality. The nose is low-key and it has a slightly heavier palate than the other DC wines. It's very soft, toasty, light-bodied and rounded. Don't serve it too cold: 12 degrees is fine. Try it with delicate smoked salmon.

Quality	▼▼▼▼
Value	★★★⤍
Grapes	pinot noir
Region	various
Cellar	▮ 3
Alc./Vol.	12.5%
RRP	$30.00 ⑤

Domaine Chandon Vintage Brut

In true Champagne tradition, this was blended from 45 base wines. Dom Perignon, who fathered that tradition, would have been proud.
CURRENT RELEASE 1994   Straw, hay, tobacco aromas are overlain by bready yeast autolysis character, and the palate has a good frothy mousse and deep, dry-finishing flavour. There are some genuine aged complexities buried deep within the wine. It's a bubbly of substantial character and depth. Try it with sushi.

Quality	▼▼▼▼⤍
Value	★★★★
Grapes	pinot noir 50%;
	chardonnay 49%;
	pinot meunier 1%
Region	various, Vic., SA &
	Tas.
Cellar	▮ 4
Alc./Vol.	12.5%
RRP	$30.00 ⑤

Domaine Chandon Vintage Brut Rosé

Rosé bubbly is often dismissed as a dilettante's wine. But in truth, some of the finest Champagnes we've tasted have been rosés. It depends on the intent of the maker . . .
CURRENT RELEASE 1994   An exciting drink, and even more complex than the standard Vintage Brut. The colour is a slightly developed pink, the nose has straw-berry, smoky pinot aromas up-front, and the palate is full of savoury, complex flavours with a creamy texture and smooth balance. It has body and richness, and the finish is long and full. Try it with salmon gravlax.

Quality	▼▼▼▼▼
Value	★★★★★
Grapes	pinot noir 60%;
	chardonnay 40%
Region	various
Cellar	▮ 3
Alc./Vol.	12.5
RRP	$30.00 ⑤

Eyton on Yarra

Quality	♟♟♟⸮
Value	★★★⸍
Grapes	chardonnay 50%; pinot noir 50%
Region	Yarra Valley, Vic.
Cellar	▮ 3
Alc./Vol.	12.8%
RRP	$20.00

A finger in every pie, and the sparkling pie is looking particularly appealing in this district. Only the classic grape varieties need apply.

CURRENT RELEASE 1993   There are apple and creamy yeast aromas on the nose, and the bubbles are lively. The palate is zesty and fresh with some Granny Smith flavours and lively acid. The finish is very crisp and palate-cleansing. Serve it well chilled as a pre-dinner drink.

Hanging Rock Macedon Cuvée V

Quality	♟♟♟♟♟
Value	★★★★
Grapes	pinot noir; chardonnay
Region	Macedon, Vic.
Cellar	▮ 2
Alc./Vol.	12.5%
RRP	$36.00

When introduced, this wine left many ambivalent about the style. It was full-on with no beg-pardons; in past editions of this book we lauded it because it dared to be different. Although the maker has turned the volume down a tad, it still dares to be wild. Maker John Ellis.

Previous outstanding vintages: all previous releases

CURRENT RELEASE *non-vintage*   The wine is meaty and intentionally aldehydic. The nose is candied with Vegemite qualities and loads of yeast. The palate is chewy with honeyed fruit and lemon flavours. The finish is soft and lively; the bubbles make for a lift. It's a good food style. Serve well chilled with Atlantic salmon.

Hardys Sir James Brut de Brut

Quality	♟♟♟
Value	★★★
Grapes	pinot noir; chardonnay
Region	not stated
Cellar	▮ 1
Alc./Vol.	12.0%
RRP	$15.00 Ⓢ

'Brut de brut' is supposed to indicate a very dry wine, in this case the driest in the Sir James portfolio. Without masking sweetness, the fruit quality stands revealed, warts and all.

CURRENT RELEASE *non-vintage*   Here's one for the sailing enthusiasts. It's a basic bubbly with some smoky, caramel and vanilla pinot-derived flavours, and the palate is straightforward and light, with a dry but balanced finish. Take it out on the yacht and mix it with orange juice.

Hardys Sir James Cuvée Brut

We can't think of this wine without remembering the pompous French *sommelier* in the TV ad. I guess that's what you call effective advertising. Maker Ed Carr.

CURRENT RELEASE *non-vintage* The medium–light yellow colour has brassy reflections, indicating pinot noir grapes. The nose initially has a hint of a struck match – a sulfur residue – while the taste is slightly sweet, soft and simple with a slight grip on the finish. This is basic bubbly but fair value at the (often-discounted) price. Serve with crumbed lamb's brains.

Quality	🍷🍷🍷
Value	★★★
Grapes	pinot noir; chardonnay
Region	not stated
Cellar	1
Alc./Vol.	12.0%
RRP	$15.00 (S)

Hardys Sir James Vintage

Hardys poached fizzicist Ed Carr from Southcorp in an effort to lift their bubblies. This is a pretty good effort to start off with.

CURRENT RELEASE 1993 Rich, nutty sparkler with bready, smoky and faintly strawberry pinot-noir-derived flavours. Aromas of candied fruits and vanilla. A softer, mouthfilling style of bubbly with a decisive finish. Serve with caviar.

Quality	🍷🍷🍷🍷½
Value	★★★½
Grapes	chardonnay; pinot noir
Region	Yarra Valley, Vic.
Cellar	2
Alc./Vol.	12.5%
RRP	$24.00 (S)

James Irvine Merlot Brut Cuvée 900

Sparkling reds made from merlot are almost as rare as hens' teeth, but it seems logical as merlot is usually a soft-finishing wine. Maker Jim Irvine.

CURRENT RELEASE *non-vintage* At first pour, the bouquet is dominated by charry oak, but as it warms in the glass the fruit comes up to give it balance. The colour is a medium red–purple and in the mouth there's a lively, lean but elegant structure. The palate carries a good dollop of sweetness and the finish winds up with quite a tannin grip. Best served with just a gentle chill. Roast turkey goes well.

Quality	🍷🍷🍷🍷
Value	★★★
Grapes	merlot
Region	Eden Valley, SA
Cellar	5+
Alc./Vol.	13.0%
RRP	$29.00

Jansz Brut Cuvée

Quality	❚❚❚❚❚
Value	★★★★
Grapes	pinot noir; chardonnay
Region	northern Tasmania
Cellar	▮ 3
Alc./Vol.	12.0%
RRP	$29.80

Gerrit Jansz skippered a ship called *Zeehan*, which accompanied Abel Tasman's *Heemskerk* on a voyage of discovery to what later became known as Tasmania. Maker Gary Ford.

Previous outstanding vintages: '91, '92

CURRENT RELEASE 1993 It's amazing what a difference time makes. Bottles of Jansz are progressively disgorged as the market demands. The last to be sold are fuller, more mellow and better balanced, while the earliest taste leaner and more acidic. Ours was a late-disgorged bottle, and shows much better than those sampled a year ago. Bready, candied fruit and herbal complexities; very fine and smooth palate; pure flavours and creamy mousse. Great with oysters.

Jeanneret Bottle Fermented Grenache

Quality	❚❚❚❚❚
Value	★★★★
Grapes	grenache
Region	Clare Valley, SA
Cellar	▮ 5
Alc./Vol.	11.0%
RRP	$20.00

Jeanneret is the name of the people who make these wines. They are from Belgium, hence the froggy-sounding handle. Very old, hand-tended, dryland bush vines are the source of the fruit.

CURRENT RELEASE *non-vintage* This is a delicious sparkling red and perhaps the use of grenache is a discovery. It has a nice deep colour and rich, ripe spice/licorice and dark plum aromas. The taste is fairly youthful but soft and smoothly rounded, with tight tannins to finish and no excess sweetness. A delicious, beautifully balanced wine. Try it with roast turkey.

Killawarra Premier Vintage Brut

It's amazing that the big wine companies can bottle-ferment, age on lees, and do everything else they do with sparkling wines such as this, and then flog 'em at such low prices. It's a big win for the consumer. This spends at least 12 months on its lees. Maker Ian Shepherd.

CURRENT RELEASE 1994 Starve the lizards if this isn't the best value bubbly around in 1997. It has a youthful light yellow colour and a bouquet of apples, straw and spice, with just a smidgin of breadiness. The taste is clean and has remarkable depth and balance for the price, which dips as low as $11.99 when discounted. It manages to combine freshness with character. Try it with sushi.

Quality	ΨΨΨΨ
Value	★★★★⊦
Grapes	pinot noir; chardonnay
Region	mainly Padthaway, Coonawarra and Barossa Valley, SA
Cellar	▲ 1
Alc./Vol.	12.0%
RRP	$13.50 Ⓢ

Miranda Sparkling Shiraz

This comes from old vines in the Barossa Valley, which means Miranda is covering all the marketing bases. It's a blend of the 1992 vintage (85%) and the 1993 vintage (15%).

CURRENT RELEASE *non-vintage* If there is such a thing as an authentic sparkling Burgundy style, this wine comes close. It has the requisite sweetness on the palate and there is plenty of black-tea-like tannin. Ripe shiraz shines through and the wine should improve with bottle-age. Serve well chilled with turkey.

Quality	ΨΨΨΨ
Value	★★★★
Grapes	shiraz
Region	Barossa valley, SA
Cellar	▲ 3
Alc./Vol.	13.0%
RRP	$15.50

Mitchell Sparkling Peppertree

Quality	🍷🍷🍷🍷🍷
Value	★★★★★
Grapes	shiraz
Region	Clare Valley, SA
Cellar	🍷 4
Alc./Vol.	13.0%
RRP	$18.00

It had to happen: a sparkling red wine from the Clare Valley, and this one is right in the middle of the Peppertree red tradition. Maker Andrew Mitchell.

CURRENT RELEASE *non-vintage*   Pepper and spice and all things nice. The colour is deep and the bubbles dance a jig on the tongue. The nose has black pepper and plum aromas. The palate is chewy with the traditional hint of sweetness, which adds bulk. The finish is dry and long. It can take the big chill and is great – sipping-style – mid-afternoon.

Mount Prior Sparkling Durif

Quality	🍷🍷🍷🍷
Value	★★★★
Grapes	durif
Region	North East Victoria
Cellar	🍷 3
Alc./Vol.	13.0%
RRP	$14.50

Here's another use for a grape variety that is usually a component of a port blend. Mount Prior is a 50-hectare vineyard originally founded in 1860. Maker Tony Lacy.

CURRENT RELEASE *non-vintage*   This is a little drier than the traditional style. The colour is a mulberry stain and the nose has strong berry aromas, plus a hint of iron tonic. The palate is restrained with hints of mulberry, and the finish shows plenty of tannin and grip. It can be served well chilled as a pre-dinner drink.

Nautilus Cuvée Marlborough

Quality	🍷🍷🍷🍷
Value	★★★
Grapes	pinot noir; chardonnay
Region	Marlborough, NZ
Cellar	🍷 1
Alc./Vol.	12.0%
RRP	$25.30

Nautilus is an Aussie venture in New Zealand's pre-eminent wine region, Marlborough. It's owned by S. Smith & Son (Yalumba).

CURRENT RELEASE *non-vintage*   This was the International Wine Challenge's bubbly of the year back in 1995. The bouquet reveals tremendous complexity of smoky, meaty, strawberry-developed pinot characters. The palate is lively and shows the same flavours, lifted by a little volatility. Serve with chat potatoes and chive cream.

Preece Pinot Chardonnay Brut

Natty miniature labels are a feature of the Preece wines. This new addition to the range has a triangular label. Maker Don Lewis.

CURRENT RELEASE 1995   A respectable but somewhat bland sparkler, which is fair value at the price. Fresh bread-dough and pear-like fruit aromas, a hint of sweetness on the palate and a lightness of touch that won't offend anyone. Try it with sushi.

Quality	♥♥♥↑
Value	★★★
Grapes	pinot noir 50%; chardonnay 50%
Region	Yarra Valley & Goulburn Valley, Vic.
Cellar	▮ 2
Alc./Vol.	12.1%
RRP	$14.65 Ⓢ

Red Hill Estate Brut

Red Hill Estate is named after a town on the peninsula, and is the retirement address of Sir Peter Derham. Maker Jenny Bright.

Previous outstanding vintages: '94

CURRENT RELEASE 1995   Very pale pink hue. The pinot theme is repeated on the bouquet, which is all about strawberry, candy and toasted bread pinot noir and yeast interactions. It's a lively drink with loads of character, the high acid bringing on a slightly hard finish, which the liqueuring struggles to balance. Don't over-chill, and serve with food. Try gravlax.

Quality	♥♥♥↑
Value	★★★
Grapes	chardonnay 60%; pinot noir 40%
Region	Mornington Peninsula, Vic.
Cellar	▮ 4
Alc./Vol.	12.5%
RRP	$22.00

Red Hill Sparkling Pinot Noir

This is Sir Peter Derham's weekender on the Peninsula that got out of control. It's now 12 hectares under vine and counting. Maker Jenny Bright.

CURRENT RELEASE *non-vintage*   The nose has the meat aroma that only pinot noir can give. Cooked bread smells also play a part. The colour is a salmon-pink with a hint of onion skin. The palate is delightfully delicate with subtle berry flavours and crisp acid. The bubbles work well, and the wine makes a very refreshing pre-dinner drink.

Quality	♥♥♥♥
Value	★★★↑
Grapes	pinot noir
Region	Mornington Peninsula, Vic.
Cellar	▮ 2
Alc./Vol.	12.5%
RRP	$23.00

Richmond Grove Pinot Chardonnay NV Brut

Quality	♉♉♉♉
Value	★★★★
Grapes	pinot noir; chardonnay
Region	not stated
Cellar	▮
Alc./Vol.	11.5%
RRP	$13.00

This is a useful and under-promoted wine that should be remembered when the whip, 'round for after-work-TGIF-drinks doesn't amount to the price of Dom Perignon.

CURRENT RELEASE *non-vintage*   The nose has fresh fruit aromas plus some cracked yeast smells. The palate is medium-bodied with some steely characters. The bubbles give a good account of themselves, and the finish is dry. It would also work well with fruit juice.

Stephen John Traugott Cuvée Sparkling Burgundy

Quality	♉♉♉♉
Value	★★★★
Grapes	not stated
Region	Clare Valley, SA
Cellar	▮ 1
Alc./Vol.	12.5%
RRP	$18.00

This is named after the maker's great-great-grandfather Traugott Benjamin John, who arrived in 1845 and settled in the Barossa Valley.

CURRENT RELEASE *non-vintage*   There is a big cherry and confectionery aroma on the nose. The palate is medium-bodied with sweet raspberry fruit flavours and lively bubbles. The finish is clean and dry. It's not as massively sweet as most sparkling burgundies. It can be served very cold with knackwurst and German mustard.

Tulloch Hunter Cuvée Brut

Quality	♉♉♉♉
Value	★★★
Grapes	semillon
Region	Hunter Valley, NSW
Cellar	▮
Alc./Vol.	11.5%
RRP	$13.55 ⓢ

Jay Tulloch, the last member of the family to work for the company that bears this proud old Hunter name, retired in 1996. The company is part of Southcorp.

CURRENT RELEASE 1992   This style is known in the trade as a 'white Burgundy with bubbles'. It has a medium–full yellow colour, an open-knit peachy/herbal nose (which has a common thread with all the Seppelt bubblies), and a light, soft, broad flavour. It falls away at the finish, but it's more than adequate at the price.

Wilson's Pinot Noir Chardonnay

This brand was started by the late Ian Wilson, who with Grant Burge revitalised Krondorf in the '80s. This wine is produced at Petaluma's Bridgewater Mill.

CURRENT RELEASE *non-vintage* Lightly toasted bready aromas combine with dried grass/straw scents and hints of candied fruit. The taste is quite full and rich with attractive, complex candy and vanilla flavours. While it may lack a little delicacy and refinement, it's a generous glass of fizz. Serve with canapés.

Quality 🍷🍷🍷🍷½
Value ★★★★
Grapes pinot noir; chardonnay
Region South Australia
Cellar 🍾 2
Alc./Vol. 12.0%
RRP $22.50

Yalumba Angas Brut Rosé

Pink was supposed to make the boys wink. These days who knows: it's the alcohol that does the work whatever the colour.

CURRENT RELEASE *non-vintage* Party-frock pink with some festive bubbles. The nose is almost neutral and the palate has a hint of sweetness. There are soft acids on the finish. A big chill will thrill. Drink it behind the water cooler at the office party.

Quality 🍷🍷🍷½
Value ★★★½
Grapes not stated
Region not stated
Cellar 🍾
Alc./Vol. 11.5%
RRP $9.90 (S)

Yalumba D

D is for D-lish-us. This is one of the pioneers of the development of premium Australian sparkling wine styles. It's now one of the most reliable brands on the market and it has settled on a house style.

Previous outstanding vintages: '90, '91, '92, '93

CURRENT RELEASE 1994 A very polished style that is showing considerable refinement. The nose has cooked bread and bakers' yeast qualities. The palate is of medium weight with citrus and meaty qualities that are enlivened by some brisk bubbles. Some bottle-age is apparent, which adds to the complexity. There is bracing acid on the finish. It can be served well chilled as a pre-dinner drink.

Quality 🍷🍷🍷🍷½
Value ★★★★
Grapes pinot noir; chardonnay
Region various, SA
Cellar 🍾 3
Alc./Vol. 12.5%
RRP $28.00

Yellowglen Yellow

Quality	♔♔♔
Value	★★★
Grapes	pinot noir; chardonnay; others
Region	not stated
Cellar	▮
Alc./Vol.	11.5%
RRP	$10.00 Ⓢ

It's party time! This is hard to take seriously, with its slash of yellow paint for a 'label' and the price is very down-market.

CURRENT RELEASE *non-vintage* Brassy colour; monotone vanilla, slightly smoky aromas; a heavy-handed palate that tastes dull and lacks life. It does have flavour, however, and it will probably find a following at its lowly price. Put some orange juice in it for a Bucks Fizz.

Fortified Wines

All Saints Show Reserve Amontillado

Put this down to old stocks dating back to the days when the Sutherland Smith family held sway over All Saints, a replica of a castle on the Firth of Mey in the Parish of All Saints, Scotland.

CURRENT RELEASE *non-vintage* This is a rich, dry fino/amontillado style with plenty of yeast character that is evident on the nutty nose. The palate shows the richness of mellow fruit, which is counterbalanced by some acid and rancio characters, and the finish lingers. It's perfect for a game consommé with a poached quail egg.

Quality	♟♟♟♟♟
Value	★★★★☆
Grapes	not stated
Region	Rutherglen, Vic.
Cellar	🍾
Alc./Vol.	19.0%
RRP	$29.00

All Saints Show Reserve Old Liqueur Muscat

The Brown Brothers have lavished much care and attention on the ancient All Saints property. It's now a showcase for the district.

CURRENT RELEASE *non-vintage* This is a marvel. The wine is incredibly concentrated, trial by muscat if you will. There are deep layers of flavour that include rancio, raisins, vanilla, malt extract and dried peels. The nose has strong berry aromas and sweet muscat smells, and the finish adds balance and freshness. It has both power and balance. Indeed, it has the armour plate to withstand stilton.

Quality	♟♟♟♟♟
Value	★★★★☆
Grapes	red frontignac
Region	Rutherglen, Vic.
Cellar	🍾
Alc./Vol.	18.5%
RRP	$45.00

All Saints Show Reserve Old Liqueur Tokay

Quality	🍷🍷🍷🍷🍷
Value	★★★⟨
Grapes	muscadelle
Region	Rutherglen, Vic.
Cellar	🍸
Alc./Vol.	17.0%
RRP	$45.00

The Terrace restaurant is another Brown Brothers innovation and it's a fine place to dine after looking at the hall of fame.

CURRENT RELEASE *non-vintage* The colour is the key and gives a clue to the age of this wine: it's deep amber with green tinges on the edge. The nose gives another clue to the age: there is a deep rancio character and ancient dried fruit. It lingers long with mellow spirit and wood. It's an outstanding style for some smelly soft cheese.

Angove's Anchorage Old Tawny Port

Quality	🍷🍷🍷⟨
Value	★★★⟨
Grapes	not stated
Region	Murray Valley, SA
Cellar	🍸
Alc./Vol.	17.4%
RRP	$11.40

Is that Anchorage, Alaska or Anchorage, Renmark? We're not sure, but the wine is good enough to keep you anchored to a comfy chair in front of an open fire.

CURRENT RELEASE *non-vintage* Fairly pale, tawny–brown colour, showing a lot of maturity. The nose is all vanilla and raisins, the taste is sweet and lean and pulls up fairly quickly. It's more about mellow aged character than fruit, and it would suit freshly shelled walnuts.

Angoves Flor Fino

Quality	🍷🍷🍷⟨
Value	★★★★
Grapes	not stated
Region	Riverland, SA
Cellar	🍸
Alc./Vol.	17.4%
RRP	$12.50

They must be worried at Renmark because the market for this wine is either being put on the wagon by the doctor or is headed for the great solero in the sky. It needs to be introduced to a more youthful consumer base.

CURRENT RELEASE *non-vintage* A pale (almost water-coloured) sherry style with a nutty, yeasty nose and a hint of mature cheese. The palate is dry and soft with a gentle salt tang, and the finish has some attractive acid, which is highlighted by chilling. Drink it pre-dinner.

Angoves 1991 Port

This is a vintage port style that spent minimal time in wood and should develop in the bottle. As could be expected, excellent brandy spirit has been used during fortification.

CURRENT RELEASE 1991   A lively style that makes much of some aged brandy. The nose is a mixture of spirit, fruit and wood. The palate is medium-bodied with sweet berry fruit flavours, warming brandy and dusty dry oak. It should be cellared and drunk with soft blue cheese and nuts.

Quality	▼▼▼▽
Value	★★★↑
Grapes	shiraz
Region	Riverland, SA
Cellar	↓ 5
Alc./Vol.	18.5%
RRP	$15.00

Baileys Winemakers Selection Old Muscat

Whither Baileys' fortifieds now that the winery is a piece of gravel in Ray King's shoe? (King is boss of Mildara Blass, which acquired Baileys in 1996. He's not one to trifle with tradition.)

CURRENT RELEASE *non-vintage*   A great Australian muscat! It's dark brown, powerfully flavoured, very concentrated and genuinely old, sitting perhaps at the sweeter end of the muscat spectrum. Malt, rose petal, brown sugar and raisins – very intense muscat character, tremendously luscious and long on the palate. Sip with stilton cheese.

Quality	▼▼▼▼▼
Value	★★★★↑
Grapes	red frontignac
Region	North East Victoria
Cellar	↓
Alc./Vol.	18.0%
RRP	$50.00

Brown Brothers Reserve Port

Is this the fate of the leftover red grapes at Browns? With five varieties, it certainly is a fruit salad.

CURRENT RELEASE *non-vintage*   This is more the royal reserve end of the line than the family reserve. It's a youthful, simple style with the accent on fruit rather than on wood-aged complexity. There are vanilla and plum aromas with hints of spice, and the palate is sweet and fruity but well balanced with a clean, dry aftertaste. Take a hipflask to the snow.

Quality	▼▼▼
Value	★★★
Grapes	shiraz; grenache; mataro; carignan; cabernet sauvignon
Region	North East Victoria
Cellar	↓
Alc./Vol.	18.0%
RRP	$11.60

Brown Brothers Very Old Port

Quality	▼▼▼▼▼
Value	★★★★⸳
Grapes	shiraz
Region	North East Victoria
Cellar	▮
Alc./Vol.	18.5%
RRP	$22.50

Based on wines from the '50s, with selected parcels from the best vintages since. It's a top-line wine for the hard-core port freaks.

CURRENT RELEASE *non-vintage*   It's no fib: this is very old indeed, with all the great depth of character and complexity that goes with extended oak ageing and careful re-blending. It has a deep tawny–red colour and a mellow bouquet of rancio, mixed peel, vanilla, chocolate and oak. Its flavours fill the mouth and linger long after it's gone down the hatch. Slinky texture is a feature. Serve with coffee and a good Havana.

Brown Brothers Very Old Tokay

Quality	▼▼▼▼▼
Value	★★★★★
Grapes	muscadelle
Region	North East Victoria
Cellar	▮
Alc./Vol.	18.5%
RRP	$28.00 ▮

Liqueur tokay may have borrowed its name from the famous wine of Hungary, but there the similarity ends. At some point in the future, a name change will have to occur as tokay is not the grape's real name.

CURRENT RELEASE *non-vintage* This is a stunning wine and at this price must be one of the best-value tokays around. Extraordinary depth of flavour, which recalls tea leaf, cedar, rancio and a hint of Vegemite. Immense power and concentration, and a finish that resonates long after it's gone. The flavour is so complex as to defy description. Great to sip meditatively while watching cricket.

Buller & Son Liqueur Muscat

Quality	▼▼▼▼
Value	★★★★
Grapes	red frontignac
Region	Rutherglen, Vic.
Cellar	▮
Alc./Vol.	17.8%
RRP	$20.00

This is a wine typical of the district and the style. It has been a cornerstone of the three Bs: Buller, Browns and Baileys, who are champions of the style.

CURRENT RELEASE *non-vintage* This is a portentous wine that can be smelled the instant the bottle is opened. The nose has strong muscat and barrel smells with a lactic hint. The palate is deep with raisiny fruit characters on the dry side as opposed to fresh berries. There are mellow wood and heady spirit aromas. It's a full-flavoured style with a stand-alone quality for after a meal.

Buller & Son Liqueur Port

Just what exactly constitutes a liqueur port? In our book it's one that has been concentrated by evaporation while being stored in a wooden cask.

CURRENT RELEASE *non-vintage* The colour is a deep mahogany and the nose is powerful with strong fruit flavours and heady spirit. As would be expected, the flavour is rich and concentrated. There is a ripe, sweet prune flavour and this is followed by clean spirit on a long finish. It's a satisfying style that has great after-dinner potential.

Quality	🍷🍷🍷🍷
Value	★★★★
Grapes	not stated
Region	Rutherglen, Vic.
Cellar	🍾
Alc./Vol.	17.9%
RRP	$20.00

Buller & Son Liqueur Tokay

This is another style that was pioneered by the Rutherglen region in Victoria's north east. It can be very delicate, yet satisfying.

CURRENT RELEASE *non-vintage* The more you taste, the more you find in the blend. The nose has a yeasty, cold-tea-like aroma. The palate is medium-bodied and quite elegant, yet there is an intensity of fruit that lingers. There are caramel, vanilla, malt and toffee flavours that are mixed with some fresh acid. It can be tipped over homemade vanilla ice-cream to great effect.

Quality	🍷🍷🍷🍷
Value	★★★★
Grapes	muscadelle
Region	Rutherglen, Vic.
Cellar	🍾
Alc./Vol.	17.8%
RRP	$20.00

Buller & Son Victoria Madeira

What makes an Australian madeira? In this case it appears to be the grape variety. This is a light, fresh style that is very easy to drink.

CURRENT RELEASE *non-vintage* The colour is a pale tawny with orange highlights. The nose has sweet fruit and delicate wood aromas. There is an attractive toffee flavour on the palate plus a hint of caraway seeds. The finish is clean and lingering with benign spirit. It could be served chilled as a summer afternoon refreshment.

Quality	🍷🍷🍷🍷
Value	★★★★
Grapes	pedro ximinez
Region	northern Victoria
Cellar	🍾
Alc./Vol.	17.8%
RRP	$14.00

Buller & Son Victoria Tawny

Quality	♟♟♟
Value	★★★
Grapes	shiraz; grenache
Region	northern Victoria
Cellar	♦
Alc./Vol.	17.8%
RRP	$14.00

This is a mid-range, drink-now style that has youthful indicators of the things that will follow if the wine is given more time in the cask.

CURRENT RELEASE *non-vintage*   A lighter, almost frisky, style. The nose has lively spirit and hints of dried fruit. The palate is medium-bodied with sweet berry flavours and old wood characters. The finish has length and clean spirit. It's a 'toss-me-back-after-a-big-lunch' style.

Buller & Son Rare Liqueur Tokay

Quality	♟♟♟♟♟
Value	★★★★⊢
Grapes	muscadelle
Region	Rutherglen, Vic.
Cellar	♦
Alc./Vol.	18.5%
RRP	$60.00 (375 ml)

This is grown on vines planted in 1920, basket-pressed and aged in small oak. The oldest component dates back to the early '40s.

CURRENT RELEASE   *non-vintage*   Deep amber/black colour and high viscosity are telltale signs of a very old blend. Classic cold-tea aged tokay bouquet of great complexity. The palate is rich and unctuous with caramel and malt flavours, which seem to linger forever on the finish. Serve with stilton.

Cambewarra Estate Chambourcin Vintage Port

Quality	♟♟♟
Value	★★★
Grapes	chambourcin
Region	Shoalhaven, NSW
Cellar	♦ 2
Alc./Vol.	18.5%
RRP	$18.00

Perhaps this is the way this variety – red wine's answer to verdelho – should be handled. It's difficult to appraise because there's nothing quite like it.

CURRENT RELEASE 1996   The colour is that of a young red wine and the nose is dominated by spirit and licorice. The palate has a medium body with raspberry and cherry flavours. It's sweet, and there is also a hint of raisins. The finish offers some drying tannins. It's hard to predict how it will develop. Drink it after dinner.

Craigmoor Rummy Port

The legend has it the style started in the '30s when there was a shortage of barrels. Old rum casks were used to age some wine and this added a flavour to it.
CURRENT RELEASE *non-vintage*   You can't exactly smell or taste the rum. There are some rancio wood characters and middle-aged fruit aromas on the nose. The medium-bodied palate has simple dried fruit flavours and lively wood. The finish is clean with acid, spirit and a hint of tannin. Use as an after-dinner drink.

Quality	♟♟♟♟
Value	★★★ℓ
Grapes	not stated
Region	Mudgee, NSW
Cellar	▮
Alc./Vol.	17.5%
RRP	$18.00

d'Arenberg Nostalgia Very Old Port

McLaren Vale built its foundations on fortified wines, and although the pendulum has swung away from fortifieds, it's still home to some of the best ports in Australia. Makers d'Arry and Chester Osborn.
CURRENT RELEASE *non-vintage*   A powerful, intensely flavoured port that has a lot of sweetness and concentration from long wood-ageing. The high acid is also a product of extended ageing. The bouquet has vanilla, caramel, raisin and prune flavours with some rancio, and the aftertaste lingers on and on. Goes well with stilton.

Quality	♟♟♟♟
Value	★★★ℓ
Grapes	grenache; shiraz
Region	McLaren Vale, SA
Cellar	▮
Alc./Vol.	18.5%
RRP	$21.00

d'Arenberg Vintage Fortified Shiraz

This unfamiliar title is an attempt to come to grips with the recent wine-labelling agreement between the Australian wine industry and the European Union, which bans the use of regional generic names such as port. This is vintage port reborn.
CURRENT RELEASE 1995   As the dense purple–red colour of this wine suggests, it needs a lot of time in the cellar. The nose has a pungency of violets, pressings-like fruit and floral spirit. There's a lot of heavily extracted tannin leading to a bitter finish, which we can only hope time will moderate. It certainly has plenty of structure. Don't open it yet!

Quality	♟♟♟♟
Value	★★★
Grapes	shiraz
Region	McLaren Vale, SA
Cellar	➥ 5–15+
Alc./Vol.	17.5%
RRP	$21.00

De Bortoli 8-Year-Old Tawny

Quality	🍷🍷🍷🍷
Value	★★★★★
Grapes	not stated
Region	Riverina, NSW & Rutherglen, Vic.
Cellar	🍷
Alc./Vol.	18.5%
RRP	$14.20

De Bortoli's premium fortifieds are some of the most under-priced on the market.

CURRENT RELEASE *non-vintage* This is a textbook Aussie tawny port. It has a medium–deep red–brown colour, and quite mellow walnutty, savoury rancio on the nose together with some oak. The taste is intense and lively and doesn't lack elegance, and there's plenty of aged character throughout. Serve with coffee and a fat cigar.

De Bortoli Old Boys Tawny Port

Quality	🍷🍷🍷🍷
Value	★★★★
Grapes	not stated
Region	Riverina, NSW
Cellar	🍷
Alc./Vol.	18.5%
RRP	$29.00

This is a new port with an arresting packaging job, but we wonder whether the Old Boys theme isn't putting port back in the stuffy old hole it's been trying to climb out of for years.

CURRENT RELEASE *non-vintage* A lovely, genuinely old port with excellent rancio complexity and power to spare. Correct tawny–brown colour; slightly fumey on the nose with a hint of staleness that doesn't mar it; and some heat from the spirit which gives a little astringency to the finish. Good aged concentration and length. Sip with after-dinner mints and coffee.

De Bortoli Show Liqueur Muscat

Quality	🍷🍷🍷🍷🍷
Value	★★★★★
Grapes	red frontignac
Region	Riverina, NSW & Rutherglen, Vic.
Cellar	🍷
Alc./Vol.	18.4%
RRP	$14.20

This is basically a 10-year-old muscat with added complexity from small amounts of both older and younger wines. Blender Steve Warne.

CURRENT RELEASE *non-vintage* **A delicious muscat which is extraordinarily good value for money! It smells of raisins, caramel and plum pudding. The younger component provides lots of fresh muscat fruit and it's well balanced and luscious in the mouth. There is also a lot of aged complexity. It's won a trophy and gold medals in open company. Serve with brandied figs and mascarpone.**

PENGUIN BEST BARGAIN FORTIFIED

Hardys Show Port

In the olden days (cue violins), this used to have a vintage date on the label, which had little to do with the actual age of the wine. HH fondly remembers the 1954; now he's showing his age . . .

CURRENT RELEASE *non-vintage*   This is one of the great tawny ports. It has marvellous depth of genuine aged material in the blend. There are dried citrus peel, nuts, vanilla and malt characters to smell, and a good dollop of rancio, which – coupled with the spirit – results in a classic dry finish. The aftertaste lingers on and on. Perfect for après-ski.

Quality	♟♟♟♟♟
Value	★★★★⊦
Grapes	shiraz; grenache
Region	McLaren Vale, SA
Cellar	🍾
Alc./Vol.	19.5%
RRP	$37.60 Ⓢ

Hardys Tall Ships Tawny Port

Did anyone know what a Tall Ship was before 1988? A fleet of them (square riggers) entered Sydney Harbour on bicentennial day and now we all know them.

CURRENT RELEASE *non-vintage*   A good foil for the Whiskers Blake, this is a contrasting style which is all about rich red-grape characters. Prune and raisin flavours mingle with vanilla and a little aged rancio. It's not overly sweet and the rich fruitcake flavours linger well. Terrific value for money. Serve with dried figs and muscatels.

Quality	♟♟♟♟
Value	★★★★★
Grapes	not stated
Region	McLaren Vale, SA
Cellar	🍾
Alc./Vol.	17.5%
RRP	$10.50 Ⓢ

Hardys Whiskers Blake Tawny Port

Those who aspire to growing a beard could do well to use the legendary Whiskers Blake's as a model. He was an employee of Hardys' Tintara winery many moons ago.

CURRENT RELEASE *non-vintage*   *Wine Spectator* magazine got very excited about this, but then the Yanks have never shown signs of understanding Australian fortifieds. This is a light-coloured, light-bodied and very sweet style, which reminds us more of what winemakers call 'sweet white' than of true Aussie tawny port. Goes well with blue cheeses.

Quality	♟♟♟
Value	★★★
Grapes	not stated
Region	McLaren Vale, Riverland & Barossa Valley, SA
Cellar	🍾
Alc./Vol.	18.0%
RRP	$13.50 Ⓢ

Kay Brothers Centenary Very Old Tawny Port

Quality	?????
Value	★★★★
Grapes	not stated
Region	McLaren Vale, SA
Cellar	1
Alc./Vol.	18.0%
RRP	$25.00 (375 ml)

The base of this limited release came from the solero of the founders Frederick and Hubert Kay. It was released in 1990 on the 100th anniversary of the winery, and is sold in 375-ml bottles.

CURRENT RELEASE *non-vintage*   The colour is a bright, polished walnut wood grain. The nose has strong spirit and rancio characters with a slight milky quality. The palate has intense concentrated dried fruit flavour, and there is solid wood with acid and rancio character on the finish. It's a sippin' style.

Lauriston Show Muscat

Quality	????
Value	★★★✦
Grapes	red frontignac
Region	not stated
Cellar	1
Alc./Vol.	19.5%
RRP	$25.00

This boasts 16 gold medals and eight trophies dating back to 1986. It's blended from wines up to 70 years old.

CURRENT RELEASE *non-vintage*   Old tawny–brown in colour, and although it lacks the aromatic muscat fruit of a good Rutherglen model, it does have intensity, power and mouth-caressing richness. Lots of viscosity and a spirit kick on the finish. Serve with moist, brandied fruitcake.

Lauriston Show Port

Quality	?????
Value	★★★★★
Grapes	not stated
Region	not stated
Cellar	1
Alc./Vol.	19.5%
RRP	$25.00

This is a brand without a home these days. When BRL Hardy owned the Angle Vale winery, home of Barossa Valley Estate, the name Lauriston was coined, apropos of nothing. BRLH kept the brand and these fabulous show fortifieds are all that remain.

CURRENT RELEASE *non-vintage*   This has textbook tawny colour and mature, wood-aged bouquet with good prune and raisin-like fruit beneath liberal aged complexity. Pleasing richness, character and length of aftertaste. Sip with coffee and a good Havana around an open fire.

Lindemans Macquarie Port

Named after Lachlan Macquarie, an early governor of the colony of New South Wales, this is the only premium fortified in the Lindemans range that is still distributed widely. Alas, a sign of the times.

CURRENT RELEASE *non-vintage* This is exactly what you'd hope for in a port of its price. The colour is the correct tawny–red, and the bouquet shows raisiny fruit from younger wines and some rancio from older wines, which come together in a most agreeable way. It's quite sweet and rich on the tongue with some oak character, and makes an excellent after-dinner sipper at a price most people can afford.

Quality	🍷🍷🍷
Value	★★★★
Grapes	grenache; shiraz
Region	mainly Barossa Valley, SA
Cellar	🍷
Alc./Vol.	18.5%
RRP	$12.25

McWilliams Show Series Amontillado

The fortified that came in from the cold. The Riverina isn't supposed to make wines as good as this – just ask the boys down the road at Rutherglen. Drink it and weep, lads . . .

CURRENT RELEASE *non-vintage* The colour is a light gold with tawny robes and green highlights. There are profound wood-age elements on the nose. The palate has nutty rancio characters and a lactic quality. The finish is mellow with a warmth of alcohol and old oak flavours. It has length and complexity – just the thing for game consommé.

Quality	🍷🍷🍷🍷🍷
Value	★★★★★
Grapes	palomino; pedro ximinez
Region	Riverina, NSW
Cellar	🍷
Alc./Vol.	18.5%
RRP	$28.00

McWilliams Show Series Liqueur Muscat

This wine is slightly more elegant than the Rutherglen equivalent, but it's no less powerful. Try smelling your hands after you've poured the wine!

CURRENT RELEASE *non-vintage* There is a deep tawny–amber colour, and the nose has raisin and treacle aromas. The palate remains elegant with a profound depth of flavour. There is a distinct malt extract character as well as dried fruits and peels. The finish is fortified with warming spirit and bracing acid, and is clean non-cloying. Great after dinner with nuts and all the trimmings.

Quality	🍷🍷🍷🍷🍷
Value	★★★★★
Grapes	red frontignac
Region	Riverina, NSW
Cellar	🍷
Alc./Vol.	18.5%
RRP	$28.00

McWilliams Show Series Oloroso

Quality	ŸŸŸŸŸ
Value	★★★★★
Grapes	palomino; pedro ximinez
Region	Riverina, NSW
Cellar	▮
Alc./Vol.	19.5%
RRP	$28.00

They use the traditional grapes in the right climate and don't stint on time in old oak stored in a cool cellar. So why are we surprised when the Riverina delivers the goods?

CURRENT RELEASE *non-vintage* The colour is a bright bronze and the nose has rich rancio plus honey and malt extract. The palate has an impact of sweetness, which is balanced by mellow wood-aged characters and hints of toffee and caramel. The finish shows some fine spirit and bracing acid. It's a beautiful drink with fruitcake.

McWilliams Vintage Port

Quality	ŸŸŸŸ
Value	★★★★
Grapes	not stated
Region	not stated
Cellar	▮ 3
Alc./Vol.	18.5%
RRP	$19.00

It's not common to find a fully developed vintage port matured under cellar conditions. For many consumers it will be a first-time experience and should not be missed.

CURRENT RELEASE 1974 The colour is a tawny–brown, and the nose has nut and orange peel aromas. The palate is medium-bodied, and there are hints of chocolate plus sweet berry fruits. The finish is very dry, introducing a Portuguese style element. The dry finish makes for an excellent after-dinner drink or one to have with soft cheese.

Morris Old Premium Liqueur Muscat

Quality	ŸŸŸŸŸ
Value	★★★★★
Grapes	red frontignac
Region	North East Victoria
Cellar	▮
Alc./Vol.	$18.5%
RRP	$38.00

If ever there was an Australian equivalent of a Kamikaze, this would be the ceremonial drink before the warrior was strapped into the cockpit for the suicide mission. This is a great Australian drink!

CURRENT RELEASE *non-vintage* The colour is a deep polished mahogany and the nose has a strong dried fruit aroma, rancio character and heady spirit. The palate is intense with dried muscat grape flavours, peels and mellow wood flavours. The finish shows evidence of fresh spirit, which adds life to the aged material. It needs to be sipped rather than gulped. Banzai!

Morris Old Premium Liqueur Tokay

There are things that only time can do. This is good ol'
Rutherglen stuff made by allowing the wine to slumber
long in old wooden casks.

CURRENT RELEASE *non-vintage*   The wine shows beautiful balance. It has a deep, lustrous tawny colour and a
nose that smells of cold black tea, rancio and dried fruit
aromas. The palate is intense and complex with aged
wood characters and raisiny fruits. The finish has been
tweaked with some younger material that had high acid.
It's a beautiful drink over and beside homemade vanilla
ice-cream.

Quality	♟♟♟♟♟
Value	★★★★⯪
Grapes	muscadelle
Region	North East Victoria
Cellar	▮
Alc./Vol.	18.0%
RRP	$38.00

Morris Old Tawny Port

This is an affordable style that gives a clue to the splen-
dours of Rutherglen. What it lacks in aged character it
compensates for in spice.

CURRENT RELEASE *non-vintage*   The colour is a bright,
young tawny–brown with hints of orange. The palate
has sweet raisin fruit flavours and there is a mildly lactic
character on the nose. The finish shows a mixture of
wood and acid. It drinks well with coffee and nuts.

Quality	♟♟♟
Value	★★★
Grapes	not stated
Region	Rutherglen, Vic.
Cellar	▮
Alc./Vol.	18.0%
RRP	$15.00

Normans King William Tawny Port

The trend is towards putting an indication of age on
port labels, and there's now a whole flotilla of 10-year-
old ports on the market. This one's 12 years old. Blender
Brian Light.

CURRENT RELEASE *non-vintage*   This has a very light
colour for a port: it's more like an old oloroso sherry
with a medium–light amber hue. The bouquet is lovely:
it's full of rancio aged complexities – oak, old leather
and nuts. The palate has plenty of sweetness and raisin
and prune flavours, which finish dry and with a long
follow-through. Serve with stilton and nuts.

Quality	♟♟♟♟♟
Value	★★★★⯪
Grapes	shiraz; grenache
Region	McLaren Vale, SA
Cellar	▮
Alc./Vol.	18.0%
RRP	$19.00 Ⓢ

Penfolds Club Port

Quality	♟♟♟
Value	★★★
Grapes	shiraz; grenache; mataro
Region	various, SA
Cellar	▮
Alc./Vol.	18.0%
RRP	$9.40 Ⓢ

What will they call port in future, now that the name is banned by the EU on anything but Portuguese wine? A creative thinking American winemaker, Andrew Quady, calls his Starboard.

CURRENT RELEASE *non-vintage* A simple, fruity young port with quite high sweetness and not a great deal of aged character. As a four- to five-year-old youngster, it has the accent on grape flavour and is a fair deal at the price. Good for Dutch courage on the ski slopes.

Penfolds Grandfather Port

Quality	♟♟♟♟♟
Value	★★★★
Grapes	shiraz; mataro
Region	Barossa Valley, SA
Cellar	▮
Alc./Vol.	19.0%
RRP	$85.00

This blend was commenced during the late Jeffrey Penfold Hyland's tenure as chairman of the company. Hence, his signature is on the label. Blender Dean Kraehenbuhl.

CURRENT RELEASE *non-vintage* A great classic Australian tawny, rich and very concentrated in every regard. The colour is a darker shade of tawny and the bouquet is a tremendous complexity of fruitcake, rancio and oak. The palate is towards the richer end of the tawny port spectrum, with truly amazing persistence. Goes well with Christmas cake.

Penfolds Reserve Club Port

Quality	♟♟♟♟
Value	★★★★
Grapes	shiraz; grenache; mataro
Region	various, SA
Cellar	▮
Alc./Vol.	18.0%
RRP	$13.20 Ⓢ

Club is the market leader in premium port, so it was only a matter of time before the canny Southcorp marketers decided to make the name work harder for them. CURRENT RELEASE *non-vintage* It's well worth paying $3 or $4 more than the common-or-garden-variety Club for this. It's a superior wine, and while still quite sweet it has more intensity and wood-aged rancio. There are dried fruit and vanilla flavours and good balance on the palate. As Dean Kraehenbuhl says, the standard Club is for weeknights and the Reserve is for your Saturday night lash-out.

Pennyweight Fino

The name Morris is not a stranger in the fortified wine lexicon. This wine comes from a new region. This is not pennyweight and pound foolish! Maker Stephen N. Morris.

CURRENT RELEASE *non-vintage* This is an excellent summer style that could be served chilled. It has a yeasty, lactic nose. The palate is very clean with austere, crisp fruit that is balanced by clean acid on a lingering finish. It's best served well chilled, and once the bottle has been opened, drink it within six weeks.

Quality	????
Value	★★★★
Grapes	not stated
Region	Beechworth, Vic.
Cellar	▮
Alc./Vol.	17.0%
RRP	$17.00

Peter Lehmann Bin AD 2015

This wine has its drinking date as part of the label. MS says he won't be around to check if the maker was right. So drink up! Maker Lehmann Wine Making Team.

Previous outstanding vintages: every label released

CURRENT RELEASE 1994 Lovely wine with all the good bits and none of the bad. The nose is heady with spirit, ripe fruit and chocolate smells. The palate is rich with ripe blackberry and licorice flavours drizzled over chocolate. There is bold tannin and warming brandy spirit on the finish, which is emphatic and lingering. It has far to go. Try it with soft blue cheese.

Quality	?????
Value	★★★★★
Grapes	shiraz
Region	Barossa Valley, SA
Cellar	➡ 10 years
Alc./Vol.	20.0%
RRP	$20.00 ▮

Pirramimma Liqueur Port

This is one of the few examples of what the Southern Vales can do with fortified wines. Pity the financial return is not sufficient to encourage more. This one took a minimum of 12 years to make.

CURRENT RELEASE *non-vintage* This is a full-flavoured style with strong raisin characters. The colour is a deep tawny, and the nose has sweet ripe fruit and damp wood aromas. The palate is rich and ripe, and the wood adds a mellow tone. The finish is clean with warming spirit. Good after dinner.

Quality	????
Value	★★★★
Grapes	grenache; shiraz
Region	McLaren Vale, SA
Cellar	▮
Alc./Vol.	18.7%
RRP	$25.00

Renmano Cromwell Tawny Port

Quality	?????
Value	★★★★
Grapes	grenache; gordo; shiraz
Region	Murray Valley, SA
Cellar	↑
Alc./Vol.	18.0%
RRP	$8.00

Did Oliver Cromwell drink port? Well, who's going to bother to question – it's just another name.

CURRENT RELEASE *non-vintage* The pedant would argue that this isn't a classic tawny as it's very sweet and has some muscat fruit character, but at $8 who's noticing? It's a very drinkable after-dinner fortified. The raisiny taste lingers well on the finish and it's hard to argue about the price. Try it with gorgonzola and bikkies.

Saint Gregory's Vineyard Private Bin Port

Quality	???
Value	★★★
Grapes	not stated
Region	Apsley, Vic.
Cellar	↑
Alc./Vol.	18.3%
RRP	$15.00

Hands up who knows where Bingalbert South is located? Search us, but this is a new Victorian label from that location. The vineyard was established in 1984 and has 2.4 hectares under vine. Maker Gregory Flynn.

CURRENT RELEASE *non-vintage* This is a bright young ruby style with fresh fruit and lively spirit. The nose is dominated by spirit and the palate has sweet berry characters, soft tannins and a warmth of alcohol. It's an after-dinner style with a dry finish.

Sandalford Sandalera

Quality	?????
Value	★★★★
Grapes	not stated
Region	Swan Valley, WA
Cellar	↑ 1
Alc./Vol.	18.0%
RRP	$25.00 (375 ml)

This is a well-kept secret from the Swan Valley. It's an aged white-wine-based fortified that has been around for yonks – literally. The new packaging looks a treat.

CURRENT RELEASE *non-vintage* There is obviously a well-matured base to this graceful fortified. The colour is a bright tawny–orange and the nose offers sweet fruit, obvious rancio and a slightly lactic aroma. The palate is substantial, with sweet fruit and rich, rancio nutty characters. These have been balanced by some fresh young material that enlivens the finish. Great after-dinner drink with brandy snaps.

Scarpantoni Reserve Tawny

Time has done its work well. This is a small maker's contribution to the realm of fortified wines. It proves you don't have to be a large company to play the game. The major ingredients are time and a co-operative bank manager.

CURRENT RELEASE *non-vintage* The colour is a bright orange with a hint of polished walnut wood grain. The nose has strong spirit and mellow wood-aged characters, and there are some complex raisin flavours with mellow oak. The finish is dry and lingering. It's a good after-dinner drink.

Quality	🍷🍷🍷🍷
Value	★★★★
Grapes	shiraz; grenache
Region	McLaren Vale, SA
Cellar	🍾
Alc./Vol.	18.0%
RRP	$18.00

Scarpantoni Vintage Port

Here's the chance to make a small investment in the future. This wine will make the usual gains in the cellar and it will be interesting to watch the changes.

CURRENT RELEASE 1993 The nose has strong spirit and blackberry aromas. The palate is middleweight with sweet blackberry and mulberry flavours that are matched by some tinder-dry tannins with plenty of grip. Age will not weary them, but they'll become more mellow. Drink after dinner with coffee.

Quality	🍷🍷🍷🍷
Value	★★★★½
Grapes	shiraz; grenache
Region	McLaren Vale, SA
Cellar	🍾 6
Alc./Vol.	18.0%
RRP	$12.50

Seppelt DP 116 Show Amontillado

This is the darling of the Seppelt show sherry set, although these days we aren't allowed to call them sherries. This wine has a formidable show record. Maker James Godfrey.

CURRENT RELEASE *non-vintage* Very complex stuff that is satisfaction in every sip. It has a bright tawny colour, and a profound nose full of rancio, vanilla and citrus peel. The palate is medium-bodied with mellow wood characters. The fruit and wood have coalesced into a mellow opus, and this is enlivened with some freshening material to give zest to the finish. The average age of the blend is 16 years, so sip with reverence.

Quality	🍷🍷🍷🍷🍷
Value	★★★★★
Grapes	palomino
Region	Barossa Valley, SA
Cellar	🍾
Alc./Vol.	22.0%
RRP	$18.50 (500 ml)

Seppelt DP 117 Show Fino

Quality	🍷🍷🍷🍷🍷
Value	★★★★★
Grapes	palomino
Region	Barossa Valley, SA
Cellar	🍶
Alc./Vol.	17.0%
RRP	$18.50 (500 ml)

Bottle freshness is the key to enjoyment. Once the bottle has been broached it should be consumed during the next eight to 10 weeks. Although the wine won't be undrinkable after that time, it loses its edge.

CURRENT RELEASE *non-vintage*   Light, clean and refreshing with great yeast and aldehyde characters. The nose has a hint of cheese and some bready yeast aromas. The palate is suitably austere with some fresh green fruit characters that are tied to crisp acid and discreet wood on a dry finish. It could be served chilled and it's perfect as the prelude to a banquet.

Seppelt DP 38 Show Oloroso

Quality	🍷🍷🍷🍷🍷
Value	★★★★★
Grapes	palomino
Region	Barossa Valley, SA
Cellar	🍶
Alc./Vol.	22.0%
RRP	$18.50 (500 ml)

It's been eight years since this book has been reporting on the outstanding DP (duty paid) fortified series. The only thing left to be said is: drink more, drink often, and make sure it's fresh.

CURRENT RELEASE *non-vintage*   It looks like an old tokay but let's call it a sweet fortified. The grace and balance are exceptional. It retains freshness with an apple character and there is a nutty aldehyde character over a sweet fruitcake nose. The palate is a mixture of walnuts, vanilla and fruitcake with a hint of glacé character. The finish shows some fresh acid and a level of dryness in keeping with the fruit on the palate. Drink with fruitcake.

St Francis Classic Port

Quality	🍷🍷🍷
Value	★★★
Grapes	cabernet sauvignon; shiraz
Region	Southern Vales, SA
Cellar	🍶
Alc./Vol.	18.5%
RRP	$14.50

Here we go again – what makes a wine a classic? There is no indication of the age of this port on the label.

CURRENT RELEASE *non-vintage*   The colour is a deep brick-red with a hint of tawny–brown. The nose is largely spirit with a hint of fruit. The palate is almost lightweight and there are some sweet dried fruit flavours. The finish is clean with warming spirit. Try it after dinner.

Tapestry Old Tawny Port

Don't tell us about wax capsules – they look cute until they are all over the tablecloth, in your hair and glass, and on your lap and you've even managed to cut yourself with a knife trying to peel the bloody thing off. Never mind, the average age of this wine is 10 years.

CURRENT RELEASE *non-vintage* The colour is a light tawny and the nose is dominated by spirit. There is evidence of rancio character on the palate as well as some dried fruit flavours. The finish is a mix of acid and spirit. It's an elegant style with an entertaining hint of spice.

Quality	▼▼▼⸱
Value	★★★⸱
Grapes	not stated
Region	McLaren Vale, SA
Cellar	▮
Alc./Vol.	17.5%
RRP	$19.00

Wirra Wirra Fine Old Tawny

Another bottle to prove the McLaren Vale district is a region for all seasons. This is a distinguished wine of considerable pedigree.

CURRENT RELEASE *non-vintage* This is a finely balanced style with a rich tawny colour and a nose like a mature fruitcake full of nuts and peel. The palate has obvious rancio character with sweet dried fruit flavours, and the finish has attractive freshness that tunes up the mouth. Drink after dinner.

Quality	▼▼▼▼⸱
Value	★★★★★
Grapes	shiraz; grenache; touriga
Region	McLaren Vale, SA
Cellar	▮
Alc./Vol.	18.0%
RRP	$18.00

Woodstock Muscat

After a few drinks with maker/proprietor Scott Collett he will be at pains to tell you 'I am a red wine maker'. He makes the other styles to keep faith with his restaurant customers.

CURRENT RELEASE *non-vintage* The colour is a polished mahogany and the nose has strong spirit aromas plus perfumed muscat fruit aromas with a hint of dried fruit. The full-bodied palate has toffee and sweet dried fruit flavours. The finish has warming spirit and loads of wood. It's good with plum pudding.

Quality	▼▼▼▼
Value	★★★★
Grapes	red frontignac; muscat [sic]
Region	McLaren Vale, SA
Cellar	▮ 1
Alc./Vol.	18.0%
RRP	$15.00

Woodstock Old Tawny Port

Quality	♟♟♟♟♟
Value	★★★★★
Grapes	shiraz; grenache
Region	McLaren Vale, SA
Cellar	🍾 1
Alc./Vol.	20.0%
RRP	$29.00

The roots of this wine hark back to Doug Collett, a devotee of fortified wines and the father of Scott Collett. Doug invested in fortified wine by putting down a base many years ago.

CURRENT RELEASE *non-vintage* The colour is bright orange with hints of polished rosewood. The nose has plenty of rancio character with aged fruit aromas. The palate is super-fine with well-integrated fruit flavours and mellow wood. There is also some lively spice. The finish is mouth-cleansing and refreshing with a hint of clean acid. It's a beautiful blend that should be sipped after a grand meal.

Woodstock Vintage Port

Quality	♟♟♟♟
Value	★★★★
Grapes	grenache
Region	McLaren Vale, SA
Cellar	🍾 4
Alc./Vol.	19.0%
RRP	$11.00

There are a few stalwart companies that indulge themselves in making a vintage port style. This is generally not understood by the modern consumer.

CURRENT RELEASE 1994 The wines keep the faith; there are many typical vintage port elements on the nose. Spirit, blackberry, plums, raspberry and chocolate are all evident. The medium-bodied palate is dominated by sweet raspberry fruit, and there is a warmth of spirit. The finish is dry and clean. Try it after dinner with a cigar.

Yalumba Clock Tower Port

Quality	♟♟♟♟
Value	★★★★
Grapes	not stated
Region	not stated
Cellar	🍾
Alc./Vol.	17.5%
RRP	$10.00 Ⓢ

If there is one symbol of the English contribution to the settlement of the Barossa Valley it would be the Clock Tower at Angaston. A little bit of England.

CURRENT RELEASE *non-vintage* This is a ruby style (although you won't find that description on the label). It's young and quite sweet. There are ripe fruit flavours with a hint of licorice, and the spirit on the finish is warming. Use it to soak raisins and eat and drink same.

Yalumba Director's Special

Quality	♟♟♟♟
Value	★★★★
Grapes	not stated
Region	Barossa Valley, SA
Cellar	▮
Alc./Vol.	17.5%
RRP	$28.00

Not sure about the time-honoured name of this tawny port. Do they serve it in Blue Stone College (where many directors end up)? Perhaps they serve it in Majorca.

CURRENT RELEASE *non-vintage* Wood-aged rancio characters and a tawny colour typecast this blend. The nose also has dried fruit and prunes, and these are the major flavours on the palate. There is acid freshening the finish. It's very fine after a power lunch in the Cayman Islands.

Yalumba Galway Pipe

Quality	♟♟♟♟♟
Value	★★★★⋆
Grapes	not stated
Region	Barossa Valley, SA
Cellar	▮
Alc./Vol.	18.7%
RRP	$28.00

Named after Sir Henry Galway and the down beat in the collectors port movement. Galway port was on ration long before any other fortified, and as with any shortage it left people wanting more.

CURRENT RELEASE *non-vintage* This is a rich, mellow and smooth old tawny port. The colour is a ruddy tawny with lots of rancio character on the nose. The palate has been handcrafted with a judicious use of aged and fresh material. The flavours are many, including raisin, caramel, vanilla, toffee and peel, and all this has some attractive acid on a clean finish. Get out the humidor and beware the Pleasure Police.

Yalumba 10 Year Old Premium Port

Quality	♟♟♟♟
Value	★★★⋆
Grapes	not stated
Region	Barossa Valley, SA
Cellar	▮
Alc./Vol.	18.5%
RRP	$19.00

MS says it's with some affection that Robert Hill-Smith (honcho of Yalumba, Hill-Smith Estate, Heggies, Pewsey Vale, don't-mention-the-war-or-the-corporate-structure) is called the 'head prefect'. He wouldn't be amused at this lavish praise about his ports ('we are not a fortified house').

CURRENT RELEASE *non-vintage* A real tawny with an amber–tawny colour and a sweet nose with aged wood and dried fruit aromas. It's medium-bodied with sweet dried fruit characters and the mellow qualities only wood age can bestow. Pour yourself a glass and settle back with a copy of *The Times*.

The Overflow

This section is an at-a-glance assessment of the wines that simply wouldn't fit in the main body of the text. The wines are in no way diminished in status because they appear in this section. The blunt fact is there were far too many good Australian wines submitted for inclusion in this book.

Reds

	Quality	Value	RRP
Andrew Harris Reserve Shiraz 1995	♟♟♟♟	★★★★	$19.30
Ashwood Grove Shiraz 1994	♟♟♟	★★★	$11.00
Bloodwood Cabernet Merlot 1994	♟♟♟	★★⊦	$18.00
Brown Brothers Family Reserve Cabernet Sauvignon 1988	♟♟♟♟	★★★	$42.75
Brown Brothers Victoria Shiraz 1995	♟♟♟♟	★★★	$16.75
Burge Family Draycott Shiraz 1995	♟♟♟♟	★★★★⊦	$15.00 (cellar door)
Cobaw Ridge Shiraz 1995	♟♟♟♟♟	★★★★	$20.00 (cellar door)
De Bortoli Melba Vineyard Barrel Select 1992	♟♟♟♟♟	★★★⊦	$50.00
De Bortoli Montage Cabernet Merlot 1996	♟♟♟	★★★⊦	$9.00 Ⓢ
De Bortoli Windy Peak Cabernet Shiraz Merlot 1995	♟♟♟♟	★★★⊦	$13.65 Ⓢ
Diamond Valley Blue Label Cabernet Merlot 1993	♟♟♟♟	★★★★⊦	$14.50
Diamond Valley Estate Cabernet 1994	♟♟♟♟	★★★	$20.00
Drayton's Bin 5555 Shiraz 1996	♟♟♟♟	★★★⊦	$14.80 Ⓢ

Draytons Cabernet Merlot 1996	🍷🍷🍷	★★★	$14.80
Draytons Cabernet Sauvignon 1996	🍷🍷🍷	★★★	$14.80
Eyton on Yarra NDC Merlot 1995	🍷🍷🍷🍷½	★★★★	$27.00
Fire Gully Pinot Noir 1996	🍷🍷½	★★★	$16.10
Hardys Tintara Grenache 1995	🍷🍷🍷🍷½	★★★★	$22.00
Hardys Tintara Shiraz 1995	🍷🍷🍷🍷🍷	★★★★	$24.00
Heemskerk Pinot Noir 1995	🍷🍷🍷🍷	★★★	$24.00
Heggies Merlot 1993	🍷🍷🍷	★★½	$19.00
Heggies Pinot Noir 1994	🍷🍷🍷	★★★	$21.00 Ⓢ
Heritage Estate Cabernet Malbec 1995	🍷🍷🍷🍷	★★★★	$14.50
Holm Oak Pinot Noir 1995	🍷🍷🍷	★★★	$19.00
Lake Breeze Cabernet Sauvignon 1995	🍷🍷🍷🍷🍷	★★★★★	$15.00 (cellar door)
Leydens Vale Merlot 1995	🍷🍷🍷	★★½	$18.00
Macedon Ridge Pinot Noir 1994	🍷🍷🍷	★★★	$22.00
Montana Cabernet Sauvignon Merlot 1995	🍷🍷🍷	★★★	$13.00
Moorilla Estate Winter Collection Merlot 1994	🍷🍷🍷🍷	★★★	$40.00
Ninth Island Pinot Noir 1996	🍷🍷🍷	★★½	$17.60
Passing Clouds Merlot Cabernet Franc 1994	🍷🍷🍷½	★★★½	$18.00
Pipers Brook Pellion Pinot Noir 1996	🍷🍷🍷🍷½	★★★½	$24.00
Plunkett Blackwood Ridge Pinot Noir 1996	🍷🍷🍷½	★★★	$19.00
Plunkett Strathbogie Ranges Cabernet Merlot 1995	🍷🍷🍷🍷	★★★★	$20.00
Riddoch Estate Cabernet Shiraz 1995	🍷🍷🍷🍷	★★★★	$14.00
Rochford Premier Pinot Noir 1995	🍷🍷🍷🍷½	★★★½	$28.00
St Matthias Cabernet Merlot 1995	🍷🍷🍷🍷	★★★	$19.00
Tait Wines Vintage Red 1994	🍷🍷🍷½	★★★★	$13.00 (cellar door)
Tatachilla Foundation Shiraz 1995	🍷🍷🍷🍷	★★★½	$24.15

	Quality	Value	RRP
Taylors Clare Valley Classic Dry Red 1996	♟♟♟	★★★	$8.90 ⓢ
Water Wheel Shiraz 1996	♟♟♟♟♟	★★★★★	$14.00
Yalumba Family Reserve Cabernet Sauvignon Merlot 1995	♟♟♟♟	★★★★	$11.00 ⓢ
Yalumba Oxford Landing Cabernet Sauvignon Shiraz 1996	♟♟♟	★★★	$8.00 ⓢ

Whites

	Quality	Value	RRP
Alkoomi Sauvignon Blanc 1997	♟♟♟	★★★	$16.50
Ashbrook Verdelho 1997	♟♟♟	★★★	$17.25
Bethany Barrel Fermented Semillon 1996	♟♟♟	★★★	$15.45
Brown Brothers Noble Riesling 1993	♟♟♟♟	★★★	$32.40
Cobaw Ridge Chardonnay 1996	♟♟♟♟	★★★★	$24.00
Cullen Reserve Sauvignon Blanc Semillon 1996	♟♟♟♟♟	★★★★	$31.00
De Bortoli Gulf Station Riesling 1994	♟♟♟♟	★★★★	$15.50 ⓢ
De Bortoli Windy Peak Chardonnay 1996	♟♟♟	★★★	$13.65 ⓢ
Devil's Lair Chardonnay 1996	♟♟♟♟♟	★★★★	$29.00
Dowie Doole Semillon Sauvignon Blanc 1996	♟♟♟	★★★	$19.35
Fox Creek Verdelho 1997	♟♟♟♟	★★★★	$15.50
Hardys Hunter Ridge Semillon 1996	♟♟♟	★★★	$12.00 ⓢ
Heggies Riesling 1994	♟♟♟	★★★	$15.00
Howard Park Chardonnay 1996	♟♟♟♟♟	★★★★★	$35.00
Karri Grove Verdelho 1997	♟♟♟	★★★	$15.00
Kumeu River Mate's Vineyard Chardonnay 1994	♟♟♟♟♟	★★★★★	$44.00
Kumeu River Sauvignon Semillon 1996	♟♟♟♟	★★★	$28.00
Lakes Folly Chardonnay 1996	♟♟♟♟♟	★★★	$35.00

Lenswood Vineyards Sauvignon Blanc 1996	♟♟♟♟♟	★★★┝	$22.20
Lillydale Vineyards Yarra Gold 1995	♟♟♟♟	★★★★┝	$12.00 (375ml)
Lowe Chardonnay 1996	♟♟♟	★★┝	$20.00
Lowe Unwooded Chardonnay 1997	♟♟♟♟	★★★┝	$17.00
Lowe Unwooded Semillon 1997	♟♟♟	★★★	$16.00
Moss Wood Chardonnay 1996	♟♟♟♟♟	★★★┝	$35.00
Mount Avoca Chardonnay 1996	♟♟♟♟	★★★★	$17.00
Nautilus Marlborough Sauvignon Blanc 1996	♟♟♟	★★★	$16.00
Ninth Island Chardonnay 1996	♟♟♟♟	★★★	$17.60
Pipers Brook Chardonnay 1996	♟♟♟♟	★★★	$28.00
Plunkett Blackwood Ridge Gewurztraminer 1997	♟♟♟♟	★★★┝	$16.00
Portree Chardonnay 1996	♟♟♟♟♟	★★★★	$22.00 (cellar door)
Richard Hamilton Synergy Natural Chardonnay 1997	♟♟♟	★★★	$12.90
Rochecombe Sauvignon Blanc 1996	♟♟♟♟	★★★┝	$17.40
Rosemount New Australian White 1996	♟♟♟	★★★	$10.60 Ⓢ
Rosemount Roxburgh Chardonnay 1995	♟♟♟♟♟	★★★	$45.00
Rosemount Semillon Lightly Oaked 1996	♟♟♟♟	★★★	$16.00
Salitage Unwooded Chardonnay 1996	♟♟♟♟♟	★★★★	$17.70
Salitage Unwooded Chardonnay 1997	♟♟♟♟	★★★	$17.70
Tait Wines Barossa Chardonnay 1996	♟♟♟♟	★★★★	$14.00 (cellar door)
Taylors Classic Dry White 1996	♟♟♟	★★★	$9.70 Ⓢ
Tyrrell's Vat 47 Chardonnay 1996	♟♟♟♟	★★★	$34.00
West End Three Bridges Botrytis Semillon 1996	♟♟♟♟	★★★★	$15.00 (375ml)

	Quality	Value	RRP
Xanadu Chardonnay 1996	🍷🍷🍷½	★★★	$21.00
Yalumba Family Reserve Botrytis Semillon 1995	🍷🍷🍷🍷	★★★★	$12.50 (375ml)
Yalumba Watervale Riesling 1995	🍷🍷🍷🍷	★★★★	$12.00
Yeringa Ridge Reserve Chardonnay 1995	🍷🍷🍷	★★★	$14.00

Sparkling

	Quality	Value	RRP
Charles Sturt University Pinot Noir Chardonnay 1994	🍷🍷🍷🍷	★★★★	$19.00
Delatite Demelza Pinot Noir Chardonnay NV	🍷🍷🍷½	★★★	$21.50 (cellar door)
Glenara Pinot Noir Brut 1995	🍷🍷🍷🍷	★★★★˧	$21.00
Killawarra Brut Champagne NV	🍷🍷🍷½	★★★★	$10.75 Ⓢ
Orlando Trilogy Cuvée Brut NV	🍷🍷🍷½	★★★★	$13.50 Ⓢ
Peter Rumball Sparkling Shiraz NV	🍷🍷🍷🍷	★★★★	$21.00
Peter Rumball The Pink Rosé NV	🍷🍷🍷🍷	★★★★	$21.00
Seaview Glass Mountain Classic Brut NV	🍷🍷½	★★˧	$11.00 Ⓢ
Seppelt Rhymney Sparkling Sauvignon Blanc 1996	🍷🍷🍷½	★★★	$18.00 Ⓢ
Seppelt Salinger 1991	🍷🍷🍷🍷	★★★★˧	$27.00
Seppelt Sunday Creek Pinot Noir Chardonnay NV	🍷🍷🍷	★★★★	$11.60 Ⓢ

Food/Wine Combinations – Reds

Antipasto

Bannockburn Saignée
Brown Brothers Tarrango
Houghton Cygnet
Xanadu Featherwhite

Beef *(air-cured; braised; carpaccio; hamburgers; kebabs; meatballs; pan-fried; pot-roast; roast; rissoles; steak; steak and kidney pie)*

Annie's Lane Shiraz
Arlewood Cabernet Sauvignon
Ashwood Grove Cabernet Sauvignon
Balgownie Estate Cabernet Sauvignon
Balgownie Estate Shiraz
Brokenwood Shiraz
Chain of Ponds Amadeus
Darling Estate Koombahla Cabernet Sauvignon
David Wynn Unwooded Shiraz
De Bortoli Yarra Valley Cabernet Sauvignon
Dromana Estate Pinot Noir
Eyton on Yarra Cabernet Merlot
Garden Gully Shiraz
Gilberts Shiraz
Hardys Bankside Grenache

Heemskerk Pinot Noir
Henschke Keyneton Estate
Jamiesons Run
Jim Barry McRae Wood Cabernet Malbec
JJ McWilliam Cabernet Sauvignon
Knight Granite Hills Shiraz
Leasingham Bin 61 Shiraz
Lindemans Padthaway Cabernet Merlot
Miranda Show Reserve Old Vine Shiraz
Montrose Black Shiraz
Montrose Poet's Corner
Passing Clouds Angel Blend
Paul Osicka Cabernet Sauvignon
Penfolds Bin 28 Kalimna
Penfolds Bin 389 Cabernet Shiraz
Penfolds Bin 407 Cabernet Sauvignon
Penfolds Koonunga Hill Shiraz Cabernet
Petaluma Coonawarra
Redbank Long Paddock Shiraz
Richard Hamilton Hut Block Cabernet
Richard Hamilton Reserve Merlot
Rosemount Mountain Blue Shiraz Cabernet
Salitage Pinot Noir
Seaview Edwards & Chaffey Shiraz
St Francis Coonawarra Cabernet Merlot
Tatachilla Cabernet Sauvignon
Tyrrell's Old Winery Shiraz
Williams Rest Granite Flats Red
Wirra Wirra Original Blend
Wynns Shiraz
Wynns John Riddoch Cabernet Sauvignon
Xanadu Cabernet Sauvignon
Yalumba The Menzies

Casseroles *(beef; cassoulet; goulash; Irish stew; kid; osso bucco; lamb; savoury mince; shepherd's pie; veal)*

Baileys 1920s Block Shiraz
Chestnut Grove Cabernet Merlot
Deakin Estate Grand Prix Shiraz Cabernet
Frankland Estate Isolation Ridge
Jenke Barossa Mourvèdre
Leeuwin Estate Prelude Cabernet Sauvignon
Madfish Bay Premium Dry Red
McWilliams Mount Pleasant Rosehill Shiraz
Morris Shiraz
Peel Estate Shiraz
Penfolds Bin 128 Coonawarra
Penfolds Magill Estate Shiraz
Pirramimma Stocks Hill Shiraz
Rosemount Orange Vineyard Cabernet Sauvignon
Rothbury Estate Reserve Shiraz
Sandalford Margaret River Mount Barker Shiraz
Taltarni Merlot Cabernet
Tatachilla Clarendon Vineyard Merlot
Tisdall Mount Helen Cabernet Merlot

Cheese

Arrowfield Hunter Valley Shiraz
Barwang Shiraz
Brands Original Vineyard Shiraz
Dalfarras Cabernets
Fermoy Estate Cabernet Sauvignon
Frankland Estate Olmo's Reward
Henschke Mount Edelstone Shiraz
Houghton Jack Mann
Howard Park Cabernet Merlot
Jasper Hill Georgia's Paddock Shiraz
Joseph Cabernet Sauvignon Merlot

Leasingham Classic Clare Shiraz
Lindemans Hunter River Steven Vineyard Reserve Shiraz
Mildara Alexanders
Penfolds Bin 707 Cabernet Sauvignon
Phillip Island Wines 'The Nobbies' Pinot Noir
Richmond Grove Coonawarra Cabernet Sauvignon
Rosemount Show Reserve Cabernet Sauvignon
Taltarni Cabernet Sauvignon
Tyrrell's Vat 9 Shiraz Aged Release
Zema Estate Family Selection Cabernet Sauvignon

Chicken

Passing Clouds Pinot Noir
Yalumba Oxford Landing Merlot

Curry

Fern Hill Estate Shiraz
Lindemans Hunter River Shiraz

Duck (confit; Peking; roast; sausages; warm salad; tea-smoked; wild)

Chapel Hill McLaren Vale Shiraz
Crofters Cabernet Merlot
Diamond Valley Estate Pinot Noir
Edwards & Chaffey Cabernet Sauvignon
Elderton Shiraz
Evans & Tate Margaret River Cabernet Sauvignon
Evans Family 'Hillside' Pinot Noir
Freycinet Pinot Noir
Kay Brothers Block 6 Shiraz
Lark Hill Pinot Noir
Lindemans Padthaway Pinot Noir

McWilliams Mount Pleasant Phillip
Mitchell Peppertree Vineyard Shiraz
Paringa Estate Pinot Noir
Saltram Barossa Reserve Shiraz
Tarrawarra Pinot Noir
Yarrawonga Estate

Fish *(fish balls; salmon; soup; tuna)*

Ashton Hills Pinot Noir
Best's Pinot Noir
Bloodwood Rosé of Malbec
Lillydale Vineyards Pinot Noir
Pattersons Pinot Noir
Wolf Blass Pinot Noir

Game *(buffalo; hare; Guinea fowl; goose; mutton bird; pheasant; pigeon; quail; rabbit; squab; venison)*

Bannockburn Pinot Noir
Bindi Pinot Noir
Blue Pyrenees Estate
Bridgewater Mill Millstone Shiraz
Canobolas-Smith Alchemy
Cassegrain Reserve Chambourcin
Cathcart Ridge Shiraz
Clonakilla Cabernet
Coldstream Hills Pinot Noir
d'Arenberg d'Arry's Original Shiraz Grenache
De Bortoli Gulf Station Cabernet Sauvignon
De Bortoli Yarra Valley Pinot Noir
Delatite R J
Elderton Command Shiraz
Fire Gully Cabernets Merlot
Ingoldby Cabernet Sauvignon
Jim Barry McRae Wood Shiraz

Kyeema Shiraz
Leeuwin Estate Art Series Cabernet Sauvignon
Lengs & Cooter Old Vines Shiraz
Leo Buring Barossa Coonawarra Cabernet Sauvignon
Lindemans Pyrus
Majella Shiraz
Mandurang Valley Cabernet Sauvignon
Morris Durif
Murray Robson Wines Cabernet Sauvignon
Pauletts The Quarry
Pegasus Bay Pinot Noir
Pipers Brook Pellion Pinot Noir
Rockford Basket Press Shiraz
Rosemount GSM
Rosemount Reserve Shiraz
Rosemount Shiraz
Sandhurst Ridge Shiraz
Stephen John Shiraz
Tim Adams Shiraz
Tim Adams The Aberfeldy
Tisdall Mount Ida Shiraz
Wendouree Shiraz
West End Three Bridges Cabernet Sauvignon
Wynns Michael Shiraz
Yalumba Octavius
Yalumba Signature Blend
Zema Estate Shiraz

Kangaroo (chargrilled; pan-fried; stewed)

Annie's Lane Cabernet Merlot
Fox Creek Reserve Shiraz
Hardys Eileen Hardy Shiraz
Helm's Cabernet Sauvignon
Leydens Vale Shiraz
Rosabrook Estate Shiraz
Tisdall Mount Ida Shiraz
Vasse Felix Shiraz

Lamb *(BBQ; chops; kebabs; Middle Eastern; mutton; pan-fried fillets; satays; shanks; smoked; spicy; tandoori)*

Alkoomi Frankland River Shiraz
Bethany Shiraz
Brands Laira Cabernet Sauvignon
Brown Brothers Cellar Door Release Graciano
Campbells Bobbie Burns Shiraz
Canobolas-Smith Alchemy Pinot Noir
Cape Mentelle Trinders Cabernet Merlot
Garrett Family Cabernet Merlot
Gralaine Vineyard Merlot
Grant Burge Cameron Vale Cabernet Sauvignon
Grant Burge Filsell Shiraz
Hardys Bankside Shiraz
Hay Shed Hill Cabernet Sauvignon
Idyll Vineyard Cabernet Sauvignon Shiraz
Karina Vineyard Cabernet Merlot
Katnook Cabernet Sauvignon
Katnook Merlot
Leconfield Cabernet
Leeuwin Estate Art Series Pinot Noir
Majella Coonawarra Cabernet
Maritime Estate Cabernet Sauvignon
Mornington Vineyards Estate Pinot Noir
Normans Chais Clarendon Cabernet Sauvignon
Orlando Russet Ridge Cabernet Shiraz Merlot
Orlando St Hugo Cabernet Sauvignon
Penley Estate Phoenix Cabernet Sauvignon
Pierro Cabernets
Plantagenet Cabernet Sauvignon
Riddoch Shiraz
Sandalford Cabernet Sauvignon
Stanley Brothers Thoroughbred Cabernet Sauvignon
Stephen John Cabernet Sauvignon
Stonyfell Metala
Tollana Show Reserve Shiraz
Tollana TR 222 Cabernet Sauvignon

Trentham Estate Cabernet Merlot
Trentham Estate Shiraz
Vasse Felix Cabernet Sauvignon
Winstead Pinot Noir
Woodstock Cabernet Sauvignon
Yarra Burn Cabernets
Yarra Edge Cabernets

Mixed Grill

J J McWilliam Shiraz

Offal *(kidneys; liver; oxtail; pâté; sweetbreads; tripe)*

Cape Mentelle Zinfandel
Cathcart Ridge Shiraz Cabernet Sauvignon
Clonakilla Shiraz Pinot Noir Viognier
Craigmoor Cabernet Sauvignon
Jingalla Reserve Shiraz
Kay's Amery Vineyards Shiraz
Killerby Cabernet Sauvignon
Laurel Bank Pinot Noir
Leconfield Cabernet
Lengs & Cooter Old Bush Vines Grenache
Morris Cabernet Sauvignon
Richard Hamilton Burton's Vineyard Grenache Shiraz
Rymill Merlot Cabernets

Pasta *(meat sauce; tomato sauce)*

Angoves Sarnia Farm Cabernet Sauvignon
Brands Laira Shiraz
Chateau Tahbilk Shiraz
Grevillea Estate Merlot
Knight Granite Hills Cabernet

Miranda High Country Merlot
Mount Ararat Estate Shiraz
Pearson Vineyards Cabernet Franc
Rosemount Shiraz Cabernet
Thomas Mitchell Triple Blend

Pizza & Takeaway Food

All Saints Aleatico
Antipodean
Cooperage Hill Estate Shiraz
Evans & Tate Gnangara Shiraz
Fiddlers Creek Cabernet Shiraz
Knight Granite Hills Shiraz
Koltz Niseda Cabernet
Lindemans Bin 50 Shiraz
Osborne's Harwood Cabernet Sauvignon
Pendarves Pinot Noir
Preece Merlot
Redman Cabernet Sauvignon Merlot
Redman Shiraz
Reynolds Hunter Orange Cabernet Merlot
Reynolds Orange Cabernet Sauvignon
Rosemount Grenache Shiraz
Seaview Shiraz
Vasse Felix Cabernet Merlot Classic Dry Red
Wolf Blass Bilyara Shiraz Grenache
Wolf Blass Brown Label Classic Shiraz
Yarra Ridge Pinot Noir

Pork

Ashwood Grove Cabernet Sauvignon
Brands Laira Cabernet Sauvignon
Brown Brothers Everton
Hungerford Hill Young/Cowra Cabernet Sauvignon

JJ McWilliam Cabernet Sauvignon
Leydens Vale Pinot Noir
Normans Bin C106 Cabernet Sauvignon
Redbank Spud Gully Pinot Noir

Risotto

Crofters Cabernet Merlot
Seville Estate Pinot Noir

Sausages

Cambewarra Estate Cabernet Sauvignon
Deakin Estate Cabernet Sauvignon
Deakin Estate Shiraz
Four Sisters Shiraz
Geoff Weaver Cabernet Merlot
Gramp's Cabernet Merlot
Normans Merlot Bin C108
Plantagenet Omrah Merlot Cabernet

Snails

Best's Pinot Meunier

Soup (oxtail)

Wyndham Estate Bin 888 Cabernet Merlot

Veal

Arrowfield Cowra Merlot

Bannockburn Shiraz
Chain of Ponds Novello Rosso
Gralaine Vineyard Merlot
Headlands Mourvèdre Shiraz
Henschke Abbotts Prayer Merlot Cabernet Sauvignon
Lenton Brae Cabernet Merlot
Mitchelton Print Label
Pankhurst Cabernet Merlot
Preece Cabernet Sauvignon
Redbank Sally's Paddock
Robertson's Well Cabernet Sauvignon
Taltarni Merlot
Yarra Ridge Merlot

Food/Wine Combinations – Whites

Antipasto

Garry Crittenden Bianco
Mildara Vintage Reserve Chardonnay
Tyrrell's Old Winery Chardonnay

Asian Food *(lightly spicy)*

Basedow Late Harvest White Frontignac
Brindabella Hills Riesling
Brown Brothers Gewurztraminer
Deakin Estate Semillon Chardonnay
Forrest Marlborough Riesling
Lillydale Vineyards Gewurztraminer
Lindemans Cawarra Classic Dry White
Rouge Homme Chardonnay

Asparagus

Coldstream Hills Semillon Sauvignon Blanc
Selaks Marlborough Sauvignon Blanc

Cheese (including soufflé)

Cloudy Bay Sauvignon Blanc
De Bortoli Gulf Station Chardonnay
Henschke Lenswood Croft Chardonnay
Lark Hill Chardonnay
Lenton Brae Chardonnay
Lillypilly Sauvignon Blanc
Lindemans Padthaway Classic Release Botrytis Riesling
Mount Avoca Sauvignon Blanc
Plantagenet Sauvignon Blanc
Riddoch Sauvignon Blanc
Rochecombe Sauvignon Blanc
Scarpantoni Botrytis Riesling

Chicken

All Saints Chenin Blanc
Angoves Butterfly Ridge Colombard Chardonnay
Angoves Chardonnay
Antipodean
Azure Bay Sauvignon Blanc Semillon
Basedow Chardonnay
Basedow Riesling
Brokenwood Graveyard Chardonnay
Brown Brothers King Valley Chardonnay
Brown Brothers Semillon
d'Arenberg The Olive Grove Chardonnay
Evans Wine Company Chardonnay
Fermoy Estate Semillon
Galafrey Rhine Riesling
Glenguin Chardonnay
Goona Warra Chardonnay
Houghton Show Reserve White Burgundy
Jimmy Watson's Chardonnay
Lindemans Padthaway Chardonnay
Macedon Ridge Chardonnay

McWilliams Mount Pleasant Verdelho
Mitchell The Growers Semillon Sauvignon Blanc
Montana Gisborne Chardonnay
Mount Avoca Classic Dry White
Mount Horrocks Semillon Sauvignon Blanc
Penfolds Clare Estate Chardonnay
Penfolds Old Vine Barossa Semillon
Poole's Rock Chardonnay
Robertson's Well Chardonnay
Scotchmans Hill Sauvignon Blanc
Seaview Chardonnay
Seville Estate Chardonnay
St Hallett Semillon Select
The Willows Semillon
Wa De Lock Chardonnay
Wirra Wirra Chardonnay
Yalumba Christobel's
Yalumba Family Reserve Chardonnay
Yalumba Reserve Verdelho

Crème Brûlée

d'Arenberg The Noble Riesling
De Bortoli Noble One Botrytis Semillon

Crustaceans (crab; crayfish; prawns; yabbies)

Allandale Hilltops Semillon
Ashton Hills Chardonnay
Bethany The Manse Dry White
Bloodwood Chardonnay
Brands Laira Chardonnay
Brands Laira Riesling
Canobolas-Smith Chardonnay
Cape Jaffa Unwooded Chardonnay
Chain of Ponds Sauvignon Blanc Semillon

Craigmoor Mudgee Chardonnay
De Bortoli Yarra Valley Chardonnay
Geoff Weaver Riesling
Hardys Eileen Hardy Chardonnay
Hay Shed Hill Semillon
Helm's Non-oaked Chardonnay
Hollick Chardonnay
Hunter's Sauvignon Blanc
Karina Vineyard Chardonnay
Lamonts Chenin Blanc
Leeuwin Estate Art Series Chardonnay
Marienberg Reserve Chardonnay
Miranda Rovalley Ridge Grey Series Chardonnay
Petaluma Chardonnay
Pierro Chardonnay
Riddoch Chardonnay
Stefano Lubiana Riesling
Tarrawarra Chardonnay
Tatachilla Sauvignon Blanc
Trentham Estate Chardonnay
Wolf Blass Classic Dry White
Wolf Blass Show Reserve Chardonnay
Yalumba Reserve Viognier
Yarra Ridge Chardonnay

Dim Sum/Sashimi/Sushi/Wontons

Brokenwood Semillon
Brokenwood Unwooded Chardonnay
Devil's Lair Fifth Leg
Penfolds Koonunga Hill Semillon Sauvignon Blanc
Sacred Hill Rhine Riesling

Fish *(battered; cakes; deep-fried; grilled; raw; smoked – all varieties)*

Allandale Hilltops Semillon
Arrowfield Chardonnay Show Reserve
Barwang Chardonnay
Bindi Kostas Rind Chardonnay
Briagolong Estate Chardonnay
Chain of Ponds Riesling
Chapel Hill Eden Valley Riesling
Chapel Hill Reserve Chardonnay
Craiglee Chardonnay
d'Arenberg White Ochre
Dalwhinnie Chardonnay
Diamond Valley Blue Label Chardonnay
Diamond Valley Estate Chardonnay
Eaglehawk Rhine Riesling
Eyton on Yarra Chardonnay
Frankland Estate Rhine Riesling
Glenara Riesling
Heritage Estate Semillon
Hill Smith Estate Chardonnay
Howard Park Riesling
Jamiesons Run Chardonnay
Jeanneret Riesling
Leasingham Bin 7 Rhine Riesling
Leconfield Twelve Rows Riesling
Leo Buring Clare Valley Semillon
Leo Buring Leonay Eden Valley Riesling
Leo Buring Leonay Watervale Riesling
McWilliams Eden Valley Rhine Riesling
Meadowbank Chardonnay
Mornington Vineyards Chardonnay
Mount Horrocks Unwooded Chardonnay
Mount Hurtle Sauvignon Blanc
Penfolds Bottle Aged Riesling
Peter Lehmann Chardonnay
Peter Lehmann Riesling

Peter Lehmann Semillon Chardonnay
Pewsey Vale Riesling
Pierro Semillon Sauvignon Blanc
Rothbury Estate Cowra Chardonnay
Stephen John Pedro Ximinez
Tyrrell's Lost Block Semillon
Tyrrell's Vat 1 Semillon
Woodstock Chardonnay
Yalumba Eden Valley Family Reserve Riesling
Yalumba Oxford Landing Chardonnay
Yarra Burn Bastard Hill Chardonnay

Fruit (including prosciutto melone)

Brokenwood Gewurztraminer Jelka Vineyard
Evans Family Pinchem Chardonnay
Freycinet Chardonnay
Glenguin Chardonnay
Koppamurra Botrytis Riesling
Lillypilly Tramillon
Plantagenet Omrah Unoaked Chardonnay
Rosemount Giant's Creek Noble Semillon
Rymill June Traminer
Tollana Botrytis Riesling
Trentham Estate Noble Taminga

Octopus/Calamari

Andrew Garrett Chardonnay
Grevillea Estate Unwooded Chardonnay
Houghton Show Reserve Verdelho
Knight Granite Hills Chardonnay
Krondorf Semillon
Madfish Bay Western Australian Premium Dry White
Montara Riesling
Peter Lehmann Semillon

Rosemount Show Reserve Chardonnay
Tisdall Mount Helen Chardonnay
Westfield Bronzewing Estate Chardonnay

Offal

Best's Riesling
Bridgewater Mill Chardonnay
Brookland Valley Chardonnay
Geoff Weaver Chardonnay
Geoff Weaver Riesling
Leasingham Bin 37 Chardonnay

Pasta

Geoff Weaver Sauvignon Blanc
Katnook Sauvignon Blanc
Murrindindi Chardonnay
Scarpantoni Chardonnay
Tatachilla Keystone Semillon Chardonnay
Taylors Chardonnay

Pâté

De Bortoli Windy Peak Spatlese Riesling
Green Point Chardonnay
Leo Buring Late Picked Riesling
Orlando St Hillary Chardonnay
Pepper Tree Traminer
West End Three Bridges Chardonnay

Pizza

Glenguin Unwooded Chardonnay
Montara Chasselas

Pork

Abbey Vale Chardonnay
Allandale Chardonnay
Bannockburn Chardonnay
Cape Mentelle Chardonnay
Miranda Golden Botrytis
Moondah Brook Chardonnay
Sandalford Mount Barker Margaret River Chardonnay
Smithbrook Chardonnay
Wolf Blass Show Reserve Chardonnay

Pudding (summer)

All Saints Late Harvest Semillon
Woodstock Botrytis Sweet White

Quiche

Brown Brothers King Valley Riesling
De Bortoli Gulf Station Chardonnay
Penfolds Koonunga Hill Chardonnay
Pepper Tree Semillon Sauvignon Blanc
Taylors Riesling

Risotto/Paella

Bulletin Place Chardonnay
Rosabrook Estate Semillon Sauvignon Blanc

Salad

Banrock Station Unwooded Chardonnay
Brokenwood Cricket Pitch
Cambewarra Estate Chardonnay
Fermoy Estate Chardonnay
Helm's Rhine Riesling Classic Dry
Hollick Unwooded Chardonnay
Lillydale Vineyards Classic Dry White
Lindemans Hunter River Semillon
Miranda High Country Sauvignon Blanc
Moondah Brook Verdelho
Plantagenet Riesling
Richmond Grove Traminer Riesling
Rosemount Yarra Valley Chardonnay
Seaview Edwards & Chaffey Chardonnay
Vasse Felix Classic Dry White
Xanadu Semillon

Sausages

Rymill March Traminer

Shellfish (mussels; oysters; pipis; scallops)

Allandale Hilltops Semillon
Allandale Riesling
Bowen Estate Chardonnay
Brown Brothers Family Reserve Riesling

Brown Brothers Whitlands Sauvignon Blanc
Craig Avon Vineyard Chardonnay
De Bortoli Windy Peak Rhine Riesling
Deakin Estate Alfred Chardonnay
Evans & Tate Chardonnay
Forrest Sauvignon Blanc
Glenguin Semillon
Goodchild Rhine Riesling
Hardys Adelaide Hills Sauvignon Blanc
Hardys Sir James Chardonnay
Heggies Chardonnay
Houghton Chablis
Hungerford Hill Tumbarumba Sauvignon Blanc
Jim Barry Watervale Riesling
Koppamurra Riesling
Lillydale Vineyards Chardonnay
Montrose Chardonnay
Moss Brothers Sauvignon Blanc
Moss Brothers Semillon
Penfolds Adelaide Hills Trial Bin Chardonnay
Pewsey Vale Sauvignon Blanc
Scotchmans Hill Chardonnay
Seaview Riesling
Shingle Peak Pinot Gris
Shottesbrooke Chardonnay
Stephen John Riesling
Stonier's Chardonnay
Taylors Clare Valley Riesling
Vasse Felix Semillon
Wirra Wirra Sauvignon Blanc
Wynns Chardonnay
Yalumba Family Reserve Chardonnay
Yarra Burn Sauvignon Blanc Semillon

Tripe

Cape Mentelle Semillon Sauvignon Blanc

Turkey

Carlyle Estate Chardonnay
Coldstream Hills Chardonnay
David Traeger Verdelho
Leeuwin Prelude Chardonnay
Lenswood Vineyards Chardonnay
Leydens Vale Riesling
Mountadam Chardonnay
Palmers Chardonnay
Stonier's Reserve Chardonnay
Westfield Bronzewing Estate Verdelho

Veal

Annie's Lane Semillon
Eyton on Yarra Chardonnay
McWilliams Maurice O'Shea Chardonnay
Rosemount Roxburgh Chardonnay

Vegetables

Banrock Station Semillon Chardonnay
Barratt Chardonnay
Dalfarras Sauvignon Blanc
Dalfarras Unoaked Chardonnay
De Bortoli Yarra Valley Semillon
Deakin Estate Chardonnay
Fox Creek Sauvignon Blanc
Hanging Rock The Jim Jim Sauvignon Blanc

Houghton Chardonnay Verdelho
Houghton White Burgundy
Pattersons Unwooded Chardonnay
Pipers Brook Pinot Gris
Taltarni Sauvignon Blanc
Twin Islands Sauvignon Blanc
Voyager Estate Semillon

Wine Terms

The following are commonly used winemaking terms.

ACID   There are many acids that occur naturally in grapes and it's in the winemaker's interest to retain the favourable ones because these promote freshness and longevity.

AGRAFE   A metal clip used to secure champagne corks during secondary bottle fermentation.

ALCOHOL   Ethyl alcohol (C_2H_5OH) is a by-product of fermentation of sugars. It's the stuff that makes people happy and it adds warmth and texture to wine.

ALCOHOL BY VOLUME (A/V)   The measurement of the amount of alcohol in a wine. It's expressed as a percentage, e.g. 13.0% A/V means there is 13.0% pure alcohol as a percentage of the total volume.

ALDEHYDE   An unwanted and unpleasant organic compound formed between acid and alcohol by oxidation. It's removed by sulfur dioxide.

ALLIER   A type of oak harvested in the French forest of the same name.

APERITIF   A wine that stimulates the appetite.

AROMATIC   A family of grape varieties that have a high terpene content. Riesling and gewurztraminer are examples, and terpenes produce their floral qualities.

AUTOLYSIS   A Vegemite or fresh-baked bread taste and smell imparted by spent yeast cells in sparkling wines.

BACK BLEND   To add unfermented grape juice to wine or to add young wine to old wine in fortifieds.

BARREL FERMENTATION   The process of fermenting a red or white wine in a small barrel, thereby adding a creamy texture and toasty or nutty characters, and better integrating the wood and fruit flavours.

BARRIQUE   A 225-litre barrel.

BAUMÉ   The measure of sugar in grape juice used to estimate potential alcohol content. It's usually expressed as a degree, e.g. 12 degrees baumé juice will produce approximately 12.0% A/V if it's fermented to dryness. The alternative brix scale is approximately double baumé and must be divided by 1.8 to estimate potential alcohol.

BENTONITE   A fine clay (drillers mud) used as a clarifying (fining) agent.

BLEND   A combination of two or more grape varieties and/or vintages. *See also* Cuvée

BOTRYTIS CINEREA   A fungus that thrives on grape vines in humid conditions and sucks out the water of the grapes thereby concentrating the flavour. Good in white wine but not so good in red. (There is also a loss in quantity.)

BREATHING   Uncorking a wine and allowing it to stand for a couple of hours before serving. This introduces oxygen and dissipates bottle odours. Decanting aids breathing.

BRIX   *see* Baumé

BRUT   The second lowest level of sweetness in sparkling wine; it does not mean there is no added sugar.

BUSH VINE   Although pruned the vine is self-supporting in a low-to-the-ground bush. (Still common in the Barossa Valley.)

CARBONIC MACERATION   Fermentation in whole (uncrushed) bunches. This is a popular technique in Beaujolais. It produces bright colour and softer tannins.

CHARMAT PROCESS   A process for making sparkling wine where the wine is fermented in a tank rather than in a bottle.

CLONE (CLONAL)   A recognisable subspecies of vine within a varietal family, e.g. there are numerous clones of pinot noir and these all have subtle character differences.

COLD FERMENTATION   (Also Controlled Temperature Fermentation) Usually applied to white wines where the ferment is kept at a low temperature (10–12 degrees Centigrade).

CORDON   The arms of the trained grapevine that bear the fruit.

CORDON CUT   A technique of cutting the fruit-bearing arms and allowing the berries to dehydrate to concentrate the flavour.

CRUSH   Crushing the berries to liberate the free-run juice (*q.v.*). Also used as an expression of a wine company's output: 'This winery has a 1000-tonne crush'.

CUVÉE   A Champagne term meaning a selected blend or batch.

DISGORGE   The process of removing the yeast lees from a sparkling wine. It involves freezing the neck of the bottle and firing out a plug of ice and yeast. The bottle is then topped up and recorked.

DOWNY MILDEW   A disease that attacks vine leaves and fruit. It's associated with humidity and lack of air circulation.

DRIP IRRIGATION   An accurate way of watering a vineyard. Each vine has its own dripper and a controlled amount of water is applied.

DRYLAND VINEYARD   A vineyard that has no irrigation.

ESTERS   Volatile compounds that can occur during fermentation or maturation. They impart a distinctive chemical taste.

FERMENTATION   The process by which yeast converts sugar to alcohol with a by-product of carbon dioxide.

FINING   The process of removing solids from wine to make it clear. There are several methods used.

FORTIFY   The addition of spirit to increase the amount of alcohol in a wine.

FREE-RUN JUICE   The first juice to come out of the press or drainer (as opposed to pressings).

GENERIC   Wines labelled after their district of origin rather than their grape variety, eg. Burgundy, Chablis, Champagne etc. These terms can no longer legally be used on Australian labels. *Cf.* Varietal.

GRAFT   Changing the nature/variety of a vine by grafting a different variety on to a root stock.

IMPERIAL   A 6-litre bottle (contains eight 750-ml bottles).

JEROBOAM   A 4.5-litre champagne bottle.

LACCASE   A milky condition on the surface of red wine caused by noble rot. The wine is usually pasteurised.

LACTIC ACID   One of the acids found in grape juice; as the name suggests, it's milky and soft.

LACTOBACILLUS   A micro-organism that ferments carbohydrates (glucose) or malic acid to produce lactic acid.

LEES   The sediment left after fermentation. It consists mainly of dead yeast cells.

MALIC ACID   One of the acids found in grape juice. It has a hard/sharp taste like a Granny Smith apple.

MALOLACTIC FERMENTATION   A secondary fermentation process that converts malic acid into lactic acid. It's encouraged in red wines when they are in barrel. If it occurs after bottling, the wine will be fizzy and cloudy.

MERCAPTAN Ethyl mercaptan is a sulfur compound with a smell like garlic, burnt rubber or asparagus water.

MÉTHODE CHAMPENOISE The French method for producing effervescence in the bottle; a secondary fermentation process where the carbon dioxide produced is dissolved into the wine.

METHOXYPYRAZINES Substances that give sauvignon blanc and cabernet sauvignon that added herbaceousness when the grapes aren't fully ripe.

MOUSSE The froth or head on sparkling wine.

MUST *see* Free-run juice

NOBLE ROT *see* Botrytis cinerea

NON-VINTAGE A wine that is a blend of two or more years.

OAK The least porous wood, genus *Quercus*, and used for wine storage containers.

OENOLOGY The science of winemaking.

ORGANIC VITICULTURE Growing grapes without the use of pesticides, fungicides or chemical fertilizers. Certain chemicals, e.g. copper sulfate, are permitted.

ORGANIC WINES Wines made from organically grown fruit without the addition of chemicals.

OXIDATION Browning caused by excessive exposure to air.

pH The measure of the strength of acidity. The higher the pH the higher the alkalinity and the lower the acidity. Wines with high pH values should not be cellared.

PHENOLICS A group of chemical compounds which includes the tannins and colour pigments of grapes. A white wine described as 'phenolic' has an excess of tannin, making it taste coarse.

PHYLLOXERA A louse that attacks the roots of a vine, eventually killing the plant.

PIGEAGE To foot-press the grapes.

PRESSINGS The juice extracted by applying pressure to the skins after the free-run juice has been drained.

PRICKED A wine that is spoilt and smells of vinegar, due to excessive volatile acidity. *Cf.* Volatile.

PUNCHEON A 500-litre barrel.

RACKING Draining off wine from the lees or other sediment to clarify it.

SAIGNÉE French for bleeding: the winemaker has run off part of the juice of a red fermentation to concentrate what's left.

SKIN CONTACT   Allowing the free-run juice to remain in contact with the skins; in the case of white wines, usually for a very short time.

SOLERO SYSTEM   Usually a stack of barrels used for blending maturing wines. The oldest material is at the bottom and is topped up with younger material from the top barrels.

SOLIDS   Minute particles suspended in a wine.

SULFUR DIOXIDE (SO₂)   (Code 220) A chemical added to a wine as a preservative and a bactericide.

SUR LIE   Wine that has been kept on lees and not racked or filtered before bottling.

TACHÉ   A French term that means to stain, usually by the addition of a small amount of red wine to sparkling wine to turn it pink.

TANNIN   A complex substance derived from skins, pips and stalks of grapes as well as the oak casks. It has a preservative function and imparts dryness and grip to the finish.

TERROIR   Arcane French expression which describes the complete growing environment of the vine, including climate, aspect, soil, etc., and the direct effect this has on the character of its wine.

VARIETAL   An industry-coined term used to refer to a wine by its grape variety, e.g. 'a shiraz'. *Cf.* Generic.

VÉRAISON   The moment when the grapes change colour and gain sugar.

VERTICAL TASTING   A tasting of consecutive vintages of one wine.

VIGNERON   A grapegrower or vineyard worker.

VINEGAR   Acetic acid produced from fruit.

VINIFY   The process of turning grapes into wine.

VINTAGE   The year of harvest, and the produce of a particular year.

VOLATILE   Excessive volatile acids in a wine.

YEAST   The micro-organism that converts sugar into alcohol.

Tasting Terms

The following terms refer to the sensory evaluation of wine.

AFTERTASTE The taste (sensation) after the wine has been swallowed. It's usually called the finish.

ASTRINGENT (ASTRINGENCY) Applies to the finish of a wine. Astringency is caused by tannins that produce a mouth-puckering sensation and coat the teeth with dryness.

BALANCE 'The state of . . . '; the harmony between components of a wine.

BILGY An unfortunate taste like the bilge of a ship. Usually caused by mouldy old oak.

BITTERNESS A sensation detected at the back of the tongue. It's not correct in wine but is desirable in beer.

BOUQUET The aroma of a finished or mature wine.

BROAD A wine that lacks fruit definition; usually qualified as soft or coarse.

CASSIS A blackcurrant flavour common in cabernet sauvignon. It refers to a liqueur produced in France.

CHALKY An extremely dry sensation on the finish.

CHEESY A dairy character sometimes found in wine, particularly sherries.

CIGAR BOX A smell of tobacco and wood found in cabernet sauvignon.

CLOUDINESS A fault in wine that is caused by suspended solids that make it look dull.

CLOYING Excessive sweetness that clogs the palate.

CORKED Spoiled wine that has reacted with a tainted cork, and smells like wet cardboard. (The taint is caused by trichloroanisole.)

CREAMY The feeling of cream in the mouth, a texture.

CRISP Clean acid on the finish of a white wine.

DEPTH   The amount of fruit on the palate.

DRY   A wine that does not register sugar in the mouth.

DULL   Pertaining to colour; the wine is not bright or shining.

DUMB   Lacking nose or flavour on the palate.

DUSTY   Applies to a very dry tannic finish; a sensation.

EARTHY   Not as bad as it sounds, this is a loamy/mineral character that can add interest to the palate.

FINESSE   The state of a wine. It refers to balance and style.

FINISH   *see* Aftertaste

FIRM   Wine with strong, unyielding tannins.

FLABBY   Wine with insufficient acid to balance ripe fruit flavours.

FLESHY   Wines of substance with plenty of fruit.

FLINTY   A character on the finish that is akin to sucking dry creek pebbles.

GARLIC   *see* Mercaptan (in Wine Terms)

GRASSY   A cut-grass odour, usually found in semillon and sauvignon blancs.

GRIP   The effect on the mouth of tannin on the finish; a puckering sensation.

HARD   More tannin or acid than fruit flavour.

HERBACEOUS   Herbal smells or flavour in wine.

HOLLOW   A wine with a lack of flavour in the middle palate.

HOT   Wines high in alcohol that give a feeling of warmth and a slippery texture.

IMPLICIT SWEETNESS   A just detectable sweetness from the presence of glycerin (rather than residual sugar).

INKY   Tannate of iron present in a wine which imparts a metallic taste.

INTEGRATED (WELL)   The component parts of a wine fit together without gaps or disorders.

JAMMY   Ripe fruit that takes on the character of stewed jam.

LEATHERY   A smell like old leather, not necessarily bad if it's in balance.

LENGTH (LONG)   The measure of the registration of flavour in the mouth. (The longer the better.)

LIFTED   The wine is given a lift by the presence of either volatile acid or wood tannins, e.g. vanillian oak lift.

LIMPID   A colour term usually applied to star-bright white wine.

MADEIRISED   Wine that has aged to the point where it tastes like a madeira.

MOULDY   Smells like bathroom mould; dank.

MOUTH-FEEL   The sensation the wine causes in the mouth; a textural term.

MUSTY   Stale, flat, out-of-condition wine.

PEPPER   A component in either the nose or the palate that smells or tastes like cracked pepper.

PUNGENT   Wine with a strong nose.

RANCIO   A nutty character found in aged fortifieds that is imparted by time on wood.

RESIDUAL SUGAR   The presence of unfermented grape sugar on the palate; common in sweet wines.

ROUGH   Unpleasant, aggressive wine.

ROUND   A full-bodied wine with plenty of mouth-feel (*q.v.*).

SAPPY   A herbaceous character that resembles sap.

SHORT   A wine lacking in taste and structure. *See also* Length

SPICY   A wine with a high aromatic content; spicy character can also be imparted by wood.

STALKY   Exposure to stalks, e.g. during fermentation. Leaves a bitter character in the wine.

TART   A lively wine with a lot of fresh acid.

TOASTY   A smell of cooked bread.

VANILLAN   The smell and taste of vanilla beans; usually imparted by oak ageing.

VARIETAL   Refers to the distinguishing qualities of the grape variety used in the wine.

Directory of Wineries

AFFLECK VINEYARD
RMB 244
Millynn Rd (off Gundaroo
  Rd)
Bungendore NSW 2651
(06) 236 9276

ALAMBIE WINES
Campbell Ave
Irymple Vic. 3498
(03) 5024 6800
fax (03) 5024 6605

ALKOOMI
Wingeballup Rd
Frankland WA 6396
(08) 9855 2229
fax (08) 9855 2284

ALL SAINTS ESTATE
All Saints Rd
Wahgunyah Vic. 3687
(03) 6033 1922
fax (03) 6033 3515

ALLANDALE
Lovedale Rd
Pokolbin NSW 2320
(049) 90 4526
fax (049) 90 1714

ALLANMERE
Lovedale Rd
Pokolbin NSW 2320
(049) 30 7387

AMBERLEY ESTATE
Wildwood & Thornton Rds
Yallingup WA 6282
(08) 9755 2288
fax (08) 9755 2171

ANDERSON WINERY
Lot 13 Chiltern Rd
Rutherglen Vic. 3685
(03) 6032 8111

ANDREW GARRETT
Kangarilla Rd
McLaren Vale SA 5171
(08) 8323 8853
fax (08) 8323 8550

ANGOVES
Bookmark Ave
Renmark SA 5341
(08) 8595 1311
fax (08) 8595 1583

ANTCLIFFE'S CHASE
RMB 4510
Caveat
via Seymour Vic. 3660
(03) 5790 4333

ARROWFIELD
Denman Rd
Jerry's Plains NSW 2330
(065) 76 4041
fax (065) 76 4144

ASHTON HILLS
Tregarthen Rd
Ashton SA 5137
(08) 8390 1243
fax (08) 8390 1243

ASHWOOD GROVE
(not open to public)
(03) 5030 5291

AVALON
RMB 9556
Whitfield Rd
Wangaratta Vic. 3677
(03) 5729 3629

BABICH WINES
Babich Rd
Henderson NZ
(09) 833 8909

BAILEYS
Taminick Gap Rd
Glenrowan Vic. 3675
(03) 5766 2392
fax (03) 5766 2596

BALDIVIS ESTATE
Lot 165 River Rd
Baldivis WA 6171
(09) 525 2066
fax (09) 525 2411

BALGOWNIE
Hermitage Rd
Maiden Gully Vic. 3551
(03) 5449 6222
fax (03) 5449 6506

BANNOCKBURN
Midland Hwy
Bannockburn Vic. 3331
(03) 5281 1363
fax (03) 5281 1349

BANROCK STATION
(*see* Hardys)

BAROSSA SETTLERS
Trial Hill Rd
Lyndoch SA 5351
(08) 8524 4017

BAROSSA VALLEY ESTATE
Heaslip Rd
Angle Vale SA 5117
(08) 8284 7000
fax (08) 8284 7219

BARRATT
(not open to public)
PO Box 204
Summertown SA 5141
(08) 8390 1788
fax (08) 8390 1788

BARWANG
(*see* McWilliam's)

BASS PHILLIP
Tosch's Rd
Leongatha South Vic. 3953
(03) 5664 3341

BERRI ESTATES
Sturt Hwy
Glossop SA 5344
(08) 8582 0300
fax (08) 8583 2224

BESTS GREAT WESTERN
Western Hwy
Great Western Vic. 3377
(03) 5356 2250
fax (03) 5356 2430

BETHANY
Bethany Rd
Bethany
via Tanunda SA 5352
(08) 8563 2086
fax (08) 8563 2086

BIANCHET
187 Victoria Rd
Lilydale Vic. 3140
(03) 9739 1779
fax (03) 9739 1277

BINDI
(not open to public)
145 Melton Rd
Gisborne Vic. 3437
(03) 5428 2564
fax (03) 5428 2564

BIRDWOOD ESTATE
PO Box 194
Birdwood SA 5234
(08) 8263 0986

BLACKJACK VINEYARD
Calder Hwy
Harcourt Vic. 3452
(03) 5474 2528
fax (03) 5475 2102

BLEASDALE
Wellington Rd
Langhorne Creek SA 5255
(08) 8537 3001

BLEWITT SPRINGS
Recreational Rd
McLaren Vale SA 5171
(08) 8323 8689

BLOODWOOD ESTATE
4 Griffin Rd
via Orange NSW 2800
(063) 62 5631

BLUE PYRENEES ESTATE
Vinoca Rd
Avoca Vic. 3467
(03) 5465 3202
fax (03) 5465 3529

BOSTON BAY
Lincoln Hwy
Port Lincoln SA 5605
(08) 8684 3600

BOTOBOLAR
Botobolar La.
PO Box 212
Mudgee NSW 2850
(063) 73 3840
fax (063) 73 3789

BOWEN ESTATE
Penola–Naracoorte Rd
Coonawarra SA 5263
(08) 8737 2229
fax (08) 8737 2173

BOYNTONS OF BRIGHT
Ovens Valley Hwy
Porepunkah Vic. 3740
(03) 5756 2356

BRANDS LAIRA
Naracoorte Hwy
Coonawarra SA 5263
(08) 8736 3260
fax (08) 8736 3208

BREMERTON LODGE
Strathalbyn Rd
Langhorne Creek SA 5255
(08) 8537 3093
fax (08) 8537 3109

BRIAGOLONG ESTATE
118 Boisdale St
Maffra Vic. 3860
(03) 5147 2322
fax (03) 5147 2400

BRIAR RIDGE
Mount View
Mt View NSW 2321
(049) 90 3670
fax (049) 98 7802

BRIDGEWATER MILL
Mount Barker Rd
Bridgewater SA 5155
(08) 8339 3422
fax (08) 8339 5253

BRINDABELLA HILLS
Woodgrove Cl.
via Hall ACT 2618
(06) 230 2583

BROKENWOOD
McDonalds Rd
Pokolbin NSW 2321
(049) 98 7559
fax (049) 98 7893

BROOK EDEN
Adams Rd
Lebrina Tas. 7254
(03) 6395 6244

BROOKLAND VALLEY
Caves Rd
Willyabrup WA 6284
(08) 9755 6250
fax (08) 9755 6214

BROWN BROTHERS
Meadow Crk Rd (off the
  Snow Rd)
Milawa Vic. 3678
(03) 5720 5500
fax (03) 5720 5511

BROWNS OF PADTHAWAY
PMB 196
Naracoorte SA 5271
(08) 8765 6063
fax (08) 8765 6083

BULLER & SONS, R L
Calliope
Three Chain Rd
Rutherglen Vic. 3685
(03) 5037 6305

BULLER (RL) & SON
Murray Valley Hwy
Beverford Vic. 3590
(03) 5037 6305
fax (03) 5037 6803
fax (03) 6032 8005

BURGE FAMILY WINEMAKERS
Barossa Hwy
Lyndoch SA 5351
(08) 8524 4644
fax (08) 8524 4444

BURNBRAE
Hargraves Rd
Erudgere
Mudgee NSW 2850
(063) 73 3504
fax (063) 73 3601

CALAIS ESTATE
Palmers La.
Pokolbin NSW 2321
(049) 98 7654
fax (049) 98 7813

CALLATOOTA ESTATE
Wybong Rd
Wybong NSW 2333
(065) 47 8149

CAMBEWARRA ESTATE
520 Illaroo Rd
Cambewarra NSW 2541
(02) 4446 0170
fax (02) 4446 0170

CAMPBELLS
Murray Valley Hwy
Rutherglen Vic. 3685
(060) 32 9458
fax (060) 32 9870

CANOBOLAS–SMITH
Cargo Rd
Orange NSW 2800
(063) 65 6113

CAPE CLAIRAULT
via Caves Rd
or Bussell Hwy
CMB Carbunup River
 WA 6280
(08) 9755 6225
fax (08) 9755 6229

CAPE MENTELLE
Wallcliffe Rd
Margaret River WA 6285
(08) 9757 3266
fax (08) 9757 3233

CAPELVALE
Lot 5
Capel North West Rd
Capel WA 6271
(08) 9727 2439
fax (08) 9727 2164

CAPERCAILLIE
Londons Rd
Lovedale NSW 2325
(02) 4990 2904
fax (02) 4991 1886

CASSEGRAIN
Fern Bank Ck Rd
Port Macquarie NSW 2444
(065) 83 7777
fax (065) 84 0353

CASTLE ROCK ESTATE
Porongurup Rd
Porongurup WA 6324
(08) 9853 1035
fax (08) 9853 1010

CHAIN OF PONDS
Gumeracha Cellars
PO Box 365
Main Rd
Gumeracha SA 5233
(08) 8389 1415
fax (08) 8336 2462

CHAMBERS ROSEWOOD
Corowa–Rutherglen Rd
Rutherglen Vic. 3685
(03) 6032 8641
fax (03) 6032 8101

CHAPEL HILL
Chapel Hill Rd
McLaren Vale SA 5171
(08) 8323 8429
fax (08) 8323 9245

CHARLES CIMICKY
Gomersal Rd
Lyndoch SA 5351
(08) 8524 4025
fax (08) 8524 4772

CHARLES MELTON
Krondorf Rd
Tanunda SA 5352
(08) 8563 3606
fax (08) 8563 3422

**CHARLES STURT
UNIVERSITY**
Boorooma St
North Wagga Wagga
 NSW 2678
(02) 6933 2435
fax (02) 6933 2107

CHATEAU REYNELLA
Reynella Rd
Reynella SA 5161
(08) 8392 2222
fax (08) 8392 2202

CHATEAU TAHBILK
Tabilk Vic. 3607
via Nagambie
(03) 5794 2555
fax (03) 5794 2360

CHATEAU YALDARA
Gomersal Rd
Lyndoch SA 5351
(08) 8524 4200
fax (08) 8524 4678

CHATSFIELD
O'Neill Rd
Mount Barker WA 6324
(08) 9851 1704
fax (08) 9841 6811

CLARENDON HILLS
(not open to public)
(08) 8364 1484

CLEVELAND
Shannons Rd
Lancefield Vic. 3435
(03) 5429 1449
fax (03) 5429 2017

CLONAKILLA
Crisps La.
Murrumbateman
  NSW 2582
(06) 251 1938 (A.H.)

CLOUDY BAY
(*see* Cape Mentelle)

CLOVER HILL
(*see* Taltarni)

COBAW RIDGE
Perc Boyer's La.
East Pastoria
via Kyneton Vic. 3444
(03) 5423 5227

COLDSTREAM HILLS
31 Maddens La.
Coldstream Vic. 3770
(03) 5964 9388
fax (03) 5964 9389

COOLANGATTA ESTATE
Coolangatta Resort
via Berry NSW 2535
(044) 48 7131
fax (044) 48 7997

COOMBEND
Swansea Tas. 7190
(03) 6257 8256
fax (03) 6257 8484

COOPERS CREEK
WINERY
Highway 16
Haupai
Auckland NZ
(09) 412 8560

COPE WILLIAMS WINERY
Glenfern Rd
Romsey Vic. 3434
(03) 5429 5428
fax (03) 5429 2655

CORIOLE
Chaffeys Rd
McLaren Vale SA 5171
(08) 8323 8305
fax (08) 8323 9136

COWRA ESTATE
Boorowa Rd
Cowra NSW 2794
(063) 42 3650

CRABTREE WATERVALE
CELLARS
North Tce
Watervale SA 5452
(08) 8843 0069
fax (08) 8843 0144

CRAIG AVON
Craig Avon La.
Merricks North Vic. 3926
(03) 5989 7465

CRAIGIE KNOWE
Cranbrook Tas. 7190
(03) 6223 5620

CRAIGLEE
Sunbury Rd
Sunbury Vic. 3429
(03) 9744 1160

CRAIGMOOR
Craigmoor Rd
Mudgee NSW 2850
(063) 72 2208

CRAIGOW
Richmond Rd
Cambridge Tas. 7170
(03) 6248 5482

CRANEFORD
Main St
Springton SA 5235
(08) 8568 2220
fax (08) 8568 2538

CRAWFORD RIVER
Condah Vic. 3303
(03) 5578 2267

CULLENS
Caves Rd
Willyabrup
via Cowaramup WA 6284
(08) 9755 5277

CURRENCY CREEK
Winery Rd
Currency Creek SA 5214
(08) 8555 4069

DALFARRAS
(see Chateau Tahbilk)

DALRYMPLE
Pipers Brook Rd
Pipers Brook Tas. 7254
(03) 6382 7222

DALWHINNIE
Taltarni Rd
Moonambel Vic. 3478
(03) 5467 2388

d'ARENBERG
Osborn Rd
McLaren Vale SA 5171
(08) 8323 8206

DARLING ESTATE
(by appointment only)
Whitfield Rd
Cheshunt Vic. 3678
(03) 5729 8396
fax (03) 5729 8396

DARLING PARK
Lot 1 Browne La.
Red Hill 3937
(03) 5989 2732
fax (03) 5989 2254

DAVID TRAEGER
399 High St
Nagambie Vic. 3608
(03) 5794 2514

DAVID WYNN
(see Mountadam)

De BORTOLI
De Bortoli Rd
Bibul NSW 2680
(069) 64 9444
fax (069) 64 9400

De BORTOLI
Pinnacle La.
Dixons Creek Vic. 3775
(03) 5965 2271

DEAKIN ESTATE
(see Katnook)

DELAMERE
4238 Bridport Rd
Pipers Brook Tas. 7254
(03) 6382 7190

DELATITE
Stoney's Rd
Mansfield Vic. 3722
(03) 5775 2922
fax (03) 5775 2911

DEMONDRILLE
RMB 97 Prunevale Rd
Prunevale
via Harden NSW 2587
(02) 6384 4272
fax (02) 6384 4292

DENNIS'S OF McLAREN VALE
Kangarilla Rd
McLaren Vale SA 5171
(08) 8323 8665
fax (08) 8323 9121

DEVIL'S LAIR
(not open to public)
PO Box 212
Margaret River WA 6285
(08) 9757 7573
fax (08) 9757 7533

DIAMOND VALLEY VINEYARDS
Kinglake Rd
St Andrews Vic. 3761
(03) 9710 1484
fax (03) 9739 1110

DOMAINE CHANDON
Maroondah Hwy
Coldstream Vic. 3770
(03) 9739 1110
fax (03) 9739 1095

DOONKUNA ESTATE
Barton Hwy
Murrumbateman
 NSW 2582
(06) 227 5885
fax (06) 227 5085

DRAYTON'S BELLEVUE
Oakey Creek Rd
Pokolbin NSW 2320
(049) 98 7513
fax (049) 98 7743

DROMANA ESTATE
Bittern–Dromana Rd
Dromana Vic. 3936
(03) 5987 3275
fax (03) 5981 0714

DUNCAN ESTATE
Spring Gully Rd
Clare SA 5453
(08) 8843 4335

EDEN RIDGE
(*see* Mountadam)

ELAN VINEYARD
17 Turners Rd
Bittern Vic. 3918
(03) 5983 1858

ELDERTON
3 Tanunda Rd
Nuriootpa SA 5355
(08) 8862 1058 or
1800 88 8500
fax (08) 8862 2844

ELGEE PARK
(no cellar door)
Junction Rd
Merricks Nth
PO Box 211
Red Hill South Vic. 3926
(03) 5989 7338
fax (03) 5989 7553

EPPALOCK RIDGE
Metcalfe Pool Rd
Redesdale Vic. 3444
(03) 5425 3135

EVANS & TATE
38 Swan St
Henley Brook WA 6055
(09) 296 4666

EVANS FAMILY
Palmers La.
Pokolbin NSW 2320
(049) 98 7333

EYTON ON YARRA
Cnr Maroondah Hwy
   & Hill Rd
Coldstream Vic. 3770
(03) 5962 2119
fax (03) 5962 5319

FERGUSSON'S
Wills Rd
Yarra Glen Vic. 3775
(03) 5965 2237

FERMOY ESTATE
Metricup Rd
Willyabrup WA 6284
(08) 9755 6285
fax (08) 9755 6251

FERN HILL ESTATE
Ingoldby Rd
McLaren Flat SA 5171
(08) 8383 0167
fax (08) 8383 0107

FIDDLER'S CREEK
(*see* Blue Pyrenees Estate)

FIRE GULLY
(*see* Pierro)

FORREST ESTATE
Blicks Rd
Renwick
Blenheim NZ
(03) 572 9084
fax (03) 572 9084

FOX CREEK
Malpas Rd
Willunga SA 5172
(08) 8556 2403
fax (08) 8556 2104

FRANKLAND ESTATE
Frankland Rd
Frankland WA 6396
(08) 9855 1555
fax (08) 9855 1549

FREYCINET VINEYARD
Tasman Hwy
Bicheno Tas. 7215
(03) 6257 8587

GALAFREY
114 York St
Albany WA 6330
(08) 9841 6533

GALAH WINES
Box 231
Ashton SA 5137
(08) 8390 1243

GARDEN GULLY
Western Hwy
Great Western Vic. 3377
(03) 5356 2400

GEOFF MERRILL
(*see* Mount Hurtle)

GEOFF WEAVER
(not open to public)
2 Gilpin La.
Mitcham SA 5062
(08) 8272 2105
fax (08) 8271 0177

GIACONDA
(not open to public)
(03) 5727 0246

GILBERT'S
Albany Hwy
Kendenup WA 6323
(08) 9851 4028
(08) 9851 4021

GLENARA
126 Range Rd Nth
Upper Hermitage SA 5131
(08) 8380 5056
fax (08) 8380 5056

GLENGUIN
Lot 8 Milbrodale Rd
Broke NSW 2330
(02) 6579 1011
fax (02) 6579 1009

GOONA WARRA
Sunbury Rd
Sunbury Vic. 3429
(03) 9744 7211
fax (03) 9744 7648

GOUNDREY
Muir Hwy
Mount Barker WA 6324
(08) 9851 1777
fax (08) 9848 1018

GRAMP'S
(*see* Orlando)

GRAND CRU ESTATE
Ross Dewell's Rd
Springton SA 5235
(08) 8568 2378

GRANT BURGE
Jacobs Creek
Barossa Valley Hwy
Tanunda SA 5352
(08) 8563 2060

GREEN POINT
(*see* Domaine Chandon)

GREENOCK CREEK
Radford Rd
Seppeltsfield SA 5360
(08) 8562 8103
fax (08) 8562 8259

GROSSET
King St
Auburn SA 5451
(08) 8849 2175

HANGING ROCK
Jim Rd
Newham Vic. 3442
(03) 5427 0542
fax (03) 5427 0310

HANSON WINES
'Oolorong'
49 Cleveland Ave
Lower Plenty Vic. 3093
(03) 9439 7425

HAPP'S
Commonage Rd
Dunsborough WA 6281
(08) 9755 3300
fax (08) 9755 3846

**HARCOURT VALLEY
  VINEYARD**
Calder Hwy
Harcourt Vic. 3453
(03) 5474 2223

HARDYS
(*see* Chateau Reynella)

HASELGROVE WINES
Foggo Rd
McLaren Vale SA 5171
(08) 8323 8706
fax (08) 8323 8049

HAY SHED HILL
Harmans Mill Rd
Willyabrup WA 6285
(08) 9755 6234
fax (08) 9755 6305

HEATHCOTE WINERY
183 High St
Heathcote Vic. 3523
(03) 5433 2595
fax (03) 5433 3081

HEEMSKERK
Pipers Brook Tas. 7254
(03) 6382 7133
fax (03) 6382 7242

HEGGIES
(*see* Yalumba)

HELM'S
Yass River Rd
Murrumbateman
    NSW 2582
(06) 227 5536 (A.H.)
(06) 227 5953

HENSCHKE
Moculta Rd
Keyneton SA 5353
(08) 8564 8223
fax (08) 8564 8294

HERITAGE WINES
Seppeltsfield Rd
Marananga
via Tununda SA 5352
(08) 8562 2880

HICKINBOTHAM
(not open to public)
(03) 9397 1872
fax (03) 9397 2629

HIGHBANK
Main Naracoorte–Penola
    Rd
Coonawarra SA 5263
(08) 8737 2020

HIGHFIELD
Brookby Rd
RD 2 Blenheim NZ
(03) 572 8592
fax (03) 572 9257

HILL SMITH ESTATE
(*see* Yalumba)

HILLSTOWE WINES
104 Main Rd
Hahndorf SA 5245
(08) 8388 1400
fax (08) 8388 1411

HOLLICK
Racecourse Rd
Coonawarra SA 5263
(08) 8737 2318
fax (08) 8737 2952

HOTHAM VALLEY
(by appointment only)
South Wandering Rd
Wandering WA 6308
(08) 9884 1525
fax (08) 9884 1079

HOUGHTON
Dale Rd
Middle Swan WA 6056
(09) 274 5100

HOWARD PARK
(not open to public)
PO Box 544
Denmark WA 6333
(08) 9848 2345
fax (08) 9848 2064

HUGH HAMILTON WINES
PO Box 615
McLaren Vale SA 5171
(08) 8323 8689
fax (08) 8323 9488

HUGO
Elliott Rd
McLaren Flat SA 5171
(08) 8383 0098
fax (08) 8383 0446

HUNGERFORD HILL
(*see* Tulloch or Lindemans)

HUNTER'S WINES
Rapaura Rd
Blenheim NZ
(03) 572 8489
fax (03) 572 8457

HUNTINGTON ESTATE
Cassilis Rd
Mudgee NSW 2850
(06) 373 3825
fax (06) 373 3730

IAN LEAMON
Calder Hwy
Bendigo Vic. 3550
(03) 5447 7995

IDYLL
Ballan Rd
Moorabool Vic. 3221
(03) 5276 1280
fax (03) 5276 1537

INGOLDBY
Kangarilla Rd
McLaren Vale SA 5171
(08) 8383 0005

INNISFAIL
(not open to public)
(03) 5276 1258

JAMES IRVINE
Roeslers Rd
Eden Valley SA 5235
PO Box 308
Angaston SA 5353
(08) 8564 1046
fax (08) 8564 1046

JASPER HILL
Drummonds La
Heathcote Vic. 3523
(03) 5433 2528

JEIR CREEK WINES
Gooda Creek Rd
Murrumbateman
   NSW 2582
(06) 227 5999

JENKE VINEYARDS
Jenke Rd
Rowland Flat SA 5352
(08) 8524 4154
fax (08) 8524 4154

JIM BARRY
Main North Rd
Clare SA 5453
(08) 8842 2261

JINGALLA
Bolganup Dam Rd
Porongurup WA 6324
(08) 9853 1023
fax (08) 9853 1023

JOHN GEHRIG
Oxley Vic. 3678
(03) 5727 3395

JOSEPH
(*see* Primo Estate)

KARINA VINEYARDS
RMB 4055
Harrisons Rd
Dromana Vic. 3936
(03) 5981 0137

KARRIVALE
Woodlands Rd
Porongurup WA 6324
(08) 9853 1009
fax (08) 9853 1129

KARRIVIEW
RMB 913
Roberts Rd
Denmark WA 6333
(08) 9840 9381

KATNOOK ESTATE
Riddoch Hwy
Coonawarra SA 5263
(08) 8737 2394
fax (08) 8737 2397

KAYS
Kays Rd
McLaren Vale SA 5171
(08) 8323 8211
fax (08) 8323 9199

KIES ESTATE
Hoffnungsthal Rd
Lyndoch SA 5351
(08) 8524 4511

KILLAWARRA
(*see* Kaiser Stuhl)

KILLERBY
Minnimup Rd
Gelorup WA 6230
(08) 9795 7222
fax (08) 9795 7835

KINGS CREEK
(not open to public)
(03) 5983 2102

KNAPPSTEIN WINES
2 Pioneer Ave
Clare SA 5453
(088) 42 2600
fax (088) 42 3831

KNIGHTS
Burke and Wills Track
Baynton
via Kyneton Vic. 3444
(03) 5423 7264
mobile 015 843 676
fax (03) 5423 7288

KOPPAMURRA
(no cellar door)
PO Box 110
Blackwood SA 5051
(08) 8271 4127
fax (08) 8271 0726

KRONDORF
Krondorf Rd
Tanunda SA 5352
(08) 8563 2145
fax (08) 8562 3055

KYEEMA
(not open to public)
PO Box 282
Belconnen ACT 2616
(02) 6254 7557

LAANECOORIE
(cellar door by
   arrangement)
RMB 1330
Dunolly Vic. 3472
(03) 5468 7260
mobile 018 518 887

LAKE'S FOLLY
Broke Rd
Pokolbin NSW 2320
(049) 98 7507
fax (049) 98 7322

LALLA GULLY
(not open to public)
(03) 6331 2325
fax (03) 6331 7948

LAMONT'S
Bisdee Rd
Millendon WA 6056
(08) 9296 4485
fax (08) 9296 1663

LANCEFIELD WINERY
Woodend Rd
Lancefield Vic. 3435
(03) 5433 5292

LARK HILL
RMB 281
Gundaroo Rd
Bungendore NSW 2621
(062) 38 1393

LAUREL BANK
(by appointment only)
130 Black Snake La.
Granton Tas. 7030
(03) 6263 5977
fax (03) 6263 3117

LAURISTON
(*see* Hardys)

LEASINGHAM
7 Dominic St
Clare SA 5453
(08) 8842 2555
fax (08) 8842 3293

LECONFIELD
Narracoorte–Penola Rd
Coonawarra SA 5263
(08) 8737 2326
fax (08) 8737 2285

LEEUWIN ESTATE
Stevens Rd
Margaret River WA 6285
(08) 9757 6253
fax (08) 9757 6364

LELAND ESTATE
PO Lenswood SA 5240
(08) 8389 6928

LENGS & COOTER
24 Lindsay Tce
Belair SA 5052
(08) 8278 3998

LENSWOOD VINEYARDS
3 Cyril John Crt
Athelstone SA 5076
(08) 8365 3766
fax (08) 8365 3766

LENTON BRAE
Caves Rd
Willyabrup WA 6280
(08) 9755 6255
fax (08) 9755 6268

LEO BURING
Stuart Hwy
Tanunda SA 5352
(08) 8563 2184
fax (08) 8563 2804

LEYDENS VALE
(*see* Blue Pyrenees Estate)

LILLYDALE VINEYARDS
Davross Crt
Seville Vic. 3139
(03) 5964 2016

LILLYPILLY ESTATE
Farm 16
Lilly Pilly Rd
Leeton NSW 2705
(069) 53 4069
fax (069) 53 4980

LINDEMANS
McDonalds Rd
Pokolbin NSW 2320
(049) 98 7501
fax (049) 98 7682

LONG GULLY
Long Gully Rd
Healesville Vic. 3777
(03) 5962 3663
fax (03) 59807 2213

LONGLEAT
Old Weir Rd
Murchison Vic. 3610
(03) 5826 2294
fax (03) 5826 2510

LOVEGROVE OF COTTLES BRIDGE
Heidelberg Kinglake Road
Cottlesbridge Vic. 3099
(03) 9718 1569
fax (03) 9718 1028

McALISTER
(not open to public)
(051) 49 7229

McGUIGAN BROTHERS
Cnr Broke & McDonalds
 Rds
Pokolbin NSW 2320
(049) 98 7400
fax (049) 98 7401

McWILLIAM'S
Hanwood NSW 2680
(069) 63 0001
fax (069) 63 0002

MADEW
(by appointment only)
Westering Vineyard
Federal Hwy
Lake George NSW 2581
(02) 4848 0026
fax (02) 4848 0026

MADFISH BAY
(*see* Howard Park)

MAGLIERI
Douglas Gully Rd
McLaren Flat SA 5171
(08) 8323 8648

MAIN RIDGE
Lot 48 Williams Rd
Red Hill Vic. 3937
(03) 5989 2686

MALCOLM CREEK
(not open to public)
(08) 8264 2255

MARIENBERG
2 Chalk Hill Rd
McClaren Vale SA 5171
(08) 8323 9666
fax (08) 8323 9600

MASSONI HOME PTY LTD
(by appointment only)
Mornington–Flinders Rd
Red Hill Vic. 3937
(03) 5989 2352

MASTERSON
(*see* Peter Lehmann)

MAXWELL
Cnr Olivers & Chalkhill
 Rds
McLaren Vale SA 5171
(08) 8323 8200

MEADOWBANK
Glenora Tas. 7140
(03) 6286 1234
fax (03) 6286 1133

MERRICKS ESTATE
Cnr Thompsons La.
 & Frankston–Flinders Rd
Merricks Vic. 3916
(03) 59898 416
fax (03) 9629 4035

MIDDLETON ESTATE
Flagstaff Hill Rd
Middleton SA 5213
(08) 8555 4136
fax (08) 8555 4108

MILBURN PARK
(*see* Salisbury Estate)

MILDARA
(various locations)
(03) 9690 9966
(head office)

MILDURA VINEYARDS
Campbell Ave
Irymple Vic. 3498

MINTARO CELLARS
Leasingham Rd
Mintaro SA 5415
(08) 8843 9046

MIRAMAR
Henry Lawson Dr.
Mudgee NSW 2850
(063) 73 3874

MIRANDA WINES
57 Jordaryan Ave
Griffith NSW 2680
(069) 62 4033
fax (069) 62 6944

MIRROOL CREEK
(*see* Miranda)

MITCHELL
Hughes Park Rd
Sevenhill via Clare SA 5453
(08) 8843 4258

MITCHELTON WINES
Mitcheltstown
Nagambie 3608
(03) 5794 2710
fax (03) 5794 2615

MONTANA
PO Box 18-293
Glen Innis
Auckland NZ
(09) 570 5549

MONTARA
Chalambar Rd
Ararat Vic. 3377
(03) 5352 3868
fax (03) 5352 4968

MONTROSE
Henry Lawson Dr.
Mudgee NSW 2850
(063) 73 3853

MOONDAH BROOK
(*see* Houghton)

MOORILLA ESTATE
655 Main Rd
Berridale Tas. 7011
(03) 6249 2949

MOOROODUC ESTATE
Derril Rd
Moorooduc Vic. 3933
(03) 5978 8585

MORNING CLOUD
(cellar door by
   appointment)
15 Ocean View Ave
Red Hill South Vic. 3937
(03) 5989 2762
fax (03) 5989 2700

**MORNINGTON
VINEYARDS**
(by appointment only)
Moorooduc Rd
Mornington Vic. 3931
(03) 5974 2097

MORRIS
off Murray Valley Hwy
Mia Mia Vineyards
Rutherglen Vic. 3685
(060) 26 7303
fax (060) 26 7445

MOSS BROTHERS
Caves Rd
Willyabrup WA 6280
(08) 9755 6270
fax (08) 9755 6298

MOSS WOOD
Metricup Rd
Willyabrup WA 6280
(08) 9755 6266
fax (08) 9755 6303

MOUNT AVOCA
Moates La.
Avoca Vic. 3467
(03) 5465 3282

MOUNT HORROCKS
PO Box 72
Watervale SA 5452
(08) 8849 2243
fax (08) 8849 2243

MOUNT HURTLE
291 Pimpala Rd
Woodcroft SA 5162
(08) 8381 6877
fax (08) 8322 2244

MOUNT LANGI GHIRAN
Warrak Rd
Buangor Vic. 3375
(03) 5354 3207
fax (03) 5354 3277

MOUNT MARY
(not open to public)
(03) 9739 1761
fax (03) 9739 0137

MOUNT PRIOR VINEYARD
Cnr River Rd & Popes La.
Rutherglen Vic. 3685
(060) 26 5591
fax (060) 26 5590

MOUNTADAM
High Eden Ridge
Eden Valley SA 5235
(08) 8564 1101

MT PLEASANT
Marrowbone Rd
Pokolbin NSW 2321
(049) 98 7505

MT WILLIAM WINERY
Mount William Rd
Tantaraboo Vic. 3764
(03) 5429 1595
fax (03) 5429 1998

MURRINDINDI
(not open to public)
(03) 5797 8217

NATTIER
(*see* Mitchelton)

NAUTILUS
(*see* Yalumba)

NEPENTHE VINEYARDS
(not open to public)
(08) 8389 8218

NGATARAWA
Ngatarawa Rd
Bridge Pa
Hastings NZ
(070) 79 7603

NICHOLSON RIVER
Liddells Rd
Nicholson Vic. 3882
(03) 5156 8241

NORMANS
Grants Gully Rd
Clarendon SA 5157
(08) 8383 6138
fax (08) 8383 6089

NUTFIELD
(*see* Hickinbotham)

OAKRIDGE ESTATE
(until Jan. '98)
Aitken Rd
Seville Vic. 3139
(after Jan. '98)
864 Maroondah Hwy
Coldstream Vic. 3770
(03) 5964 3379
fax (03) 5964 2061

OAKVALE WINERY
Broke Rd
Pokolbin NSW 2320
(049) 98 7520

OLD KENT RIVER
Turpin Rd
Rocky Gully WA 6397
(08) 9855 1589
fax (08) 9855 1589

ORLANDO
Barossa Valley Way
Rowland Flat SA 5352
(08) 8521 3111
fax (08) 8521 3102

PALMER WINES
Caves Rd
Willyabrup WA 6280
(08) 9797 1881
fax (08) 9797 0534

PANKHURST WINES
Woodgrove Rd
Hall ACT 2618
(06) 230 2592

PARADISE ENOUGH
(weekends & holidays only)
Stewarts Rd
Kongwak Vic. 3951
(03) 5657 4241

PARINGA ESTATE
44 Paringa Rd
Red Hill South Vic. 3937
(03) 5989 2669

**PARKER COONAWARRA
ESTATE**
Penola Rd
Coonawarra SA 5263
(Contact Leconfield)
(08) 8737 2946
fax (08) 8737 2945

PASSING CLOUDS
Powlett Rd
via Inglewood
Kingower Vic. 3517
(03) 5438 8257

PATTERSONS
St Werburghs Rd
Mount Barker WA 6324
(08) 9851 2063
fax (08) 9851 2063

PAULETT'S
Polish Hill River Rd
Sevenhill SA 5453
(08) 8843 4328
fax (08) 8843 4202

PEEL ESTATE
Fletcher Rd
Baldivis WA 6210
(08) 9524 1221

PEGASUS BAY
Stockgrove Rd
Waipara
Amberley RD 2
North Canterbury NZ
(03) 314 6869
fax (03) 355 5937

PENDARVES ESTATE
Lot 12 Old North Rd
Belford NSW 2335
(065) 74 7222

PENFOLDS
(*see* Southcorp Wines)

PENLEY ESTATE
McLean's Rd
Coonawarra 5263
(08) 8736 3211
fax (08) 8736 3211

PEPPERS CREEK
Cnr Ekerts & Broke Rds
Pokolbin NSW 2321
(049) 98 7532

PEPPER TREE WINES
Halls Rd
Pokolbin NSW 2320
(02) 4998 7539
fax (02) 4998 7746

PETALUMA
(not open to public)
(08) 8339 4122
fax (08) 8339 5253

PETER LEHMANN
Para Rd
Tanunda SA 5352
(08) 8563 2500
fax (08) 8563 3402

PETERSONS
PO Box 182
Mount View Rd
Mount View NSW 2325
(049) 90 1704

PFEIFFER
Distillery Rd
Wahgunyah Vic. 3687
(060) 33 2805
fax (060) 33 3158

PHILLIP ISLAND WINES
Lot 1 Berrys Beach Rd
Phillip Island Vic. 3922
(03) 5956 8465

PIBBIN FARM
Greenhill Rd
Balhannah SA 5242
(08) 8388 4794

PICARDY
(not open to public)
(08) 9776 0036
fax (08) 9776 0036

PICCADILLY FIELDS
(not open to public)
(08) 8390 1997

PIERRO
Caves Rd
Willyabrup WA 6280
(08) 9755 6220
fax (08) 9755 6308

PIKES POLISH HILL ESTATE
Polish Hill River Rd
Seven Hill SA 5453
(08) 8843 4370
fax (08) 8843 4353

PIPERS BROOK
3959 Bridport Hwy
Pipers Brook Tas. 7254
(03) 6382 7197
fax (03) 6382 7226

PIRRAMIMMA
Johnston Rd
McLaren Vale SA 5171
(08) 8323 8205
fax (08) 8323 9224

PLANTAGENET
Albany Hwy
Mount Barker WA 6324
(08) 9851 2150
fax (08) 9851 1839

PLUNKETT'S
Cnr Lambing Gully Rd &
    Hume Fwy
Avenel Vic. 3664
(03) 5796 2150
fax (03) 5796 2147

PORT PHILLIP ESTATE
261 Red Hill Rd
Red Hill Vic. 3937
(03) 5989 2708
fax (03) 5989 2891

PORTREE VINEYARD
RMB 700
Lancefield Vic. 3435
(03) 5429 1422
fax (03) 5429 2205

PREECE
(*see* Mitchelton)

PRIMO ESTATE
Cnr Old Port Wakefield
& Angle Vale Rds
Virginia SA 5120
(08) 8380 9442

PRINCE ALBERT
Lemins Rd
Waurn Ponds Vic. 3221
(03) 5243 5091
fax (03) 5241 8091

QUEEN ADELAIDE
(*see* Seppelt)

QUELLTALER ESTATE
Main North Rd
Watervale SA 5452
(08) 8843 0003
fax (08) 8843 0096

REDBANK
Sunraysia Hwy
Redbank Vic. 3478
(03) 5467 7255

RED HILL ESTATE
53 Red Hill–Shoreham Rd
Red Hill South Vic. 3937
(03) 5989 2838

REDMAN
Riddoch Hwy
Coonawarra SA 5263
(08) 8736 3331
fax (08) 8736 3013

RENMANO
Renmark Ave
Renmark SA 5341
(08) 8586 6771
fax (08) 8586 5939

REYNOLDS YARRAMAN
Yarraman Rd
Wybong NSW 2333
(02) 6547 8127
fax (02) 6547 8013

RIBBON VALE ESTATE
Lot 5 Caves Rd
via Cowaramup
Willyabrup WA 6284
(08) 9755 6272

RICHARD HAMILTON
Willunga Vineyards
Main South Rd
Willunga SA 5172
(08) 8556 2288
fax (08) 8556 2868

RICHMOND GROVE
(*see* Orlando)

RIDDOCH
(*see* Katnook)

ROBERT THUMM
(*see* Chateau Yaldara)

ROBINVALE WINES
Sealake Rd
Robinvale Vic. 3549
(03) 5026 3955
fax (03) 5026 1123

ROCHECOMBE
(*see* Heemskerk)

ROCHFORD
Romsey Park
via Woodend Rd
Rochford Vic. 3442
(03) 5429 1428

ROCKFORD
Krondorf Rd
Tanunda SA 5352
(03) 8563 2720

ROMSEY PARK
(*see* Rochford)

ROMSEY VINEYARDS
(*see* Cope Williams)

ROSABROOK ESTATE
Rosa Brook Rd
Margaret River WA 6285
(08) 9757 2286
fax (08) 9757 3634

ROSEMOUNT
Rosemount Rd
Denman NSW 2328
(065) 47 2467
fax (065) 47 2742

ROTHBURY ESTATE
Broke Rd
Pokolbin NSW 2321
(049) 98 7555
fax (049) 98 7553

ROUGE HOMME
(*see* Lindemans)

ROWAN
(*see* St Huberts)

RYECROFT
Ingoldby Rd
McLaren Flat SA 5171
(08) 8383 0001

RYMILL COONAWARRA WINES
The Riddoch Run
  Vineyards (off Main Rd)
Coonawarra SA 5263
(08) 8736 5001
fax (08) 8736 5040

SADDLERS CREEK WINERY
Marrowbone Rd
Pokolbin NSW 2321
(049) 91 1770
fax (049) 91 1778

SALISBURY ESTATE
(*see* Alambie)

SALITAGE
Vasse Hwy
Pemberton WA 6260
(08) 9776 1599
fax (08) 9776 1504

SALTRAM
Angaston Rd
Angaston SA 5353
(08) 8563 8200

SANDALFORD
West Swan Rd
Caversham WA 6055
(09) 274 5922
fax (09) 274 2154

SANDSTONE VINEYARD
(cellar door by
  appointment)
Caves & Johnson Rds
Willyabrup WA 6280
(08) 9755 6271
fax (08) 9755 6292

SCARBOROUGH WINES
Gillards Rd
Pokolbin NSW 2321
(049) 98 7563

SCARPANTONI
Kangarilla Rd
McLaren Flat SA 5171
(08) 8383 0186
fax (08) 8383 0490

SCHINUS
(*see* Dromana Estate)

SCOTCHMAN'S HILL
Scotchmans Rd
Drysdale Vic. 3222
(03) 5251 3176
fax (03) 5253 1743

SEAVIEW
Chaffeys Rd
McLaren Vale SA 5171
(08) 8323 8250

SEPPELT
Seppeltsfield
via Tanunda SA 5352
(08) 8562 8028
fax (08) 8562 8333

SEVENHILL
College Rd
Sevenhill
via Clare SA 5453
(088) 43 4222
fax (088) 43 4382

SEVILLE ESTATE
Linwood Rd
Seville Vic. 3139
(03) 5964 4556
fax (03) 5943 4222

SHANTELL
Melba Hwy
Dixons Creek Vic. 3775
(03) 5965 2264
fax (03) 9819 5311

SHAREFARMERS
(*see* Petaluma)

SHAW & SMITH
(not open to public)
(08) 8370 9725

SHOTTESBROOKE
(*see* Ryecroft)

SIMON HACKET
(not open to public)
(08) 8331 7348

SIMON WHITLAM
(*see* Arrowfield)

SKILLOGALEE
Skillogalee Rd
via Sevenhill SA 5453
(08) 8843 4311
fax (08) 8843 4343

SMITHBROOK
(not open to public)
(08) 9772 3557
fax (08) 9772 3579

SOUTHCORP WINES
Tanunda Rd
Nuriootpa SA 5355
(08) 8560 9389
fax (08) 8560 9669

ST FRANCIS
Bridge St
Old Reynella SA 5161
(08) 8381 1925
fax (08) 8322 0921

ST HALLETT'S
St Halletts Rd
Tanunda SA 5352
(08) 8563 2319
fax (08) 8563 2901

ST HUBERTS
Maroondah Hwy
Coldstream Vic. 3770
(03) 9739 1118
fax (03) 9739 1015

ST LEONARDS
St Leonard Rd
Wahgunyah Vic. 3687
(060) 33 1004
fax (060) 33 3636

ST MARY'S VINEYARD
V and A La.
via Coonawarra SA 5263
(08) 8736 6070
fax (08) 8736 6045

STANTON & KILLEEN
Murray Valley Hwy
Rutherglen Vic. 3685
(060) 32 9457

STEPHEN JOHN WINES
Government Rd
Watervale SA 5452
(08) 8843 0105
fax (08) 8843 0105

STEVENS CAMBRAI
Hamiltons Rd
McLaren Flat SA 5171
(08) 8323 0251

STONELEIGH
Corbans Wines
Great Northern Rd
Henderson NZ
(09) 836 6189

**STONEY VINEYARD/
DOMAINE A**
Teatree Rd
Campania Tas. 7026
(03) 6260 4174
fax (03) 6260 4390

STONIER'S WINERY
362 Frankston–Flinders Rd
Merricks Vic. 3916
(03) 5989 8300
fax (03) 5989 8709

SUMMERFIELD
Main Rd
Moonambel Vic. 3478
(03) 5467 2264
fax (03) 5467 2380

SUTHERLAND
Deasey's Rd
Pokolbin NSW 2321
(049) 98 7650

TALTARNI VINEYARDS
off Moonambel–Stawell Rd
Moonambel Vic. 3478
(03) 5467 2218
fax (03) 5467 2306

TAMBURLAINE WINES
McDonalds Rd
Pokolbin NSW 2321
(049) 98 7570
fax (049) 98 7763

TANGLEWOOD DOWNS
Bulldog Creek Rd
Merricks North
(03) 5974 3325

TAPESTRY
Merrivale Wines
Olivers Rd
McLaren Vale SA 5171
(08) 8323 9196
fax (08) 8323 9746

TARRAWARRA
Healesville Rd
Yarra Glen Vic. 3775
(03) 5962 3311
fax (03) 5962 3311

TATACHILLA WINERY
151 Main Rd
McLaren Vale SA 5171
(08) 8323 8656
fax (08) 8323 9096

TAYLORS
Mintaro Rd
Auburn SA 5451
(088) 49 2008

TEMPLE BRUER
Angas River Delta
via Strathalbyn SA 5255
(08) 8537 0203
fax (08) 8537 0131

T'GALLANT
Lot 2 Mornington–Flinders
  Rd
Main Ridge Vic. 3937
(03) 5989 6565
fax (03) 5989 6577

THALGARA ESTATE
De Beyers Rd
Pokolbin NSW 2321
(049) 98 7717

TIM ADAMS
Wendouree Rd
Clare SA 5453
(08) 8842 2429
fax (08) 8842 2429

TIM GRAMP
PO Box 810
Unley SA 5061
(08) 8379 3658
fax (08) 8338 2160

TISDALL
Cornelia Creek Rd
Echuca Vic. 3564
(03) 5482 1911
fax (03) 5482 2516

TOLLANA
(*see* Penfolds)

TORRESAN ESTATE
Manning Rd
Flagstaff Hill SA 5159
(08) 8270 2500

TRENTHAM ESTATE
Sturt Hwy
Trentham Cliffs
via Gol Gol NSW 2738
(050) 24 8888
fax (050) 24 8800

TULLOCH
De Beyers Rd
Pokolbin NSW 2321
(049) 98 7503
fax (049) 98 7682

TUNNEL HILL
(*see* Tarrawarra)

TURKEY FLAT
James Rd
Tanunda SA 5352
(08) 8563 2851
fax (08) 8563 3610

TYRRELL'S
Broke Rd
Pokolbin NSW 2321
(049) 98 7509
fax (049) 987 723

VASSE FELIX
Cnr Caves & Harmans Rds
Cowaramup WA 6284
(08) 9755 5242
fax (08) 9755 5425

VERITAS
94 Langmeil Rd
Tanunda SA 5352
(08) 8563 2330

VIRGIN HILLS
(not open to public)
(03) 5423 9169

VOYAGER ESTATE
Stevens Rd
Margaret River WA 6285
(08) 9757 6358
fax (08) 9757 6405

WANDIN VALLEY ESTATE
Wilderness Rd
Rothbury NSW 2321
(049) 30 7317
fax (049) 30 7814

WANINGA
Hughes Park Rd
Sevenhill
via Clare SA 5453
(088) 43 4395
fax (08) 232 0653

WANTIRNA ESTATE
(not open to public)
(03) 9801 2367

**WARDS GATEWAY
CELLARS**
Barossa Valley Hwy
Lyndoch SA 5351
(08) 8524 4138

WARRAMATE
27 Maddens La.
Gruyere Vic. 3770
(03) 5964 9219

WARRENMANG
Mountain Ck Rd
Moonambel Vic. 3478
(03) 5467 2233
fax (03) 5467 2309

**WATERWHEEL
VINEYARDS**
Lyndhurst St
Bridgewater-on-Loddon
Bridgewater Vic. 3516
(03) 5437 3060
fax (03) 5437 3082

WELLINGTON WINES
34 Cornwall St
Rose Bay Tas. 7015
(03) 6248 5844

WENDOUREE
Wendouree Rd
Clare SA 5453
(088) 842 2896

WESTFIELD
Memorial Ave
Baskerville WA 6056
(09) 296 4356

WIGNALLS KING RIVER
Chester Pass Rd
Albany WA 6330
(08) 9841 2848

WILD DUCK CREEK
Springflat Rd
Heathcote Vic. 3523
(03) 5433 3133

WILDWOOD
St Johns La.
via Wildwood Vic. 3428
(03) 9307 1118

WILLESPIE
Harmans Mill Rd
Willyabrup WA 6280
(08) 9755 6248
fax (08) 9755 6210

WILLOWS VINEYARD, THE
Light Pass Rd
Barossa Valley SA 5355
(08) 8562 1080

WILSON VINEYARD, THE
Polish Hill River
via Clare SA 5453
(088) 43 4310

WILTON ESTATE
Whitton Stock Route
Yenda NSW 2681
(069) 68 1303
fax (069) 68 1328

WINCHELSEA ESTATE
C/- Nicks Wine Merchants
(03) 9639 0696

WING FIELDS
(*see* Water Wheel)

WIRILDA CREEK
Lot 32 McMurtrie Rd
McLaren Vale SA 5171
(08) 8323 9688

WIRRA WIRRA
McMurtrie Rd
McLaren Vale SA 5171
(08) 8323 8414
fax (08) 8323 8596

WOLF BLASS
Sturt Hwy
Nuriootpa SA 5355
(08) 8562 1955
fax (08) 8562 2156

WOODSTOCK
Douglas Gully Rd
McLaren Flat SA 5171
(08) 8383 0156
fax (08) 8383 0437

WOODY NOOK
Metricup Rd
Metricup WA 6280
(08) 9755 7547
fax (08) 9755 7547

WYANGA PARK
Baades Rd
Lakes Entrance Vic. 3909
(03) 5155 1508
fax (03) 5155 1443

WYANGAN ESTATE
(*see* Miranda)

WYNDHAM ESTATE
Dalwood Rd
Dalwood NSW 2321
(049) 38 3444
fax (049) 38 3422

WYNNS
Memorial Dr.
Coonawarra SA 5263
(08) 8736 3266

XANADU
Terry Rd (off Railway Tce)
Margaret River WA 6285
(08) 9757 2581
fax (08) 9757 3389

YALUMBA
Eden Valley Rd
Angaston SA 5353
(08) 8561 3200
fax (08) 8561 3392

YARRA BURN
Settlement Rd
Yarra Junction Vic. 3797
(03) 5967 1428
fax (03) 5967 1146

YARRA RIDGE
Glenview Rd
Yarra Glen Vic. 3775
(03) 9730 1022
fax (03) 9730 1131

YARRA VALLEY HILLS
Old Don Rd
Healesville Vic. 3777
(03) 5962 4173
fax (03) 5762 4059

YARRA YERING
Briarty Rd
Gruyere Vic. 3770
(03) 5964 9267

YELLOWGLEN
White's Rd
Smythesdale Vic. 3351
(03) 5342 8617

YERING STATION
Melba Hwy
Yering Vic. 3775
(03) 9730 1107
fax (03) 9739 0135

YERINGBERG
(not open to public)
(03) 9739 1453
fax (03) 9739 0048

ZEMA ESTATE
Narracoorte–Penola Rd
Coonawarra SA 5263
(08) 8736 3219
fax (08) 8736 3280